This book comes with access to more content online.

Quiz yourself, track your progress, and improve your grammar!

Register your book or ebook at
www.dummies.com/go/getaccess

Select your product, and then follow the prompts
to validate your purchase.

You'll receive an email with your PIN and instructions.

English Grammar

ALL-IN-ONE

WITHDRAWN

by Geraldine Woods

A Wiley Brand

English Grammar All-in-One For Dummies®

Published by: **John Wiley & Sons, Inc.,** 111 River Street, Hoboken, NJ 07030-5774, www.wiley.com

Copyright © 2023 by John Wiley & Sons, Inc., Hoboken, New Jersey

Published simultaneously in Canada

For general information on our other products and services, please contact our Customer Care Department within the U.S. at 877-762-2974, outside the U.S. at 317-572-3993, or fax 317-572-4002. For technical support, please visit https://hub.wiley.com/community/support/dummies.

Wiley publishes in a variety of print and electronic formats and by print-on-demand. Some material included with standard print versions of this book may not be included in e-books or in print-on-demand. If this book refers to media such as a CD or DVD that is not included in the version you purchased, you may download this material at http://booksupport.wiley.com. For more information about Wiley products, visit www.wiley.com.

Library of Congress Control Number: 2023931512

ISBN 978-1-394-15944-4 (pbk); ISBN 978-1-394-15949-9 (ebk); ISBN 978-1-394-15950-5 (ebk)

SKY10043634_022423

Table of Contents

Introduction

Does this resemble the inside of your head when you're preparing to talk with an authority figure?

> *Glad to have met . . . to be meeting . . .* Uh-oh. Maybe just *Hi! How's it going?* No, that's too friendly. New direction: *You asked to see whoever . . . whomever . . . wrote the report.* Or is it *had written?*

If you answered yes, you're in the right place. *English Grammar All-in-One For Dummies* helps you navigate the sea of grammar without wrecking your grades, your career, or your mind. I mention grades and career because the ability to speak and write according to the rules of Standard English gives you an advantage in school and in the working world. This book presents the latest guidelines for Standard English. Yes, latest. When an English teacher is pounding them into your head, the rules of Standard English usage seem set in stone. But language is anything but static. It moves along just as people do — sometimes quickly and something at the speed of a tired snail. To keep you sharp in every 21st century situation, *English Grammar All-in-One For Dummies* gives you information and then practice with the current, commonly accepted language of texts, tweets, presentation slides, emails, and more traditional forms of writing.

About This Book

In *English Grammar All-in-One For Dummies*, I address all your grammar questions about written and spoken language, including a few you didn't know you had. I do so without loading you up with obscure terminology, defining terms only when you need them to understand what you're supposed to do as well as why you're supposed to do it. I also explain which rules of formal English you can and should ignore in various situations. The goal is to ensure that the language you use conveys your ideas accurately and makes a good impression on your reader or listener.

Every chapter but one provides

>> Explanations of grammar rules and common usage

>> Sample questions with answers

>> A slew of extra practice questions (and more online)

>> Chapter quizzes with answers and explanations

Are you wondering which chapter breaks this pattern? It's the first. Instead of a quiz, Chapter 1 ends with a diagnostic tool — a chart of common grammatical dilemmas (*capital letter or lowercase? gave or had given? comma or colon?* and the like) and points you toward the chapter addressing that topic. You can turn immediately to the chapters that meet your needs, or you can work through the book in order, moving from an overview of grammar and style to parts of speech, parts of a sentence, and onward to punctuation, capitalization, and common errors. The last unit focuses on useful information for writing at school and on the job, with special attention to electronic media.

Foolish Assumptions

I assume you're reading this book because you want one or more of the following:

>> Skill in communicating exactly what you mean

>> Better grades or a better job

>> Speech and writing that serves you well in formal situations

>> A good score on standardized exams

Of course, you may be reading this book because an authority figure has threatened to fail, fire, or ground you if you don't. Even so, I hope you'll learn something — and smile along the way.

Icons Used in This Book

Five types of icons steer your journey:

TIP

Wherever you see this icon, you'll find helpful strategies for understanding the structure of the sentence or for choosing the correct word form.

WARNING

Not every grammar point has a built-in trap, but some do. This icon tells you how to avoid common mistakes as you construct a sentence.

EXAMPLE

You can test your knowledge of a topic by trying a sample question or two, checking your answers, and reading the accompanying explanations.

YOUR TURN

Put on your thinking cap when you see this icon, because it identifies a set of practice questions. Answers and explanations appear in a separate section near the end of the chapter.

REMEMBER

This icon identifies key grammar points to deposit in your memory bank.

Beyond the Book

For additional reference material and writing tips, check out www.dummies.com to find the accompanying Cheat Sheet for this book. Just type "English Grammar All-in-One For Dummies cheat sheet" in the search box.

You can also test yourself with online quizzes oriented to a single chapter or to a heftier amount of information. To gain access to the online practice, all you have to do is register. Just follow these simple steps:

1. **Register your book or ebook at Dummies.com to get your PIN. Go to** www.dummies. com/go/getaccess.
2. **Select your product from the drop-down list on that page.**
3. **Follow the prompts to validate your product, and then check your email for a confirmation message that includes your PIN and instructions for logging in.**

If you don't receive this email within two hours, please check your Spam folder before contacting us through our Technical Support website at https://support.wiley.com or by phone at 877-762-2974.

Now you're ready to go! You can come back to the program as often as you want. Simply log in with the username and password you created during your initial login. No need to enter the access code a second time.

Where to Go from Here

To the refrigerator for a snack. Nope. Just kidding. Take the grammar diagnostic in Chapter 1, or simply think for a few moments about the aspects of writing or speaking that make you pause. Then select the chapters that meet your needs. If you're unsure whether a topic is a problem, no problem! Look for the example icons and try a couple of questions. If you get the right answer — or if you don't but the explanation cleared up your confusion — move on. If you stub your toe, work on the practice questions or take an online quiz until you master the topic. And you will!

A NOTE ABOUT PRONOUNS

Much has changed in the world of pronouns in the past few years. Change isn't always comfortable, but it's here and, I believe, necessary and good.

Let me explain. A pronoun is a word that stands in for a noun or another pronoun. Pronouns streamline language, allowing you to say "George said that he forgot his phone" instead of "George said that George forgot George's phone." A pronoun is supposed to match, or agree, with the word it refers to: Singular pairs with singular, plural with plural. Gender also matters. Some pronouns are masculine *(he, him, his)*; some are feminine *(she, her, hers)*; and others are neuter *(it, they* when referring to objects, ideas, or places). The rules for these pronouns have stayed the same. Ditto for gender-neutral pronouns referring to a group *(they, them, their, theirs).*

(continued)

(continued)

The rules have shifted, though, when you refer to one person whose gender is unspecified — a *person* or a *senator* or an *insurance agent*, perhaps — or to a person who does not identify gender as binary (male or female) or who identifies as gender fluid. For an increasing number of grammarians and editors, *they, them, their,* and *theirs* have become the preferred pronouns for these situations. In other words, these pronouns may be either singular or plural, depending on the word they refer to. Take a look at some examples:

Someone forgot their homework; therefore, the teacher will give them a failing grade. (pairs the singular pronoun *someone* with the singular pronouns *their* and *them*)

Each applicant should explain their reasons for leaving their previous job. (The singular noun *applicant* pairs with the singular pronoun *their*.)

Alix arrived late because they were stuck in a traffic jam. (The singular noun *Alix*, the name of a person who identifies as nonbinary, pairs with the singular pronoun *they*.)

It's worth noting that this "change" in the usage of *they, them,* and *their* in the first two examples is actually a return to tradition. From the 14th century onward, ordinary people, as well as great writers (Chaucer, Shakespeare, and Austen, to name three) treated *they, them, their,* and *theirs* as flexible, gender-neutral pronouns, a grammatically correct way to refer to one person or to a group, just as the pronoun *you* does. In the 18th century, though, influential grammarians declared that the pronouns *they, them, their,* and *theirs* were correct only for references to a group. According to these grammarians, the forms *he, him,* and *his* and *she, her,* and *hers* were the only appropriate references to one person. If the gender was unknown, masculine pronouns were said to be the proper choice. In 1850, the British Parliament went so far as to enact that grammar rule into law! You can imagine how popular this decision was with supporters of women's equality. In the late 20th century, many writers reserved *they, them, their,* and *theirs* for plural references but, in an effort to be more inclusive, turned to pairs — *he or she, him or her,* and *his or her* — for singular references. That practice often results in sentences like this: "A student should ask his or her teacher about his or her pronoun policy during the first meeting with him or her." As you see, providing two choices can result in a clunky sentence! Paired pronouns also ignore people who identify as nonbinary or gender fluid.

To solve these problems, some people have invented gender-neutral pronouns, such as *ze* and *zir*. These new words may catch on, but at the moment they're not common. Much more widespread is the use of *they, them, their,* and *theirs* in both singular and plural situations. I've employed this usage in *English Grammar All-in-One For Dummies*, a decision that Wiley, the publisher of *For Dummies* books, supports.

It may take a while to get used to the singular *they*. If you're expecting one dinner guest and hear "they're on the way," you may panic and cook an extra portion of pasta before you remember that *they* is your guest's preferred pronoun and *they* would never bring a friend without asking first. You may also find yourself writing for an authority figure who insists on restricting *they, them, their,* and *theirs* to plural situations. In that situation, you have some options. You can shift from third person (talking about someone) to second person (talking to the person with the flexible pronoun *you*):

If you forget to do the homework, you will receive a failing grade.

You can also reword and avoid the pronoun entirely:

Someone forgot to do the homework and will receive a failing grade.

Each applicant should explain the reasons for leaving a previous job.

Alix arrived late because of traffic.

1

Exploring Grammar and Style

In This Unit . . .

Chapter **1**

Sampling the Ingredients of Grammar and Style

In the Middle Ages, *grammar* meant the study of Latin, the language of choice for educated people. The word soon came to refer to any kind of learning, the definition that applies when people of grandparent-age talk about their *grammar school,* not their elementary school. The term *grammar school* is a leftover from the old days. The very old days.

These days, the word *grammar* refers to the nuts and bolts of language — specifically, how words are put together to create meaning. Most people also apply the term to a set of rules you have to follow in order to speak and write in Standard English, what society has set as — surprise! — the standard for "correct" speech and writing. I placed *correct* in quotation marks because the way people speak and write changes according to situation, audience, and purpose. (More on this in Chapter 2.) In this chapter, I take you on a whirlwind tour of the elements of grammar and style and direct you to chapters that meet your needs.

What This Year's Sentence Is Wearing: Understanding Grammar and Style

Fresh from the shower, you're standing in front of your closet. What should you select? Some options aren't open to you. You can't show up at the office wearing nothing — not if you want to keep your job and, in addition, stay out of jail. That's a law (in the real world) and a rule (in the world of grammar). You *can* choose a bright purple jacket and a fluorescent green scarf. The fashion police may object, but real cops will leave you alone. In both the real world and Grammar Land, this sort of decision is a matter of *style.* A style point is more flexible than a grammar rule. Take that jacket-scarf selection. Your friends may suggest a subtler color combination, or praise you if your school colors are purple and green and you're cheering at a pep rally.

The grammar rules of proper English can and do change, but not often — maybe a few times every 500 years. Style, on the other hand, shifts much more frequently. A sentence from the early 20th century may look odd to 21st-century readers, and a sentence from the 19th century will seem even stranger. Style also changes with context. Science publications and literary journals, for example, capitalize titles differently. Geography matters, too. In the United States, a comma often appears before *and* in a list of three or more items. British writers generally omit that comma.

TIP

In *English Grammar All-in-One For Dummies,* I discuss the most common style points. If I tackled every situation, though, you'd be reading a thousand-page book. For your most important writing projects, you may want to consult a manual of style. Many institutions publish this sort of book, listing their preferences for punctuation, capitalization, and a whole bunch of other -*ations.* A few popular style manuals are the *Modern Language Association Handbook* (for academic writing in the humanities), *The Chicago Manual of Style* (for general writing), the *Publication Manual of the American Psychological Association,* and the *MIT Guide to Science and Engineering Communication* (for science writing).

These examples illustrate the difference between grammar and style:

> SENTENCE: Am going basketball game I to the.
>
> WHAT'S NOT STANDARD: The word order is scrambled.
>
> GRAMMAR OR STYLE? Grammar.
>
> STANDARD ENGLISH: I am going to the basketball game.
>
> SENTENCE: She was born on March 18 2009.
>
> WHAT'S NOT STANDARD: Most writers would insert a comma after *18.*
>
> GRAMMAR OR STYLE? Style.
>
> ALTERNATIVE VERSIONS: She was born on March 18, 2009. Or, She was born on 18 March 2009.

SENTENCE: Them enjoy playing baseball.

WHAT'S NOT STANDARD: The word *them* isn't appropriate for that spot in the sentence.

GRAMMAR OR STYLE: Grammar.

STANDARD ENGLISH: They enjoy playing baseball.

SENTENCE: Ann spends too much time surfing the Internet.

WHAT'S NOT STANDARD: When it was first invented, *Internet* was generally capitalized. These days, most publications prefer lowercase *(internet)*.

GRAMMAR OR STYLE: Style.

NEW VERSION: Ann spends too much time surfing the internet.

TIP

Standard English isn't the "best" form of the language; nor is it the best choice in many situations. To find out more, turn to Chapter 2.

Getting to Know the Elements of Grammar and Style

When you bake a cake, you need all the right ingredients. If you forget one, the cake is tasteless. English has a number of ingredients, too. You can't ignore any if you want to express yourself correctly in Standard English. Here are the basics:

>> **Parts of speech:** Words, like people, base a portion of their identity on the work they do. Words that name people or things, for example, are *nouns.* English teachers call the identity of a word the *part of speech.* Understanding how to select the appropriate part of speech is an important aspect of grammar.

>> **Parts of a sentence:** Words seldom like to be alone, another quality that words and people have in common. When words join together, they form *sentences.* Complete sentences are essential in formal writing.

>> **Mechanics:** Surprised? Usually, mechanics repair cars and other machines. In language, the term *mechanics* refers to the little things that help readers understand what you mean. Spelling and capitalization are included in mechanics. So is *punctuation,* the placement of periods, commas, question marks, and other symbols. With faulty mechanics, your writing may suffer.

>> **Word order:** In English, location partly determines meaning. *The dog bit John* is different from *John bit the dog.* In the first version, the dog is in trouble. In the second, John has a problem. You should know the rules that govern the placement of words.

>> **Word choice:** Some words sound alike (*eye* and *I,* for example). Others are nearly twins (for instance, *affect* and *effect*). Selecting the wrong word can wreck your writing.

>> **Word forms:** Today *I walk.* Yesterday *I walked.* The form of the word *walk* changes to reveal the time period of the action. Knowing the correct form is essential.

These are the main ingredients that cook up proper English. The next sections examine each in turn.

Parts of speech

According to one computer analysis, the English language includes more than a million words. All those words can be sorted into one of eight boxes: the *parts of speech*. Take a look at the Big Eight:

» Nouns

» Pronouns

» Verbs

» Adjectives

» Adverbs

» Prepositions

» Conjunctions

» Interjections

Not every box has the same number of words in it. The *interjection* container is light. The *noun* and *verb* containers are huge. The other boxes fall somewhere in between.

Check out these sentences, in which the parts of speech are underlined and labeled:

Nora likes algebra. (*Nora* and *algebra* are nouns.)

I told you the story already. (*I* and *you* are pronouns.)

The baby shook the rattle. (*Shook* is a verb.)

Great speeches require intense practice. (*Great* and *intense* are adjectives.)

Glen wrote his name carefully and correctly. (*Carefully* and *correctly* are adverbs.)

A play by that author received great reviews from the critics. (*By* and *from* are prepositions.)

Nora and Fred like opera, but Sal prefers jazz. (*And* and *but* are conjunctions.)

Wow, those tickets are cheap! (*Wow* is an interjection.)

You may ask, "Why should anyone bother labeling parts of speech?" Good question! Most of the time, you think about the meaning of a word, not its part of speech. Most of the time, your writing is correct. However, some important grammar rules depend upon knowing the difference between one part of speech and another. For example, an *adjective* is a word that describes people, places, or things. An *adverb* is also a description, but it can't do an adjective's job.

Take a look at these examples. Pay close attention to the underlined words:

NONSTANDARD: Today the weather is <u>beautifully</u>.

WHY IT'S NOT STANDARD: *Beautifully* is an adverb. You need an adjective here.

STANDARD: Today the weather is <u>beautiful</u>.

WHY IT'S STANDARD: The adjective *beautiful* works well here.

NONSTANDARD: Bill and Tina <u>agenda</u> the next meeting.

WHY IT'S NOT STANDARD: *Agenda* is a noun. You need an action word (a verb).

STANDARD: Bill and Tina <u>will write</u> the agenda for the next meeting.

WHY IT'S STANDARD: The verb *will write* provides the action. *Agenda* correctly appears as a noun.

NONSTANDARD: The puppy lifted <u>it's</u> paw.

WHY IT'S NOT STANDARD: You need a pronoun in this spot. *It's* means "it is."

STANDARD: The puppy lifted <u>its</u> paw.

WHY IT'S STANDARD: *Its* is a pronoun.

NONSTANDARD: The rumor spread <u>threw</u> the class.

WHY IT'S NOT STANDARD: *Threw* is a verb. An action word doesn't belong here.

STANDARD: The rumor spread <u>through</u> the class.

WHY IT'S STANDARD: The verb has been replaced by a preposition, a word that relates ideas. In this sentence, it relates *spread* and *class,* showing where the rumor *spread.*

In Unit 2, you find in-depth information on every part of speech. Well, every part of speech except for interjections. An *interjection* is a word that briefly comments on the rest of the sentence. *Ouch, wow,* and *oh* are interjections. I don't provide in-depth commentary on interjections. They have no depth! They simply add a little interest to your conversation.

TIP

Every dictionary tells you the part of speech of the word, usually right in front of the definition. Some words may have several labels because they change their identity in different sentences. For more information on how to understand every part of a dictionary definition, see Chapter 16.

Parts of a sentence

A judge sentences criminals to prison, where inmates must follow many rules. You may feel that English sentences are prisons, too, because so many rules apply to them. But English sentences are *not* prisons; they're structures to hold your thoughts. They help your reader differentiate one idea from another. Take a peek at this paragraph:

going to the beach bad idea no pets allowed want take the dog he does not bite you
know kind and friendly he is to the park instead

Oh, my! That paragraph resembles a closet with no hangers. Take another look at the same paragraph, this time with sentences:

> Going to the beach is a bad idea. No pets are allowed. I want to take the dog. He does not bite. You know how kind and friendly he is! We should go to the park instead.

This one is easier to understand, isn't it? The extra words, capital letters, and punctuation are like hangers. They organize your thoughts into complete sentences. In doing so, they sort out ideas the way hangers sort out clothing.

TIP

Complete and proper sentences aren't always necessary. When you speak with your friends, for instance, you may use half-sentences.

Read this conversation. Imagine that Joe and Barbara are speaking to or texting each other:

> Joe: Want to go to the beach?
>
> Barbara: Not without my dog.
>
> Joe: Okay, the park instead.

These comments work well because Joe and Barbara are not in a formal situation. To find out when formal English is necessary and when conversational English is acceptable, turn to Chapter 2. For more about grammar and texting, see Chapter 25.

In creating sentences that are grammatically correct in Standard English, you should pay attention to verbs, subjects, complements, and descriptions.

Verbs

Every sentence has at least one word that expresses action or being. That word is a *verb*. In these sentences, the verbs are underlined:

> Candice <u>loves</u> her engagement ring. (*loves* = action word)
>
> Duke <u>ate</u> every dog biscuit in the box. (*ate* = action word)
>
> She <u>will be</u> pleased with your work. (*will be* = being words)
>
> <u>Were</u> the lights on? (*Were* = being word)

Selecting the verb form that is correct in Standard English is important. Glance at these examples. Notice the underlined verbs:

> NONSTANDARD: You <u>was</u> wrong.
>
> WHY IT'S NOT STANDARD: In Standard English, the verb form *was* does not pair with *you*.
>
> STANDARD: You <u>were</u> wrong.
>
> WHY IT'S STANDARD: *Were* is the verb form that matches *you*. (To learn more about this topic, see Chapter 5.)

NONSTANDARD: The mayor <u>speaked</u> to voters yesterday.

WHY IT'S NOT STANDARD: *Speaked* is not correct in Standard English.

STANDARD: The mayor <u>spoke</u> to voters yesterday.

WHY IT'S STANDARD: *Spoke* is the irregular verb form you need in this sentence. (For more information about irregular verb forms, see Chapter 12.)

NONSTANDARD: John <u>studying</u> for his exam.

WHY IT'S NONSTANDARD: The verb form *studying* is not complete.

STANDARD: John <u>is studying</u> for his exam.

WHY IT'S STANDARD: Now the verb is complete. (See Chapter 8 for more about these verb forms.)

Subjects

In a sentence, someone or something does the action or exists in the state of being. That word is the *subject.* Notice the underlined subjects in these sample sentences:

<u>Cindy</u> arrived at 10 o'clock. (*Cindy* = subject)

<u>We</u> had sandwiches for lunch. (*We* = subject)

The <u>sandwiches</u> were delicious. (*sandwiches* = subject)

Do <u>you</u> like peanut butter? (*you* = subject)

<u>It</u> is smooth and sticky. (*It* = subject)

<u>Jelly</u> and <u>jam</u> go well with peanut butter. (*Jelly* and *jam* = subjects)

Most times, you know who or what you're writing about. The subject, in other words, is usually easy to select. When the subject is a pronoun, errors often occur. Examine these examples. Pay special attention to the underlined words:

NONSTANDARD: <u>Him</u> and John failed the Latin test.

WHY IT'S NOT STANDARD: *Him* can't be a subject.

STANDARD: <u>He</u> and John failed the Latin test.

WHY IT'S STANDARD: *He* is a proper subject.

NONSTANDARD: Are <u>youse</u> ready?

WHY IT'S NOT STANDARD: *Youse* is not the plural of *you*. <u>*Youse*</u> is not a Standard English form.

STANDARD: Are <u>you</u> ready?

WHY IT'S STANDARD: *You* is Standard English. *You* is both singular (one) and plural (more than one).

NONSTANDARD: <u>Us</u> friends should stick together.

WHY IT'S NOT STANDARD: <u>Us</u> is not a proper subject.

STANDARD: <u>We</u> friends should stick together.

WHY IT'S STANDARD: *We* is a proper subject in Standard English.

Chapter 14 explains which pronouns work as subjects.

Pairing subjects with verbs can also cause trouble. Check these examples. Pay attention to the underlined words in these example sentences:

NONSTANDARD: Mr. Smith and Ms. Jones <u>has been promoted</u>.

WHY IT'S NOT STANDARD: *Has been promoted* pairs up with one person. In this sentence, you have two people: *Mr. Smith and Ms. Jones.*

STANDARD: Mr. Smith and Ms. Jones <u>have been promoted</u>.

WHY IT'S STANDARD: The verb *have been promoted* properly pairs with *Mr. Smith and Ms. Jones.* Both are plural (more than one).

NONSTANDARD: The list of grammar rules <u>are</u> too long.

WHY IT'S NOT STANDARD: The subject of the sentence is *list,* a singular word. It can't pair with *are,* a plural verb form. Did you focus on *rules? Rules* is not the subject of this sentence. It's part of a description, *of grammar rules.*

STANDARD: The list of grammar rules <u>is</u> too long.

WHY IT'S STANDARD: The singular verb form, *is,* pairs correctly with the singular subject, *list.*

To find out more about matching singular subjects to singular verb forms and plural subjects to plural verb forms, check out Chapter 13.

Complements and descriptions

Your thoughts are rich and varied. You want to say more than "Mary is" or "I run." Some elements, called *complements,* complete ideas. Have a look at these example sentences. The complements are underlined:

Mary is <u>happy</u>.

Deborah mailed the <u>letter</u>.

Cathy and Drew are always <u>nervous</u> in the dentist's office.

Give <u>Jean</u> her <u>pizza</u>.

Did you tell <u>Barbara</u> the <u>secret</u>?

Usually, complements fall into place correctly. Pronouns can cause problems when they act as complements. (Have you noticed that pronouns are troublemakers?) For more information on complements, check out Chapter 9. To sort out pronouns as complements, see Chapter 14.

Your writing would be very boring without descriptions. Notice the underlined descriptions in these examples:

Every morning I run through the park.

Pink paint covered the bumpy wall.

Silk thread is more expensive than cotton thread.

Wind in that area blows the fallen leaves away.

The book of speeches helped me prepare for graduation.

Singing, the choir entered the church.

As you see, descriptions come in many shapes and sizes. Chapter 6 explains short descriptions, and Chapter 15 tackles longer ones.

Small but important: Punctuating, capitalizing, and spelling

Punctuation marks, capital letters, and spelling may seem unimportant, but they add more to your writing than you may expect. Take punctuation, for example. A few years ago, truck drivers in Maine won $5 million in a lawsuit because of a missing comma!

Punctuation

I once saw a television show in which a conversation similar to this one took place:

Angel (waving a thick stack of paper): I am writing a book.

Angel's friend (looking at the first page): What is this? I can't read it. There's no punctuation.

Angel: Oh, I'll worry about that stuff later.

Angel's friend: I don't think so! You need punctuation now!

Angel's friend is right. You can't read without punctuation, the little marks that show the reader where to pause, when someone is speaking, and so on. These are the basic punctuation marks you should know:

>> **Apostrophe:** This is a little curved hook above the line. An apostrophe, along with the letter s, shows possession:

- Ellen's car (Ellen owns the car.)

- the boys' locker room (The locker room belongs to the boys.)

- my cousin's shoes (My cousin owns the shoes.)

- the vice president's staff (The staff belongs to the vice president.)

- states' rights (The rights belong to the states.)

>> Apostrophes also shorten words:

- Annie does<u>n't</u> ice-skate. (*Doesn't* is short for *does not*)

- <u>I'm</u> excited that vacation is finally here. (*I'm* is short for *I am.*)

- Olivia could<u>n't</u> ride the roller coaster. (In this sentence, *couldn't* is short for *could not.*)

- Is<u>n't</u> that lemonade too cold? (*Isn't* is short for *is not.*)

>> To learn more about apostrophes, turn to Chapter 17.

>> **Period, question mark, exclamation point:** These three punctuation marks signal the end of a sentence. A *period* is a little dot; it follows a sentence that makes a statement. A *question mark* is made from a curve and a dot; it follows a sentence that asks a question. An *exclamation point* is a vertical line and a dot; it shows emphasis — the punctuation mark that shouts. Look at these punctuation marks in action:

- Mary's socks are blue. (The period ends the statement.)

- Are Tim's shoes blue also? (The question mark ends the question.)

- No, they are not! (The exclamation point adds emphasis.)

>> To learn more about these three important punctuation marks, see Chapter 10.

>> **Comma:** A comma tells the reader to pause. This little curved hook starts on the line and reaches below. Notice the commas in these sentences:

- Katie, my friend, is visiting from Chicago.

- Katie arrived yesterday, but she has to leave tomorrow.

- Chicago, which is in the state of Illinois, is a large city.

- Tim, have you ever visited Chicago?

>> If you read these sentences aloud, you can hear the short silences that appear at each comma. If commas trouble you, check out Chapter 19.

>> **Quotation marks:** Quotation marks are pairs of curved marks that appear above the line. Their most common job is to mark off the exact words that someone said or wrote. Notice the quotation marks in these examples:

- "Be quiet," said the librarian.

- The children cried, "We were not very loud."

- "In the library," replied the librarian, "any noise is too loud."

>> To use quotation marks properly, you must follow many rules. Turn to Chapter 18 for everything you need to know about quotation marks.

Capitalization

Have you ever seen a very old piece of writing? Capital letters show up in strange places. The U.S. Declaration of Independence is more than 200 years old. In the middle of one sentence, you see a famous phrase:

the pursuit of Happiness

These days, *happiness* would appear in lowercase (noncapitals). The founders of the country could place a capital wherever they wanted, but you don't have the same freedom. Glance at these situations, which require capital letters:

>> **Speaker or writer:** The pronoun *I* always refers to the person who is writing. It is always capitalized. Check these examples:

  ● When I am asleep, I don't snore.

  ● Gene and I love to sail on the lake.

  ● Do I have to pay extra for my suitcase?

>> By the way, poets sometimes place the pronoun *I* in lowercase. Poets break rules whenever they want. Outside of a poem, however, use a capital letter for *I*.

>> **First word in a sentence:** A capital letter begins every sentence. The letter serves as a signal that one sentence has ended and another has begun. Read these examples:

  ● Nana sings to the baby. She has a terrible voice! The baby does not mind. He loves her anyway.

  ● Palm trees grow in my yard. Warm weather suits them. Rainstorms water the trees. They require little care.

TIP

>> Are you curious about numbers? You can't capitalize *22* or *15* or any numeral. Are you wondering what happens when a number appears at the beginning of a sentence? Good question! The answer is that you should not begin a sentence with a numeral. If you need a number there, use the word:

  ● WRONG: 22 people live in that building.

  ● RIGHT: Twenty-two people live in that building.

>> **Names:** I am *Geraldine Woods,* not *geraldine woods.* Nearly all names require capital letters. (Some companies choose lowercase letters for products. The *iPad* is an example of a name that doesn't begin with a capital letter.)

Of course, these aren't the only rules that govern capital letters. Turn to Chapter 21 for more information.

Spelling

Spelling — placing every letter in the right spot — is important. Take a close look at the following paragraph. Can you identify five misspelled words?

> Jenny enjoys sewing. She pushs the needle into the cloth with her thum. Tina, who is makeing a new skirt, offen chats with Jenny wen they sew.

Before you check your answers, think for a moment. The preceding paragraph contains proper sentences. It clearly states the facts. Yet it's not a good piece of writing. The misspelled words turn a good paragraph into a bad one. Here are the correctly spelled words: *pushes, thumb, making, often, when.*

In Chapter 16, you find some rules for English spelling. Unfortunately, many, many English words don't follow those rules. To check your spelling, you may need help from the dictionary. Chapter 16 also explains how to understand and use the dictionary.

TIP

Many words sound the same but have different spellings and meanings. Other words are nearly alike in appearance or sound, but their definitions are not alike. Check Chapter 23 for help with these confusing words.

Recognizing Your Grammar Profile

No one else in the universe is exactly like you. Even your identical twin, if you have one, differs from you in some way. Your biology and experiences are unique. So is your grammar profile. Some aspects of grammar you know very well, and others may puzzle you. Your strengths and weaknesses form your grammar profile.

Table 1-1 is a checklist of common grammar problems. Next to each problem is a chapter number. If you say, "I know that already," consider skipping that chapter. If you say, "I need help with this one," you probably need to read the chapter listed in Column 3, labeled "Help Needed?" Once you have filled out the checklist, you have a road map through *English Grammar All-in-One For Dummies* and a clear route to a better command of the English language.

Table 1-1   Checklist of Common Grammar Problems

Problem	Chapter(s) Covering This Topic	Help Needed?
that boxes or *those boxes?*	3	
you was or *you were?*	4	
will you had or *will you have? we does* or *we do?*	5	
should be nearby or *could be nearby?*	5	
real good or *really good?*	6	
feels bad or *feels badly?*	6	
an apple or *a apple?*	6	
both strict but kind or *both strict and kind?*	7	
Mary buying or *Mary is buying?*	8	
The pie is or *The pie is delicious?*	9	
John sang, I danced. Correct?	10	
It snowed, however, I went anyway. Correct?	10	
had been asked or *has been asked? have did* or *have done?*	12	
Yesterday he walk or *Yesterday he walked?*	12	
One plus one is two or *One plus one was two?*	12	
river flow or *river flows?*	13	
pen and pencil was or *pen and pencil were? stick or stone is* or *stick or stone are?*	13	
Everyone are or *Everyone is? Here are three books* or *Here is three books? Some of the pie was* or *Some of the pie were?*	13	

Problem	Chapter(s) Covering This Topic	Help Needed?
John and I went or *John and myself went? Helen told me* or *Helen told I?*	14	
easier or *more easier? less difficult* or *least difficult?*	15	
bought only one shirt? or *only bought one shirt?*	15	
Abraham Lincoln is better than any president. Correct or incorrect?	15	
monkies or *monkeys? touches* or *touchs? independant* or *independent?*	16	
childrens' clothing or *children's clothing? I dont know* or *I don't know?*	17	
its or *it's? your* or *you're? who's* or *whose?*	17	
Sally said, I love that movie. Correct?	18	
boys, girls, and parents or *boys, girls and parents? No I will not* or *No, I will not?*	19	
beautifully made clothing or *beautifully-made clothing?*	20	
, or : Which is correct?	20	
Director of Security or *director of security?*	21	
the amazon river or *the Amazon River?*	21	
affect your mood or *effect your mood? Sometimes* or *Some times?*	23	
too, to, or *two?*	23	
can't hardly or *can hardly? Didn't do nothing* or *Didn't do anything?*	23	
Having played, he left or *Playing, he left?*	24	
to swim, to dive, and floating or *swimming, diving, and floating?*	24	
Text LOL? or *Text I am joking?*	25	
The problem is: Correct punctuation?	25	

Chapter **2**

Adapting Language to Every Situation

Presumably, you're reading this book because you want to learn good grammar. Excellent plan! The only problem is that *good grammar* is a moving target. What works in one situation may be completely inappropriate in another. In this chapter, I explain how to tailor your speech and writing to suit any purpose, medium, and situation. In Chapter 25, I go into more detail on the opportunities and demands of electronic communication — texts, tweets, posts, and presentation slides.

Grasping the Power and Limits of Standard English

During my grammar lessons, students sometimes ask me who made the rules I'm explaining. My answer: "*You* did." That's a collective *you*, however. When I state that *made* refers to an action in the past and *make* to an action in the present, I'm relaying what millions of English speakers have agreed on. If one person decides to fashion a new rule — say, that every sentence must begin with three exclamation points — it's likely to puzzle whoever is on the receiving end of the communication. !!!Do you see what I mean?

Here's where standards come in, closely followed by English teachers who are eager to explain, enforce, and, if need be, hammer their version of the rules into students' heads. When enough people agree on what to capitalize and how verb tenses designate time, English teachers teach that rule and grammar-book writers write about it. We're always a little behind, though, because language continues to change. So we catch up, groaning about how in *our* student days we met higher standards. But we didn't. We just met different standards, about which our own teachers undoubtedly complained.

A few English teachers and linguists have at times pulled grammatical power away from the people. Inventing or rewriting rules, they somehow convinced influential people that following those rules was a sign of a well-educated person. That idea lives on. If you speak and write according to the rules of Standard English, you're more likely to receive higher grades in school or status at work. That's not necessarily fair, but it's true. Standard English has power and advantages. It also has limitations. Some of the best, most inventive language comes from those who break the rules in a creative way. Beauty and energy often characterize nonstandard expression, and our verbal life would be very dull if rule-breaking were somehow eliminated.

What all this adds up to, I hope, is vibrant language that communicates your intended meaning in a way that suits your audience and purpose. My recommendation is to follow the rules when they serve your interests and break them when they don't. How? Read on.

Adjusting Language to Suit Your Audience

How many "Englishes" do you know? Chances are you're familiar with some version of these three:

> Wanna see the Yankees crush the Sox this afternoon? (friendspeak)
>
> Took the car. Back by 6. Bringing dinner! (conversational English)
>
> I am very sorry, Officer. I did not realize the road around the stadium was closed on game days. Please don't give me a ticket. (Standard English)

Can you see how the language in each example moves up the ladder of formality? In the first, the speaker is talking to a pal. I call this sort of language friendspeak. In the second, the writer leaves a note for a family member. This is conversational English, the go-to choice for everyday exchanges. The third is Standard English, the most formal level of language and a good choice for remarks to authority figures, such as the police.

TIP

There are gradations on the formality ladder, of course, as well as regional and community dialects. All can enrich communication. In this book, I concentrate on the rules of Standard English and the ways in which they may be eased or broken without impairing your message.

Wanna get something to eat? Friendspeak

When you relax, you probably take off your school or business outfit and put on comfortable clothing. Sweats and an old T-shirt signal that you have no obligations. You can do whatever you like. You're in charge! Language works the same way. *Friendspeak*, my term for the language you use when you're off duty, shows that it's time for fun.

Friendspeak works well when the power level is balanced. The people you're talking with or writing to are your peers. Look at these two conversations, both of which took place in my classroom:

STUDENT to TEACHER: George and I went to the gym. He did 60 push-ups. I can't do nearly as many.

TEACHER to STUDENT: George exercises regularly. That's why he's strong.

SAME STUDENT to ANOTHER STUDENT: Me and George went to the gym. He did 60 push-ups, and I'm like, no way.

OTHER STUDENT: Dude, he like, lives in the gym.

These two conversations say the same thing, but not in the same way. In speaking with teachers, students usually know they must follow the rules. The teacher also follows grammar rules. Why? The teacher–student relationship is a formal one. In the second conversation, breaking the rules is the point. The speakers have nothing to prove to each other. They're comfortable with each other's mistakes. In fact, they make mistakes on purpose, to show that they have a personal, friendly relationship.

TIP

Standard English, which follows the rules strictly, often gives you an advantage in life. When you speak with friends, though, perfectly proper sentences may sound snobby. For this reason, more casual language (either friendspeak or conversational English, which I cover in the next section) is sometimes more suitable than Standard English.

I don't deal with friendspeak in this book. Chances are, you already know it. This level of language is fine in these situations:

>> Talking with friends

>> Chatting with close family members, especially those who are the same age

>> Writing to friends in emails and texts

WARNING

Many people use the friendspeak level of English for posts on social media. This practice sounds harmless. After all, you're writing to people who, on that website, are your friends. Be careful! Employers and school officials sometimes check social media when they're considering your application for a job or for admission to a school. True, they understand that you aren't aiming for perfect grammar when you post. However, if you come across as ignorant — or worse, offensive — you may decrease your chances of acceptance. Even more important, you may hurt your readers!

REMEMBER

Employ friendspeak only when you're sure that the people you're addressing are comfortable with this type of language.

Conversational English

One step higher on the ladder of formality is conversational English. Instead of sweats and tees, think of conversational English as well-fitting jeans and a reasonably nice shirt. The language is comfortable, but not as messy as friendspeak. Conversational English is the language just about everyone uses for — surprise! — conversations. In this level of language, the people speaking probably know each other. They relax, but not completely.

Conversational English has a breezy sound. Letters are dropped in contractions (*don't, I'll, would've,* and so forth). In written form, conversational English breaks punctuation rules, too. Sentences run together, and commas connect all sorts of things. Multiple punctuation marks (two or three exclamation points, for example) show strong emotion, especially in social media posts and texts.

I use conversational English in this book because, as I write, I imagine that I am speaking with you, the reader. I pretend that I know you and that we are spending some free time together. I don't see myself as a teacher in a formal classroom situation.

Conversational English is suitable for these situations:

» Chats with friends and family

» Conversations with neighbors and other acquaintances

» Notes, emails, instant messages, letters, and texts to friends and family

» Comments posted on social media

» Informal conversations with teachers

» Remarks to co-workers

WARNING The last two items on this list are tricky. In a school or business situation, you can be friendly, but not too friendly. Suppose a teacher is in the middle of a lesson. In this situation, don't employ conversational English. Questions and remarks during class are best phrased in Standard English. If you're chatting with a teacher after class, though, you don't need formal language. At work, conversational English is fine for lunch and coffee breaks. During meetings at work, you should be more careful to follow the rules of grammar.

TIP At work or at school, check the level of language before you speak. How formal are others' remarks? Listen, and adapt your own language to match the group's preferred style.

Standard English

Standard English is similar to the clothing you select when you want to look your best. Imagine a business suit or an outfit you would wear to a dinner party. When you employ Standard English, your readers or listeners grasp that you know the rules of grammar. You demonstrate that you have a strong vocabulary.

You should speak and write in Standard English when you're addressing someone who has more power and authority than you do. This level of English adds dignity to every interaction. It signals that you're taking things seriously and putting forth your best effort. Use Standard English for these situations:

>> Business letters

>> Emails to clients, colleagues, and teachers

>> Letters to the editor or to government officials

>> Written reports (on paper or on websites)

>> Memos

>> Homework assignments

>> Notes or emails to teachers

>> Speeches, presentations, and oral reports

>> Important conversations (job interviews, admissions interviews, and the like)

In any situation in which you're being judged, begin with Standard English. You can always ease up if you discover that your reader or listener prefers a different, less formal style.

REMEMBER

You have to know the rules of Standard English before you decide that it's okay to break them. As you read *English Grammar All-in-One For Dummies*, keep track of the rules. Practice so that you can be perfect when the need arises.

EXAMPLE

Q. Can you recognize rungs on the ladder of formality? Place these expressions in order, moving from the most formal to the least. *Note:* Two expressions may tie. For example, your answer may be "1 and 2, 3." In that answer, the first and second statements have the same level of formality, and the third statement is less formal than the first two.

(1) You just don't get it.

(2) You do not comprehend the situation.

(3) You don't understand what happened.

A. **2, 3, 1** Expression 2 is the most formal, with no contractions, such as *don't*, which you see in 3. Expression 2 also includes a fairly sophisticated word, *comprehend*. Option 3 is a little more relaxed than 2, with the contraction *don't* and *what happened* instead of *the situation*. Expression 1 includes slang: *get it* means "understand." Slang is always informal.

YOUR TURN

Place these expressions in order, moving from the most formal to the least. *Note:* Two expressions may tie.

1   (1) I provide herein

(2) I enclose

(3) Here's

2   (1) Don't worry about that issue.

(2) Hey, don't flip out!

(3) Forget it, please.

3   (1) does not exercise

(2) total couch potato

(3) never exercises

4   (1) My bad.

(2) Oops! Sorry.

(3) I apologize.

5   (1) Does this interest you?

(2) r u in? (*Note:* This is equivalent to "Are you in?")

(3) Are you in?

In addition to recognizing levels of formality, you have to decide when each is the best choice. Consider the power balance: Communicating with someone who has more power than you generally requires more formal expression. With peers, you can ease up. Also think about your purpose. Do you want to be perceived as knowledgeable and professional? Friendly and relaxed? If you answered yes to the first question, move higher on the formality ladder. If the second is true, take it down a notch.

EXAMPLE

Q. Which remarks from a student to a teacher are acceptable?

(A) no hw — ttyl

(B) Just a note to let you know I didn't do the homework. I'll explain later! Ralph

(C) Dear Ms. Smith,

I was not able to do my homework last night. I will speak with you about this matter later.

Sincerely,

Ralph

A. **(B) or (C)** The correct answer depends on a few factors. How willing are you to be stuck sitting in the corner of the classroom for the rest of the year? If your answer is "very willing," send A, a text written in friendspeak. (By the way, *hw* is short for homework, and *ttyl* means "Talk to you later.") Does your teacher come to school in jeans and sneakers? If so, (B) is probably acceptable because it's written in conversational English. Is the teacher prim and proper, expecting you to follow every rule ever created, including a few that only professional copyeditors know? If so, (C), which is written in Standard English, is your best bet.

Which choice(s), if any, would be appropriate for the situation described?

YOUR TURN

6 blog post written by a cookbook reviewer

   (A) I cooked three chickens tonight, and I'm now on page 5567 of *How to Cook Everything.* It was terrible. Don't ever put a sardine near a chicken.

   (B) i cooked three chickens tonight and im now on p 5567 of How to Cook Everything. It was terible. Don't ever put a sardine near a chicken ever.

   (C) 3 chix w/ sards tonight p 5567 *How Cook Everything* terrible

   (D) None

7 note to boss

   (A) Met client. Deal okay if shipping included. Your thoughts?

   (B) shp deal brAkr ok?

   (C) The client has accepted the deal on the condition that all shipping costs are included in the price we quoted. I wonder if you would mind getting back to me, at your earliest convenience, so that I have some idea whether this stipulation is all right with you.

   (D) None

8 ad directed at undecided voters, written by a lobbyist

   (A) No on #toothpastebill

   (B) no toothpaste bill #myteethRmine

   (C) Tell your representative to vote no on the bill to ban toothpaste.

   (D) None

9 note to teacher from student

   (A) no hw cat 8 it better tmrw leo

   (B) Mr. Smarva, sorry, can't hand in my homework my cat ate it I'll do better tomorrow your friend Leo

   (C) cat ate hw do bettrr tomorrow leo

   (D) None

10 written comments about an excavation, from archaeologist to colleagues

(A) The horizontal strips of a metallic substance and the marks of a crude pickax suggest that this was a prehistoric mine.

(B) Horizontal strips of metal + pickax marks = prehistoric mine

(C) I ascertain from the evidence that the site was consistent with a prehistoric mine. The aforementioned evidence (the horizontal strips of a metallic substance and the marks of a crude pickax) appears incontrovertible.

(D) None

11 message to a potential employer from a person interviewing for a job

(A) can't come now maybe later.

(B) not now, maybe L8R

(C) I cannot come now, maybe later.

(D) None

12 text to close friend

(A) I will have to get back to you. The professor just arrived. I will text again after the class ends.

(B) prof l8r

(C) prof here ttyl

(D) None

13 handwritten note on a thank-you card

(A) Hi, Grandpa. The speaker was great. Thanks for arranging her visit. Love, Alice

(B) Grandpa the speaker great thanks for arranging

(C) great speaker thx

(D) None

14 opinion piece about a musical performance, published in a school paper

(A) BB's last set = epic fail — where do they find those chords?

(B) Bl Bk's last set didn't work. Were do thA find those chords?

(C) Blue Beak's last set was a problem. Seriously, where do they find those notes?

(D) None

15 tweet to high school students from the class president

(A) tlion 9s only

(B) #library is 9s only

(C) Library is open now for 9th graders only!

(D) None

Practice Questions Answers and Explanations

(1) **1, 2, 3** Expression 1 uses an old-fashioned, totally formal word, *herein*. Expression 2 is more modern and less formal. Expression 3 is a contraction (*here's* is short for *here is*). The contraction makes this expression the least formal of the three.

(2) **1, 3, 2** All three of these statements attempt to reassure the listener or reader. Expression 1 is the most formal, with a complete sentence including a dignified phrase, *that issue*. Expression 2 employs slang (*flip out = get upset*), as well as the informal greeting *hey*. Somewhere in the middle is Expression 3, which attaches *please* to a complete sentence.

(3) **1 and 3, 2** Expressions 1 and 3 are Standard English, on the same level of formality. Expression 2 is slang. (A *total couch potato* is someone who never gets off the couch.) Expression 2 is the least formal.

(4) **3, 1 and 2** *I apologize* is grammatically correct and proper for all occasions. Expressions 1 and 2 are less formal because they include slang (*my bad = my mistake*, understood as an apology, and *oops*, an expression admitting an accident or error).

(5) **1, 3, 2** Expression 1 has no contractions or slang, so it's formal. Expression 3, on the other hand, uses a shortened form of the expression — close to slang. *Are you in?* means *Are you interested?* and is conversational. The least formal is Expression 2, which uses texting abbreviations, *r (are)* and *u (you)*.

(6) **(A)** Option (B) is filled with problems. No matter who your reader is, you should avoid incorrect spelling (*terible*). Also, why lowercase the personal pronoun *I*? It's not much harder or time-consuming to add an apostrophe to *I'm*. Option (C) is worse because it includes abbreviations and shortened words (*chix*) that would be better for a text to a friend than a post on a website. Option (A) obeys the rules of standard English — not a bad idea for someone who wants to be taken seriously as a reviewer.

(7) **(A)** You don't have to write all the information in option (C). By the time the boss finishes reading all those unnecessary words, the client may have moved to another supplier in sheer frustration. The same information comes through in option (A), which is shorter, and though not formal, stays close enough to Standard English to please a boss. Option (B) is far too informal for a message to someone with more power than you. Also, *brAkr (breaker)* isn't standard and may be incomprehensible.

(8) **(C)** The meaning as expressed in option (C) is clear, and because the lobbyist wants to convince voters that the ideas are the product of an intelligent being, proper grammar and spelling are a plus. The other two choices are vague and more suited for a community that expects informality. The hashtags (the # symbols) are intended to rally like-minded readers to join together, but it's hard to gather support for an ill-defined cause.

(9) **(D)** If Leo seriously wants to be excused for missing a homework assignment, he should unearth every bit of grammar knowledge he has, because a teacher is an authority figure and deserves Standard English.

(10) **(A)** Option (C) is far too wordy and stuffy, even for academia. Option (B) is too informal. The plus and equal signs don't belong in a post about archeology from someone who wants to be respected as a professional in that field.

(11) **(D)** Writing in a business setting should be more formal than options (A), (B), and (C). Furthermore, if you're postponing an interview, courtesy demands a reason (the building's on fire, you broke your leg, a comet's about to strike Earth — *something*).

(12) **(C)** Option (A) isn't wrong, exactly, but a close friend doesn't need complete and proper sentences, especially when the professor has arrived and you're supposed to be ready for class. Your peers probably understand the words you shortened, especially an abbreviation such as *ttyl* ("talk to you later") that frequently appears in texts and informal posts on social media. Option (B) is a little too vague.

(13) **(A)** In option (A), the punctuation is correct, and the sentences make sense. Grandpa will be proud. The others may be acceptable (grandparents tend to give their grandchildren a lot of leeway), but it's not particularly polite to leave your best grammar on the shelf when writing to someone older than you, especially when that person has done you a favor.

(14) **(C)** The tone of option (C) is conversational, but that's usually fine in a school paper. The other options are better suited to friend-to-friend text.

(15) **(C)** The senior class president should come across as friendly, but a bit serious also. Not to mention clear! A tweet to teens can include all sorts of abbreviations. But *tlion,* which appears in option (A), is an abbreviation I made up. Inside my head. Just me! It means "the library is open now." Option (B) doesn't include all the information. Only option (C) has a clear meaning and sounds friendly but informal.

Whaddya Know? Chapter 2 Quiz

If you're ready to test your skills a bit more, take the following chapter quiz that incorporates all the chapter topics.

Which of these statements, if any, are suitable in the specified situation? *Note:* The statement may be excerpted from a longer conversation or piece of writing.

1. Situation: Student's email to a teacher asking for a letter of recommendation

   (A) Would you please write a letter of recommendation?

   (B) You get me. Wanna write for me?

   (C) r u ok to write 4 me?

2. Situation: Letter of complaint from a customer to a company about a recent purchase

   (A) Your vacuum stinks. I want my money back now!

   (B) The vacuum doesn't work, so I want a refund.

   (C) Vacuum = busted. Refund = mine.

3. Situation: Text from Lily, who has known Anthony since preschool, commenting on a mutual friend's unexpected offer to help with a school project

   (A) 2G2BT

   (B) rly? r u sure?

   (C) 4 real?

4. Situation: Co-worker speaking to a peer at a committee meeting chaired by their supervisor

   (A) The marketing stuff's epic, but the neighborhood's sketchy.

   (B) Whassup with the neighborhood? The marketing's okay.

   (C) The marketing is fine, but the neighborhood is questionable.

5. Situation: Phone call from a parent to another parent about a playdate for their children

   (A) Saturday okay with you? Maybe the beach? Or the playground? Could be fun.

   (B) How about I take the kids to the beach or the playground on Saturday for a fun afternoon?

   (C) Would it be permissible for me to take our children on an excursion this Saturday, perhaps to the beach or to the playground, so that they can amuse each other for a while?

6. Situation: Alice speaking with a traffic patrol officer who has pulled her over to the side of the road

   (A) You gotta problem?

   (B) What's the problem, Officer?

   (C) Is there a problem?

7 Situation: Text from a boss to an assistant, requesting a file they've been working on

(A) get me file asap

(B) need file now

(C) file – now

8 Situation: Comment to a citizen from a clerk in a government agency

(A) What's your DOB and SSN?

(B) Tell me your date of birth and social security number.

(C) When were you born, and what's your social?

9 Situation: Email from broker to customer who asked for information quickly

(A) Spoke with Jacobs. Deal's OK with him.

(B) I had a chance to speak with Mr. Jacobs, as you asked. I called him immediately, as you were in a rush. He indicated that the deal is fine with him.

(C) Re Jacobs: deal's okay with him.

10 Situation: Email to co-workers from their union representative about a possible job action. It's illegal for the union members to strike

(A) Tomorrow we should all call in "sick," if that's how the vote turns out at the meeting tonight.

(B) Important vote at tonight's meeting. Please attend.

(C) We're getting the flu tomorrow, depending on tonight's vote.

Answers to Chapter 2 Quiz

1 **(A)**

A teacher has more power than a student, and so does anyone who's doing you a favor. Statement (B) — which a student actually sent! — is too informal. Statement (C) is never acceptable in an email, text, or instant message to anyone other than a close friend.

2 **(A) and (B)**

Statement (A) is rude, but it does get the point across. (Courtesy, of course, is always best, but grammatically this one works.) Statement (B) conveys the message more politely. It, too, is fine. Statement (C) probably won't be taken seriously by a manufacturer. (Would *you* send money to someone who uses this sort of language?)

3 **All of the statements**

Because Lily and Anthony are close friends, they probably text each other often and understand these abbreviations. Grammarians usually detest such shortcuts, but realists know that abbreviations and shortened words convey meaning — and they aren't going away anytime soon. For those who don't text, 2G2BT means *too good to be true, rly* means *really, r u sure* means *are you sure?*, and *4 real* means *for real*.

4 **(C)**

Because the supervisor is present, the speaker should steer clear of slang such as *epic* (impressive, great), *sketchy* (borderline, not quite safe or correct), and *whassup* (a short form of *What's up?* or *What's going on?*). The third statement is fine.

5 **(A) and (B)**

Parents are peers, so conversational English, which you see in Statements (A) and (B), is fine. Statement (C) is far too formal and stiff.

6 **(B) and (C)**

A cop who is ordering you around has more power. Statement (A) is for peers, not the traffic patrol. Statements (B) and (C) are sufficiently formal for the situation.

7 **(A) and (B)**

When a boss speaks to an assistant, the boss has more power and can break the rules of conventional grammar, as long as the intended meaning is clear. The first and second statements are okay, assuming that the assistant knows which file the boss wants. (*ASAP* is a common acronym meaning "as soon as possible." It's safe to assume that most people understand it.) Statement (C) is unclear. Does the boss want the assistant to file away information for the boss, work on the file, or bring the file to the boss? More than one meaning is possible, so Statement (C) is unacceptable.

8 **(B)**

The acronyms DOB and SSN aren't universally understood. Similarly, your social may be mystifying. Only Statement (B) is completely clear.

9 **(A) and (C)**

A customer usually merits your most formal writing, but if the customer wants something fast (and this one does), a condensed message is actually better than a drawn-out statement. Statements (A) and (C) give the facts — and the impression that the broker rushed the message to the customer as rapidly as possible. Both are better than Statement (B), which meanders toward meaning.

10 **(B)**

Email should never be used for communications you want to keep private. In Statements (A) and (C), the union representative hints at a planned strike. Those emails could lead to a court case. Statement (B) is more neutral and less likely to appear as evidence.

2

Exploring Parts of Speech

In This Unit . . .

Chapter **3**

People to See, Places to Go, Things to Remember: Recognizing Nouns

Watch very young children learning to speak. Their first words are usually the names of important people, places, or things: *Mama, Dada, home,* or *toy.* I imagine that language started in the same way. Our ancient relatives probably talked about what mattered to them — *cave, fire,* or *bear,* and, of course, *Mama* and *Dada.* Parents are always important people.

In this chapter, you learn about the first part of speech that young children use — nouns. You identify nouns and sort out those that name one (*singular* nouns) from those that name more than one (*plural* nouns). You also see how to attach other words — *that, this, those,* and *these* — to nouns.

Identifying Nouns

Important people, places, and things need names. The part of speech that names them is a *noun*.

Before you do anything with nouns — change them from singular to plural or the other way around, capitalize them, or place them in sentences — you have to find them. In this section, you search for nouns when they name people, places, things, events, ideas, or emotions.

Naming people with nouns

Who are you? You are, right now, a <u>reader</u>. You may also be some of these: a <u>man</u>, a <u>woman</u>, a <u>student</u>, or a <u>worker</u>. You may be a <u>mother</u> or <u>father</u>, a <u>son</u> or <u>daughter</u>, a <u>cousin</u>, or a <u>grandparent</u> or <u>grandchild</u>. Perhaps you're a famous <u>actor</u>. (If you're famous, please autograph something for me. I can make a lot of money selling autographed items on eBay.)

Every underlined word in the paragraph above is a general term for a person and also a *noun*. Other nouns for people include:

singer

writer

New Yorker

lawyer

neighbor

Can you guess which nouns apply to me? You really, really don't want to hear me sing, and I know nothing about the law. I do write, and I live in New York. I can use <u>writer</u>, <u>New Yorker</u>, and <u>neighbor</u> to talk about myself. All these nouns refer to me, a <u>person</u>. (The word *person*, by the way, is also a noun.)

Of course, I can also use my name to talk about myself. I'm <u>Geraldine Woods</u>. My friends call me <u>Gerri</u>. (People who don't like me have names for me, too, but I won't print those names here.) All names are nouns, including these:

Abraham Lincoln

Queen Elizabeth I

Mary Watson

Spider-Man

Do I have to tell you that nothing on this list applies to me? I am sorry to disappoint you, but I am not a queen (like Elizabeth I), a president (like Abraham Lincoln), or a superhero (like Spider-Man).

TIP

Did you notice that the names in the preceding list begin with capital letters? Specific names (*John Smith*) are capitalized. General names (*customer*) are not capitalized. To find out more about when a name should be capitalized, turn to Chapter 21.

EXAMPLE

Q. Identify the nouns in the following paragraph:

Jenny is a plumber. She told William that her last customer, Arthur Smith, was cheap. He wanted to pay her less than Gene Muller did, and Gene is a poor man.

A. **Jenny, plumber, William, customer, Arthur Smith, Gene Muller, Gene, man** All these words name people, so all are nouns.

REMEMBER

Both general and specific names for people are nouns.

Naming places with nouns

Where are you? I am in my <u>bedroom</u>, in the <u>corner</u> that I use as an <u>office</u>, in an <u>apartment</u> in <u>Manhattan</u> in <u>New York State</u> in the <u>United States of America</u>. A few years ago I visited <u>London</u> and <u>Madrid</u> after retiring from my <u>school</u>, which is located in another <u>area</u> of the <u>city</u>.

The underlined words in the preceding paragraph are places. Words that name places, even when they are general terms, are nouns. Here are several more:

> river
>
> mountain
>
> continent
>
> theater
>
> street

Names of specific places are also nouns:

> Sahara Desert
>
> Antarctica
>
> Greenwich Village
>
> Sierra Nevada
>
> Jupiter

The places that nouns name can be very large (the *universe*) or very small (my *closet*). Size doesn't matter. (Well, size doesn't matter in grammar! You decide whether it matters in other areas.)

TIP

Capital letters do matter. The name of a specific place is capitalized (*Atlantic Ocean*). General names of places are not (*island*). For more information about capitalizing the names of places, see Chapter 21.

Q. Identify the nouns in the following paragraph:

In Canada, which is a large country in North America, he often visits Montreal, a beautiful city on the Saint Lawrence River, near Mont Tremblant, a popular place to ski.

A. **Canada, country, North America, Montreal, city, Saint Lawrence River, Mont Tremblant, place** All these words name places (including the word *place* itself), so all are nouns.

Naming things with nouns

As I look out my <u>window</u>, I see many <u>things</u>: <u>buildings</u>, <u>cars</u>, an occasional <u>bus</u>, and <u>construction</u> on the <u>terrace</u> nearby, where someone has planted a tiny <u>garden</u> consisting of three <u>bushes</u> with pink <u>flowers</u>.

Yes, even in the middle of New York City, you can find a garden! A garden is a thing, and so are all the underlined words in the preceding paragraph. Words that name things are nouns.

TIP

When I say "thing," I don't mean only things that you can buy in a store and put on a shelf. You probably noticed that one of the underlined nouns *(construction)* is an activity. Nouns can name activities as well as objects. Here are other nouns that name things:

tables

exams

marriage

pollution

The names of events are also nouns:

vacation

New Year's Eve

birthdays

the Revolutionary War

exams

As you see, nouns may name events in general terms *(birthdays)*. Other nouns name specific events *(New Year's Eve, the Revolutionary War)*.

TIP

The name of a specific event is usually capitalized *(Great Depression)*. General names for events are normally written without capital letters *(anniversary)*. The name of an object may be capitalized if it's a brand *(Cadillac)* unless the company decides not to use a capital letter *(iPad)*. To find out more about when you should capitalize the name of an event or object, see Chapter 21.

EXAMPLE

Q. Identify the nouns in the following paragraph:

Nearly everyone who enjoys crafts buys glue, crayons, and cloth to make decorations for holidays and other celebrations, such as Halloween and Thanksgiving.

A. **crafts, glue, crayons, cloth, decorations, holidays, celebrations, Halloween, Thanksgiving** All these words name things, so all are nouns.

The names of things, activities, and events are nouns.

REMEMBER

Naming ideas and emotions with nouns

I feel <u>loyalty</u> to those I love and <u>gratitude</u> to everyone who has ever helped me. I believe that <u>love</u> and <u>friendship</u> are always better than <u>hatred</u> and <u>rejection</u>. Do you agree with these <u>thoughts</u>, or is your <u>opinion</u> different?

Ideas and emotions are real and extremely powerful, even though you can't touch them, and their names — all the underlined words in the preceding paragraph — are nouns. Take a look at a few more nouns naming ideas and emotions:

confusion

idealism

viewpoint

joy

anger

The names of belief systems, such as a religion (*Catholicism*, for example), are nouns. The names of causes, such as *environmentalism*, are also nouns.

Sometimes you need a capital letter for a particular system of belief (*Islam* or *Judaism*, for example), and sometimes you do not (*democracy*, for instance). For more information on capitalizing the names of ideas or beliefs, turn to Chapter 21.

TIP

Q. Identify the nouns in the following sentence:

EXAMPLE

He was filled with happiness when she explained her thoughts on freedom, because he also worked to bring about justice and equality in society.

A. You should have found six nouns: *happiness, thoughts, freedom, justice, equality, society.* All these words name ideas or feelings, so all are nouns.

Many words that describe feelings and ideas have other forms that are not nouns. For example, *equality* is a noun, but *equal* is not. The noun (*equality*) names the concept. The other form (*equal*) acts as a description (*equal opportunity*).

WARNING

YOUR TURN

Identify the nouns in these sentences.

1. Oscar loves spaghetti, which is his favorite food.

2. He cooks hamburgers in his well-equipped kitchen or, if the weather is nice, in his yard over an open fire.

3. Oscar stores charcoal in a large plastic tub that used to belong to his grandpa.

4. He's known for his passionate belief in environmentalism, a cause his Aunt Emma also supports.

5. Her garbage can is very small because she recycles or reuses things instead of throwing them out.

6. Aunt Emma trains thoroughbred horses that Oscar rides at racetracks around the country.

7. Oscar rode her three favorite horses in Buenos Aires recently.

8. Both Oscar and his aunt are animal lovers and treat the animals like royalty.

9. Because Oscar is sentimental, he dedicates each race to his mother and father.

10. He wrote a song about the filly that was born on his birthday.

11. The jockeys guiding their horses to the starting gate became annoyed by Oscar's song, which he sang in an extremely loud voice.

12. The problem is that Oscar can't stay in tune when he sings.

Sorting Out Singular and Plural Nouns

Smile! You're having a <u>baby</u>. Smile more! You're having three <u>babies</u>.

Baby is a singular noun. *Babies* is a plural noun. When you become a parent, the difference between singular (one) and plural (more than one) is rather important. It's important in grammar also. Why? Within a sentence, singular nouns match up with other singular words, and plurals pair with other plurals. In this section, you examine the singular and plural forms of nouns.

Adding the letters S or ES to form plurals

Take a look at these singular and plural nouns. Notice the difference between them:

Singular	Plural
fork	forks
television	televisions
shoe	shoes
infant	infants
horse	horses
officer	officers
photo	photos

Now check out these singular and plural nouns. Notice how they differ:

Singular	Plural
brush	brushes
match	matches
kiss	kisses
tax	taxes
witch	witches
loss	losses
bush	bushes

The rule for forming regular plurals is simple: When the singular noun ends in *sh*, *ch*, *ss*, or *x*, add the letters *es* to form the plural noun. If the singular noun ends in any other letter, add *s*.

Q. Write the form that is missing in the following table. You should add or take away either *s* or *es*:

Singular	Plural
mess	
	lions
switch	
	boxes
zoo	
	gorillas
eyelash	

A. **messes, lion, switches, box, zoos, gorilla, eyelashes** The words *mess, switch, box,* and *eyelash* employ the letters *es* to form the plural. The other words form plurals with the letter *s* alone.

Words that end with the letter *o* sometimes add a simple *s* (*zoos, avocados*) and sometimes *es* (*potatoes, heroes*). Words that end with the letter *y* form the plural with a simple *s* or with a change from *y* to *i* and the addition of *es*. For more information on *y*-ending words, turn to Chapter 16. Check the dictionary if you're unsure how to form any plural.

TIP

Plurals that break the rules

Are you a rebel, or do you usually follow the rules? I wrote *usually* because my experience tells me that no one follows the rules all the time. The English language also breaks the rules occasionally and creates strange plural forms. Read these sentences, paying attention to the underlined words:

> Help! One little <u>sheep</u> is eating my lunch! I'm joking. Only a few <u>sheep</u> live near me, all in zoos.

The first underlined word, *sheep*, is singular. The clues are *one*, which always signals a singular noun, and *is*, a singular verb. The second underlined word looks exactly the same. However, this time *sheep* is plural, indicating more than one animal. The clues are *a few*, which signals a plural noun; the word *live*, a plural verb. English is odd, isn't it? Sometimes the same word can be either singular or plural, depending on how it's used.

You can't memorize every plural form in the English language — not if you want to have time to eat, sleep, and have an actual life. However, you should know some common irregular plurals:

Singular	Plural	Singular	Plural
half	halves	moose	moose
loaf	loaves	deer	deer
knife	knives	mouse	mice
leaf	leaves	goose	geese
man	men	tooth	teeth
woman	women	information	information
child	children	editor-in-chief	editors-in-chief

TIP

Your best path through the world of irregular plurals is to remember those you use often. You may want to keep a list of your personal favorites. You can look up other plurals in the dictionary when you need them.

EXAMPLE

Q. Write the irregular plural form of each word. If you're unsure, check the dictionary.

Singular	Plural
ox	
hoof	
scarf	
runner-up	
crisis	
aircraft	
foot	

A. oxen, hooves, scarves, runners-up, crises, aircraft, feet

When you come across a word with a hyphen (a short line separating two words, such as *runner-up* or *brother-in-law*), look at the most important part of the word — the section that carries the main meaning *(runner, brother)*. Make that word plural *(runners, brothers)* and leave the rest of the word alone *(runners-up, brothers-in-law)*.

The dictionary is your friend when you're writing plural forms. Look up any noun to find its plural form or instructions for creating its plural.

Fill in the blanks with the plural or singular form of these nouns:

Singular	Plural
13. kindness	
14.	mice
15. cello	
16. itch	
17. commander-in-chief	
18. question	
19.	watches
20. tomato	

Attaching "This," "These," and Other Words to Nouns

Nouns often come with descriptions attached. In some languages, every description has a singular and a plural form, but descriptions in English usually keep the same form whether they attach to singular or plural nouns. You can correctly write about one *fine day* and five *fine days*. A few words, though, do change depending on whether the noun they're attached to is singular or plural. Take a look at these examples:

<u>this</u> book (singular)

<u>these</u> books (plural)

<u>that</u> orange (singular)

<u>those</u> oranges (plural)

<u>this</u> country (singular)

<u>these</u> countries (plural)

<u>that</u> dog (singular)

<u>those</u> dogs (plural)

As you see in this list, *this* and *that* pair up with singular nouns. *These* and *those* pair with plural nouns.

WARNING

I often hear people attach the word *them* to nouns (*them books* or *them cars*). In Standard English, *them* always stands alone and never joins a noun in this way.

TIP

Two tiny words, *a* and *an*, attach only to singular nouns. You can say *a rug* or *an apple*, but not *a rugs* or *an apples*. (If you're curious about the difference between *a* and *an*, turn to Chapter 6.) I am happy to tell you that another common word that attaches to nouns, *the*, works for both singular and plural nouns.

EXAMPLE

Q. In the following paragraph, underline the correct word from each pair:

Alex put (this/these) folder in (that/those) drawer. He locked up all (this/these) files because all (that/those) information is secret. Anne took (them/those) keys and opened (that/those) drawers. She was very interested in (this/these) file about salaries.

A. **this** folder, **that** drawer, **these** files, **that** information, **those** keys, **those** drawers, **this** file. The singular nouns (*folder, drawer, information, file*) pair with the singular words *this* and *that*. The plural nouns (*files, keys, drawers*) pair with the plural words *these* and *those*.

YOUR TURN

Select the word in Column 1 that correctly pairs with the word or words in Column 2.

21. this/these	pineapples
22. that/those	lamp
23. that/those	firefighter
24. this/these	symphonies
25. this/these	dictionary
26. that/those	iron kettles
27. this/these	sorts of situations
28. that/those	type of chair

Practice Questions Answers and Explanations

(1) **Oscar, spaghetti, food** These nouns name a person (*Oscar*) and two things (*spaghetti, food*).

(2) **hamburgers, kitchen, weather, yard, fire** These nouns name two places (*kitchen, yard*) and three things (*hamburgers, weather, fire*).

(3) **Oscar, charcoal, tub, grandpa** Did you underline *plastic*? That word can sometimes function as a noun, but here it's acting as a description of *tub*. Descriptions are adjectives. (For more information on adjectives, see Chapter 6.)

(4) **belief, environmentalism, cause, Aunt Emma** The first three are abstract, but they're still nouns. The last is the name of a person.

(5) **can, things** Did you underline *garbage*? That word can function as a noun, but here it's a description of *can*.

(6) **Aunt Emma, horses, Oscar, racetracks, country** Two people, one thing, two places — all nouns!

(7) **Oscar, horses, Buenos Aires** In this sentence, nouns name people, animals, and cities.

(8) **Oscar, aunt, lovers, animals, royalty** Why is *animals* but not *animal* a noun in this sentence? *Animal* is attached to *lover* as a description. *Animals* stands alone as a noun.

(9) **Oscar, race, mother, father** *Race* can function as a verb — an action — but in this sentence it's a noun.

(10) **song, filly, birthday** A *filly* is a young female horse — and a noun.

(11) **jockeys, horses, gate, Oscar's, song, voice** *Oscar's* is the possessive form of the noun *Oscar*. It's a possessive noun, but still a noun.

(12) **problem, Oscar, tune** Give yourself a gold star if you identified *tune* as a noun. The word names a thing you can unfortunately hear but not touch.

(13) **kindnesses** Because the singular noun *kindness* ends in *s*, you add *es* to make the noun plural.

(14) **mouse** The singular noun *mouse* has an irregular plural, *mice*.

(15) **cellos** When a singular noun ends in *o*, check the dictionary to find out whether you add *s* or *es* to form the plural. Here, *s* does the job.

(16) **itches** The singular noun *itch* ends with an *h*, so you add *es* to form the plural.

(17) **commanders-in-chief** To form the plural of a hyphenated noun, focus on the most important word — in this case, *commander*. The plural of *commander* is *commanders*.

(18) **questions** A simple *s* changes the singular noun *question* to the plural *questions*.

(19) **watch** A singular noun ending in *h* needs *es* to form the plural. Subtract those letters from the plural noun *watches* and you've got your answer.

(20) **tomatoes** To make the singular noun *tomato* plural, add *es*.

(21) **these** pineapples

(22) **that** lamp

(23) **that** firefighter

(24) **these** symphonies

(25) **this** dictionary

(26) **those** iron kettles Did I fool you with this one? The important word here is *kettles,* which is plural, so *those* is the plural word you're looking for.

(27) **these sorts of situations**

(28) **that** type of chair

If you're ready to test your skills a bit more, take the following chapter quiz that incorporates all the chapter topics.

Whaddya Know? Chapter 3 Quiz

Quiz time! Complete each problem to test your knowledge of the various topics covered in this chapter. You can then find the solutions and explanations in the next section.

Twins Alix and Andrew have made a list of birthday presents they hope to receive. Before they make a million copies and distribute them to their family and friends, underline the nouns and correct all the errors.

What we want for these birthday:

>> two orange watchs

>> one complete sets of dominos

>> three fire extinguisheres

>> ten reindeer

>> seven videoes about gooses

>> two partridge in these pear tree

Answers to Chapter 3 Quiz

> What we want for (1) these [this] (2) <u>birthday</u>:
>
> » two orange (3) watchs [<u>watches</u>]
>
> » one complete (4) sets [<u>set</u>] of (5) <u>dominos</u>
>
> » three fire (6) extinguisheres [<u>extinguishers</u>]
>
> » ten (7) <u>reindeer</u>
>
> » seven (8) videoes [<u>videos</u>] about (9) gooses [<u>geese</u>]
>
> » two (10) <u>partridges</u> in (11) these [this] pear (12) <u>tree</u>

1. **this** The noun *birthday* is singular, so attach the singular word *this* rather than the plural word *these*.

2. **birthday** This is a noun.

3. **watches** This is a plural noun. Because the singular form ends in *h*, add *es* to form the plural.

4. **set** There's only one, so you need the singular noun *set*, not the plural, *sets*.

5. **dominos** This plural noun is correctly spelled.

6. **extinguishers** The singular noun *extinguisher* ends in *r*, so simply add *s* to make it plural.

7. **reindeer** This is an irregular plural; the singular and plural nouns are the same.

8. **videos** This plural noun is formed by adding *s* to the singular noun *video*.

9. **geese** This is an irregular plural noun.

10. **partridges** This plural noun is formed by adding *s* to the singular noun *partridge*.

11. **this** You have one *pear tree*, so you need the singular form *this* rather than the plural, *these*.

12. **tree** This is a singular noun. If you underlined *pear*, you made a mistake, because in this sentence it's a description of *tree*, not a noun.

Chapter **4**

Meeting the Pronoun Family

I t is hard to imagine the English language without pronouns. They are everywhere, including in the first two sentences of the paragraph you're reading now — specifically, *it, them, they,* and *you.* Pronouns tend to be small words, but they have caused big fights, now and in the past. I discuss current issues concerning pronouns in the Introduction to this book. In this chapter, I go over pronoun basics — what they are and do, as well as what characteristics shape their identity.

Working Hard: Pronouns and Their Jobs

Some people have two or three jobs. Their reward: enough money to live on. Pronouns have five jobs, though not all at the same time. Their reward: an essential role in the English language. This section surveys what pronouns do.

Replacing nouns

Read this paragraph:

> John accompanied John's best friend, Alice, to Alice's house after the party. John asked Alice whether Alice would give John the recipe for the cookies John and Alice had eaten at the party. Alice reluctantly gave the recipe to John. "Excellent," said John to John. "Alice's recipe is the best!"

What a boring piece of writing! I suspect that you want to change the paragraph so that the same words do not appear over and over again. So do I, and because I am writing this book, I can change the words. Here's the revised paragraph:

> John accompanied <u>his</u> best friend, Alice, to <u>her</u> house after the party. <u>He</u> asked <u>her</u> whether <u>she</u> would give <u>him</u> the recipe for the cookies <u>they</u> had eaten at the party. <u>She</u> reluctantly gave <u>it</u> to <u>him</u>. "Excellent," said John to <u>himself</u>. "<u>Her</u> recipe is the best."

That paragraph isn't very exciting either, but it doesn't repeat as many words. The words I removed from the first paragraph are nouns. The underlined words I substituted in the second paragraph are *pronouns*. Here are the nouns and the pronouns that replace them, paired up:

John's→his

Alice's→her

John→he

Alice→she

John→him

John and Alice→they

Alice→she

recipe→it

John→him

John→himself

Alice's→her

For those who like grammar terminology: The noun the pronoun replaces is the pronoun's *antecedent*.

Q. Identify the pronouns and their antecedents.

EXAMPLE   The parakeet's sharp beak is its best defense against hungry cats, except for flying away from them.

A. its→parakeet's, them→cats

Replacing pronouns

Here's another paragraph for you to read:

> All of the zookeepers had to bring all of the zookeepers' lunches from home today, because the cafeteria was closed. Some of the zookeepers forgot some of the zookeepers' sandwiches. A few at another table brought extra sandwiches to share. Everyone expressed everyone's gratitude.

Here's the same paragraph, this time with pronouns, which are underlined:

> <u>All</u> of the zookeepers had to bring <u>their</u> lunches from home, because the cafeteria was closed today. <u>Some</u> of the zookeepers forgot <u>their</u> sandwiches. A few at another table brought extra sandwiches to share. <u>Everyone</u> expressed <u>their</u> gratitude.

The pronouns pair up with antecedents (the pronouns they replace) this way:

their→All

their→Some

few→they

Everyone→their

TIP

Pronouns that end in *-one* (*everyone, someone, anyone*) or *-body* (*everybody, somebody, anybody*) have no identifiable antecedent. You can think of them as replacing the name of every person in the group (*everyone, everybody*), one unidentified person in the group (*someone, anyone, somebody, anybody*), or excluding the group (*no one, nobody*). These pronouns have paired up with various partners through the years. In the very old days, these pronouns were commonly paired with *their* in situations expressing ownership. A hundred years or so ago, *their* gave way to *his*, which was supposed to represent all genders. In the recent past, *his or her* became the go-to expression. Now, more and more grammarians (including me) have returned to *their*, because it's an inclusive word. For more information, see the Introduction.

EXAMPLE

Q. Identify the pronouns and their antecedents.

All knew their fate.

A. **their→All**

Doubling back with -self pronouns

Some pronouns — those that end in *-self* or *-selves* — can double back or emphasize, as you see in these sentences:

> Gina told <u>herself</u> not to worry. (*herself* doubles back to *Gina*)

> Despite having practiced yoga for only ten minutes, Gina <u>herself</u> led the yoga class and sprained only four muscles. (*herself* emphasizes *Gina's* role)

The new plumbers reminded <u>themselves</u> that leaks are not, in fact, popular. *(themselves doubles back to plumbers)*

We *ourselves* have been drenched and enraged by a leak they forgot to plug. *(ourselves emphasizes the speakers' authority to speak about plumbing problems)*

The *-self* pronouns, in case you're interested, are called *reflexive* pronouns.

WARNING

Don't use a *-self* pronoun for anything other than the two jobs described earlier, in the section "Working Hard: Pronouns and Their Jobs":

WRONG: Gene and myself cleaned the house.

WHY IT IS WRONG: *Myself* cannot replace *I*. For emphasis, it may follow *I*.

RIGHT: Gene and I cleaned the house.

EXAMPLE

Q. Identify the pronouns and their antecedents.

The chefs asked themselves whether the dish was spicy enough to please Peter.

A. themselves→chefs

Creating connections, asking questions

A small number of hard-working pronouns do two jobs at the same time: replace and connect. Check out this paragraph:

Paul, <u>who</u> swallowed a pencil, went to the emergency room last night. "<u>What</u> on earth were you thinking?" asked the doctor, <u>whose</u> eyes were wide with shock. "Any object <u>that</u> is long and pointy can cause serious injury!" The hospital bill, <u>which</u> wiped out Paul's entire college fund, shocked Paul and his parents, to <u>whom</u> Paul apologized repeatedly.

The pronouns *who, whom, whose, what, that,* and *which* are called *relative pronouns* because they relate two or more things. Here are the replacements and connections from the preceding example:

who→Paul, connects *who swallowed a pencil* to *Paul*

whose→doctor, connects *whose eyes were wide with shock* to *doctor*

that→object, connects *that is long and pointy* to *object*

which→bill, connects *which wiped out Paul's entire college fund* to *bill*

whom→parents, connects *to whom Paul apologized repeatedly* to *parents*

The pronoun *what* asks a question in the sample paragraph. *Who, whose,* and *whom* may also ask questions, as may *whoever* and *whatever*. In informal speech, *whatever* may also be an exit line, a signal that the speaker has no interest in continuing the conversation:

After 15 apologies, Paul muttered, "Whatever," and stomped out of the room.

Q. Identify the pronouns and their antecedents.

EXAMPLE Paul's parents, who are not wealthy, grounded Paul for a minimum of five years.

A. **who→parents**

YOUR
TURN

Identify the pronouns and their antecedents (speaker, spoken to, or the name of the people or things spoken about). This set of questions forms one story; the antecedent may be in a preceding sentence:

1. "What did you say?" I asked Lola.

2. She didn't answer until Henry tapped her on her shoulder.

3. He waved his hand, which was rather muddy, in her direction.

4. "Sorry," she replied. "I was thinking about the motorcycle that I bought today."

5. Jack and Elena, who are not motorcycle fans, frowned. "Whatever makes you happy is fine with us," Elena commented in an unconvincing way.

6. They prefer public transportation to gas-powered vehicles.

7. Lola, whose love for motorcycles is fanatical, ignored everyone.

8. "Nobody but me gets to ride on it!" Lola asserted forcefully. "It is mine!"

9. I told myself to calm down.

10. Lola would give me a ride after I washed her motorcycle and polished its chrome.

Tracing Pronoun Traits

If a pronoun sat down to create a dating profile, the pronoun would have to list a few essential traits — not "loves long walks with verbs" or "prefers capital letters," but these:

>> **person** In grammar lingo, there are three possible "persons." *First person* refers to the one speaking (*I, we, me, my,* for example). *Second person* is reserved for the one spoken to (*you, your, yours, yourself, yourselves*). *Third person* is for whoever or whatever is spoken about (*he, she, it, they,* for example).

>> **number** The number may be *singular* (referring to one person or thing) or *plural* (referring to more than one person or thing) or either, depending on context.

>> **gender** This topic is in flux, as are many ideas about gender. Traditionally, some pronouns are masculine *(he, him, his)*, and some are feminine *(she, her, hers)*. Some aren't gender-specific *(you, your, yours, they, them, their, theirs)*. Some are neuter (the official grammar term for a neutral pronoun), representing nonliving things *(it, its)*.

>> **case** Pronouns change depending on whether they're acting (<u>I</u> told Henry), being acted on (Henry told <u>me</u>), or possessing (<u>his</u> story). That quality is known as *case.*

Anyone dating — sorry, selecting — a pronoun has to pick the one with a matching profile. In the following section, I explain these traits in more detail.

Person and number

How do you rank your own importance? Most people, I suspect, place themselves first. Perhaps that's why pronouns for speaking or writing about oneself are called *first-person* pronouns, which I've underlined in these sentences:

<u>I</u> love to play the piano.

Andrew gave <u>me</u> an enormous grand piano.

<u>I</u> practice on <u>my</u> piano daily, from 2 to 3 a.m.

<u>I</u> have taught <u>myself</u> five new songs.

<u>I</u> promise <u>I</u> won't play at night anymore! Don't take the piano! That instrument is <u>mine</u>!

In the preceding examples, the pronouns are all singular, because they refer to only one person. If you talk or write about yourself as part of a group, you need a different set of first-person pronouns, which are underlined in these sentences:

May <u>we</u> play music in the show?

George told <u>us</u> that life is too short to waste time listening to <u>our</u> songs.

"The audience will enjoy <u>our</u> music," <u>we</u> replied.

After <u>we</u> offered to provide earplugs, George finally gave <u>us</u> permission to play.

<u>We</u> told <u>ourselves</u> not to be nervous.

After the show, fame will be <u>ours</u>!

The underlined words are all pronouns, and all refer to a group that includes the person speaking or writing.

Q. Which of these pronouns are singular? Which are plural?

EXAMPLE   us, myself, me, I, mine, ourselves, we, our, my, ours

A. **Singular:** *myself, me, I, mine, my* **Plural:** *us, ourselves, we, our, ours*

Select the appropriate pronoun for each blank in the following sentences. All pronouns should refer to the speaker or writer. The letter *S* after a blank tells you that you need a singular pronoun. The letter *P* means you need a plural pronoun.

11 _____ (S) am going to work now. **12** _____ (S) told **13** _____ (S) that

14 _____ (S) must hurry, because **15** _____ (S) boss told **16** _____

(S) that lateness is a problem. **17** _____ (S) spoke with my friends in the

office. **18** _____ (P) all agreed that **19** _____ (P) want **20** _____ (P) boss

to leave **21** _____ (P) alone. **22** _____ (P) prefer to be by **23** _____ (P).

In Standard English, the pronoun *I* is always capitalized. For more information about capital letters, see Chapter 21.

Second-person pronouns stand in for the name of the person being addressed. Take a look at the underlined, second-person pronouns in these sentences:

Are <u>you</u> going shopping for new shoes?

<u>Your</u> shoes look comfortable, but orange-and-green plaid is an insult to the eye.

Are those purple sneakers <u>yours</u>, too?

Did <u>you</u> buy them for <u>yourself</u>, or did <u>your</u> color-blind cousins help?

Usually, the three of <u>you</u> buy clothing and shoes by <u>yourselves</u>, but this time a consultant might help.

The pronouns *you* and *your* may replace the name of one person or the names of more than one person. In other words, *you* and *your* may be either singular or plural. Use *yourself* for one person and *yourselves* for more than one.

Sometimes people try to change the pronoun *you* into a different form to show that it's plural. I often hear *y'all, you guys, youse,* and other expressions. These terms are not correct in Standard English. Use them with friends, if you like, but stay away from these words when you're in a formal situation at work or at school. Let context indicate whether the pronoun *you* is singular or plural.

Q. Sort the following pronouns into three categories: Singular (referring to one person), Plural (referring to more than one person), or Singular and Plural (correct when referring to one or more than one).

you, yourselves, your, yours, yourself

A. **Singular:** *yourself.* **Plural:** *yourselves.* **Singular and Plural:** *you, your, yours.*

Insert a pronoun into each blank in the following paragraph, always referring to the person or people being addressed. The letters in parentheses after each blank tell you whether the pronoun is singular (S) or plural (P).

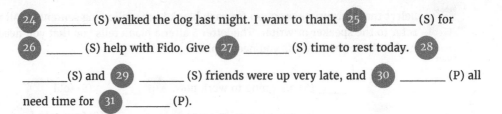

24 _____ (S) walked the dog last night. I want to thank 25 _____ (S) for 26 _____ (S) help with Fido. Give 27 _____ (S) time to rest today. 28 _____(S) and 29 _____ (S) friends were up very late, and 30 _____ (P) all need time for 31 _____ (P).

Talking about objects is simple, but talking about other people — in real life and in grammar — can be complicated, and so can third-person pronouns. Pronoun gender is a hot topic, which I'll discuss a moment. For now, take note of the underlined, third-person pronouns in this paragraph:

> He placed his painting on the wall. He had done all the work himself. Now he waited to hear their opinions. They all cheered! One of them said it was great. He looked at Mary. Did she like his art? If she said it was good, he would give the artwork to her. The painting would be hers forever.

Gender and number

All first-person pronouns (the "*I* family") work for any gender, as do all second-person pronouns (the "*you* family"). Third-person pronouns have recently become more flexible. That's why you may be asked about your pronoun preferences and why others may offer this information to you. I appreciate both the question and the information, and I do my best to respect others' wishes, in the same way I want others to respect mine.

Traditionally, pronouns for one person who identifies as male are *he, him, his,* and *himself.* Female singular pronouns are *she, her, hers,* and *herself.* Singular pronouns for nonliving objects are *it, its,* and *itself.* The pronouns *they, them, their, theirs,* and *themselves* aren't gender specific and, in commonly accepted modern usage, may be either singular or plural. In other words, pronouns from the "*they* family" may refer to a group of things, a group of males, a group of females, a mixed-gender group, or one person whose gender isn't known or who identifies as nonbinary or gender fluid.

TIP

Is *themself* a word in Standard English? The word was used, though rarely, from the 16th to the 19th centuries, and no one flapped about it. Then some influential grammarians deemed *themself* nonstandard. Some grammarians now prefer *themselves* for both singular and plural situations. Others use *themself* for singular, gender-neutral references and reserve *themselves* for plurals.

EXAMPLE

Q. What pronoun may replace the underlined words?

The telephone rang.

William and Ellen wrote letters to each other.

The insurance agent said flood damage was not covered.

A. **The telephone→It** (singular, neuter), **William and Ellen→They** (plural, any gender), **The insurance agent→they, he, or she.** The last answer depends on context. If you know that the agent identifies as male, insert *he*, a singular masculine pronoun. If you know that the agent identifies as female, insert *she*, a singular feminine pronoun. If the person is nonbinary or gender fluid, or if you don't know the gender, the pronoun *they* is a good choice.

What pronouns may replace the underlined words? Note: William and James identify as male, Ellen and Anne identify as female, and Alix identifies as nonbinary.

32 <u>William and Ellen</u> wrote letters to each other.

33 <u>William's and Ellen's</u> letters were seldom boring, because <u>William and Ellen</u> make up outlandish stories.

34 James can't resist the temptation to spy on <u>James's</u> friends; <u>James</u> said <u>the letters</u> were full of juicy gossip.

35 <u>James</u> told <u>Anne</u>, the girl most likely to post everything <u>Anne</u> hears on social media, about <u>a scandal</u>.

36 <u>Anne's</u> friend Alix spread the word. <u>Alix</u> can't resist gossip, either!

Case

In some languages, words change form to deliver meaning, and their position in the sentence is fairly flexible. English words tend to remain the same, and word order matters:

> Mary defeated John.

> John defeated Mary.

English pronouns often change form, but generally not their position. Consider *I, me,* and *my*. In Standard English you can say

> I sing like an eagle with a bad cold.

but not

> Me sing like an eagle with a bad cold.

or

> My sing like an eagle with a bad cold.

Why not? Because *I, me,* and *my* are different cases. In Chapter 14 I tell you more than you ever wanted to know about case. Here I ask you just to recognize that it exists and that it can be a complete pain in the neck.

Q. Fill in the blanks with additional forms of the pronoun provided.

EXAMPLE   he _____ _____

A. **him, his, or himself**

Fill in the blanks with additional forms of the pronoun provided.

YOUR
TURN

37 she _____ _____ _____

38 us _____ _____ _____

39 their _____ _____ _____

40 it _____

41 your _____ _____ _____ _____

42 I _____ _____ _____ _____

The pronouns I discuss in this chapter are the words that generally come to mind when this part of speech is mentioned. But did you know that *other* may function as a pronoun? How about *neither* or *each? Anybody? Someone? These? Nothing?* You most likely know the words and how to use them, but perhaps you didn't know that they were pronouns. Potential pronouns, I should say. The identity of a word depends on how it's used in a sentence. For information about these and lots more pronouns, check out Chapters 13 and 14.

TIP

Practice Questions Answers and Explanations

(1) **What** (pronoun that asks a question, no antecedent), **you** (spoken to), **I** (speaker)

(2) **She, her, her** (*Lola*)

(3) **He, his** (*Henry*), **which** (*hand*), **her** (*Lola's*)

(4) **she** (*Lola*), **I, I** (speaker), **that** (*motorcycle*)

(5) **who** (*Jack and Elena*), **Whatever** (no antecedent), **you** (person spoken to), **us** (people speaking)

(6) **They** (*Jack and Elena*)

(7) **whose** (*Lola*), **everyone** (no antecedent)

(8) **Nobody** (no antecedent), **me** (speaker), **it, It** (*motorcycle*), **mine** (speaker's)

(9) **I, myself** (speaker)

(10) **me, I** (speaker), **her** (*Lola's*), **its** (*motorcycle's*)

(11) **I**

(12) **I**

(13) **myself**

(14) **I**

(15) **my**

(16) **me**

(17) **I**

(18) **We**

(19) **we**

(20) **our**

(21) **us**

(22) **We**

(23) **ourselves**

(24) **You**

(25) **you**

(26) **your**

(27) **yourself**

(28) **You**

(29) **your**

(30) **you**

(31) **yourselves**

(32) **They** The plural *they* refers to two people, *William* and *Ellen*.

(33) **Their, they** The plural forms *their* and *they* refer to two people, *William* and *Ellen*.

(34) **his, he, they** The directions tell you that *James* identifies as male, so the singular masculine pronouns *his* and *he* are correct. The possessive form, *his*, replaces *James's*. The plural pronoun *they* replaces *the letters*.

(35) **He, her, she, it** The masculine singular pronoun *He* replaces *James*. The directions tell you that *Anne* identifies as female, so *her* and *she* correctly replace the nouns. The neuter singular pronoun *it* replaces *a scandal*.

(36) **Her** refers to *Anne*, identified in the directions as female. The directions tell you that *Alix* identifies as nonbinary, so *they* is the pronoun for this spot.

(37) **her, hers, or herself**

(38) **we, our, ours**

(39) **they, them or themselves**

(40) **its**

(41) **you, yours, yourself, or yourselves**

(42) **me, my, mine, myself**

If you're ready to test your skills a bit more, take the following chapter quiz, which incorporates all the chapter topics.

Whaddya Know? Chapter 4 Quiz

Quiz time! Complete each problem to test your knowledge on the various topics covered in this chapter. You can then find the solutions and explanations in the next section.

Read this parent's letter to her aunt. Identify the pronouns and their antecedents. Also label each pronoun as singular (S) or plural (P).

This morning the children and I visited the zoo. Benjamin is 12, and his energy level is truly amazing. That little boy raced back and forth in front of a lioness, who was napping! Benjamin finally caught her attention. The zookeeper begged him not to annoy the lions. "Their roar can be heard for miles!" he said. The zookeeper told us to behave or be thrown out. Anne chose that moment to pick up a stick and jab it at the unfortunate man. I grabbed Benjamin and Anne and pulled them away. The children said they were sorry, and I myself apologized also. Tomorrow should be easier. Our trip to the museum that recently opened will surely be a success. The children themselves have welcomed this fine opportunity to interact with art. By the way, do you know how much a museum might charge if anyone happens to splash apple juice on a Picasso sketch? No one here knows.

Answers to Chapter 4 Quiz

This morning the children and **(1-S)** I visited the zoo. Benjamin is 12, and **(2-S)** his energy level is truly amazing. That little boy raced back and forth in front of a lioness, **(3-S)** who was napping! Benjamin finally caught **(4-S)** her attention. The zookeeper begged **(5-S)** him not to annoy the lions. **(6-P)** "Their roar can be heard for miles!" **(7-S)** he said. The zookeeper told **(8-P)** us to behave or be thrown out. Anne chose that moment to pick up a stick and jab **(9-S)** it at the unfortunate man. **(10-S)** I grabbed Benjamin and Anne and pulled **(11-P)** them away. The children said **(12-P)** they were sorry, and **(13-S)** I **(14-S)** myself apologized also. Tomorrow should be easier. **(15-P)** Our trip to the museum **(16-S)** that recently opened will surely be a success. The children **(17-P)** themselves have welcomed this fine opportunity to interact with art. By the way, do **(18-S)** you know how much a museum might charge if **(19-S)** anyone happens to splash apple juice on a Picasso sketch? **(20-S)** No one here knows.

Chapter **5**

Existing and Acting with Verbs

magine that a friend returns from vacation. If you're like most people, the first thing you do is ask some version of these two questions:

How are you?

What did you do?

In grammar terms, you requested *verbs* from your friend, because verbs are the part of speech that expresses state of being or action. Verbs come in all shapes and sizes, and grammarians have come up with a few dozen names for them, such as *predicates, modals, transitive, intransitive,* and others. Don't worry about terminology. What's important is to understand how verbs express meaning.

In this chapter, I define important verb traits and show you how to sort verbs into two families: *linking verbs,* which express a state of being, and *action verbs,* which communicate what's happening. I also discuss the role of helping verbs and take you on a tour of the most common irregular verbs.

Expressing Meaning with Verbs

Verbs do much more than express a state of being or an action. They tell time, give commands, form questions, and convey duty, habit, possibility, and many other shades of meaning. How? Read on.

Tense

To find out what time it is, you can check a clock, your watch, your phone, or a verb. Surprised by that last one? Verbs situate action and states of being on a timeline. Grammarians call this trait *tense*. Check out the italicized verbs in these examples. Notice what the verb in each sentence tells the reader or listener about time:

> Mark *spilled* ink on the quilt. (*spilled* — past)
>
> Mark's mom *is* upset. (*is* — present)
>
> Mark *will wash* the quilt, or his mom *will murder* him. (*will wash* and *will murder* — future)

For a tour of regular verb forms in each tense and a detailed explanation of when to use them, turn to Chapter 12.

Number

Like nouns and pronouns, verbs can be singular or plural. The form you need depends on the subject — who or what is in the state of being or is performing the action. If the subject is singular (just one), the verb is singular. If the subject is plural (more than one), the verb is plural. In these examples, the subject of the sentence is in bold type and the verb is italicized:

> The **poster** *is* on the wall of Sam's bedroom. (*poster* and *is* — singular)
>
> Sam's **pets** *hate* the poster. (*pets* and *hate* — plural)
>
> Sam's **cat** *has chewed* one corner of the poster. (*cat* and *has chewed* — singular)
>
> My well-behaved **dogs** *do* not *chew* posters. (*dogs* and *do chew* — plural)

TIP

In the last example, did you notice that the word *not* isn't italicized? *Not* changes the meaning of the verb from positive to negative, but it isn't an official part of the verb. It's an adverb.

For help with matching singular subjects to singular verbs and plural subjects to plural verbs, read Chapter 13.

Mood

Are you in a mood? Probably, though I suspect you don't recognize that fact unless your mood is extreme — down in the dumps or walking on air. The same is true of verbs. The everyday, nothing-to-see-here mood is called *indicative*:

Indicative verbs *make* statements and *ask* questions. (*make, ask* = indicative)

Every verb you *have read* in this section *is* in the indicative mood. (*have read, is* = indicative)

Do you *see* how easy indicative mood *is*? (*Do see, is* = indicative)

The *imperative* mood gives you a command. It's easy — at least in terms of grammar. Whether you obey the command is up to you! Here are two examples, with the imperative verb in italics:

Do not *worry* about the fancy terminology. (*Do worry* = imperative)

Give commands with imperative verbs. (*Give* = imperative)

You probably already know everything you need to know about indicative and imperative verbs. One mood, though, is more complicated. It's *subjunctive*, and you use it for a sentence that expresses something contrary to fact:

If I *were* the queen of grammar, I'd outlaw apostrophes. (*were* = subjunctive)

Subjunctive verbs also give indirect commands:

I demand that grammar *be* taught immediately! (*be* = subjunctive)

Chapter 12 goes into depth on subjunctive mood.

Voice

Verbs have two possible voices: *active* and *passive*. Lend an ear to these examples:

The window *was broken* yesterday. (*was broken* = passive)

I *broke* the window yesterday. (*broke* = active)

The passive verb says what happened but not who did the deed. The active verb names the culprit. Check out Chapter 12 for more on active and passive voice.

Meeting the Families: Linking and Action Verbs

As everyone in a romantic relationship knows, when things turn serious, it's time to meet the family — the cousins, grandparents, and other relatives you'll be eating holiday dinners with for the rest of your life. Your relationship with verbs may not be romantic, but it *is* serious, because you can't make a sentence without a verb. In this section, you meet the two verb "families" — linking and action. You don't have to share meals, but you do have to recognize and deal with the families.

Linking verbs: A giant equal sign

Linking verbs are also called *being verbs* because they express states of being — what is, will be, or was. Here's where math intersects with English. Linking verbs are like giant equal signs plopped into the middle of a sentence. For example, you can think of the sentence

> Ralph's uncle *is* a cannibal with a taste for finger food.

as

> Ralph's uncle = a cannibal with a taste for finger food.

Or, in shortened form,

> Ralph's uncle = a cannibal

Just as in an algebra equation, the word *is* links two ideas and says that they are the same. Thus, *is* is a linking verb. Read on to find out about all sorts of linking verbs.

Forms of "be"

Most linking verbs are forms of the verb *be*, an essential but annoying verb that changes form frequently, depending on the subject of the sentence. Have a look at these examples:

> Lulu *will be* angry when she hears about the missing sculpture.
>
> Lulu = angry (*will be* is a linking verb)

> I *am* unhappy about the theft also!
>
> I = unhappy (*am* is the linking verb)

> Stan *was* the last surfer to leave the water when the tidal wave approached.
>
> *Stan* = last surfer (*was* is a linking verb)

> Edgar *has been* depressed ever since the fall of the House of Usher.
>
> Edgar = depressed (*has been* is a linking verb)

Charts with all forms of the irregular verb *be* appear later in this chapter.

Synonyms of "be"

Be is not the only linking verb, just the most popular. Here are a few more:

> A jail sentence for a misplaced comma *appears* harsh.
>
> jail sentence = harsh (*appears* is a linking verb in this sentence)

> The penalty for making a grammar error *remains* severe.
>
> penalty = severe (*remains* is a linking verb in this sentence)

Loch Ness *stays* silent whenever monsters are mentioned.

Loch Ness = silent (*stays* is a linking verb in this sentence)

With his sharp toenails and sneaky smile, Bigfoot *seemed* threatening.

Bigfoot = threatening (*seemed* is a linking verb)

Appears, remains, stays, and *seemed* are similar to forms of the verb *be* in that they express states of being. They also add shades of meaning to the basic concept. Reread the last example, about Bigfoot. Now take a look at what happens if you change *seemed* to a different linking verb:

With his sharp toenails and sneaky smile, Bigfoot *was* threatening.

Seemed leaves room for doubt, but *was* is more definite. Similarly, *remains* (in the second example) adds a time dimension to the basic expression of being. The sentence implies that the penalty was and still is severe.

The most common words that express shades of meaning in reference to a state of being are *appear, seem, grow, remain,* and *stay.*

TIP

Savoring sensory verbs

Sensory verbs — verbs that express information you receive through the senses of sight, hearing, smell, taste, and so forth — may also be linking verbs:

Two minutes after shaving, Ralph's chin *feels* scratchy.

Ralph's chin = scratchy (*feels* is a linking verb)

The ten-year-old lasagna in your refrigerator *smells* disgusting.

lasagna = disgusting (*smells* is a linking verb)

The ten-year-old lasagna in your refrigerator also *looks* disgusting.

lasagna = disgusting (*looks* is a linking verb)

Needless to say, the ten-year-old lasagna in your refrigerator *tastes* great!

lasagna = great (*tastes* is a linking verb)

Verbs that refer to the five senses are linking verbs only if they act as an equal sign in the sentence. If they aren't equating two ideas, they aren't linking verbs. In the preceding example about Ralph's chin, *feels* is a linking verb. Here's a different sentence with the same verb:

WARNING

With their sensitive fingers, Lulu and Stan *feel* Ralph's chin.

In this sentence, *feel* is not a linking verb because you're not saying that

Lulu and Stan = chin.

Instead, you're saying that Lulu and Stan don't believe that Ralph shaved, so they checked by placing their fingers on his chin.

Some sensory verbs that function as linking verbs are *look*, *sound*, *taste*, *smell*, and *feel*.

Q. Identify the linking verbs in these sentences.

That annoying new clock sounds extremely loud at 4 o'clock in the morning.

That annoying new clock sounds the hour with a loud heavy metal song.

Oscar is awake, and he is not happy.

A. **sounds; no linking verb; is, is** If you treated the first sentence like a math problem, you'd get *clock = extremely loud*. Therefore, *sounds* is a linking verb. In the second sentence, the clock is doing something — sounding the hour. In this context, *sounds* is an action verb. The third sentence can be rewritten this way: *Oscar = awake, he = not happy*. Therefore, *is* is a linking verb in both parts of the sentence.

Identify the linking verbs in these sentences.

1. Larry is single now, but not for long.

2. He looks happy, but I am doubtful.

3. In the past, Larry has been alone only for short periods.

4. "Did you go shopping for another engagement ring?" I asked Larry, because I am always curious about his love life.

5. "You will be sorry if you continue to pry!" he exclaimed angrily.

6. "I feel sorry now," I replied, "but not as sorry as your next spouse will be."

Lights! Camera! Action verb!

Linking verbs are important, but unless you've won the lottery, you just can't sit around being all the time. You have to do something. (And even if you do win the lottery, you'll be bored without some activity.) Here's where action verbs enter the picture. Everything that is not *being* is *action*, at least in the verb world. Unlike the giant equal sign associated with linking verbs (see the preceding section), something *happens* with an action verb:

Drew *slapped* the thief who *stole* the briefcase. (*Slapped* and *stole* are action verbs.)

Fred *will run* to third base as soon as his sneezing fit *ends*. (*Will run* and *ends* are action verbs.)

According to the teacher, Roger *has shot* at least 16 spitballs in the past ten minutes. (*Has shot* is an action verb.)

WARNING

Don't let the name *action* fool you. Some action verbs aren't particularly energetic: *think, sit, stay, have, sleep, dream*, and so forth. Besides describing my ideal vacation, these words are also action verbs. Think of the definition this way: If the verb is *not* a giant equal sign (a linking verb), it's an action verb.

EXAMPLE

Q. Identify the action verbs in these sentences.

Larry bought a diamond ring for Lola, who plays darts with him every Friday night.

Larry knelt in front of the dart board and asked her to marry him.

Lola threw a dart at Larry and screamed, "Do not interrupt the game!"

A. **bought, plays, knelt, asked, threw, screamed, do interrupt** The first sentence has two actions: *bought* and *plays. Larry* performs the first action, and *Lola* performs the second. The second sentence also expresses two actions *(knelt, asked)*, both paired with *Larry.* The third sentence expresses three actions. *Lola* does the first two *(threw, scream).* The third action is a command *(do not interrupt).* The word *not* isn't part of the verb, so the action verb is *do interrupt.*

YOUR TURN

Identify the action verbs in these sentences:

7 Everyone in the bar quieted when Larry spoke.

8 They wondered what Lola would do when the dart game ended.

9 Lola likes Larry, but she does not love him.

10 She adores his new motorcycle, however, and if she marries him, she can use it whenever she wants.

11 I think Lola will say no.

12 She has saved her money and can buy a new motorcycle for herself.

Pop the Question: Locating the Verb

Here's a quick and surefire way to identify the verb in a sentence. Ask two questions:

» What's happening?

» What is? (or, What word is a "giant equal sign"?)

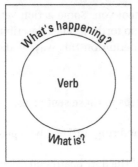

If you get an answer to the first question, you have an action verb. If you get an answer to the second question, you have a linking verb.

Take a look at this sentence:

Archie flew around the room and then swooped into his cage for a birdseed snack.

You ask, "What's happening?" and your answer is *flew* and *swooped. Flew* and *swooped* are action verbs.

If you ask, "What is?" you get no answer, because there's no linking verb in the sentence.

Try another:

Lola's new tattoo will be larger than her previous 15 tattoos.

What's happening? Nothing. You have no action verb. What is? *Will be. Will be* is a linking verb.

Q. Pop the question and find the verbs in the following sentences. Identify the verbs as action or linking.

EXAMPLE

Michelle scratched the cat almost as hard as the cat had scratched her.

After months of up-and-down motion, Lester is taking the elevator sideways, just for a change of pace.

The twisted frown on Larry's face seems strange because of the joyful background music.

A. *scratched, had scratched, is taking* (**action verbs**), *seems* (**linking verb**)

You may hear English teachers say, "the verb *to sweep*" or some such expression. But *to be* is not actually a verb. It's an infinitive. An *infinitive* is *to + a verb.* (Some grammarians see the *to* as an add-on and count only the verb as an infinitive.) Don't worry about the terminology. The

REMEMBER most important thing to know about infinitives is this: When you pop the question to find the verb, don't choose an infinitive as the answer. If you do, you'll miss the real verb or verbs in the sentence. Other than that, forget about infinitives!

Pop the question and find the verbs in these sentences. Identify them as action (A) or linking (L).

13 The sofa is wide, and the window is narrow.

14 After one hard push, the sofa flew out the window and onto the lawn.

15 "Carry it to the truck," ordered the supervisor.

16 Unfortunately, the movers had brought their smallest van.

17 The sofa has been sitting on the lawn all night.

Calling the Help Line for Verbs

You might have noticed that some verbs I identify in this chapter are single words and others are made up of several words. The extra words are called *helping verbs*. They don't carry out the trash or dust the furniture, but they do help the main verb express meaning. In this section, I list all forms of three important helpers — *be, do,* and *have* — and explain how they function in questions and negative statements. I also discuss how other helping verbs (*can, could, must,* and so forth) affect meaning.

The big three

Challenge: Write one paragraph without using any form of *be, do,* or *have.* Are you done? How did it go? I have often taken on this challenge, but I have never succeeded. In fact, I have used forms of all three helping verbs in the paragraph you're now reading.

The verb "be"

The most important and basic part of life is *being* alive. That makes *be,* in all its forms, the most important verb. It follows no rules. When you match this verb with various subjects (the person or thing that is "being"), the form often changes. Here are three tables to help you figure out *be.* The first places *be* forms in the present, the second moves to the past, and the third goes into the future. Get ready for some time travel.

Present: Singular Form	Present: Plural Form	Present: Singular/Plural Form
I am	we are	
		you are
he is		
she is		
it is		they are
Past: Singular Form	*Past: Plural Form*	*Past: Singular/Plural Form*
I was	we were	
		you were
he was		

Present: Singular Form	Present: Plural Form	Present: Singular/Plural Form
she was		
it was		they were
Future: Singular Form	*Future: Plural Form*	*Future: Singular/Plural Form*
I will be	we will be	
		you will be
he will be		
she will be		
it will be		they will be

TIP

In each of the preceding tables, the last box of the first column contains the masculine (male) pronoun *he*, the feminine (female) pronoun *she*, and the pronoun for things, *it*. These pronouns represent any masculine noun, any feminine noun, and a noun naming any and every object in the entire world. I could have placed *Henry is, the actress was, the secretary will be* — and many more examples. In the same way, the last box of the third column could also grow. *They* can stand in for any plural noun or for a singular noun when the gender is unknown or nonbinary.

EXAMPLE

Q. In the following table, the first column contains a subject. In the second column is a time period — past, present, or future. Your job is to write the correct form of the verb *be* in the third column.

Subject	Time	Be Verb
pillow	future	

A. **will be**

YOUR TURN

Write the correct form of the verb be in the last column.	Subject	Time	"Be" Verb
18.	Ellen	present	
19.	horses	past	
20.	I	future	
21.	the box	present	
22.	you (singular, for one person)	past	
23.	puppies	future	
24.	you (plural, for more than one person)	present	

The verb "do"

"Don't just sit there! *Do* something!" Have you heard these lines from an actor in a film, perhaps as a car's brakes fail and it heads toward a cliff? The command to "do something" seems to be a basic fact of human life. The verb *do* is also basic. Take a close look at the following three tables, which cover the verb *do* in the present, past, and future time.

Present: Singular Form	Present: Plural Form	Present: Singular/Plural Form
I do	we do	
		you do
he does		
she does		
it does		they do
Past: Singular Form	*Past: Plural Form*	*Past: Singular/Plural Form*
I did	we did	
		you did
he did		
she did		
it did		they did
Future: Singular Form	*Future: Plural Form*	*Future: Singular/Plural Form*
I will do	we will do	
		you will do
he will do		
she will do		
it will do		they will do

You probably noticed that *do* changes only in the present tense, when you're talking about someone or something doing an action. How nice that this verb is easier than other irregular verbs!

TIP

I listed the masculine pronoun *he,* the feminine pronoun *she,* and the pronoun for things, *it,* in the last box of the first column of each table. If you want to pair the verb *do* with a noun that names one male, use the form for *he.* For the name of one female, use the form for *she.* The name of one thing pairs with the form of the verb listed for *it. They* can stand in for any plural noun or for a singular noun when the gender is unknown or nonbinary.

EXAMPLE

Q. Try your hand at pairing a form of the verb *do* with each subject in the first column, selecting a verb for the time period in the second column.

Subject	Time	Form of the Verb "Do"
Ballerinas	past	

A. **did**

Select a verb to match the subject and time period.

YOUR TURN

	Subject	Time	Form of the Verb "Do"
25.	the snake	present	
26.	I	past	
27.	you (referring to many people)	future	
28.	awards	present	

	Subject	Time	Form of the Verb "Do"
29.	boxer	past	
30.	we	future	
31.	a bird	present	

The verb "have"

You may *have* lots of things — friends, a cold, books, fun — and many, many other things. You therefore need to know the correct forms of the verb *have*. (This verb also helps to create some tenses, or time indicators. See Chapter 12 to find out more.)

Present: Singular Form	Present: Plural Form	Present: Singular/Plural Form
I have	we have	
		you have
he has		
she has		
it has		they have
Past: Singular Form	*Past: Plural Form*	***Past: Singular/Plural Form***
I had	we had	
		you had
he had		
she had		
it had		they had
Future: Singular Form	*Future: Plural Form*	***Future: Singular/Plural Form***
I will have	we will have	
		you will have
he will have		
she will have		
it will have		they will have

Did you notice that the verb *have* changes form only in the present tense, when you're talking about one person or thing? The other forms stay the same. Take care not to confuse *has* and *have*.

TIP

The verb form that matches the masculine pronoun works for any masculine noun. The verb form that matches the feminine pronoun works for any feminine noun. The form that pairs with *it* is the form you use for any noun that names one thing. The verb form paired with the pronoun *they* works for all plural nouns and for singular nongendered or nonbinary nouns.

Q. In the following table, the first column contains a subject, and the second column contains a time. Fill in the third column with a form of the verb *have*.

EXAMPLE

Subject	Time	Form of the Verb "Have"
blanket	present	has

Fill in the form of the verb *have* that fits the subject and time.

	Subject	Time	Form of the Verb "Have"
32.	firefighter	present	
33.	tigers	past	
34.	artist	future	
35.	I	present	
36.	you	past	
37.	everyone	future	
38.	Michael	present	

Timing is everything: Creating a time frame with helping verbs

Helping verbs often signal when the action or state of being is occurring. Here are some sentences with helping verbs that create a timeline:

Alice *will sing* five arias from that opera tomorrow evening.

(*Sing* is the main verb, and *will* is a helping verb. *Will* places the action at some point in the future.)

Gwen *had moved* the vase, but the baseball *hit* it anyway.

(*Moved* is the main verb, and *had* is a helping verb. *Hit* is a main verb with no helping verbs. *Had* places the action of moving sometime in the past.)

Bob and Ellen *are admiring* Lola's new tattoo.

(*Admiring* is the main verb, and *are* is a helping verb. *Are* places the action in the present moment.)

Verb tense can be complicated. Check out Chapter 12 for more information.

Don't ask! Questions and negative statements

To make your life more complicated, English often throws in a helping verb or two in order to form questions and negative statements. Usually, the helping verb and the main verb are separated in this sort of sentence. In questions, the subject (the person or thing performing the action) comes between the helper and the main verb. In negative statements, the adverb *not* shows up between the helper and the main verb. Check out these examples of questions and negative statements with helping verbs:

Does the ring in Lulu's belly button *rust* when she showers? (*Does* = helping verb, *rust* = main verb, *ring* =subject)

No, belly button rings *do* not *rust*. (*Do* = helping verb, *rust* = main verb, *rings* = subject)

Did Larry and Ella *need* a good divorce lawyer? (*Did* = helping verb, *need* = main verb, *Larry* and *Ella* = subjects)

Do Zoe's friends *play* the same song for eight hours? (*Do* = helping verb, *play* = main verb, *friends* = subject)

Will George *remember* all the old familiar places? (*Will* = helping verb, *remember* = main verb, *George* = subject)

You've probably figured out that the main verbs in these examples of questions and negative statements are action verbs, with the helpers *does, did, do,* or *will.* You can't go wrong with *did* and *will,* because those helpers are the same for singular and plural subjects. The other two, unfortunately, change according to the subject of the sentence. *Does* and *has* match all singular subjects (when only one person is performing the action). *Do* and *have* work best in plural sentences, when more than one person is performing the action. *Have* and *do* are also the helpers you want when the subject is *I* or *you.* (For more on matching singular and plural subjects and verbs, turn to Chapter 13.)

TIP

Questions or negative statements with *be* or *have* as the main verb don't always need *do* or *does.* In these examples, the verb is italicized:

Is grammar a popular subject?

Am I a good grammarian?

Were the grammarians *analyzing* that sentence?

Have you any spare cash for Ella's lawyer?

I have no cash at all!

EXAMPLE

Q. Change this statement into a question:

Ella visited Larry's parents today.

A. **Did Ella visit Larry's parents today?** To form the question, add the helping verb *did.*

Q. Change this statement into a negative (opposite).

George gave me help during the grammar test.

A. **George did not give me help during the grammar test.** You form the negative with the helping verb *did.*

YOUR TURN

Change these sentences to questions or negative statements, as indicated in the parentheses.

39 The grammarians complained about that statement. (question)

40 The killer *bees* chase Roger. (negative)

41 They are afraid of him. (question)

42 They should be. (question)

43 Ella wears protective clothing near the beehive. (negative)

Adding shades of meaning with helping verbs

Helping verbs also change the meaning of a sentence by adding a sense of duty, probability, willingness, and so forth. Concentrate on the italicized verbs in these examples. All are add-ons, or *helping verbs*. The main verbs appear in bold type. Notice how the meaning changes:

Rita *may* **attend** the party. Her boss *might* **be** there.

(The helping verbs *may* and *might* express possibility: Rita will go if she's in a good mood and stay home if she isn't. Same thing for her boss.)

Rita's father checked out the party and said that she *may* **go**.

(In this sentence, the helping verb *may* expresses permission: In other words, the father okayed the outing.)

Rita *should* **attend** every official event. She *must* **go**.

(The helping verbs *should* and *must* mean that attending is a duty or an obligation. Even if Rita prefers to sit on her sofa and knit socks, she has to attend.)

She *can* **sleep** during the show, though. (The helping verb *can* refers to ability.)

Rita *would* **stay** home if she *could* **do** so.

(The helping verb *would* shows willingness or preference here. The helping verb *could* makes a statement about ability.)

Every Saturday when she was little, Rita would stay home and knit. (In this sentence, *would* communicates repeated past actions.)

Lola *can* **dance**. Lola *could* **perform** on Broadway, because she is extremely talented.

(*Can* and *could* imply ability — to *dance* and *perform* in the preceding example.)

WARNING
Some grammarians are quite strict about the difference between some pairs of helpers — *can/may, can/could,* and *may/might.* They see *can* as ability only and *may* as permission. Similarly, a number of grammarians allow *can* and *may* for present actions only, with *might* and *could* reserved for past tense. These days, most people interchange all these helpers and end up with fine sentences. Don't worry too much about these pairs.

Q. Add a helper to the main verb. The information in parentheses after the fill-in-the-blank sentence explains what meaning the sentence should have.

Lisa said that she _____ consider running for Parks Commissioner, but she hasn't made up her mind yet. (possibility)

A. **might** or **may**. The helping verbs (*might* or *may*) show that Lisa hasn't ruled out a run.

44 The mayor, shy as ever, said that she _____ go to the tree planting ceremony only if the press agreed to stay outside the forest. (*condition*)

45 Kirk, a reporter for the local radio station, _____ not agree to any conditions, because the station manager insisted on eyewitness coverage. (*ability*)

46 Whenever he met with her, Kirk _____ always urge the mayor to invite the press to special events, without success. (*repeated action*)

47 The mayor _____ make an effort to be more open to the press. (*duty*)

48 Lisa, who writes the popular *Trees-a-Crowd* blog, explained that she _____ rely on her imagination to supply details. (*possibility*)

49 Lisa knows that Kirk _____ leap to fame based on his tree-planting report, and she doesn't want to miss an important scoop. (*ability*)

50 All good reporters _____ know that if a tree falls or is planted in the forest, the sound is heard by a wide audience only if a radio reporter is there. (*duty*)

51 Sound engineers, on the other hand, _____ skip all outdoor events if they _____ do so. (*condition, ability*)

Practice Questions Answers and Explanations

1. **is** *Larry* = **single**

2. **looks, am** *He* = *happy*, *I* = *doubtful* Did I trick you with this one? The sentence implies that Larry isn't actually happy; he just looks that way. Nevertheless, *looks* is a linking verb because it links *He* to *happy*.

3. **has been** *Larry* = *alone*

4. **am** *I* = *curious*

5. **will be** *You* = *sorry*

6. **feel, will be** *I* = *sorry, next spouse* = *sorry*

7. **quieted, spoke** The first verb expresses what *Everyone* did (*quieted*). The second tells what *Larry* did (*spoke*).

8. **wondered, would do, ended** *They* pairs with the action *wondered*, *Lola* with *would do, and game* with *ended*. All are actions.

9. **likes, does love.** The first verb expresses what *Lola* does (*likes*) and the second what *she* does (*does love*). *Not* isn't part of the verb.

10. **adores, marries, can use, wants** Four action verbs for a very busy *Lola*, who is also referred to as *she* in this sentence.

11. **think, will say** The first verb expresses an action that *I* do. The second action is what *Lola* will do.

12. **has saved, can buy** These two actions pair with *she*.

13. **is (L), is (L)**

14. **flew (A)**

15. **Carry (A), ordered (A)**

16. **had brought (A)**

17. **has been sitting (A)**

18. **is**

19. **were**

20. **will be**

21. **is**

22. **were**

(23) **will be**

(24) **are**

(25) **does**

(26) **did**

(27) **will do**

(28) **do**

(29) **did**

(30) **will do**

(31) **does**

(32) **has**

(33) **had**

(34) **will have**

(35) **have**

(36) **had**

(37) **will have**

(38) **has**

(39) **Did the grammarians complain about that statement? or Have the grammarians complained about that statement?** The helping verbs *did* and *have* create questions.

(40) **The killer bees do not chase Roger.** *Do* is necessary for a question about a group *(bees)*.

(41) **Are they afraid of him?** You don't need a helping verb to form a question with a linking verb *(are)*.

(42) **Should they be?** No action verb, and therefore no helper needed to form a question!

(43) **Ella does not wear protective clothing near the beehive.** Because *Ella* is only one person, you need the helping verb *does* to make a negative statement.

(44) **would** The going is dependent on the press arrangement. Thus, *would* is the best choice.

(45) **could** *Can* or *could* are the helpers that express ability.

(46) **would** This helping verb expresses repeated actions in the past.

(47) **should** or **must** To imply duty, *should* or *must* is the helper you want.

(48) **may** or **might** Lisa, if she's in the mood, will cover the tree-cutting without seeing it. This possibility is expressed by the helpers *may* or *might*.

(49) **can** You need to express ability in the present tense, which *can* can do.

(50) **should** or **must** Duty calls, and *should* or *must* answers.

(51) **would, could** *Would* expresses a condition, and *could* adds ability to the sentence.

If you're ready to test your skills a bit more, take the following chapter quiz that incorporates all the chapter topics.

Whaddya Know? Chapter 5 Quiz

Quiz time! Complete each problem to test your knowledge of the various topics covered in this chapter. You can then find the solutions and explanations in the next section.

It's verb–hunting time. Read this instruction manual for Gadget–Go, a new product. Find 10 linking verbs and 15 action verbs. (These numbers don't count helping verbs separately.) Also list the helping verbs that express possibility, duty, or ability.

Congratulations on your purchase of Gadget-Go Model 55-33. You will be very happy. This model is much better than our other models. Only three have exploded since we changed the battery type. The new battery has been stable in temperatures ranging from 70 to 72 degrees Fahrenheit. Warning: Above or below that temperature, flames may shoot out from the Gadget-Go. Keep a fire extinguisher where you can reach it quickly.

Assembly instructions: First, lay out all the parts. There should be 459 pieces, plus our special G-G Frame. If the G-G Frame appears discolored or smells like fish, return it to our factory right away. Buy liability insurance first. The G-G Frame can be dangerous! One customer complained about poisonous ooze that seeped through the wrapping. When you have connected all the parts, turn on your new Gadget-Go. It should sound like a heavy metal band and feel warm to the touch. If you are happy with your purchase and your neighbors are not suing you, post a photo of your Gadget-Go on social media. Our priority has always been customer satisfaction.

Answers to Chapter 5 Quiz

The verbs are underlined and labeled L (for linking) and A (for action).

Congratulation on your purchase of Gadget-Go Model 55-33. You (1L) <u>will be</u> very happy. This model (2L) <u>is</u> much better than our other models. Only three (1A) <u>have exploded</u> since we (2A) <u>changed</u> the battery type. The new battery (3L) <u>has been</u> stable in temperatures ranging from 70 to 72 degrees Fahrenheit. Warning: Above or below that temperature, flames (3A) <u>may shoot</u> out from the Gadget-Go. (4A) <u>Keep</u> a fire extinguisher where you (5A) <u>can reach</u> it quickly.

Assembly instructions: First, (6A) <u>lay</u> out all the parts. There (4L) <u>should be</u> 459 pieces, plus our special G-G Frame. If the G-G Frame (5L) <u>appears</u> discolored or (6L) <u>smells</u> like fish, (7A) <u>return</u> it to our factory right away. (8A) <u>Buy</u> liability insurance first. The G-G Frame (7L) <u>can be</u> dangerous! One customer (9A) <u>complained</u> about poisonous ooze that (10A) <u>seeped</u> through the wrapping. When you (11A) <u>have connected</u> all the parts, (12A) <u>turn</u> on your new Gadget-Go. It (8L) <u>should sound</u> like a heavy metal band and (9L) <u>feel</u> warm to the touch. If you (10L) <u>are</u> happy with your purchase and your neighbors (14A) <u>are</u> not <u>suing</u> you, (15A) <u>post</u> a photo of your Gadget-Go on social media. Our priority (10L) <u>has</u> always <u>been</u> customer satisfaction.

Helping verbs: may (3A), can (5A, 7L), should (4L, 8L)

Chapter **6**

Two ~~Real~~ Really Good Parts of Speech: Adjectives and Adverbs

The artist paints.

Workers build houses.

Children play games.

C ould these sentences be any more boring? True, they give information, but most people want to know more:

The *massively successful* artist paints *carefully*.

Skilled, underpaid workers build *fancy, expensive* houses.

Noisy children play *video* games *frequently*.

The italicized words are adjectives and adverbs, parts of speech that add meaning and interest to sentences. In this chapter, I explain how adjectives and adverbs function — which words they attach to and what kind of information they supply. I also explain the proper use of three tiny but important words: *the, a,* and *an.* In other words, this chapter covers the basics. In Chapter 15, I discuss advanced topics relating to adjectives and adverbs — placement, comparisons, and irregular forms.

Clarifying Meaning with Descriptions

In case you doubt the significance of descriptive words, take a look at this sentence:

> Gloria was walking past Neiman Marcus when the sight of a Ferragamo Paradiso pump paralyzed her.

What must the reader know in order to understand this sentence fully? Here's a list:

>> The reader should know that Neiman Marcus is a department store.

>> The reader should be able to identify Ferragamo as an upscale shoe label.

>> The reader should be familiar with a Paradiso pump (a shoe style I made up).

>> The reader should know that a pump is a type of shoe.

If all these pieces are in place, or if the reader has a good imagination and the ability to use context clues, your message will get through. But sometimes you can't trust the reader to understand the specifics of what you're trying to say. Descriptive words can fill in the gaps. Here's Gloria, version 2:

> Gloria was walking *slowly* past the *stately* Neiman Marcus *department* store when the sight of a *fashionable, green, low-heeled dress* shoe with the *ultrachic Ferragamo* label paralyzed her.

Okay, I overdid it a bit, but you get the point. The descriptive words clarify the meaning of the sentence, particularly for the fashion-challenged.

Adding Adjectives

An *adjective* is a descriptive word that changes the meaning of a noun or a pronoun. An adjective adds information about number, color, type, and other qualities to your sentence.

TIP

Where do you find adjectives? In the adjective aisle of the supermarket. Just kidding. Most of the time you find them in front of the word they're describing, but adjectives can also roam around a bit. Here's an example:

George, *sore* and *tired,* pleaded with Lulu to release him from the headlock she had placed on him when he called her *"fragile."*

Sore and *tired* tell you about *George. Fragile* tells you about *her.* (Well, *fragile* tells you what George thinks of *her.* Lulu lifts weights every day and is anything but fragile.) As you see, these descriptions come after the words they describe, not before.

Adjectives describing nouns

The most common job for an adjective is describing a noun. Consider the adjectives *poisonous, angry,* and *rubber* in these sentences. Then decide which sentence you would like to hear as you walk through the zoo.

> There is a *poisonous* snake on your shoulder.
>
> There is an *angry, poisonous* snake on your shoulder.
>
> There is a *rubber* snake on your shoulder.

The last one, right? In these three sentences, those little descriptive words certainly make a difference. *Angry, poisonous,* and *rubber* all describe *snake* and give you information that you would really like to have. See how diverse and powerful adjectives can be?

Q. Find the adjectives in this sentence.

With a shiny cover and a large screen, the new phone drew huge crowds when it went on display.

A. **shiny** (describing *cover*), **large** (describing *screen*), **new** (describing *phone*), **huge** (describing *crowds*).

Adjectives describing pronouns

Adjectives can also describe *pronouns* (words that substitute for nouns). When they're giving you information about pronouns, adjectives usually appear after the pronoun they're describing:

> There's something *strange* on your shoulder. (The adjective *strange* describes the pronoun *something.*)
>
> Everyone *conscious* at the end of Ronald's play made a quick exit. (The adjective *conscious* describes the pronoun *everyone.*)
>
> Anyone *free* must report to the meeting room immediately. (The adjective *free* describes the pronoun *anyone.*)

Q. Find the adjectives in this sentence.

Anybody new and wise asks a lot of questions, which someone inexperienced and foolish answers.

A. **new, wise** (describing *anybody*), **inexperienced, foolish** (describing *someone*)

Adjectives attached to linking verbs

Adjectives may also follow linking verbs, in which case they describe the subject of the sentence. Because a linking verb functions like a giant equal sign, it links what comes before the verb with what comes after it. (See Chapter 5 for a full discussion of linking verbs.)

The adjectives are italicized in these sentences with linking verbs:

Lulu's favorite dress is *orange* and *purple.* (The adjectives *orange* and *purple* describe the noun *dress.*)

The afternoon appears *gray* because of the smoke from Roger's cigar. (The adjective *gray* describes the noun *afternoon.*)

George's latest jazz composition sounds *awful.* (The adjective *awful* describes the noun *composition.*)

EXAMPLE

Q. Find the adjectives in this sentence.

Lola seemed angry when she realized the ballroom was empty.

A. **angry** (describing *Lola*), **empty** (describing *ballroom*)

Pop the question: Identifying adjectives

Here's a trick to help you find adjectives: Go to the words they describe — nouns and pronouns. Start with the noun or pronoun and ask three questions:

>> How many?

>> Which one?

>> What kind?

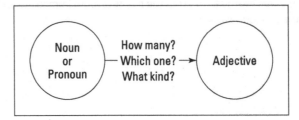

© *John Wiley & Sons, Inc.*

Take a look at this sentence:

George posted three new photos on his favorite website.

You see three nouns: *George, photos,* and *website.* George has led a colorful life, but you can't find the answer to the following questions: How many *Georges?* Which *George?* What kind of *George?* No words in the sentence provide that information, so no adjectives describe *George.*

When you try these three questions on *photos* and *website,* you do come up with something: How many *photos?* Answer: *three. Three* is an adjective. Which *photos?* What kind of *photos?* Answer: *new. New* is an adjective. The same goes for *website:* What kind? Answer: *favorite. Favorite* is an adjective.

You may have noticed that *his* answers one of the questions. (Which *website?* Answer: *his web-site.*) *His* is working as an adjective, but *his* is also a pronoun. Normal people don't have to worry about whether *his* is a pronoun or an adjective. Only English teachers care, and they divide into two camps — the adjective camp and the pronoun camp. Needless to say, each group feels superior to the other. (I'm a noncombatant. As far as I'm concerned, you can call *his* a parakeet for all I care. Just spell it correctly and you're fine.)

Look at another sentence:

The angry reaction thrilled George's rotten, little, hard heart.

This sentence has three nouns. One *(George's)* is possessive. If you ask how many *George's,* which *George's,* or what kind of *George's,* you get no answer. The other two nouns, *reaction* and *heart,* do yield an answer. What kind of *reaction? Angry reaction.* What kind of *heart? Rotten, little, hard heart.* So *angry, rotten, little,* and *hard* are all adjectives.

Q. Find the adjectives in these sentences.

1 The overworked waiter brought us cold soup.

2 Annoyed diners complained loudly about tasteless meals.

3 The embarrassed owner apologized to disappointed customers.

4 Someone mean posted a terrible review on social media.

5 Smart owners hire extra waiters and pay high salaries, because a sufficient, well-paid staff is happy.

Articles: Not just for magazines

If you ran a computer program that sorted and counted every word in this book, you'd find that *articles,* a branch on the adjective family tree, are the most common words, even though the article-branch includes only *a, an,* and *the.* Though these words collectively contain only six letters, they affect meaning.

Melanie wants *the* answer to question 12, and you'd better be quick about it.

The preceding statement means that Melanie is stuck on problem 12, and Mom won't let her leave until her homework is perfect. Melanie's friends are at the basketball game, and now she's texting, demanding *the* answer to number 12 so that she can join them. Now look at the same sentence, with one small change:

Melanie wants *an* answer, and you'd better be quick about it.

This statement means that Melanie doesn't care about accuracy. She just wants *an* answer, any answer, so that she can finish her homework and go to the game.

To sum up: Use *the* when you're speaking specifically and *an* or *a* when you're speaking more generally.

WARNING

A apple? An book? A precedes words that begin with consonant sounds (all the letters except *a, e, i, o,* and *u*). *An* precedes words beginning with the vowel sounds *a, e, i,* and *o*. The letter *u* is a special case. If the vowel sounds like *you,* choose *a.* If the word sounds like someone kicked you in the stomach — *uh* — choose *an.* Another special case is the letter *h.* If the word starts with a hard *h* sound, as in *horse,* choose *a.* If the word starts with a silent letter *h,* as in *herb,* choose *an.* Here are some examples:

an almanac (*a* = vowel)

a belly (*b* = consonant)

an egg (*e* = vowel)

a UFO (*U* sounds like *you*)

an unidentified flying object (*u* sounds like *uh*)

a helmet (hard *h*)

an hour (silent *h*)

TIP

Special note: People stuck in the past say *an historic event* because that word, a couple of centuries ago, used to begin with a silent *h.* The rest of us say *a historic event,* matching *a* with the modern pronunciation of *historic,* which includes a hard *h.*

EXAMPLE

Q. Fill in each blank with *the, a,* or *an.*

When Lulu asked to see _____ wedding pictures, she didn't expect _____ twelve-hour slide presentation.

A. **the, a** In the first half of the sentence, Lulu is asking for something specific. Also, *wedding pictures* is a plural expression, so *a* and *an* are out of the question. In the second half of the sentence, something more general is appropriate. Because *twelve* begins with the consonant *t, a* is the article of choice.

YOUR TURN

Q. Fill in each blank with *the, a,* or *an.*

6   Although Lulu was mostly bored out of her mind, she did like _____ picture of Annie's Uncle Fred snoring in the back of the church.

7   _____ nearby guest, one of several attempting to plug their ears, can be seen poking Uncle Fred's ribs.

8   At Annie's wedding, Uncle Fred wore _____ antique tie clip that he bought in _____ department store next-door to his apartment building.

9   _____ clerk who sold _____ tie clip to Uncle Fred secretly inserted _____ microphone and _____ miniature radio transmitter.

10 Uncle Fred's snores were posted on _____ obscure website that specializes in embarrassing moments.

11 Annie, who didn't want to invite Uncle Fred but was forced to do so by her mother, placed _____ buzzer under his seat.

12 Annie's plan was to zap him whenever he snored too loudly; unfortunately, Fred chose _____ different seat.

Stalking the Common Adverb

Adjectives aren't the only descriptive words. *Adverbs* — words that alter the meaning of a verb, an adjective, or another adverb — are another type of description. Check these out:

> The boss *regretfully* said no to Phil's request for a raise.
>
> The boss *furiously* said no to Phil's request for a raise.
>
> The boss *never* said no to Phil's request for a raise.

If you're Phil, you care whether the words *regretfully*, *furiously*, or *never* are in the sentence. *Regretfully*, *furiously*, and *never* are all adverbs. Notice how adverbs add meaning in these sentences:

> Lola *sadly* sang George's latest song. (Perhaps Lola is in a bad mood.)
>
> Lola sang George's latest song *reluctantly*. (Lola doesn't want to sing.)
>
> Lola *hoarsely* sang George's latest song. (Lola has a cold.)
>
> Lola sang George's latest song *quickly*. (Lola is in a hurry.)

Pop the question: Finding the adverb

Adverbs mostly describe verbs, giving more information about an action. Nearly all adverbs — enough that you don't have to worry about the ones that fall through the cracks — answer one of these four questions:

>> How?

>> When?

>> Where?

>> Why?

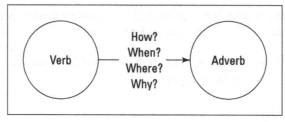

© John Wiley & Sons, Inc.

To find the adverb, go to the verb and pop the question. (For more information on locating verbs, see Chapter 5.) Look at this sentence:

Ella secretly swiped Sandy's slippers yesterday and then happily went home.

You note two verbs: *swiped* and *went*. Take each one separately. *Swiped* how? Answer: *swiped secretly*. *Secretly* is an adverb. *Swiped* when? Answer: *swiped yesterday*. *Yesterday* is an adverb. *Swiped* where? No answer. *Swiped* why? No answer.

Go on to the second verb in the sentence. *Went* how? Answer: *went happily*. *Happily* is an adverb. *Went* when? Answer: *went then*. *Then* is an adverb. *Went* where? Answer: *went home*. *Home* is an adverb. *Went* why? You find no answer in the sentence.

Here's another example:

Bill soon softly sighed and delicately slipped away.

You identify two verbs again: *sighed* and *slipped*. First one up: *sighed*. *Sighed* how? Answer: *sighed softly*. *Softly* is an adverb. *Sighed* when? Answer: *sighed soon*. *Soon* is an adverb. *Sighed* where? No answer. *Sighed* why? No answer again. Now for *slipped*. *Slipped* how? Answer: *slipped delicately*. *Delicately* is an adverb. *Slipped* where? Answer: *slipped away*. *Away* is an adverb. *Slipped* when? No answer. *Slipped* why? No answer. The adverbs are *soon, delicately*, and *away*.

Adverbs can be lots of places in a sentence. If you're trying to find them, rely on the questions *how, when, where,* and *why,* not on the location. Similarly, a word may be an adverb in one sentence and something else in another sentence. Check out this example:

Gloria went *home* in a huff because of that slammed door.

Home is where the heart is, unless you're in George's cabin.

Home plate is *not* the umpire's favorite spot.

In the first example, *home* tells you where Gloria went, so *home* is an adverb in that sentence. In the second example, *home* is a place, so *home* is a noun in that sentence. In the third example, *home* is an adjective, telling you what kind of *plate.* Also in the third example is the adverb *not,* which reverses the meaning of the verb from positive to negative. Loosely speaking, *not* answers the question *how.* (*How* are you going to the game? Oh, you're *not* going!)

EXAMPLE

Q. Which adverbs describe verbs?

Johnny often lost his temper.

A. **often** This adverb describes the verb *lost,* answering the question *lost* when?

YOUR TURN

Q. Which adverbs describe verbs?

13. Andrew never tells lies, though he is sometimes tempted.

14. I usually believe him completely, but yesterday I was not sure.

15. I arrived home, checked the refrigerator, and yelped joyfully.

16. "You actually baked me a birthday cake!" I screamed.

17. Normally, he forgets my birthday.

18. Andrew did not reply immediately.

19. "Unfortunately, I did not remember," Andrew admitted reluctantly.

20. He quietly added, "Your mom brought it here."

Adverbs describing adjectives and other adverbs

Adverbs also describe other descriptions, usually making the description more or less intense. (A description describing a description? Give me a break! But it's true.) Here's an example:

An extremely unhappy Larry collapsed when the stock market crashed.

How *unhappy?* Answer: *extremely unhappy. Extremely* is an adverb describing the adjective *unhappy.*

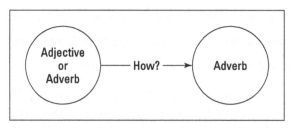

© John Wiley & Sons, Inc.

TIP

Sometimes, the questions you pose to locate adjectives and adverbs are answered by more than one word in a sentence. In the previous example, if you ask, "*Seemed* when?" the answer is *when the stock market crashed.* Don't panic. Longer answers may be prepositional phrases (see Chapter 7) or clauses. In the last example, *when the stock market crashed* is a clause (see Chapter 11). Phrases and clauses are just different members of the adjective and adverb families.

Now back to work. Here's another example:

Once he began to speak, Mary's very talkative pet parrot wouldn't shut up.

How *talkative?* Answer: *very talkative. Very* is an adverb describing the adjective *talkative.*

And another:

Larry's frog croaked *quite hoarsely.*

This time, an adverb is describing another adverb. *Hoarsely* is an adverb because it explains how the frog *croaked.* In other words, *hoarsely* describes the verb *croaked.* How *hoarsely?* Answer: *quite hoarsely. Quite* is an adverb describing the adverb *hoarsely,* which in turn describes the verb *croaked.*

EXAMPLE

Q. Which adverbs describe an adjective or another adverb?

The very hungry horse ate a bale of hay and then hiccoughed rather loudly.

A. **very, rather** *Very* describes the adjective *hungry. Rather* describes the adverb *loudly.*

YOUR TURN

Q. Which adverbs describe an adjective or another adverb?

21 Much earlier, Bert had made a very rude comment to Ellen.

22 Ellen answered Bert extremely firmly but less rudely.

23 "I am totally confident," Ellen told me a little later.

24 Ellen is really good at handling particularly sticky situations.

25 Especially now that he has an Oscar for Worst Actor, Bert feels extra needy.

Choosing Between Adjectives and Adverbs

Does it matter whether a word is an adjective or an adverb? Some of the time, no. When you were a toddler, you demanded, "I want milk NOW, Mama." You didn't know you were adding an adverb to your sentence. For that matter, you didn't know you were making a sentence! Now that you're past toddlerhood, you should know the difference between these two parts of speech so that you can select the form you need. The best way to tell whether a word is an adjective or an adverb is to "pop" the adjective questions (how many? which one? what kind?) and adverb questions (how? when? where? why?), as I explain earlier in this chapter.

TIP

Many adverbs end in *-ly*, but not all. *Strictly* is an adverb, and *strict* is an adjective. *Nicely* is an adverb, and *nice* is an adjective. *Generally* is an adverb, and *general* is an adjective. *Lovely* is a — gotcha! You were going to say *adverb*, right? Wrong. *Lovely* is an adjective. (That's why I started this paragraph with *many*, not *all*.) *Soon, now, home, fast, not,* and many other words that don't end in *-ly* can be adverbs, too.

REMEMBER

Adjectives describe nouns or pronouns, and adverbs describe verbs, adjectives, or other adverbs.

EXAMPLE

Q. Identify the adjectives and adverbs in the following sentences.

Thank you for the presents you gave us yesterday.

The lovely perfume you gave us smells like old socks.

The presents you kindly gave us are very rotten.

A. In the first sentence, *yesterday* is an adverb, describing when *you gave* the presents. The second sentence has no adverbs. *Lovely* is an adjective describing the noun *perfume. Old* is an adjective describing *socks.* In the third sentence, the adverb *kindly* describes the verb *gave,* and the adverb *very* describes the adjective *rotten. Rotten* is an adjective describing *presents.*

YOUR TURN

Q. Identify the adjectives and adverbs in the following sentences.

26 Slipping onto her comfortable old sofa, Lola quickly grabbed the black plastic remote.

27 "I arrived early because I desperately want to watch that new motorcycle show," she said to George.

28 George, who was intently watching the latest news, turned away silently.

29 Everyone present knew that Lola would get her way. She always did!

30 George struggled fiercely, but he was curious about the show, which features a different motorcycle weekly.

31 If he held out a little longer, he knew that Lola would offer something nice to him.

32 Lola's purse always held a few goodies, and George was extremely fond of chocolate brownies.

33 He could almost taste the sweet, hazelnut flavor that Lola sometimes added to the packaged brownie mix.

34 George sighed loudly and waved a long, thin hand.

35 "You can watch anything good," he remarked in a low, defeated voice, "but first give me two brownies."

Sorting out "good" and "well"

If I am ever elected emperor of the universe, one of the first things I'm going to do (after I get rid of apostrophes — see Chapter 17) is drop all irregular forms. Until then, you may want to read about *good* and *well*.

Good is an adjective, and, except when you're talking about health, *well* is an adverb. Take a look at this sentence:

> I am *good.*

The adjective *good* in this sentence means *I have the qualities of goodness* or *I am in a good mood*. In informal, conversational English, the sentence may also mean *Everything is fine with me, I don't need anything*, or *My health is good*. (The sentence may also be the world's worst pickup line.) Now look at another statement:

> I am *well.*

Well is an adjective here. The sentence means *I am not sick*. One more:

> I play the piano *well.*

This time, *well* is an adverb. It describes how I play. In other words, the adverb *well* describes the verb *play*. The sentence means that I no longer have to practice.

EXAMPLE

Q. Which sentence is correct?

(A) Egbert did not perform good on the crash test.

(B) Egbert did not perform well on the crash test.

A. **B** The adverb *well* correctly describes the verb *did perform*, which you see when you pop the question *Did perform* how? Answer: *did perform well*.

Dealing with "bad" and "badly"

Bad is a bad word, at least in terms of grammar. Confusing *bad* and *badly* is one of the most common errors. Check out these examples:

I felt badly.

I felt bad.

Badly is an adverb, and *bad* is an adjective. Which one should you use? Well, what are you trying to say? In the first sentence, you went to the park with your mittens on. The bench had a sign on it: "WET PAINT." The sign looked old, so you decided to check. You put your hand on the bench, but the mittens were in the way. You felt *badly* — that is, not accurately. In the second sentence, you sat on the bench, messing up the back of your coat with dark green stripes. When you saw the stripes, you felt *bad* — that is, you were sad. In everyday speech, of course, you're unlikely to express much about *feeling badly*. Few people walk around testing benches, and even fewer talk about their ability to feel something physically. So 99.99 percent of the time you feel *bad* — unless you're in a good mood.

TIP

In conversational English, *I feel badly* is becoming an acceptable way to express regret, as in *I feel badly about setting fire to the chem lab.* In formal English, opt for *I feel bad* — and in either situation, be careful with flammable material!

EXAMPLE

Q. Which sentence is correct?

(A) Lola felt bad when she discovered a dent in her motorcycle.

(B) Lola felt badly when she discovered a dent in her motorcycle.

A. **A** Lola loves her Harley, and every scratch or dent depresses her. Therefore, *bad* is an adjective describing Lola (actually, Lola's state of mind). In sentence B, *badly* is an adverb, so it would have to describe Lola's ability to feel. That meaning makes no sense.

Q. Which sentence is correct?

(A) Lola did bad in her negotiations with the insurance company.

(B) Lola did badly in her negotiations with the insurance company.

A. **B** The adverb *badly* describes the verb *did*. Did how? Answer: *did badly.*

YOUR TURN

Q. Choose the correct word from the choices in parentheses.

36 The trainer works (good/well) with all types of dogs, especially those that don't outweigh him.

37 My dog Caramel barks when he has run (good/well) during his daily race with the letter carrier.

38 The letter carrier likes Caramel and feels (bad/badly) about beating him when they race.

39 Caramel tends to bite the poor guy whenever the race doesn't go (good/well).

40 Caramel's owner named him after a type of candy she thinks is (good/well).

41 The letter carrier thinks high-calorie snacks are (bad/badly).

Practice Questions Answers and Explanations

1. **overworked** (describing *waiter*), **cold** (describing *soup*)

2. **Annoyed** (describing *diners*), **tasteless** (describing *meals*)

3. **embarrassed** (describing *owner*), **disappointed** (describing *customers*)

4. **mean** (describing *Someone*), **terrible** (describing *review*), **social** (describing *media*)

5. **Smart** (describing *owners*), **extra** (describing *waiters*), **high** (describing *salaries*), **sufficient, well-paid, happy** (describing *staff*)

6. **the** The sentence implies that one particular picture caught Lulu's fancy, so *the* works nicely here. If you chose *a*, no problem. The sentence would be a bit less specific but still acceptable. The only true clinker is *an*, which must precede words beginning with vowels (except for a short *u*, or "uh" sound) — a group that doesn't include *picture*.

7. **A** Because the sentence tells you that several guests are nearby, *the* doesn't fit here. The more general *a* is best.

8. **an** or **the, the** In the first blank, you may place either *an* (which must precede a word beginning with a vowel) or *the*. In the second blank, *the* is best because it's unlikely that Fred is surrounded by several department stores. *The* is more definitive, pointing out one particular store.

9. **The, the, a, a** Lots of blanks in this one! The first two seem more particular (one *clerk*, one *tie clip*), so *the* fits well. The second two blanks imply that the clerk selected one from a group of many, not a particular microphone or transmitter. The more general article is *a*, which precedes words beginning with consonants.

10. **an** Because the website is described as *obscure*, a word beginning with a vowel, you need *an*, not *a*. If you inserted *the*, don't cry. That article works here also.

11. **a** The word *buzzer* doesn't begin with a vowel, so you have to go with *a*, not *an*. The more definite *the* could work, implying that the reader knows that you're talking about a particular buzzer, not just any buzzer.

12. **a** He chose any old seat, not a particular one, so *a* is what you want.

13. **never** → *tells*, **sometimes** → *tempted*

14. **usually, completely** → *believe*, **yesterday** → *sure*, **not** → *was*

15. **home** → *arrived*, **joyfully** → *yelped*

16. **actually** → *baked*

17. **Normally** → *forgets*

18. **not, immediately** → *did reply*

19. **unfortunately, not** → *did remember*, **reluctantly** → *admitted*

20. **quietly** → *added*, **here** → *brought*

(21) **Much** →adverb *earlier,* **very** → adjective *rude*

(22) **extremely** → adverb *firmly,* **less** → adverb *rudely*

(23) **totally** → adjective *confident,* **little** → adverb *later*

(24) **really** → adjective *good,* **particularly** → adjective *sticky*

(25) **Especially** → adverb *now,* **extra** → adjective *needy*

(26) **comfortable (ADJ), old (ADJ), quickly (ADV), black (ADJ), plastic (ADJ).** The adjectives *comfortable* and *old* tell you what kind of *sofa.* The adverb *quickly* tells you how Lola *grabbed.* The adjectives *black* and *plastic* tell you what kind of *remote.*

(27) **early (ADV), desperately (ADV), new (ADJ), motorcycle (ADJ).** The adverb *early* tells you when she *arrived.* The adverb *desperately* tells you how she *wanted.* The adjectives *new* and *motorcycle* answer the question *what kind of show?*

(28) **intently (ADV), latest (ADJ), away (ADV) silently (ADV).** The adverb *intently* answers the question *watching how? Latest,* an adjective, tells you *what kind of news. Away* and *silently,* both adverbs, answer *turned how?*

(29) **present (ADJ) always (ADV).** *Present* is an adjective describing the pronoun *everyone.* This adjective breaks the pattern because it appears after the word it describes, not before. It also doesn't fit perfectly into the adjective questions (how many? which one? what kind?), but it serves the same purpose. It limits the meaning of *everyone.* You aren't talking about everyone in the universe, just *everyone present. Always* answers the question *did when?* and is therefore an adverb. You may be wondering about *her. Her* is a possessive pronoun, functioning as a description of *way.* What kind of *way? Her way.*

(30) **fiercely (ADV), curious (ADJ) different (ADJ), weekly (ADV).** *Fiercely,* an adverb, answers the question *struggled how? Curious* is an adjective appearing after a linking verb *(was). Curious* describes the pronoun *he. Different* is an adjective answering the question *which motorcycle? Weekly,* an adverb, answers the question *features when?*

(31) **little (ADV), longer (ADV), nice (ADJ).** The adverb *little* changes the intensity of another adverb, *longer.* Together they answer the question *held out when? Nice,* an adjective, describes the pronoun *something.*

(32) **few (ADJ), extremely (ADV), fond (ADJ), chocolate (ADJ).** How many goodies? *A few* goodies. *Few* is an adjective. (*A* is an article, which is technically an adjective.) The adverb *extremely* intensifies the meaning of the adjective *fond. Fond,* which appears after a linking verb, describes *George. Extremely* answers the question *how fond?* The adjective *chocolate* answers *what kind of brownies?*

(33) **almost (ADV) sweet (ADJ), hazelnut (ADJ) sometimes (ADV), packaged (ADJ), brownie (ADJ).** The adverb *almost* answers the question *taste how?* What kind of *flavor? Sweet, hazelnut.* Both are adjectives. *Added* when? *Sometimes* — an adverb. What kind of *mix? Packaged, brownie mix.* Both *packaged* and *brownie* are adjectives.

(34) **loudly (ADV), long (ADJ), thin (ADJ).** *Loudly,* an adverb, answers *sighed how? Long and thin,* adjectives, tell you what kind of *hand.*

(35) **good (ADJ), low (ADJ), defeated (ADJ), first (ADV), two (ADV).** *Good* is an adjective describing the pronoun *anything. Low* and *defeated* are adjectives answering *what kind of voice? First* is an adverb answering *give when? Two* is an adjective answering *how many brownies?*

(36) **well** How does the trainer work? The word you need must be an adverb because you're giving information about an action *(work)*, not a noun.

(37) **well** The adverb *well* tells you how Caramel *has run*.

(38) **bad** This sentence illustrates a common mistake. The description tells you nothing about the letter carrier's ability to *feel* (touching sensation). Instead, it tells you about his state of mind. Because the word is a description of a person, not of an action, you need an adjective, *bad.*

(39) **well** The adverb *well* describes the verb *go*.

(40) **good** What is her opinion of chocolate caramels? She *thinks* they are *good*. The adjective is needed because you're describing the noun *candy.*

(41) **bad** The description *bad* applies to the *snacks*, not to the verb *are*. Hence, an adjective is what you want.

Whaddya Know? Chapter 6 Quiz

In this page from a clothing catalog, a number of words are underlined. If they're correct, leave them alone. If you find an adjective or adverb error, correct the mistake.

Dollar Clothing: Fashions That Work!

(1) <u>Surprising</u> (2) <u>comfortable</u> suits for work and leisure are on sale! (3) <u>Easily</u>-to-clean polyester in a (4) <u>real</u> fashionable color goes from the (5) <u>office</u> grind to an (6) <u>extreme</u> (7) <u>trendy</u> club without a pause. Imagine yourself in these (8) <u>beautifully</u> clothes that are made (9) <u>well</u>.

Jacket: Stun your coworkers with (10) <u>a</u> (11) <u>astonishingly</u> elegance of (12) <u>deeply</u> eggplant. (13) <u>Gently</u> curves follow (14) <u>an</u> (15) <u>real</u> natural outline to accentuate your figure. The (16) <u>silkily</u> lining, in (17) <u>delightful</u> (18) <u>loud</u> shades of orange, gives a strong message: I am (19) <u>good</u> at my job and I will feel (20) <u>badly</u> if I don't succeed.

Answers to Chapter 6 Quiz

1. **Surprisingly** The adverb *surprisingly* is what you need attached to the description *comfortable*, an adjective.

2. **Correct** The adjective *comfortable* answers *what kind of suits? Suits* is a noun.

3. **Easy** *Easily* is an adverb, but the three-word description is attached to a noun, *polyester. Easy* is an adjective and is the word you want here. Are you wondering why this phrase is hyphenated? Check Chapter 20 for more information.

4. **really** The adjective *fashionable* is intensified by the adverb *really. Real*, an adjective, is out of place here.

5. **Correct** *Office* can be a noun, but here it functions as an adjective, describing the noun *grind.*

6. **extremely** How *trendy? Extremely trendy.* Intensifiers are adverbs.

7. **Correct** The adjective *trendy* describes the noun *club.*

8. **beautiful** *Beautiful* is an adjective describing *clothes.*

9. **Correct** You need an adverb to describe the verb *made.*

10. **the** *Elegance* is defined in a specific way in this sentence. It's *deep eggplant.* Because you're being specific, *the* is the best article here.

11. **astonishing** *Astonishing* is an adjective attached to the noun *elegance.*

12. **deep** To refer to the noun *eggplant*, which is a color here and not a vegetable, use the adjective *deep.*

13. **Gentle** *Gentle* is an adjective, just what you need to describe the noun *curves.*

14. **a** Before a word beginning with a consonant, such as *r*, place *a.*

15. **really** *Natural* is an adjective, which you intensify with the adverb *really.*

16. **silky** *Lining* is a noun, so you describe it with the adjective *silky.*

17. **delightfully** To intensify the adjective *loud*, use the adverb *delightfully.*

18. **Correct** This adjective *loud* describes the noun *shades.*

19. **Correct** The adjective *good* describes the speaker, *I.*

20. **bad** You need an adjective to describe the mood, not an adverb to describe an action.

Chapter **7**

Tiny but Mighty: Prepositions, Conjunctions, and Interjections

ull disclosure: Not all prepositions, conjunctions, and interjections are tiny. But whether they're nine letters long or two, they're all mighty. They connect ideas, define relation-ships, and enhance the flow of your writing. In this chapter, I explain everything you always wanted to know about identifying and employing these parts of speech properly.

Proposing Relationships: Prepositions

Imagine that you encounter two nouns: *elephant* and *book*. (A *noun* is a word for a person, place, thing, or idea.) How many ways can you connect the two nouns to express different ideas?

the book *about* the elephant

the book *by* the elephant

the book *behind* the elephant

the book *in front of* the elephant

the book *near* the elephant

the book *under* the elephant

The italicized words relate two nouns to each other. These relationship words are called *prepositions. Prepositions* may be defined as any word or group of words that relates a noun or a pronoun to another word in the sentence.

Sometime during the past millennium when I was in grammar school, I had to memorize a list of prepositions. (How quaint, right? We had inkwells, too.) I don't think memorizing prepositions is worth your time, but a familiarity would be nice. Take a look at Table 7-1 for a list of some common prepositions.

Table 7-1   **Common Prepositions**

about	above	according to	across
after	against	along	amid
among	around	at	before
behind	below	beside	besides
between	beyond	by	concerning
down	during	except	for
from	in	into	like
of	off	on	over
past	since	through	toward
underneath	until	up	upon
with	within	without	

Prepositional phrases

Prepositions never travel alone; they're always with an object. In the examples in the preceding section, the object of each preposition is *elephant.* Just to get all the annoying terminology over with at once, a *prepositional phrase* consists of a preposition and an object. The object of a preposition is always a noun or a pronoun, or perhaps one or two of each. (A *pronoun* is a word that takes the place of a noun, such as *him* for *Raymond* or *it* for *hotel.* See Chapter 4 for more about pronouns.)

Take a look at this sentence:

In the afternoon, the snow pelted Raymond on his little bald head.

This sentence has two prepositions: *in* and *on. Afternoon* is the object of the preposition *in,* and *head* is the object of the preposition *on.*

Why, you may ask, is the object *head* and not *little* or *bald?* (Sigh.) I was hoping you wouldn't notice. Okay, here's the explanation. You can throw a few other words inside a prepositional phrase — mainly descriptive words. Check out these variations on the plain phrase *of the elephant:*

> of the *apologetic* elephant
>
> of the *always annoying* elephant
>
> of the *antagonizingly argumentative* elephant

Despite the different descriptions, each phrase is still basically talking about an *elephant.* Also, *elephant* is a noun, and only nouns and pronouns are allowed to be objects of the preposition. So in the *Raymond* sentence, you need to choose the most important word as the object of the preposition. Also, you must choose a noun, not an adjective. Examine *his little bald head* (the words, not Raymond's actual head, which is better seen from a distance). *Head* is clearly the important concept, and *head* is a noun. Thus, *head* is the object of the preposition.

Sometimes, a preposition may have more than one object, as in this sentence:

> Little Jane bounced the rubber ball in the hallway and bedroom.

In this sentence, *hallway* and *bedroom* are objects of the preposition *in.* You can think of this sentence as an abbreviated form of

> Little Jane bounced the rubber ball in the hallway and in the bedroom.

When you attach two or more objects to one preposition, you must be sure that both objects pair well with the preposition. Take a look at this sentence:

> Little Jane bounced the rubber ball in the street and the wall.

If you expand this sentence, you get

> Little Jane bounced the rubber ball in the street and in the wall.

How can you bounce a ball *in the wall?* You can't, unless you're talking about a half-built house. You bounce a ball *on* or *against the wall.* The moral of the story is that a preposition with more than one object must make sense with each object separately. If it doesn't, write two separate prepositional phrases.

WARNING Also be careful when you're choosing a pronoun as the object of a preposition. The pronouns cleared to act as objects of the preposition are *me, you, him, her, it, us, them, whom,* and *whomever.* Stay away from *I, we, she, he, they, who,* and *whoever.* Those pronouns are for subjects and subject complements. (Turn to Chapter 14 for more information.)

Pop the question: Questions that identify the objects of the prepositions

All objects — of a verb or of a preposition — answer the questions *whom?* or *what?* To find the object of a preposition, ask *whom?* or *what?* after the preposition.

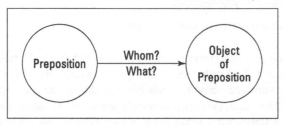

© *John Wiley & Sons, Inc.*

Marilyn thought that the selection of the elephant for the show was unfair.

In this sentence, you see two prepositional phrases. The first preposition is *of. Of* what? *Of the elephant. Elephant* is the object of the preposition *of.* The second preposition is *for. For* what? For the *show. Show* is the object of the preposition *to.*

WARNING

When a noun — the name of a person, place, or thing — is the object of a preposition, everything is easy. Nouns work as subjects and objects without changing form. Most pronouns — words that substitute for nouns — change form depending on whether they're functioning as a subject or an object. For more information on object pronouns, see Chapter 14.

Why pay attention to prepositions?

Choosing the wrong preposition may be embarrassing:

Person 1: May I sit *next* to you?

Person 2: (smiling) Certainly.

Person 1: May I sit *under* you?

Person 2: (sound of slap) Help! Police!

The task of selecting the proper preposition is often difficult because common expressions differ, depending on the country or even area of a country in which the language is spoken. In New York City, for example, polite people wait *on line.* (Impolite people push through the crowd.) In other parts of the United States, people wait *in line.* Also, sometimes more than one preposition is acceptable. You can *browse over* or *browse through* a magazine, reading bits here and there and deciding what you'd like to investigate thoroughly. Both prepositions, *over* and *through,* are correct.

Omitting a preposition can also change meaning. Do you see the difference between these two sentences?

> Shirley swam the ocean.
>
> Shirley swam in the ocean.

In the first example, Shirley swam across the entire ocean — from, say, California to Japan or from New York to Ireland. The second example expresses a more likely meaning, that Shirley went to the beach and swam for a while in ocean water.

Placement may also matter. Check out these sentences:

> He went by bicycle <u>to the game</u>, saw the winning goal, and returned afterward.
>
> He went by bicycle, saw the winning goal, and returned <u>to the game</u> afterward.

Do you see the difference? In the first sentence, *he* traveled *to the game* first. Then he *returned* to his starting point. In the second sentence, *he* traveled somewhere else. Then he *returned to the game*. The meaning changes because one phrase, *to the game*, moves.

TIP

Pay attention to prepositional phrases when you're checking subject-verb pairs. Why? So you can ignore them. No word in a prepositional phrase ever acts as a subject. Once you mentally subtract the prepositional phrases from a sentence, you can focus on the real subject-verb pair and match them up correctly. For more information on subjects, see Chapter 8.

You may also find it helpful to recognize prepositional phrases, because sometimes, when you "pop the question" to find an adjective or an adverb, the answer is a prepositional phrase. That's not a mistake. Prepositional phrases are just another form of description. (See Chapter 6 for more on adjectives and adverbs.)

One thing you don't have to worry about is ending a sentence with a preposition. Years ago, some of the strictest grammarians would scold anyone who wrote a sentence like this:

> Tell me whom he spoke *about.*

They insisted on this version:

> Tell me *about* whom he spoke.

Both sentences are now considered correct, with the second being a bit more formal.

EXAMPLE

Q. Identify the prepositional phrase.

The heroic teacher pounded grammar rules into her students' tired brains.

A. **into** (preposition) **her students' tired brains** (object) When you pop the question — *into* whom? *into* what? — the answer is *her students' tired brains.* The most important word is *brains*, which is a noun.

YOUR TURN

Q. Identify the prepositional phrases.

1. Take the cat to the veterinary clinic now because Fifi is moaning in pain.

2. The dog food bag in the closet is empty, and the bag has a long rip across the bottom.

3. Fifi probably stole food from Spot's supply of doggie treats.

4. During the night, I heard noises in the kitchen.

5. The flashlight on my nightstand was broken, so I saw nothing of interest.

6. Before midnight, I had searched inside every cabinet, without success, but I had forgotten to look in the closet.

Connecting with Conjunctions

Are you a matchmaker? Do you pair up your friends, hoping lonely individuals will find happiness joined together? If so, you will love conjunctions, a part of speech that joins. Take a look at these sentences:

> Lola's cousin Rob gave her a bobsled, <u>but</u> she is afraid of ice <u>and</u> snow. <u>Because</u> bobsleds don't move well on cement, the bobsled will stay in her garage, <u>or</u> she'll donate it to an Olympic sledder.

The four underlined conjunctions in the preceding paragraph — *but, and, because, or* — connect ideas (much better than Rob connects with Lola).

Improving flow and adding meaning with conjunctions

As any plumber can tell you, good connections improve flow. Have a look at this paragraph:

> Short sentences are boring. Short sentences are childish. Combining them is a good idea. Selecting the proper conjunction can be tricky.

Are you still awake? Now add conjunctions:

> <u>Because</u> short sentences sound boring <u>and</u> childish, combining them is a good idea, <u>but</u> selecting the proper conjunction can be tricky.

Better, right? Here are the connections, with the conjunction in bold type:

> *boring* ↔ **and** ↔ *childish*
>
> *short sentences sound boring and childish* ↔ ***because*** ↔ *combining them is a good idea*
>
> *combining them is a good idea* ↔ ***but*** ↔ *selecting the proper conjunction can be tricky*

As you see, whether conjunctions connect single words (*boring, childish*) or complete sentences, they create a smoother style.

When you combine ideas with a conjunction, you must be careful to choose the correct word, because each conjunction gives a different meaning. Consider these two statements:

> Sentence 1: Sarah wants to speak with her brother.
>
> Sentence 2: He is annoyed.

How should you combine these ideas? It depends on what you want to say. Look at this sentence:

> Sarah wants to speak with her brother, but he is annoyed.

This sentence hints that Sarah will wait until later, when her brother is in a better mood. Now check out this one:

> Sarah wants to speak with her brother because he is annoyed.

Now you know that Sarah is not going to wait for a smile from her brother. She is going to have a conversation about his mood or whatever caused his annoyance. How about this one:

> Sarah wants to speak with her brother although he is annoyed.

In this version, Sarah has something to say. Her brother's mood does not matter. She will speak with him whether he is in a good mood or a bad mood. Look at one more:

> Sarah wants to speak with her brother when he is annoyed.

Now Sarah comes across as a bossy sister. She calls her brother or drops in for a chat because she thinks she can calm him down.

With the appropriate conjunction, you can emphasize one idea and downplay another, establish an order of events, show cause-and-effect, and do so much more. Chart 7-1 lists some common conjunctions.

and	but	nor	or	yet
after	before	since	although	because
while	so	until	if	for
even though	whether	than	unless	as though

Don't worry about labeling the part of speech; just employ every technique you can to make your writing interesting!

Q. Identify the conjunction and what it connects.

Peter and Rebecca will cook the turkey.

A. **and** (conjunction) **Peter ↔ Rebecca** (connected elements)

Q. Identify the conjunction and what it connects.

I think we should dine out or order in.

A. **or** (conjunction) **eat** ↔ **order** (connected elements)

YOUR TURN

Q. Identify the conjunctions and what they connect.

⑦ Peter was no chef, nor was Rebecca a good cook.

⑧ The turkey was dry yet tasty.

⑨ We will eat a lot of turkey, and we will not complain.

⑩ The meal is not great, but it is free.

⑪ The leftovers will go to the dog, the cat, or the piglet.

⑫ Mary canceled the parade because it is raining.

⑬ While Roger was at the dentist, his sister called.

⑭ The farmers worked until darkness fell.

⑮ Although the current mayor is popular, many voters favor another candidate.

⑯ Candice always sounds happy when she is talking with Tom.

Pairing up conjunctions

Sometimes conjunctions work in pairs. (Perhaps they're lonely all by themselves?) *Or* often appears with *either. Nor* partners with *neither. Both* may show up with *and. Not only* works with *but also.*

Observe these pairs in their natural setting, a sentence:

> Neither George nor Helen went to Florida last winter. (conjunction pair = *Neither, nor;* ideas connected = *George, Helen* — both nouns)

> We must act either now or never. (conjunction pair = *either, or;* ideas connected = *now, never* — both adverbs)

> Hugh can both dance and sing. (conjunction pair = *both, and;* ideas connected = *dance, sing* — both verbs)

Did you notice that everything connected by paired conjunctions has the same grammatical identity? You do not need to know the labels, but you should be sure that everything you connect with these conjunction pairs matches. How do you detect a match? Listen! Suppose the last sentence was *Hugh can both dance and he sings.* Do you hear the mismatch? One is just an action (*dance*), and the other is a person and an action (*he sings*). In Chapter 13, I discuss how to make good grammatical matches when paired conjunctions connect ideas.

Q. Identify the conjunctions and what they connect.

EXAMPLE Not only Larry but also his bride yearned for a day at the beach.

A. **Not only, but also** (conjunction pair) **Larry** ↔ **his bride**

 Q. Identify the conjunctions and what they connect.

YOUR TURN

 17 Either you or I must break the news about the fake diamond to Larry.

 18 Neither Ralph nor I have brought a proper present to Larry's wedding.

 19 Both because he stole the garter and because he lost the ring, Roger is no longer welcome as best man.

 20 Lulu will go with Larry either to the bachelor party or to the shower, but she will not attend both.

 21 Lulu mocked neither Larry nor his bride about the fact that the bride's mother has a terrible singing voice.

22 Both her graceful dancing and superb acting skills convinced Michael to award Lola a starring role in Michael's new musical, *The Homework Blues.*

Interjections Are Easy!

Grammarians usually give every part of speech a lot of attention — well, every part of speech except one. Interjections tend to fade into the background when you're analyzing a sentence grammatically. That's the opposite of what interjections do when you're listening to or reading a sentence that includes one. Why? *Interjections* are exclamations that often express intense emotion. These words or phrases aren't connected grammatically to the rest of the sentence, but they add lots of meaning. Check out these examples, in which the interjections are italicized:

Ouch. I caught my finger in the hatch of that submarine.

Curses, foiled again.

Yes! We've finally gotten to a topic that is foolproof.

Interjections may be followed by commas, but sometimes they're followed by exclamation points or periods. The separation by punctuation shows the reader that the interjection is a comment on the sentence, not a part of it. (Of course, in the case of the exclamation point or period, the punctuation mark also indicates that the interjection is not a part of the sentence at all.)

You can't do anything wrong with interjections, except perhaps overuse them. Interjections are like salt: A little salt sprinkled on dinner perks up the taste buds; too much sends you to the telephone to order takeout.

Practice Questions Answers and Explanations

(1) **to the veterinary clinic, in pain** The prepositions are *to* and *in*. The objects are *clinic* and *pain*.

(2) **in the closet, across the bottom** The prepositions are *in* and *across*. The objects are *closet* and *bottom*.

(3) **from Spot's supply, of doggie treats** The prepositions are *from* and *of*. The objects are *supply* and *treats*.

(4) **During the night, in the kitchen** The prepositions are *during* and *in*. The objects are *night* and *kitchen*.

(5) **on my nightstand, of interest** The prepositions are *on* and *of*. The objects are *nightstand* and *interest*.

(6) **Before midnight, inside every cabinet, without success, in the closet** The prepositions are *before, inside, without,* and *in*. The objects are *midnight, cabinet, success,* and *closet*. Did I catch you with *to look*? In this sentence, *look* is a verb, not a noun, so this can't be a prepositional phrase, because there's no object. *To look* is an infinitive, a fancy word for what you get when you add *to* to a verb. (More on infinitives appears in Chapter 24.)

(7) **nor** (conjunction) **Peter was no chef** ↔ **Rebecca was a good cook** Did you notice how the conjunction affects the meaning of the sentence? The second statement implies that you'd enjoy dinner at Rebecca's house, but not Peter's, but *nor* makes it negative.

(8) **yet** (conjunction) **dry** ↔ **tasty** The conjunction *yet* introduces a redeeming quality of the cooking.

(9) **and** (conjunction) **We will eat a lot of turkey** ↔ **we will not complain** The conjunction connects two complete sentences.

(10) **but** (conjunction) **The meal is not great** ↔ **it is free.** Another connection between complete sentences.

(11) **or** (conjunction) **dog** ↔ **cat** ↔ **piglet** The conjunction appears before the last item, but it connects all three.

(12) **because** (conjunction) **Mary canceled the parade** ↔ **it is raining** The conjunction introduces a reason.

(13) **While** (conjunction), **Roger was at the dentist** ↔ **his sister called** The conjunction adds a time element.

(14) **until** (conjunction), **The farmers worked** ↔ **darkness fell** The conjunction adds a time element.

(15) **Although** (conjunction) **the current mayor is popular** ↔ **many voters favor another candidate** The conjunction introduces a condition.

(16) **when** (conjunction), **Candice always sounds happy** ↔ **she is talking with Tom** The conjunction introduces a time element or condition.

(17) **Either, or** (conjunction pair) **you** ↔ **I**

(18) **Neither**, **nor** (conjunction pair) **Ralph** ↔ **I** Did you notice that this pair connects a noun and a pronoun? This doesn't break the rule that the halves of the pair must have the same grammatical identity, because pronouns can take the place of nouns.

(19) **Both**, **and** (conjunction pair) **because he stole the garter** ↔ **because he lost the ring**

(20) **either, or** (conjunction pair) **to the bachelor party** ↔ **to the shower**

(21) **neither, nor** (conjunction pair) **Larry** ↔ **his bride**

(22) **Both**, **and** (conjunction pair) **her graceful dancing** ↔ **superb acting skill**

Whaddya Know? Chapter 7 Quiz

Q. Identify the conjunctions, prepositional phrases, and interjections in this evaluation form. You should find ten conjunctions (counting paired conjunctions as a single unit), ten prepositional phrases, and two interjections.

LearnNot University Evaluation Form

We at LearnNot University care about your well-being. Please answer these questions concerning your experience in Cooking 101, the class you took during the last academic year.

Which statement expresses your feelings about Cooking 101?

Oh, I just loved the class and the teacher!

When I measured the boredom level, I considered dropping the course.

I have no opinion because I cut every class.

What did you think of the teacher's grading practices?

Neither my parents nor my grandparents donated a building, and I therefore failed the course.

Both my parents and my grandparents bribed the teacher directly, yet I still failed the course.

Because I never open my mail, I don't know my grade.

Why did you choose Cooking 101?

After ten minutes, the teacher leaves and class is over.

Alas! I am banned for life from all other courses because of the stapler incident.

I like eating while I am studying.

Answers to Chapter 7 Quiz

Prepositional phrases, conjunctions, and interjections are underlined and labeled. The letter *P* means "prepositional phrase," the letter C means "conjunction, and the letter I means "interjection."

We (P1) <u>at LearnNot University</u> care (P2) <u>about your well-being</u>. Please answer these questions (P3) <u>concerning your experience</u> (P4) <u>in Cooking 101</u>, the class you took (P5) <u>during the last academic year</u>.

Which statement expresses your feelings (P6) <u>about Cooking 101</u>?

(I 1) <u>Oh</u>, I loved the class (C1) <u>and</u> the teacher.

(C2) <u>When</u> I calibrated the boredom level, I considered dropping this course.

I have no opinion (C3) <u>because</u> I cut every class.

What did you think (P6) <u>of the teacher's grading practices</u>?

(C4) <u>Neither</u> my parents (C4) <u>nor</u> my grandparents donated a building, (C5) <u>and</u> I therefore failed the course.

(C6) <u>Both</u> my parents (C6) <u>and</u> my grandparents bribed the teacher directly, (C7) <u>yet</u> I still failed the course.

(C8) <u>Because</u> I never open my mail, I don't know my grade.

Why did you choose Cooking 101?

(P7) <u>After ten minutes</u>, the teacher leaves (C9) <u>and</u> class is over.

(I 2) <u>Alas</u>, I am banned (P8) <u>for life</u> (P9) <u>from all other courses</u> (P10) <u>because of the stapler incident</u>.

I like eating (C10) <u>while</u> I am studying.

3

Basic Elements of a Sentence

In This Unit . . .

Chapter **8**

Who's Doing What? Identifying the Subject-Verb Pair

Imagine a sentence as a flatbed truck carrying your meaning to the reader or listener. Verbs are the wheels of the truck. Subjects are the drivers. Unless you have both, you're in for a wild ride. In this chapter, I discuss these essential elements of a sentence.

Baring the Bones of a Sentence: The Subject–Verb Pair

At the heart of every sentence is the *verb*, the word or words expressing action or state of being. Verbs are a finicky part of speech. If you get one little thing wrong — writing *sneeze* rather than *sneezed* or *sneezes*, for example — your intended message may crash and burn. For this reason, I devote several chapters solely to various aspects of verbs: the basics in Chapter 5, tense in Chapter 12, and agreement in Chapter 13. In this chapter, I tackle verbs in relation to their most important partner, subjects.

The *subject* is *who* or *what* you're talking about in relation to the action or state of being expressed by the verb. Think about it for a moment and you'll see why a subject is crucial: You can't have an action in a vacuum. Nor can you have a naked, solitary state of being. There must be someone or something doing the action or in the state of being.

TIP

A "someone" must be a person, and a "something" must be a thing, place, or idea. So guess what? The subject is usually a noun, because a noun is a person, place, thing, or idea. I say *usually* because sometimes the subject is a pronoun — a word that substitutes for a noun or another pronoun — *he, they, it,* and so forth. (For more on pronouns, see Chapter 4.)

The subject–verb pair is the main idea of the sentence, stripped to essentials. Check out these sentences:

> *Jasper gasped* at the mummy's sudden movement.

In this sentence, *Jasper gasped* is the main idea; it's also the subject–verb pair.

You should spot two subject–verb pairs in the following sentence: *Justin will judge* and *girlfriend competes*:

> *Justin will judge* the beauty contest only if *his girlfriend competes*.

Now try a sentence without action. This one describes a state of being, so it employs a linking verb:

> *Jill has* always *been* an extremely efficient worker.

The subject–verb pair is *Jill has been.* Did you notice that *Jill has been* sounds incomplete? *Has been* is a linking verb, and linking verbs always need something after the verb to complete the idea. The subject–verb pair in action-verb sentences may usually stand alone, but the subject–verb pair in linking verb sentences may not. (More on completions for linking-verb sentences appears in Chapter 9.)

When One Is Not Enough: Compound Subjects and Verbs

Subjects and verbs pair off, but sometimes you get two (or more) for the price of one. You can have two subjects (or more) and one verb. The multiple subjects are called *compound subjects.* Here's an example:

> *Dorothy* and *Justin* went home in defeat.

Here you notice one action *(went)* and two people *(Dorothy, Justin)* doing the action. So the verb *went* has a compound subject.

Now take a look at some additional examples:

Lola and *Lulu* prepared breakfast for George yesterday. (*prepared* = verb; *Lola*, *Lulu* = subjects)

The *omelet* and *fries* were very salty. (*were* = verb; *omelet*, *fries* = subjects)

Snow White and *Doc accepted* Sneezy and Dopey into their band, but *they rejected* Snort and Squirm. (*accepted* = verb; *Snow White*, *Doc* = subjects)

Another variation is one subject paired with two (or more) verbs. For example:

Alex *screamed* and *cried* after the contest.

You have two actions (*screamed*, *cried*) and one person doing both (*Alex*). *Alex* is the subject of both *screamed* and *cried*.

Here are some additional samples of double verbs, which in grammatical terms are called *compound verbs*:

George *snatched* the flash drive and quickly *stashed* it in his pocket. (*snatched, stashed* = verbs; *George* = subject)

Larry *complained* for hours about Ella's insult and then *crept* home. (*complained, crept* = verbs; *Larry* = subject)

Ella *looked* and *sounded* awful. (*looked, sounded* = verbs, *Ella* = subject)

Luke *came* to school last week but *didn't stay* there. (*came, did stay* = verbs; *Luke* = subject)

Pop the Question: Locating the Subject–Verb Pairs

Allow me to let you in on a little trick for pinpointing the subject–verb pair of a sentence: Pop the question! (No, I'm not asking you to propose.) Pop the question tells you what to ask in order to find out what you want to know. The correct question is all-important in the search for information, as all parents realize.

WRONG QUESTION FROM PARENT: What did you do last night?

TEENAGER'S ANSWER: Nothing.

RIGHT QUESTION FROM PARENT: When you came in at midnight, were you hoping that I'd ignore the fact that you went to the Carleton Club?

TEENAGER'S ANSWER: I didn't go to the Carleton Club! I went to the mall.

PARENT: Aha! You went out on a school night. You're grounded.

In Chapter 5, I explain that the first question to ask is not "Will this be on the test?" but rather "What's the verb?" (To find the verb, ask "what's happening?" or "what is?") After you uncover the verb, put *who* or *what* in front of it to form a second question. The answer is the subject.

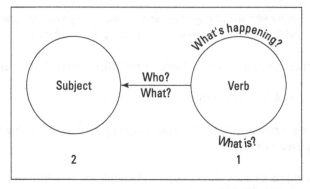

© John Wiley & Sons, Inc.

Check out this example: Jack polishes his diving technique during hours of practice.

1. Pop the question: What's happening? Answer: *polishes. Polishes* is the verb.

2. Pop the question: Who or what *polishes?* Answer: *Jack polishes. Jack* is the subject.

Ready for another?

The pool has been closed by the health department.

1. Pop the verb question: What's happening? Answer: *has been closed. Has been closed* is the verb.

2. Pop the subject question: Who or what *has been closed?* Answer: *pool. Pool* is the subject.

 Did you notice anything different about the last example? The verb, *has been closed*, asks about something that happened to the pool, not about something the pool did. *Has been closed* is a passive verb (the action happens to the subject), not an active one (the subject does the action). Fortunately, "pop the question" works the same way for sentences with either active or passive verbs.

TIP

 Sometimes when you pop the question to find the verb, you come up with a verb form that's not functioning as the verb in the sentence. Not a problem! Simply pop the subject question. If you can't find an answer, you've found a verbal. For more information on verbals, read "Don't Get Faked Out: Avoiding Fake Verbs and Subjects," later in this chapter.

WARNING

Popping the question for questions

Popping the question works for questions, too. In that situation, you're likely to find a helping verb and a main verb with the subject tucked somewhere in the middle. For that reason, you may find it helpful to rewrite the question as a statement before you pop the question. Don't add any words. The statement will sound a bit strange, but it helps you see the sentence structure more clearly. Here's an example:

> Did you eat your cookie?

1. Rearrange the question so that it resembles a statement: You did eat your cookie.
2. Pop the verb question: What's happening? Answer: *did eat. Did eat* is the verb.
3. Pop the subject question: Who or what *did eat*? Answer: *you. You* is the subject.

Try another:

> Will you eat my cookie?

1. Rearrange the question so that it resembles a statement: You will eat my cookie.
2. Pop the verb question: What's happening? Answer: *will eat. Will eat* is the verb.
3. Pop the subject question: Who or what *will eat*? Answer: *you. You* is the subject.

One more:

> Does Connie often steal other people's cookies?

1. Rearrange the question so that it resembles a statement: Connie often does steal other people's cookies.
2. Pop the verb question: What's happening? Answer: *does steal. Does steal* is the verb.
3. Pop the subject question: Who or what *does steal*? Answer: *Connie. Connie* is the subject.

EXAMPLE

Q. What are the subjects and verbs in the following sentence?

Roger will soon be smiling because of all the treasure on his ship.

No matter what the weather, Roger never even considers wearing a hat.

Does Roger hate hats, or is he afraid of messy hair?

A. will be smiling (V), Roger (S)

A. considers (V), Roger (S)

A. does hate (V), Roger (S); is (V), he (S)

Unusual word order

As I explain in the preceding section, the word order in a question differs from the word order in a statement. But statements may vary, too. Most follow the normal subject–verb order, which is (surprise!) subject–verb. In other words, the subject usually comes before the verb. Sometimes, though, a subject hides out at the end of the sentence or in some other weird place.

If you pop the question and answer it according to the meaning of the sentence — not according to the word order — you'll be fine. The key is to put the subject questions (who? what?) in front of the verb. Then think about what the sentence is actually saying and answer the questions. Like magic, your subject will appear.

Try this one:

> Up the avenue and around the park trudged Godzilla.

1. Pop the question: What's happening? What is? Answer: *trudged. Trudged* is the verb.

2. Pop the question: Who *trudged?* What *trudged?* Answer: *Godzilla. Godzilla* is the subject. (I'll let you decide whether Godzilla is a who or a what.)

If you were answering by word order, you'd say *park.* But the *park* did not *trudge; Godzilla trudged.* Pay attention to meaning, not to placement in the sentence, and you can't go wrong.

 Q. What are the subjects and verbs in the following sentences?

EXAMPLE

Alas, what a sadly inadequate grammarian am I!

Over the river and through the woods to the grammarian's house go Ella and Larry.

A. am (V), I (S)

A. go (V), Ella (S) Larry (S)

Not missing in action: Detecting you-understood

"Sit still."

"Eat your vegetables."

"Clean your room."

What do these sentences have in common? Yes, they're all nagging comments you've heard all your life. More importantly, they're all commands. The verbs give orders: *sit, eat, clean.* Where's the subject in these sentences?

If you pop the question, here's what happens:

1. Pop the question: What's happening? What is? Answer: *sit, eat, clean.*

2. Pop the question: Who *sit, eat, clean?* Answer: Uh. . . .

The second question appears to have no answer, but appearances can be deceiving. The answer is *you. You* sit still. *You* eat your vegetables. *You* clean your room. What's that you say? *You* is not in the sentence? True. *You* is not written, but it's implied. And when your mom says, "Eat your vegetables," you understand that she means *you.* So grammarians say that the subject is *you-understood.*

Q. Find the subject–verb pairs in these three sentences:

EXAMPLE

Stop dancing the cha-cha, Ella!

Sit down now, please.

Don't attempt any more new dance moves.

A. **stop (V), sit (V), Do attempt, you-understood (S)** In the first sentence, the remark is addressed to *Ella*, but *you-understood* is still the subject, as it is in the next two sentences. In the last sentence, *don't* is a shortened form of *do not*. Because *not* isn't a verb, you have to expand *don't attempt* to *do not attempt* and extract the verb, *do attempt*.

What are the subjects and verbs in the following sentences?

YOUR TURN

1. The fire engine raced down the street.

2. Do not chase it!

3. Around the curve, just ahead of the railroad tracks, stood seven donkeys.

4. One of the donkeys was frightened by the noise of the siren and ran away.

5. Come back right now, donkey!

6. Another looked worried but did not move.

7. Was he brave or was he determined to defend his herd?

8. Most likely, the animal did not notice the noise or did not care.

9. I think another donkey was eating George and Anna's lawn.

10. Eat something else, please.

11. Their house was not on fire, but several buildings on the street were burning.

12. George and Anna left the donkey alone and went inside for an extra-long lunch.

13. George and Anna, for goodness' sake, act responsibly for once in your life!

14. Because of the donkey, they did not mow their lawn.

15. Will the homeowners association fine them for "unlawful possession of a donkey"?

16. If the donkey runs away, George and Anna's problem will be solved.

17. However, the animal appears content, and Anna has posted adorable photos of him on her social media accounts.

18. Her posts have attracted much attention and have been widely shared.

19. In one obscure corner of the internet is the homeowners association statement.

20. "We love animals," the statement says, "but we do not allow braying."

21. "Send the donkey to a farm!" the association demanded.

22. George and Anna are training Donkey King, their new pet, to be silent.

23. Their lawyer has challenged the homeowners association.

24. "Lawnmowers are louder than donkeys," the lawyer says.

25. What will the judge decide?

Don't Get Faked Out: Avoiding Fake Verbs and Subjects

As I walk through New York City, I often see "genuine" Rolex watches (retail price: $10,000 or so) for sale from street peddlers for "$15 — special today only!" You need to guard against fakes when you're on the city streets (no surprise there). Also (and this may be a surprise), you need to guard against fakes when you're finding subject–verb pairs.

Verbals

Verbs can be sneaky sometimes. You may ask *who?* or *what?* in front of a verb and get no answer, or at least no answer that makes sense. When this happens, you probably haven't really found a verb. Instead, you've stumbled upon a lookalike, or, as I call it, a "fake verb." Here's an example:

> Wiping his tears dramatically, Alex pleaded with the teacher to forgive his lack of homework.

Suppose you pop the verb question *(What's happening? What is?)* and get *wiping* for an answer. A reasonable guess. But now pop the subject question: *Who wiping? What wiping?* The questions don't sound right, and that's your first hint you haven't found a real verb. The question is not important; the answer is. And there is no real answer in the sentence. You may try *Alex,* but when you put *Alex* with the "verb," it doesn't match: *Alex wiping.* (*Alex is wiping* would be okay, but that's not what the sentence says.) So now you know for sure that your first "verb" isn't really a verb. Put it aside and keep looking. What's the real verb? *Pleaded.*

To sum up: Lots of words in the sentence express action or being, but only some of these words function as verbs. (Most are what grammarians call verbals; check out Chapter 24 for more on verbals.) If you get no answer to your pop-the-subject question, just ignore the "fake" verb and look for the real one.

Q. Find the subject and verb in these sentences.

Alex's teacher, annoyed by the salty tears dripping into his coffee, denied the request for forgiveness.

A. **denied (V), teacher (S)** When you pop the question to find the verb, you may have come up with three answers: *annoyed, dripping,* and *denied.* When you pop the question to find the subject, you encounter a problem: "Who or what *annoyed?*" In the real world, the answer to that question would be *Alex,* but *Alex* isn't in the sentence. If you ask, "Who or what *dripping?*" you might answer *tears dripping.* Can you hear the mismatch? *Tears are dripping* works, but not *tears dripping.* Because you have no subject for *annoyed* and *dripping,* you know you have "fake" verbs. The real subject–verb pair is *teacher denied.*

Q. Identify the subject–verb pairs.

Dumping out his salty coffee, the teacher "accidentally" spilled a few drops on Alex's shoes.

Alex, hopping up and down and screaming about the stains, plans a lawsuit.

A. **spilled (V), teacher (S)** If you ask, "Who or what *dumping?*" you get no answer. Fake verb! Asking "Who or what *spilled?*" yields *teacher spilled,* your subject–verb pair.

A. **plans (V), Alex (S)** Did you opt for *hopping* or *screaming?* They're "fake" verbs with no matching subjects. The true verb is *plans.* Who or what *plans? Alex plans.*

"Here" and "there" sentences

Someone comes up to you and says, "Here is ten million dollars." What's the first question that comes into your mind? I know, good grammarian that you are, that your question isn't "Where can I buy a good yacht?" but rather "What's the subject of that sentence?" Try to answer your question in the usual way, by popping the question:

Here is ten million dollars.

1. Pop the question: What's happening? What is? Answer: *is.*
2. Pop the question: Who *is?* What *is?* Answer: *ten million dollars.*

What did you say? *Here is?* Wrong. *Here* can't be a subject. Neither can *there.* Both of these words are "fake" subjects. What's the real answer to the question *What is? Ten million dollars. Here* and *there* are fill-ins, place markers; they aren't what you're talking about. *Ten million dollars* — that's what you're talking about!

If you write *here* and *there* sentences, be sure to choose the correct verb. Because *here* and *there* are never subjects, you must always look *after* the verb for the real subject. When you match a subject to a verb (a topic I discuss in detail in Chapter 13), be sure to use the real subject, not *here* or *there.* Example:

Here are ten anteaters. *Not* Here is ten anteaters. (anteaters = subject)

If you want to check your choice of verb, try reversing the sentence. In the preceding sentence, say *ten anteaters is/are*. Chances are your "ear" will tell you that you want *ten anteaters are*, not *ten anteaters is*.

EXAMPLE

Q. Identify the subjects and verbs in these sentences.

There are 50 reasons for my complete lack of homework.

Here's a note from my mom about my homework allergy.

A. **are (V), reasons** (S) In a sentence beginning with *there*, the subject appears after the verb.

A. **is (V), note (S)** *Here's* is short for *here is*. Only *is* is the verb. The subject, *note*, follows the verb.

YOUR TURN

Identify the subjects and verbs in these sentences:

26. Ana and Max, cramming for finals, spend all their free time in the library.

27. Max, having grown quite tall, has not adjusted to his new size.

28. There was a book under the library table.

29. Max, helping Anna in every way, reached under the table.

30. Holding the book and standing up quickly, Max smashed his head on the bottom of the table.

31. There is a Max-size dent in the table now.

32. There's also a table-size dent in Max's head.

33. Possessing thick hair and an equally thick skull, Max is protected from most head injuries.

34. However, the table, destabilized by the collision, collapsed and broke Ana's toe.

35. "Here's an ice pack," Max offered helpfully.

Practice Questions Answers and Explanations

1. **raced (V), fire engine (S)** Pop the verb question "what's happening?" and you locate the verb, *raced*. Popping the subject question "who or what *raced*?" yields *fire engine*, or just *engine*.

2. **Do chase (V), you-understood (S)** The subject is implied in this command, not stated.

3. **stood (V), donkeys (S)** Did I catch you on this one? *Donkeys* answers the question "who stood?" so it's the subject. *Curve* and *tracks* appear in front of the verb, the usual position for subjects, but they aren't subjects.

4. **was frightened, ran (V), one (S)** Did you think "donkeys" was the subject? Pop the question: who was frightened? who ran? Not the *donkeys*. *One was frightened* and *one ran*. Therefore, the subject is *one*.

5. **come (V), you-understood (S)** The subject isn't *donkey*, though whoever is giving the command is addressing the *donkey*. In grammar terms, *donkey* is a direct address. The subject is *you-understood*.

6. **looked (V), did move (V), another (S)** The subject, *another*, is paired with two verbs.

7. **was (V), he (S); was (V), he (S)** This short sentence packs in two matching subject–verb pairs, *he was*.

8. **did notice (V), did care (V), animal (S)** Negative statements often rely on forms of the verb *do*. Here you find *did notice* and *did care*, both of which pair with the subject, *animal*.

9. **think (V), I (S); was eating (V), donkey (S)** You have two subject–verb pairs here. *Donkey* is the most important word in the second portion of the sentence, but if you identified the subject as *another donkey*, count yourself correct.

10. **Eat (V), you-understood (S)** The subject of a command sentence is always *you-understood*.

11. **was (V), house (S); were burning (V), buildings (S)** Did you correctly identify *buildings* as the subject of *were burning*? It appears in the usual spot before the verb, but a description, *on the street*, may have distracted you. As always, rely on the question: who or what *were burning*? Not the street, but *several buildings*. The most important word in that expression is *buildings*.

12. **left (V), went (V), George** and **Anna (S)** In this sentence, the compound (double) subject *George* and *Anna* pairs with a compound verb, *left* and *went*.

13. **Act (V), you-understood (S)** The command to *act* is addressed to *George and Anna*, but the subject is *you-understood*.

14. **did mow (V), they (S)** The word *not* is not part of the verb.

15. **will fine (V), homeowners association (S)** When you ask, "Who *will fine*?" the answer is a group, *homeowners association*, not a person. Nevertheless, that's the subject.

16. **runs (V), donkey (S); will be solved (V), problem (S)** Did you choose *George and Anna* as subjects? They won't be solved — the *problem* will. *Problem* is the subject.

17. **appears (V), animal (S); has posted (V), Anna (S)** When you encounter a sentence with two separate ideas in it, you probably have two separate subject–verb pairs.

(18) **have attracted (V), have been shared (V), posts (S)** Did you include *widely* when you identified the verb? It's a description, not an action or a state of being.

(19) **is (V), statement (S)** The subject in this sentence follows the verb, but it's the answer to the question "what is?" and therefore is the subject.

(20) **love (V), We (S); says (V), statement (S); do allow (V), we (S)** This sentence has three subject–verb pairs. *Braying* at first glance appears to be an action, but in this sentence it's a thing the association does not allow.

(21) **send (V), you-understood (S); demanded (V), association (S)** The quotation is a command, so *you-understood* is the subject. The tag identifies the speaker, *association*, which is the subject of the verb *demanded*.

(22) **are training (V), George** and **Anna (S)** In case you're curious, *to be silent* isn't functioning as a verb in this sentence. It's an infinitive. For more information on infinitives, see "Don't Get Faked Out: Avoiding Fake Verbs and Subjects," earlier in this chapter.

(23) **has challenged (V), lawyer (S)** This sentence may be easier than most because the subject, *lawyer*, is doing what lawyers do — challenging!

(24) **are (V), Lawnmowers (S); says (V), lawyer (S)** This sentence has two parts: a quotation and a tag identifying the speaker. The quotation has a subject and a verb (*lawnmowers are*) and so does the tag (*lawyer says*).

(25) **will decide (V), judge (S)** Rearrange the question into a statement: *the judge will decide what.* The subject–verb pair immediately stands out.

(26) **spend (V), Anna** and **Max (S)** I hope you avoided the "fake" verb *cramming.*

(27) **has adjusted (V), Max (S)** Here the distraction is *having grown.* If you pop the subject question for that verb form, though, you get no answer. The real verb is *has adjusted*, which pairs with *Max.*

(28) **was (V), book (S)** *Here* and *there* are never subjects. In this sort of sentence, the subject generally follows the verb.

(29) **reached (V), Max (S)** Ignore the distracting verbal, *helping*, and focus on the real verb, *reached.*

(30) **smashed (V), Max (S)** More to ignore: the verbals *holding* and *standing.*

(31) **is (V), dent (S)** *There* can't be a subject. Check after the verb and you see that *dent is.*

(32) **is (V), dent (S)** You have to tease out the verb from the contraction *there's*, which is short for *there is.* Once you have the verb, pop the question and you see that *dent is.*

(33) **is protected (V), Max (S)** Two verbals — not verbs — begin this sentence, but the real verb follows the subject, *Max.*

(34) **collapsed, broke (V), table (S)** The descriptive phrase, *destabilized by the collision*, contains a verbal, not a verb.

(35) **is (V), pack (S); offered (V), Max (S)** Pull the *is* from the contraction *here's*, short for *here is.* Pop the subject question to find *pack*, or *ice pack.* In the second part of the sentence, *Max offered.*

If you're ready to test your skills a bit more, take the following chapter quiz, which incorporates all the chapter topics.

Whaddya Know? Chapter 8 Quiz

Quiz time! Complete each problem to test your knowledge on the various topics covered in this chapter. You can then find the solutions and explanations in the next section.

Here's a portion of the welcome packet offered to guests staying in a short-term rental. Check the underlined words. Identify them as verbs (V), subjects (S), or neither (N).

We at Alpine Shores (1) <u>welcome</u> you to your luxurious accommodations! (2) <u>Here</u> are a few suggestions for your comfort, as well as one or two small, easy-to-follow (3) <u>rules</u>:

» The (4) <u>room</u> (5) <u>is designed</u> for two guests, but up to 24 (6) <u>people</u> will fit, if you (7) <u>exercise</u> some creativity with (8) <u>sleeping</u> arrangements.

» There's a queen-size (9) <u>bed</u>, which (10) <u>can be expanded</u> by (11) <u>removing</u> the mattress and placing it on the floor. Two or even three (12) <u>guests</u> can sleep on the mattress and a similar number on the box spring.

» (13) <u>Remove</u> the sofa pillows, place (14) <u>them</u> on the floor, and you have additional (15) <u>beds</u> for children or short adults. If you need a bigger bed, try (16) <u>lashing</u> two pillows together. Bungee (17) <u>cords</u> for this purpose (18) <u>may be found</u> in the closet.

» (19) <u>Smoking</u> is not permitted.

» (20) <u>Leave</u> the apartment as clean as you found it, please!

Answers to Chapter 8 Quiz

(1) **V**

(2) **N** *Here* is never a subject. The real subject, *suggestions,* appears after the verb, *is.*

(3) **N** This word is part of a descriptive expression (*as well as . . . rules*) and is neither a subject nor a verb.

(4) **S**

(5) **V**

(6) **S** *People* is the subject of the verb *will fit.*

(7) **V**

(8) **N** This verb form functions as a description. How do you know? If you ask, "Who or what *sleeping?*" you get no answer.

(9) **S** In a sentence beginning with *here* or *there*, the subject often follows the verb.

(10) **V**

(11) **N** This verb form doesn't function as the verb in the sentence. It's the object of the preposition *by.*

(12) **S**

(13) **V**

(14) **N** *Them* is the object, not the subject. (For more on objects, see Chapter 9.)

(15) **N** Another object! The subject of the sentence is *you.*

(16) **N** Although *lashing* is a verb form, you get no answer when you pop the subject question: who or what *lashing.* Because no answer appears, you know you have found a "fake" verb. *Lashing* is a verbal; for more information on verbals, see Chapter 24.

(17) **S**

(18) **V**

(19) **S** Surprised? *Smoking* is an action, but here it answers the subject question: who or what *is* not *permitted?*

(20) **V**

Chapter **9**

Handling Complements

In Chapter 8 I compare a sentence to a flatbed truck carrying meaning to the reader. If verbs are the wheels and the subject is the driver, complements are the less essential parts of the vehicle — perhaps the defroster or the speedometer. These words are a little more important than those fuzzy dice some people hang from their rearview mirrors or bumper stickers, declaring "I stop at railroad tracks." (What do they think the rest of us do? Leap over the train?) You can sometimes create a sentence without complements, but their presence is generally part of the driving — sorry, I mean *communicating* — experience.

Four kinds of complements show up in sentences: direct objects, indirect objects, objective complements, and subject complements. This chapter explains all of them. The first three types of complements are related to the object of a sentence. (Notice that the word *object* is part of the name.) The fourth type of complement is related to the subject of a sentence. (Thus the word *subject* is part of its name.) Distinguishing between these two groups helps you choose the proper pronoun whenever the sentence calls for that part of speech. A complement (not to be confused with a compliment, or expression of praise) completes the idea that the subject and verb begin.

Getting a Piece of the Action: Complements for Action Verbs

Action verbs express — surprise! — action. No action verb needs a complement to be grammatically legal, but an action-verb sentence without a complement may sound bare. The complements that follow action verbs — the direct object, indirect object, and objective complement — enhance the meaning of the subject-verb pair.

Receiving the action: Direct objects

Imagine that you're holding a baseball, ready to throw it to your friend. In your fantasy, you're facing a Hall of Fame hitter. You go into your windup and pitch. The ball arcs gracefully against the clear blue sky — and crashes right through the kitchen window.

> You broke the kitchen window!

Before you can retrieve the ball, your phone rings. It's your mom, who has radar for situations like this. "What's going on?" she asks. You mutter something containing the word *broke*. (There's the verb.) "Broke? Who broke something?" she demands. You admit that *you* did. (There's the subject.) "What did you break?" You hesitate. You consider a couple of possible answers: a bad habit, the world's record for the hundred-meter dash. Finally, you confess: the *window*. (There's the complement.)

Here's another way to think about the situation (and the sentence). *Broke* is an action verb because it tells you what happened. The action comes from the subject *(you)* and goes to an object *(the window)*. As some grammarians phrase it, *the window* receives the action expressed by the verb *broke*. Conclusion? *Window* is a *direct object* because it receives the action directly from the verb.

Try another:

> With the force of 1,000 hurricanes, you pitch the baseball.

Pitch is an action verb because it expresses what is happening in the sentence. The action goes from the subject *(you, the pitcher)* to the object *(the baseball)*. In other words, *baseball* receives the action of *pitching*. Thus, baseball is the direct object of the verb *pitch*.

Here are a few examples of sentences with action verbs. The direct objects are underlined:

> The defective X-ray machine took strange <u>pictures</u> of my toe. (*took* = verb, *X-ray machine* = subject)
>
> George hissed the secret <u>words</u> to a fellow spy. (*hissed* = verb, *George* = subject)
>
> My best crayons draw beautiful <u>lines</u>. (*draw* = verb, *crayons* = subject)
>
> Leroy's laser printer spurted <u>toner</u> all over his favorite shirt. (spurted = *verb*, printer = *subject*)

You may be able to recognize direct objects more easily if you think of them as part of a pattern in the sentence structure: subject (S) – action verb (AV) – direct object (DO). This S–AV–DO pattern is one of the most common in the English language; it may even be the most common. (I don't know whether anyone has actually counted all the sentences and figured it out!) At any rate, think of the parts of the sentence in threes, in the S–AV–DO pattern:

> machine took pictures
>
> George hissed words
>
> crayons draw lines
>
> printer spurted toner

Of course, just to make your life more difficult, a sentence can have more than one direct object. Check out these examples, in which the direct objects are underlined:

Alfred autographed <u>posters</u> and <u>books</u> for his many admirers.

Roger will eat a dozen <u>doughnuts</u> and a few <u>slabs</u> of cheesecake for breakfast.

The new president of the Healthy Heart Society phoned <u>Egbert</u> and his <u>brother</u>.

George threw stained <u>shirts</u> and smelly <u>socks</u> across his bedroom.

Ella bought orange juice, tuna, aspirin, and a coffee table.

Some sentences have no direct object. Take a look at this example:

Throughout the endless afternoon and into the lonely night, Alfred sighed sadly.

No one or nothing receives the sighs, so the sentence has no direct object. Perhaps that's why Alfred is lonely.

The easiest way to find the direct object is to "pop the question." Locate the subject and the verb first. (I explain how to pop the question for verbs in Chapter 5 and for subjects in Chapter 8.) Say the subject and verb and tack on these questions:

Who or whom?

What?

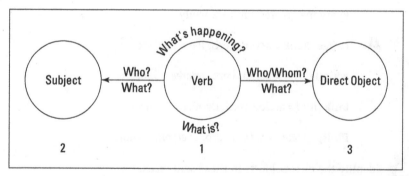

© John Wiley & Sons, Inc.

Watch these questions in action:

Flossie maintains the cleanest teeth in Texas.

1. Pop the verb question: What's happening? Answer: *maintains. Maintains* is the action verb.

2. Pop the subject question: Who or what *maintains?* Answer: *Flossie maintains. Flossie* is the subject.

3. Pop the complement question: *Flossie maintains* who/whom? *No answer. Flossie maintains* what? Answer: Flossie maintains *the cleanest teeth in Texas* (*teeth* = the most important word). *Teeth* is the direct object.

TIP

Sometimes when you pop the subject question, you find no answer. If the sentence is a command, the subject is understood to be *you*. If the sentence is not a command, you may have found a verb form that is functioning as a description. This sort of verb form — a *verbal* — may have a direct object, too. If you find one, good for you! Here's an example:

Mattie, having crushed all the grapes, washed her feet.

The verb in this sentence is *washed*, which pairs with the subject, *Mattie*. The direct object of *washed* is *feet*. If you chose *having crushed* as the verb and popped the subject questions: who *having crushed*? what *having crushed*? you got no answer. (*Mattie having crushed* doesn't work.) The verb form *having crushed* functions as a description of *Mattie*. Now ask the direct object questions: *having crushed* whom? *having crushed* what? The answer is *grapes*, which is the direct object of the verbal *having crushed*.

Q. Identify the direct object(s).

EXAMPLE

Joe drank coffee every morning.

The referee blew the whistle.

Carmen filled the tank with gas.

Everyone greeted Philip warmly.

A. **coffee** *drank* = action verb, *Joe* = subject

whistle *blew* = action verb, *referee* = subject

tank *filled* = action verb, *Carmen* = subject

Philip *greeted* = action verb, *Everyone* = subject

YOUR TURN

Identify the direct objects in these sentences.

1 He knew someone in the government.

2 Bert played guitar and banjo in the show.

3 A gifted writer, Simon read several stories to his class yesterday.

4 Simon has also written poems, novels, and plays.

5 Hannah is chewing steak and broccoli.

6 Somebody should use more soap and deodorant!

Rare, but sometimes there: Indirect objects

Another type of object is *indirect* because the action doesn't flow directly to it. The *indirect object*, affectionately known as the IO, is an intermediate stop along the way between the action verb and the direct object. Read this sentence, in which the indirect object is underlined:

Knowing that I'm on a diet, Maggie sent me some nonfat snacks.

The action is *sent*. My friend *Maggie* performed the action, so *Maggie* is the subject. What received the action? *Snacks*. *Snacks* is the direct object. That's what was *sent*, what received the action of the verb directly. But *me* also received the action, indirectly. *Me* received the sending of the snacks. *Me* is the indirect object.

The sentence pattern for indirect objects is subject (S) – action verb (AV) – indirect object (IO) – direct object (DO). Notice that the indirect object always precedes the direct object: S–AV–IO–DO. Here are a few sentences, with the indirect objects underlined:

Gloria will tell me the whole story tomorrow. (*will tell* = verb, *Gloria* = subject, *story* = direct object)

As a grammarian, I should have given you better examples. (*should have given* = verb, *I* = subject, *examples* = direct object)

Ella impulsively sent Larry a harsh text. (*sent* = verb, *Ella* = subject, *text* = direct object)

The opponent's coach unwisely offered Annie a bribe for dropping out of the race. (*offered* = verb, *coach* = subject, *bribe* = direct object)

Indirect objects, like salesclerks in a discount store, don't appear very often. When indirect objects do show up, they're always in partnership with a direct object. Unless you're a fan of grammar terminology, you don't need to worry about distinguishing between direct and indirect objects. As long as you understand that these words are objects, completing the meaning of an action verb, you recognize the basic components of a sentence.

Though indirect objects seldom appear, you can check for them with another "pop the question." After you locate the action verb, the subject, and the direct object, ask

To whom? For whom?

To what? For what?

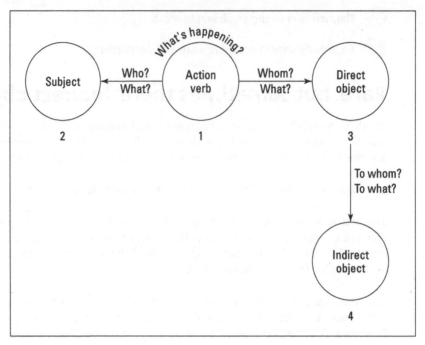

© John Wiley & Sons, Inc.

If you get an answer, it should reveal an indirect object. Here's an example:

Mildred will never tell me the gossip.

1. Pop the verb question: What's happening? Answer: *will tell. Will tell* is an action verb.

2. Pop the subject question: Who will tell? Answer: *Mildred. Mildred* is the subject.

3. Pop the direct object question: *Mildred will tell* whom? or what? Answer: *Mildred will tell the gossip. Gossip* is the direct object.

4. Pop the indirect object question: *Mildred will tell the gossip* to whom? Answer: to *me. Me* is the indirect object.

TIP

You may come up with a different answer when you pop the DO question in step 3 (*Mildred will tell* whom? or what?). You can answer *Mildred will tell me.* True. The only problem is that the sentence then has *gossip* flapping around with no label. Your attempt to determine the sentence structure has reached a dead end. Luckily for you, all you need to know is that both are objects. Only obsessive grammarians like me worry about which one is direct and which one is indirect.

EXAMPLE

Q. Identify the indirect objects in these sentences.

Mark gave Maria some water.

Brad wrote me a letter.

Chris will buy everyone a present.

Gardeners gave the plants and trees extra water.

A. **Maria** *gave* = verb, *Mark* = subject, *water* = direct object

me *wrote* = verb, *Brad* = subject, *letter* = direct object

everyone *will buy* = verb, *Chris* = subject, *present* = direct object

plants, trees *gave* = verb, *Gardeners* = subject, *water* = direct object

Identify the indirect objects in these sentences.

7 Gus told her a secret.

8 Did Lola bring Lulu more coffee?

9 No, Lulu had not given Lola enough money for coffee.

10 Without sufficient caffeine, Lulu will certainly give her friend a hard time.

No bias here: Objective complements

Finally, a grammar rule that's hard to bungle. Here's the deal: Sometimes a direct object doesn't get the whole job done. A little more information is needed or desired, and the writer doesn't want to bother adding a whole new subject–verb pair. The solution? An *objective complement* — an added fact about the direct object.

The objective complement (underlined in the following sentences) may be a person, place, or thing. In other words, the objective complement may be a noun:

> Egbert named Lester <u>editor</u> of the Healthy Heart Society Bulletin. (*named* = verb, *Egbert* = subject, *Lester* = direct object)

> Gloria and the other club members unanimously elected Roger <u>president</u>. (*elected* = verb, *Gloria and members* = subjects, *Roger* = direct object)

> Alfred called his dog <u>Alfred-Too</u>. (*called* = verb, *Alfred* = subject, *dog* = direct object)

The objective complement may also be a word that describes a noun. (A word that describes a noun is called an *adjective*; see Chapter 6 for more information.) Take a peek at these sample sentences, in which the objective complement is underlined:

> Nancy considered her <u>unqualified</u> for the job. (*considered* = verb, *Nancy* = subject, *her* = direct object)

> George dubbed Alred-Too <u>ridiculous</u>. (*dubbed* = verb, *George* = subject, *Alfred-Too* = direct object)

> Roger called George <u>heartless</u>. (*called* = verb, *Roger* = subject, *George* = direct object)

As you see, the objective complements in each of the sample sentences give the sentence an extra jolt. You know more with it than you do without it, but the objective complement isn't a major player in the sentence.

Q. Identify the objective complement in these sentences.

George declared Nancy ineligible and unqualified for the "Best Grammarian" contest.

Nancy had appointed George judge of the contest!

Now she called him "hopelessly inadequate."

A. **ineligible, unqualified** *declared* = verb, *George* = subject, *Nancy* = direct object

judge *had appointed* = verb, *Nancy* = subject, *George* = direct object

inadequate *called* = verb, *she* = subject, *him* = direct object (**Note:** *hopelessly* is a description, explaining exactly how *inadequate* Nancy thinks George is.)

Identify the objective complements in these sentences.

11. The other contestants considered Nancy strange.

12. They deemed George unfair.

13. A mediator named Alfred chief grammarian.

14. Everyone considered Alfred annoyingly accurate in his judging.

Completing the Equation: Subject Complements

Subject complements are major players in sentences powered by linking verbs. A *linking verb* begins a word equation; it expresses a state of being, linking two ideas. The complement completes the equation. Because a complement following a linking verb tells you something about the *subject* of the sentence, it is called a *subject complement*. In each of the following sentences, the first idea is the subject, and the second idea (underlined) is the complement:

Ms. McAnnick is <u>upset</u> by the bankruptcy of the auto-parts manufacturer. *(Ms. McAnnick = upset)*

Gloria was a <u>cheerleader</u> before the dog bite incident. *(Gloria = cheerleader)*

The little orange book will be <u>sufficient</u> for all your firework information needs. *(book = sufficient)*

It is <u>I</u>, the master of the universe. *(It = I)*

Subject complements can take several forms. Sometimes the subject complement is a descriptive word (an *adjective*, in case you like to know the correct terminology). Sometimes the subject complement is a *noun* (person, place, thing, or idea) or a *pronoun* (a word that substitutes for a noun). The first sample sentence equates *Ms. McAnnick* with a description (the adjective *upset*). The second equates *Gloria* with a position (the noun *cheerleader*). In the third sample sentence, the subject *book* is described by the adjective *sufficient.* The last sentence equates the subject *it* with the pronoun *I.* Don't worry about these distinctions. They don't matter! As long as you can find the subject complement, you're grasping the sentence structure.

TIP

The linking verbs I mention in the preceding paragraph are forms of the verb *be.* Other verbs that give sensory information (*feel, sound, taste, smell,* and so on) may also be linking verbs. Likewise, *appear* and *seem* are linking verbs. (For more information on linking verbs, see Chapter 5.) Have a look at a couple of sentences with sensory linking verbs. The complements are underlined:

> Larry sounds <u>grouchier</u> than usual today. *(Larry = grouchier)*
>
> After solving an algebra problem, Anna feels <u>proud</u>. *(Anna = proud)*

To find a subject complement, you employ the same questions that locate a direct object: *who? what?* after the subject–verb pair.

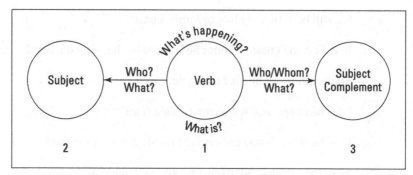

© *John Wiley & Sons, Inc.*

Here's an example of "pop the question" for linking verbs:

> The actor recovering from the flu appeared tired and worn.

1. Pop the verb question: What's happening? No answer. What is? Answer: *Appeared. Appeared* is the linking verb.

2. Pop the subject question: Who or what *appeared?* Answer: *Actor appeared. Actor* is the subject.

3. Pop the complement question: *Actor appeared* who? No answer. *Actor appeared* what? Answer: *Tired* and *worn. Tired* and *worn* are the subject complements.

EXAMPLE

Q. Identify the subject complements in these sentences.

Molly seems cheerful.

Our house has been a beloved home.

The stew tastes salty.

The secretaries are Grace and Pete.

The new rug is soft but durable.

A. **cheerful** *Molly* = subject, *seems* = linking verb

home *has been* = linking verb, *house* = subject

salty *tastes* = linking verb, *stew* = subject

Grace, Pete *are* = linking verb, *secretaries* = subject

soft, durable *is* = linking verb, *rug* = subject

YOUR
TURN

Identify the subject complements in these sentences.

15 The traffic on the expressway is terrible, as usual!

16 We will be extremely late to Annie's party.

17 John was the guest of honor because of his heroism during the fire.

18 Annie will never be his host again.

19 John had been anxious about Annie's reaction.

20 Now he was relieved because the music sounded too loud.

21 Also, the cake looked disgusting and tasted awful.

WARNING

In Standard English, you can't mix types of subject complements that complete the meaning of the same verb. (English teachers refer to this rule as *parallelism*. For more about parallelism, check out Chapter 24.) Use all descriptions or all nouns and pronouns. Take a look at these examples:

WRONG: Gramps is grouchy but a good artist.

RIGHT: Gramps is a grouch but a good artist.

ALSO RIGHT: Gramps is grouchy and artistic.

WRONG: Lester's pet spider can be annoying and a real danger.

RIGHT: Lester's pet spider can be an annoyance and a real danger.

ALSO RIGHT: Lester's pet spider can be annoying and really dangerous.

Objects follow action verbs, and subject complements follow linking verbs.

REMEMBER

Q. Label the underlined words O (for direct objects, indirect objects, or objective complements) or S (for subject complements).

Sal seemed <u>soggy</u> after his final water polo match.

The referee gave <u>him</u> a <u>towel</u>.

The loser shot the <u>referee</u> a dirty <u>look</u>.

A. **soggy = subject complement** (*seemed* = linking verb, *Sal* = subject)

towel = direct object, him = indirect object (*gave* = action verb, *referee* = subject)

look = direct object, referee = indirect object (*shot* = action verb, *loser* = subject)

Label the underlined words as objects or subject complements.

22 During the annual softball game between two branch offices of our company, Lola swung the <u>bat</u> with all her strength.

23 She is extremely <u>strong</u> because she exercises for two hours every day.

24 The bat hit the <u>ball</u> and lifted <u>it</u> over the outfield fence.

25 Spectators felt <u>joyful</u> and even <u>hopeful</u> after Lola's hit.

26 The applause always sounds <u>louder</u> during Lola's games.

27 Compared to Lola, the next batter seemed <u>small</u> and <u>weak</u>.

28 He is the <u>president</u> of the company, and he looks <u>powerful</u>.

29 He has <u>power</u> over our paychecks!

30 The pitcher tossed the <u>president</u> a slow <u>ball</u>.

31 Who would challenge <u>him</u>?

32 Our opponents called the <u>pitch</u> <u>unfair</u>.

33 Despite the slow pitch, the president smacked the <u>ball</u> only a few feet.

34 He reached third <u>base</u> anyway because no one would tag <u>him</u>.

35 I consider <u>him</u> <u>incompetent</u>, especially on the playing field.

Practice Questions Answers and Explanations

(1) **someone** (*knew* = verb, *He* = subject)

(2) **guitar, banjo** (*played* = verb, *Bert* = subject)

(3) **stories** (*read* = verb, *Simon* = subject)

(4) **poems, novels, plays** (*has written* = verb, *Simon* = subject)

(5) **steak, broccoli** (*is chewing* = verb, *Hannah* = subject)

(6) **soap, deodorant** (*should use* = verb, *Somebody* = subject)

(7) **her** (*told* = verb, *Gus* = subject, *secret* = direct object)

(8) **Lulu** (*Did bring* = verb, *Lola* = subject, *coffee* = direct object)

(9) **Lola** (*had given* = verb, *Lulu* = subject, *money* = direct object)

(10) **friend** (*will give* = verb, *Lulu* = subject, *time* = direct object)

(11) **strange** (*considered* = verb, *contestants* = subject, *Nancy* = direct object)

(12) **unfair** (*deemed* = verb, *They* = subject, *George* = direct object)

(13) **grammarian** (*named* = verb, *mediator* = subject, *Alfred* = direct object)

(14) **accurate** (*considered* = verb, *Everyone* = subject, *Alfred* = direct object)

(15) **terrible** (*is* = verb, *traffic* = subject)

(16) **late** (*will be* = verb, *We* = subject)

(17) **guest** (*was* = verb, *John* = subject)

(18) **host** (*will be* = verb, *Annie* = subject)

(19) **anxious** (*had been* = verb, *John* = subject)

(20) **relieved, loud** (*was* = verb, *he* = subject; *sounded* = verb, *music* = subject)

(21) **disgusting, awful** (*looked, tasted* = verbs, *cake* = subject)

(22) O **(direct object;** *swung* = action verb, *Lola* = subject)

(23) S **(subject complement;** *is* = linking verb, *She* = subject)

(24) O, O **(direct object, direct object;** *hit, lifted* = action verbs, *bat* = subject)

(25) S, S **(subject complement, subject complement;** *felt* = linking verb, *Spectators* = subject)

(26) S **(subject complement;** *sounds* = linking verb, *applause* = subject)

(27) S, S **(subject complement, subject complement;** *seemed* = linking verb, *batter* = subject)

(28) S, S **(subject complement, subject complement;** *is, looks* = linking verbs; *he, he* = subjects)

(29) O **(direct object;** *has* = action verb, *He* = subject)

(30) O, O **(indirect object, direct object;** *tossed* = action verb, *pitcher* = subject)

(31) O **(direct object;** *would challenge* = action verb, *Who* = subject)

(32) O, O **(direct object, objective complement;** *called* = action verb, *opponents* = subject)

(33) O **(direct object;** *smacked* = action verb, *president* = subject)

(34) O, O **(direct object, direct object;** *reached* = action verb, *he* = subject; *would tag* = action verb, *no one* = subject)

(35) O, O **(direct object, objective complement;** *consider* = action verb, *I* = subject)

If you're ready to test your skills a bit more, take the following chapter quiz, which incorporates all the chapter topics.

Whaddya Know? Chapter 9 Quiz

Quiz time! Complete each problem to test your knowledge on the various topics covered in this chapter. You can then find the solutions and explanations in the next section.

Identify the complements in this course description. You should find 22 direct objects (DO), 4 indirect objects (IO), 2 objective complements (OC), and 6 subject complements (SC).

Introduction to Gravity (3 credits) Professor Angus Newton

Do you like gravity? Are you fond of this force? If so, send me an enrollment form. This course examines our planet's gravitational pull. During the first class, each student will drop an apple from the roof and observe its path through the air. The students will record the apples' direction — up, down, left, right — and form a hypothesis about gravity. Next, students will email each other a detailed plan for another gravitational experiment. For example, students may pick up our expensive, extremely thick textbook and test the power of gravity with their muscles. All students write lab reports and send me their findings. (Spoiler alert: Most experiments have found gravity powerful and one-directional.) As a capstone project, students will investigate any aspect of gravity. This is a thrilling opportunity! Last year, one project was an analysis of gravity and running shoes. The student measured no increase in gravity at mile 17 of a marathon, despite the runner's claims. Another research project was a daring but unsuccessful attempt to reverse gravity. Does this project seem interesting? If so, you are perfect for this course!

This class requires one lecture and two hours of field work per week. If students work diligently and reach their goals, I drop the final. If students cut class, I give them a midterm test and an extremely hard final.

Answers to Chapter 9 Quiz

Introduction to Gravity (3 credits)

Do you like **gravity (DO-1)**? Are you **fond (SC-1)** of this force? If so, send **me (IO-1)** an enrollment **form (DO-2)**. This course examines our planet's gravitational **pull (DO-3)**. During the first class, each student will drop an **apple (DO-4)** from the roof and observe its **path (DO-5)** through the air. The students will record the apples' **direction (DO-6)** — up, down, left, right — and form a **hypothesis (DO-7)** about gravity. Next, students will email **each other (IO-2)** a detailed **plan (DO-8)** for another gravitational experiment. For example, students may pick up our expensive, extremely thick **textbook (DO-9)** and test the **power (DO-10)** of gravity with their muscles. All students write lab **reports (DO-11)** and send **me (IO-3)** their **findings (DO-12)**. (Spoiler alert: Most experiments have found **gravity (DO-13) powerful (OC-1)** and **one-directional (OC-2)**.) As a capstone project, students will investigate any **aspect (DO-14)** of gravity. This is a thrilling **opportunity (SC-2)**! Last year, one project was an **analysis (SC-3)** of gravity and running shoes. The student measured no **increase (DO-15)** in gravity at mile 17 of a marathon, despite the runner's claims. Another research project was a daring but unsuccessful **attempt (SC-4)** to reverse gravity. Does this project seem **interesting (SC-5)**? If so, you are **perfect (SC-6)** for this course!

This class requires one **lecture (DO-16)** and two **hours (DO-17)** of field work per week. If students work diligently and reach their **goals (DO-18)**, I drop the **final (DO-19)**. If students cut **class (DO-20)**, I give **them (IO-4)** a midterm **test (DO-21)** and a **final (DO-22)**.

Chapter **10**

When All Is Said and Done: Complete Sentences

E veryone knows this important rule of English grammar: All sentences must be complete. But everyone breaks the rule. I just did! *But everyone breaks the rule* is not a complete sentence; it's a sentence *fragment*. At times, fragments are perfectly acceptable — in texts or tweets, for example. The other extreme — more than one complete sentence improperly glued together — is a *run-on sentence*. A run-on sentence — and its variation, a *comma splice* — are grammatical felonies. Never fear: In this chapter, I explain how to join ideas without risking a visit from the Grammar Police. I also provide everything you need to know about *end marks*, the punctuation separating one sentence from another.

Completing Sentences: The Essential Subjects and Verbs

A complete sentence has at least one subject–verb pair. They're a pair because they match. They both enjoy taking long walks on the beach, playing video games, and making fun of reality-show contestants. Just kidding. They match because, well, they work smoothly as a team. One half of the pair, the *verb*, expresses action or being, and the other half, the *subject*, is whatever or whoever does the action or exists in the state of being. (Chapter 8 provides a step-by-step process for identifying subjects and verbs.)

A few subject–verb pairs that match are

> Egbert scrambled
>
> Ms. McAnnick has repaired
>
> Eva will be

Just for comparison, here are some mismatches:

> Egbert scrambling
>
> Ms. McAnnick having repaired
>
> Eva being

How do you know when a pair matches? If you have spent a lot of time listening to or reading Standard English, you may sense a mismatch. Scanning the regular-verb charts in Chapter 5 might also help you decide. Still in doubt? Keep reading. In the following sections I explain some common mistakes in pairing up subjects and verbs.

Not flying solo: Verb forms ending in –ing

The *–ing* form of a verb expresses an action in progress or an ongoing state of being, but it can't carry out this task alone. It requires help from a form of the verb *be*. Take a look at this chart of subject–verb pairs, sorted according to the rules of Standard English. The verb forms are underlined:

Matching Pair	Nonmatching Pair
bird is flying	bird flying
Henry is going	Henry going
I am swimming	I swimming
the prince and his wife are being	the prince and his wife being
mirrors are reflecting	mirrors reflecting
the river is flowing	the river flowing
musicians are playing	musicians playing

REMEMBER

To act as a proper verb in a subject–verb pair, the *–ing* form of a verb must be attached to *is, are, was, were, will be, had been,* or another form of the verb *be*.

Remember that the guidelines in this section apply only to subject–verb pairs. The *–ing* form of a verb, all alone, may be correct in other roles, as in this example:

WARNING

> WRONG: Sam riding his bike.
>
> WHY IT IS WRONG: *Sam riding* is not a proper subject–verb pair.

RIGHT: Sam, riding his bike, hit a tree.

WHY IT IS RIGHT: In this sentence, *riding* is not paired with *Sam*. *Riding* adds information about *Sam*. *Sam hit* is the real subject–verb pair in this sentence.

Another example:

WRONG: Hitting a bump.

WHY IT IS WRONG: The "sentence" has no subject and no true verb.

RIGHT: Hitting a bump, Sam fell off his bike.

WHY IT IS RIGHT: In this sentence, *hitting a bump* gives more information about *Sam*. The subject–verb pair is *Sam fell*.

Q. Choose the correct verb from the parentheses.

EXAMPLE   You (are going, going) away tomorrow.

A. **are going**

Choose the correct verb from the parentheses.

YOUR TURN

1. His sister (is waiting, waiting) for a new credit card.

2. My toe (has been aching, aching) for three days.

3. Zina (telling, was telling) an amazing story to her friends.

4. The mansion (is standing, standing) on top of that hill.

5. He (is admiring, admiring) your new hairstyle.

Past verb forms that can't stand alone

Have you ever <u>spoken</u> to your friends about grammar? Probably not! Grammar has never <u>been</u> a topic to bring up at a party. When I discussed grammar at a party, I looked around and saw that everyone had <u>fallen</u> asleep!

The underlined words in the preceding paragraph are fine as part of a verb. However, they cannot match with a subject unless they have a helping verb. In the preceding paragraph, these underlined verbs do have helpers:

have <u>spoken</u>

has <u>been</u>

had <u>fallen</u>

With their helpers, the sentences are correct in Standard English. Without the helpers, you do not have a proper subject–verb pair.

Look at this set of matches and mismatches, according to the rules of Standard English.

Matching Pair	Nonmatching Pair
Ross has written	Ross written
Anne had gone	Anne gone
ducks have swum	ducks swum
bricks had fallen	bricks fallen
he was done	he done
vases were stolen	vases stolen
president has spoken	president spoken

Do you see that the matching pair always includes *was, were, has, have,* or *had?* The verb forms here, and many others, do not work all by themselves as part of a subject–verb pair. These forms must have helpers attached. Because of this rule, *he was done* is correct in Standard English, but *he done* is not.

TIP

In grammar terms, these forms are called *irregular past participles.* Don't waste brain cells remembering that term! Check Chapter 12 for a list of the most common irregular forms.

WARNING

Sometimes a participle is not part of the verb in a sentence. Instead, the participle adds information. If the participle acts as a description, it's fine by itself. Here's an example:

WRONG: Elsa frozen on the iceberg.

WHY IT IS WRONG: *Elsa frozen* is not a proper subject–verb pair.

RIGHT: Elsa, frozen on the iceberg, called for help.

WHY IT IS RIGHT: In this sentence, *frozen* is not paired with *Elsa. Frozen* adds information about *Elsa. Elsa called* is the true subject–verb pair in this sentence.

EXAMPLE

Q. Select the verb form that's correct in Standard English.

The sky (was covered, covered) with clouds.

A. **was covered**

YOUR TURN

Select the verb form that's correct in Standard English.

6 We (have done, done) the work.

7 Those ants (have gone, gone) away.

8 Sid (taken, has taken) the test twice.

9 The ball (was thrown, thrown) to the pitcher.

10 The horse (been ridden, has been ridden, ridden) in three races.

Do not "be" alone

Another type of subject–verb pair that's often mismatched in Standard English places the verb *be* all by itself. In formal situations, *be* always changes form or has a helping verb attached when it functions as the verb in a sentence. Look at this chart.

Matching Pair	Nonmatching Pair
Margie will be	Margie be
the polar bear is	the polar bear be
I am	I be
the teenagers on the train are talking	the teenagers on the train be talking
Ned has been chopping	Ned be chopping
the singers will be performing	the singers be performing

As you see in the table, sometimes *be* changes form when it is part of the matching pair *(is, am)*. At other times, *be* has a helping verb *(will, are, has)*. To see all forms of *be*, turn to Chapter 5.

TIP

Another usage that breaks the rules of Standard English is dropping the *be* verb entirely. Take a look at this example:

WRONG: She happy.

WHY IT IS WRONG IN STANDARD ENGLISH: The statement has no verb.

CORRECTION: She is happy.

WHY IT IS CORRECT IN STANDARD ENGLISH: The sentence now has a verb, *is.* Any other verb that pairs with *she* would also work: *She was happy. She will be happy. She seems happy. She sounds happy.*

EXAMPLE

Q. Select the verb form that's correct in Standard English.

Jack (is, be) hungry.

A. is

YOUR TURN

Select the verb form that's correct in Standard English.

 11 Robin (be, will be) at school today.

12 (Are, Be) you pleased with the decorations?

13 Archers (been, be, have been) part of that competition since ancient times.

14 Everyone (should be, be) kind to animals.

15 The mountains (be, are, been) very snowy.

When texting, tweeting, or IMing (instant-messaging), many people opt for "sentences" that lack subjects. That's fine as long as the meaning is clear. Check out these sample texts:

> Fed cow
>
> Cleaned barn
>
> Went home

The missing subject, *I*, is obvious. If you're talking about someone else, however, you need to supply a subject:

> Abner fed cow
>
> Julia cleaned barn
>
> I went home

Now the person receiving the message understands that Abner and Julia did all the work, not the texter — who, of course, was too busy texting to tackle chores. By the way, I used capital letters in the preceding examples. Lots of people opt for lowercase in messages like these, and many also omit periods, as I did. Check Chapter 25 for a guide to grammar and electronic media.

You may find some mismatches in your sentences when you go subject–verb hunting. Mismatches are not necessarily wrong; they're simply not subject–verb pairs. Take a look at a subject–verb mismatch *(Egbert scrambling)*, properly tucked inside a sentence:

> Egbert, scrambling for a seat at the counter, knocked over an omelet plate.

When you're checking a sentence for completeness, ignore the mismatches. Keep looking until you find a subject–verb pair that belongs together. If you can't find one, you don't have a complete sentence.

Q. Subject–verb pair or mismatch?

Dorothy fiddled

snake slithering

doctor will examine

paper having been written

A. **pair, mismatch, pair, mismatch**

Subject–verb pair or mismatch?

16 butterfly flew

17 Celeste singing

18 sun shining

19 planet appeared

20 cactus plant was

21 Arthur having dreamed

22 employees will strike

23 party being over

24 candles blown out

25 dogs had barked

Complete Thoughts, Complete Sentences

What's an incomplete sentence? It's the moment in the television show just before the last commercial. You know what I mean. *The hero slowly edges the door open a few inches, peeks in, gasps, and . . . FADE TO DANCING CEREAL BOX.* You were planning to switch to a different show, but instead you wait to see whether the villain stabs the hero. You haven't gotten to the end, and you don't know what's happening. A complete sentence is the opposite of that moment in a television show. You have reached the end, and you do know what's happening. In other words, a complete sentence must express a complete thought. (You've probably noticed that grammar terminology isn't terribly original.)

Check out these complete sentences. Notice how they express complete thoughts:

Despite Egbert's fragile appearance, he proved to be a tough opponent.

Ms. McAnnick will repair your car while you wait.

I can't imagine why anyone would want to ride on top of a bus.

Did Lola apply for a job as a tattoo artist?

For comparison, here are a few incomplete thoughts:

The reason I wanted a divorce was.

Because I said so.

I can guess what you're thinking. Both of those incomplete thoughts may be part of a longer conversation. In context, those incomplete thoughts may indeed express a complete thought:

Sydney: So the topic of conversation was the team's chances for a trophy?

Alice: No! The reason I wanted a divorce was!

and

> Nick: Why do I have to do this dumb homework?
>
> Nick's mom: Because I said so.

Fair enough. You can pull a complete thought out of the examples. However, the context of a conversation isn't enough to satisfy the complete thought / complete sentence rule. To be "legal," your sentence must express a complete thought.

Check out these examples:

> The reason I wanted a divorce was the topic of our conversation, even though his real interest was the team's chances for a trophy.
>
> You have to do this dumb homework because I said so.

Final answer: Every complete sentence has at least one subject–verb pair and must express a complete thought.

WARNING

In deciding whether you have a complete sentence, you may be led astray by words that resemble questions. Consider these three words: *who knits well.* A complete thought? Maybe yes, maybe no. Suppose those three words form a question:

> Who knits well?

This question is understandable and its thought is complete. Verdict: legal. Suppose these three words form a statement:

> Who knits well.

Now they don't make sense. This incomplete sentence needs more words to make a complete thought:

> The honor of making Elizabeth's sweater will go to a person who knits well.

REMEMBER

Don't change the meaning of what you're saying when deciding whether a thought is complete. If you're *questioning*, consider your sentence as a *question*. If you're *stating*, consider your sentence as a *statement*.

TIP

Occasionally a complete sentence ends with an ellipsis — three spaced dots. Such sentences show up in dramatic works, to add suspense or to indicate hesitation or confusion. These sentences appear incomplete, but because they fulfill the author's purpose, they *are* complete. For more information on ellipses, see "Reaching the End of the Line: End Marks," later in this chapter.

EXAMPLE

Q. Complete or incomplete thought?

Martin sings.

Martin, who hopes to sing professionally someday but can't get beyond the do-re-mi level despite 15 years with an excellent teacher and many hours of practice.

A. **complete, incomplete** Even though it is short, the first sentence states a complete thought. The second statement starts with *Martin* and tacks on a long description, but the reader doesn't know what *Martin* is doing. To put it in grammar terms, no verb pairs with the subject, *Martin*.

Complete or incomplete thought?

26. What happened.

27. The basketball lying on the shelf and getting dusty.

28. Somebody should play.

29. While the players were practicing.

30. What does coach say?

31. Enough already.

32. Roger is tall but hates basketball.

33. Tony, although he is short, can jump higher than everyone else on the team.

34. The team, winning the championship because of Tony.

35. The crowd cheered.

Reaching the End of the Line: End Marks

When you speak, your body language, silences, and tone act as punctuation marks. You wriggle your eyebrows, stop at significant moments, and raise your voice when you ask a question.

When you write, you can't raise an eyebrow or stop for a dramatic moment. No one hears your tone of voice. That's why sentences need end marks. This punctuation takes the place of live communication and tells your reader how to "hear" the words correctly. Plus, end marks close sentences legally in formal, written English. (The rules for texting and tweeting, as well as other forms of electronic communication, are different. See Chapter 25.)

Traditional, formal sentences end with a period (.), question mark (?), exclamation point (!), or ellipsis (. . .). The following examples show how to use end marks correctly in Standard English.

The period is for ordinary statements, declarations, and commands:

I can't do my homework.

I refuse to do my homework.

Do not assign homework again.

The question mark is for questions:

> Why are you torturing me with this homework?

> Is there no justice in the world for students?

> Does no one know how much work is listed in my assignment pad?

The exclamation point adds a little drama to sentences that would otherwise end in periods:

> I can't do my homework!

> I absolutely positively refuse to do it!

> Oh, the agony of homework I've seen!

An ellipsis (three dots) signals that something has been left out of a sentence. When missing words occur at the end of a complete sentence, use four dots (three for the missing words and one for the end of the sentence):

> Michael choked, "No, not that . . ."

> Roger complained, "The door opened. . . ."

TIP

In formal writing, don't put more than one end mark at the end of a sentence, unless you're trying to create a comic effect:

> He said my cooking tasted like what?!?!?!

Don't put any end marks in the middle of a sentence. You may find a period inside a sentence as part of an abbreviation; in this case, the period is not considered an end mark. If the sentence ends with an abbreviation, let the period after the abbreviation do double duty. Don't add another period:

> WRONG: When Ella woke me, it was 6 a.m..

> RIGHT: When Ella woke me, it was 6 a.m.

Blog posts and comments on internet sites often follow the standard end mark rules, but those that are just for fun (not business or academic sites) often follow different standards. You may see periods within a sentence to make the statement more emphatic (*Best. Cat video. Ever.*) Some posters type double or triple (or even more) question marks and exclamation points to express strong emotion. "I'm here!" is less excited than "I'm here!!!" Some writers also combine question marks and exclamation points to show doubt or amazement: "You're there?!?!?"

WARNING

Be careful when you stray from formal English rules for punctuation. If you're writing to a boss or teacher or anyone else who may expect Standard English, creative use of end marks may count against you.

Q. Add end marks to these sentences.

EXAMPLE

Who's there

Pick 12 pumpkins and leave the carving to me

I can't believe you said that

A. **Who's there?**

Pick 12 pumpkins and leave the carving to me.

I can't believe you said that!

Add end marks to these sentences.

YOUR
TURN

 36 Did you plant potatoes this year

 37 The deer will stay away from that garden

 38 Does he know much about geography

39 The map showed every river and stream in the area

 40 I am shocked that there are so many sources of water

Connecting Ideas

William Faulkner's acclaimed novel *Absalom, Absalom!* includes a sentence that's rather long — 1,287 words long, to be precise. I doubt you'll ever want to cram that many words into a single sentence, but chances are you'll sometimes want to express more than one idea before you reach an end mark. After all, spooling out ideas in small sentences makes you sound like a toddler: *I played with clay. I went to the zoo. I took a nap.* Even when the activities remain the same, you sound more mature if you write *After I played with clay, I went to the zoo, and then I took a nap.*

Connecting ideas in a grammatically correct fashion isn't hard. In this section, I explain a few simple rules.

Conjunctions

To join two complete sentences, use a conjunction (*and, but, since, because,* and so forth). Say you start with these two statements:

His hand shook

The house of cards fell.

You can connect them (and add a shade of meaning) with conjunctions, which I've underlined in these sentences:

His hand shook, <u>and</u> the house of cards fell.

His hand shook <u>when</u> the house of cards fell.

<u>Because</u> his hand shook, the house of cards fell.

Surprised by the last example sentence? The conjunction can appear at the beginning of either statement, so long as the connection is logical. (For more about conjunctions, see Chapter 7.)

WARNING

Some words appear to be strong enough to join sentences, but in reality, they're just a bunch of couch potatoes who've never seen the inside of a gym. They may look good, but the minute you need them to pick up a truck or something, they're history. False joiners include *however, consequently, therefore, moreover, then, also,* and *furthermore.* Use these words to add meaning to your sentences but not to glue the sentences together.

WRONG: Lennie gobbled the steak, consequently, Robbie had nothing to eat.

CORRECTED VERSION #1: Lennie gobbled the steak; consequently, Robbie had nothing to eat.

CORRECTED VERSION #2: Lennie gobbled the steak. Consequently, Robbie had nothing to eat.

TIP

With your sharp eyes, you probably spotted a comma after *consequently* in each of the preceding examples. Grammarians argue about whether you must place a comma after a false joiner. (For the record, false joiners are *conjunctive adverbs.* No one in the entire universe needs to know that term.) Some grammarians say that the comma is necessary. Others (I'm one) see the comma as optional — a question of personal style. If you're writing for authority figures, ask what they prefer. If you have no one to please but yourself, insert or omit a comma whenever you want.

EXAMPLE

Q. Correct or incorrect in Standard English?

Matty built a block tower, and Lola knocked it over.

Matty built a block tower, however, Lola knocked it over.

A. **correct, incorrect** In the first sentence, the conjunction *and* properly connects two complete sentences. In the second sentence, *however* incorrectly attaches one statement to the other.

Semicolons

The semicolon (;), which looks like a dot on top of a comma, functions as a pit stop between one idea and another. It's not as strong as a period, which in Britain is called a *full stop* because, well, a period stops the reader and signals the end of a statement. A semicolon lets the reader take a rest, but just for a moment. This punctuation mark is strong enough to attach one complete sentence to another.

I've seen writing manuals that proclaim, "Never use semicolons!" with the same intensity of feeling as, say, "Don't blow up the world with that nuclear missile." I've also read articles proclaiming (with no proof whatsoever) that only people old enough to collect a pension use this punctuation mark and that no sane person ever places one in a text. My advice is to use semicolons if you like them. Avoid them if you don't.

If you do put a semicolon in your sentence, be sure to attach related ideas. Here's an example:

> RIGHT: George was born in Delaware; he moved to Virginia when he was 4.

> WRONG: I put nonfat yogurt into that soup; I like Bob Dylan's songs.

In the first example, both parts of the sentence are about George's living arrangements. In the second, those two ideas are, to put it mildly, not in the same universe. (At least not until Bob Dylan writes a song about a container of yogurt. Hey, it could happen.)

Q. Punctuate the following sentence so that it follows the rules of Standard English, adding or subtracting words as needed:

Abner will clip the thorns from that rose stem he is afraid of scratches.

A. **Abner will clip the thorns from that rose stem. He is afraid of scratches.** or **Abner will clip the thorns from that rose stem; he is afraid of scratches.**

Don't connect complete sentences with just a comma. This error is so common that it has its own name: *comma splice*.

> NONSTANDARD COMMA SPLICE: Lucy gathered the cards, it was Lola's turn.

> STANDARD: Lucy gathered the cards; it was Lola's turn.

> WHY IT'S STANDARD: A semicolon attaches one complete sentence to another.

> ALSO STANDARD: Lucy gathered the cards although it was Lola's turn.

> WHY IT'S ALSO STANDARD: A conjunction, *although*, connects two complete sentences.

In informal writing, it's fine to connect two sentences with a dash. (More on dashes appears in Chapter 20.)

Relative pronouns

Another useful technique for combining short sentences legally is "the pronoun connection." (A *pronoun* substitutes for a noun, which is a word for a person, place, thing, or idea. See Chapter 4 for more information.) Check out these combinations:

> Sentence 1: Amy read the book.

> Sentence 2: The book had a thousand pictures in it.

> Joining: Amy read the book *that* had a thousand pictures in it.

Sentence 1: The paper map stuck to Will's shoe.

Sentence 2: The map will help us take over the world.

Joining: The paper map, *which* will help us take over the world, stuck to Will's shoe.

Sentence 1: Margaret wants to hire a carpenter.

Sentence 2: The carpenter will build a new ant farm for her tiny pets.

Joining: Margaret wants to hire a carpenter *who* will build a new ant farm for her tiny pets.

Sentence 1: The tax bill was passed yesterday.

Sentence 2: The tax bill will lower taxes for the top .00009% income bracket.

Joining: The tax bill *that* was passed yesterday will lower taxes for the top .00009% income bracket.

Alternate joining: The tax bill that was passed yesterday will lower taxes for Bill Gates, Elon Musk, and Mark Zuckerberg. (I interpreted a little.)

That, which, and *who* are pronouns. In the combined sentences, each takes the place of a noun. (*That* replaces *book, which* replaces *map, who* replaces *carpenter, that* replaces *tax bill.*) These pronouns serve as thumbtacks, attaching a subordinate or less important idea to the main body of the sentence. For grammar trivia contests: *that, which,* and *who* (as well as *whom* and *whose*) are pronouns that may relate one idea to another. When they do that job, they are called *relative pronouns.*

EXAMPLE

Q. Combine these sentences with a pronoun.

Sentence 1: Charlie slowly tiptoed toward the poisonous snakes.

Sentence 2: The snakes soon bit Charlie on the tip of his nose.

A. **Charlie slowly tiptoed toward the poisonous snakes, which soon bit Charlie on the tip of his nose.** The pronoun *which* replaces *snakes* in sentence 2.

Which sentences are correct in Standard English? You may find one, more than one, or none.

YOUR TURN **(A)** Kathy broke out of jail, five years for illegal sentence-joining was just too much for her.

(B) Kathy broke out of jail; five years for illegal sentence-joining was too much for her.

(C) Kathy broke out of jail because five years for illegal sentence-joining was just too much for her.

42 **(A)** The grammarian-in-chief used to work for the Supreme Court, therefore his word was law.

(B) The grammarian-in-chief used to work for the Supreme Court, and therefore his word was law.

(C) The grammarian-in-chief used to work for the Supreme Court, consequently, his word was law.

43 **(A)** His nickname, "Mr. Grammar," which had been given to him by the court clerks, was not a source of pride for him.

(B) His nickname, "Mr. Grammar," had been given to him by the court clerks, and it was not a source of pride for him.

(C) His nickname, "Mr. Grammar," had been given to him by the court clerks, it was not a source of pride for him.

44 **(A)** Nevertheless, he did not criticize those who used the term, as long as they did so politely.

(B) Nevertheless, he did not criticize those who used the term; as long as they did so politely.

(C) Nevertheless, he did not criticize those who used the term, and as long as they did so politely.

45 **(A)** He often wore a lab coat embroidered with parts of speech, for he was truly devoted to the field of grammar.

(B) He often wore a lab coat embroidered with parts of speech, he was truly devoted to the field of grammar.

(C) He often wore a lab coat embroidered with parts of speech because he was truly devoted to the field of grammar.

46 **(A)** His assistant's escape wounded him deeply; he ordered the grammar cops to arrest her as soon as possible.

(B) His assistant's escape wounded him deeply, and he ordered the grammar cops to arrest her as soon as possible.

(C) His assistant's escape wounded him deeply, consequently he ordered the grammar cops to arrest her as soon as possible.

47 **(A)** The assistant hid in a basket of dirty laundry; then she held her breath as the truck passed the border.

(B) The assistant hid in a basket of dirty laundry, and then she held her breath as the truck passed the border.

(C) The assistant hid in a basket of dirty laundry, then she held her breath as the truck passed the border.

(A) The grammarian-in-chief passed the border of sanity some time ago, although he is able to break a grammar rule if he really tries.

(B) The grammarian-in-chief passed the border of sanity some time ago, even so he is able to break a grammar rule if he really tries.

(C) The grammarian-in-chief passed the border of sanity some time ago, but he is able to break a grammar rule if he really tries.

Breaking Away from Sentence Fragments

I use incomplete sentences, or *fragments,* here and there throughout this book, and (I hope) these incomplete sentences aren't confusing. Especially in electronic communication, quick cuts and short comments are the rule. Fragments, though, sometimes *aren't* the best choice. To decide when fragments are acceptable, read on.

Placing fragments in the right context

In conversational English (see Chapter 2), fragments are usually acceptable. The most common type of fragment begins with the words *and, or, but,* or *nor.* These words are *conjunctions.* As I explain in an earlier section, "Connecting Ideas," these conjunctions may combine two complete sentences (with two complete thoughts) into one longer sentence:

Egbert went to his doctor for a cholesterol check, *and* then he scrambled home.

For centuries, writers have begun sentences with *and, or, but,* and *nor,* especially in informal writing or for dramatic effect. For example, the preceding sentence may be turned into

Egbert went to his doctor for a cholesterol check. And then he scrambled home.

No one misunderstands the meaning. The fragment's separation creates a punch line and adds a bit of drama. Verdict: This fragment is fine.

So are fragments that make sense in the context of a larger conversation, especially in conversational English. Have a look at this example:

MARIA: Is that toaster on sale now?

JOE: No, next week.

Joe's comment is clear only because Maria led the way. If Joe suddenly declares, "No, next week" without context, he's likely to be met with a puzzled look. (See "Complete Thoughts, Complete Sentences," earlier in this chapter, for more examples and additional explanation.)

Fragments are especially useful in electronic media — in some situations. When you're texting, complete sentences may appear overly formal and even disrespectful of your reader's time. Why make your reader plow through a complete sentence on a tiny screen when a few words can make the same point? Take a look at these texts between two friends making plans for the evening. For the sake of comparison, the complete, grammatically correct version appears in parentheses after each text:

LOLA: tonight? (What are the plans for tonight?)

GEORGE: dinner at my house (We are eating at my house.)

LOLA: bringing wine (I am bringing wine.)

GEORGE: ordered food (I ordered the food.)

English teachers may groan, but George and Lola understand each other perfectly. Fragments are perfectly acceptable here.

Steering clear of inappropriate fragments

Don't write sentence fragments that a reader may misunderstand, as in these examples:

When it rained

As if he were king of the world

After the ball was over but before it was time to begin the first day of the rest of your life and all those other clichés that you hear every day in the subway on your way to work

Before Alfred left

Because I want to

Whether you like it or not, and despite the fact that you don't like it, although I am really sorry that you are upset

If hell freezes over

and so on.

Avoid fragments when your most formal English is necessary. If your reader expects perfect grammar, place fragments on your avoid-at-all-costs list.

EXAMPLE

Q. Which is a sentence fragment? Which is a complete sentence? Which is a comma splice (a run-on)?

(A) Cedric sneezed.

(B) Because Cedric sneezed in the middle of the opera, just when the main character removed that helmet with the little horns from on top of her head.

(C) Cedric sneezed, I pulled out a handkerchief.

A. Choice (A) is a complete sentence. Choice B is a fragment with no complete idea. Choice (C) is a comma splice because it contains two complete thoughts joined only by a comma.

Analyze each sentence and label it as follows:

>> **Correct** The sentence is complete.

>> **Fragment** If the sentence lacks a subject-verb pair or a complete thought, it's a fragment.

>> **Missing end mark** If the sentence has no end mark, choose this label.

>> **Run-on** If more than one complete sentence is improperly joined, call it a run-on.

49 Bill's holiday concert, occurring early in October, honors the longstanding tradition of his hometown and the great Elvis Presley.

50 The holiday, which is called Hound Dog Day in honor of a wonderful dog breed.

51 Tradition calls for blue suede shoes.

52 Having brushed the shoes carefully with a suede brush, which can be bought in any shoe store.

53 The citizens lead their dogs to the town square, Heartbreak Hotel is located there.

54 "Look for the ghost of Elvis," the hotel clerk tells every guest, "Elvis has often been seen haunting these halls."

55 Elvis, ghost or not, apparently does not attend the Hound Dog Day festivities, because no one has seen a singer in a white jumpsuit there.

56 Why should a ghost attend Bill's festival

57 How can you even ask?

58 The blue suede shoes are a nostalgic touch, consequently, the tourists always wear them.

59 Personally, I prefer blue patent leather pumps, but my opinion isn't important.

60 Just stay off of my shoes!

61 While we were talking about shoes, Bill was creating a playlist for the Hound Dog Concert.

62 You should plan to arrive early, everyone in town will be there.

Practice Questions Answers and Explanations

1. **is waiting**

2. **has been aching**

3. **was telling**

4. **is standing**

5. **is admiring**

6. **have done**

7. **have gone**

8. **has taken**

9. **was thrown**

10. **has been ridden**

11. **will be**

12. **Are**

13. **have been**

14. **should be**

15. **are**

16. **Pair**

17. **Mismatch** Possible correction: *Celeste is singing.*

18. **Mismatch** Possible correction: *sun will be shining.*

19. **Pair**

20. **Pair**

21. **Mismatch** Possible correction: *Arthur dreamed.*

22. **Pair**

23. **Mismatch** Possible correction: *party was over.*

24. **Mismatch** Possible correction: *candles have been blown out.*

25. **Pair**

26. **Incomplete** With a question mark, this would be a complete thought.

27. **Incomplete** Possible correction: The basketball was lying on the shelf and getting dusty.

(28) **Complete**

(29) **Incomplete** Possible correction: *While the players were practicing, the coach was snoring.*

(30) **Complete**

(31) **Incomplete** Possible correction: *The captain declared, "Enough already!"*

(32) **Complete**

(33) **Complete**

(34) **Incomplete** Possible correction: *The team won the championship because of Tony.*

(35) **Complete**

(36) **Did you plant potatoes this year?**

(37) **The deer will stay away from that garden.**

(38) **Does he know much about geography?**

(39) **The map showed every river and stream in the area.**

(40) **I am shocked that there are so many sources of water!** A period would also be acceptable here.

(41) **B, C** The problem with choice (A) is that a comma can't unite two complete thoughts. In choice (B), the comma has been correctly changed to a semicolon. Choice (C) works because the conjunction *because* connects the two ideas correctly.

(42) **B** In choices (A) and (C), you have two complete thoughts. Everything before the comma equals one complete thought; everything after the comma is another complete thought. A comma isn't strong enough to hold them together, and *nevertheless* or *consequently* can't do the job. In choice (B), the conjunction *and* connects the two thoughts correctly.

(43) **A, B** Choices (A) and (B) are correct in Standard English. In choice (A), the extra information about the nickname *(which had been given to him by the court clerks)* is a description, not a complete thought, so it can be tucked into the sentence next to the word it describes *(nickname)*. The pronoun *which* ties the idea to *nickname*. In choice (B), the conjunction *and* links the two complete sentences. In choice (C), a comma tries to do that job, but it's not strong enough.

(44) **A** The *nevertheless* in choice (A) is not used as a joiner, so it's legal. In choice (B), you see an unnecessary semicolon. In choice (C), the *and* isn't needed.

(45) **A, C** Did I get you with choice (A)? The word *for* has another, more common grammatical use in such expressions as *for you, for the last time,* and so on. However, *for* is a perfectly fine joiner of two complete thoughts when it means *because.* Speaking of *because,* it legally joins two thoughts in choice (C). Choice (B) bombs because the comma isn't an appropriate punctuation mark to join two complete thoughts.

(46) **A, B** Sentence (A) uses a semicolon to join two complete thoughts correctly. Choice (B) employs the conjunction *and* for the same job. In choice (C), *consequently* tries to link these ideas, but it's not a conjunction and therefore not correct in Standard English.

(47) **A, B** To connect these two ideas, choice (A) uses a semicolon and choice (B) the conjunction *and*. Choice (C) fails because a comma can't link complete sentences.

(48) **A, C** The conjunction *although* joins one thought to another, more important, main idea about the grammarian-in-chief's sanity, so choice (A) is correct. So is choice C) because *but* does the job there. Choice (B) doesn't work, because *even so* isn't a conjunction.

(49) **Correct** This one has everything: subject-verb pair *(concert, honors)*, complete thought, and an end mark. One description *(occurring early in October)* is properly tucked into the sentence, near the word it describes *(concert)*.

(50) **Fragment** The sentence is incorrect because it gives you a subject *(the holiday)* and a long description *(which is called Hound Dog Day in honor of a wonderful dog breed)* but doesn't pair any verb with *holiday*. Several corrections are possible. Here's one: The holiday, which is called Hound Dog Day in honor of a wonderful dog breed, requires each citizen to attend dog obedience school.

(51) **Correct** You have a subject-verb pair *(tradition, calls)*, a complete thought, and an end mark. No problems here!

(52) **Fragment** This sentence has no subject. No one is doing the brushing or the buying. One possible correction: Having brushed the shoes carefully with a suede brush, which can be bought in any shoe store, Bill proudly displayed his footwear.

(53) **Run-on** This sentence is a run-on (comma splice), because a comma can't join two complete thoughts. Change it to a semicolon or reword the sentence. Here's a possible rewording: The citizens lead their dogs to the town square, where Heartbreak Hotel is located.

(54) **Run-on** The two quoted sections are jammed into one sentence, but each is a complete thought. Change the comma after *guest* to a period.

(55) **Correct** Here you have two complete thoughts *(Elvis, ghost or not, apparently does not attend the Hound Dog Day festivities* and *no one has seen a singer in a white jumpsuit there)*. A conjunction, *because*, connects them properly.

(56) **Missing end mark** The sentence is incorrect because it has no end mark. Add a question mark.

(57) **Correct** This one is a proper question, with a subject-verb pair *(you can ask)*, a complete thought, and a question mark.

(58) **Run-on** *Consequently* looks like a fine, strong word, but it can't join two complete thoughts, which you have in this sentence. To correct it, add a semicolon after *touch* and dump the comma.

(59) **Correct** Two complete thoughts are joined by the conjunction *but*.

(60) **Correct** Surprised? This sentence gives a command. The subject is *you*, even though *you* doesn't appear in the sentence. It's implied.

(61) **Correct** The conjunction *(while)* properly connects these two ideas, even though the conjunction appears at the beginning of the sentence.

(62) **Run-on** The comma can't connect two complete sentences.

If you're ready to test your skills a bit more, take the following chapter quiz, which incorporates all the chapter topics.

Whaddya Know? Chapter 10 Quiz

Quiz time! Complete each problem to test your knowledge on the various topics covered in this chapter. You can then find the solutions and explanations in the next section.

Read this letter introducing a new employee to customers. Check each sentence for completeness and label it correct or incorrect according to the rules of Standard English.

To Our Valued Customers:

(1) Announcing that Abner Grey is our new Director of Customer Satisfaction, effective immediately. Abner brings a wealth of experience to our company. (2) He served as assistant vice president of marketing for Antarctic Icebergs, Inc., until last year, when the cold finally became too much for him. (3) His first task, to introduce himself to every customer, finding out what has been done in the past and how our relationship may be improved. (4) Expect a phone call or a personal visit from him soon! (5) Recognizing that our previous director was not always attentive to your needs (occupied as she was with the lawsuit, prison, and so forth), we have told Abner to work at least 90 hours per week. (6) No embezzlement, either! (7) Call him whenever you have a problem. (8) You will not be disappointed, furthermore, Abner will actually anticipate your needs. (9) Rest assured. (10) That this Director of Customer Satisfaction will never see the inside of a jail cell.

Answers to Chapter 10 Quiz

1. **incorrect** The sentence lacks a subject/verb pair. To correct it, drop *Announcing that* or add *I am* to the beginning of the sentence.

2. **correct**

3. **incorrect** Although it has two long descriptions, this sentence doesn't complete the thought begun by *His first task.*

4. **correct**

5. **correct**

6. **incorrect** This sentence has neither a subject nor a verb. You could correct this one by adding *We'll have* to the beginning of the sentence.

7. **correct**

8. **incorrect** The word *furthermore* is not a conjunction. Place a semicolon in front of *furthermore* and you're fine.

9. **correct** Short sentences can still be complete, as this command sentence is.

10. **incorrect** This sentence does not express a complete thought. If you tack it to the end of the sentence 9, however, you end up with one complete, correct sentence.

Chapter **11**

No Santas but Plenty of Clauses

Say I give you a new car. What do you do? Open the hood and check the engine or hop in and drive away? The engine-checkers and the drive-awayers are subgroups of car owners. The engine-checkers have to know what's going on inside the machine. The other group doesn't care about fuel injection and spark plugs. They just want the car to run.

You can also divide language learners into two groups. Some people want to understand what's going on inside the sentence, but most just want to communicate. In this chapter, I provide some information for each — the lift-the-hood-of-the-sentence group and the drive-English-to-where-I-need-to-go clan. The first part of this chapter digs into the structure of the sentence, defining clauses. Then I show you how manipulating clauses can change the meaning and effect of a sentence.

Grasping the Basics of Clause and Effect

No matter what food you put between two pieces of bread, you've got a sandwich. That's the definition of *sandwich*: bread plus filling. Clauses have a simple definition, too: subject plus verb. Any subject-verb combination creates a clause. The reverse is also true: no subject or no verb = no clause. You can throw in some extras (descriptions, lettuce, tomato — whatever), but the basic subject-verb combination is key. Some sentences have one clause, in which case the whole sentence is the clause, and some have more than one.

TIP

Check your sentences for completeness. In formal English, each sentence should contain at least one subject–verb pair and express a complete thought, expressed in a way that can stand alone. In grammar terms, each sentence must contain at least one independent clause. (For more information on complete sentences, see Chapter 10.)

Here are a few examples of one-clause sentences:

Has Sherlock cracked The Case of the Missing Chicken? (subject = *Sherlock,* verb = *has cracked*)

Lulu crossed the Alps on foot in the dead of winter. (subject = *Lulu,* verb = *crossed*)

Sid and his parents have reached an agreement about his chores. (subjects = *Sid and his parents,* verb = *have reached*)

Alfred swam for 15 minutes and rowed for an hour before nightfall. (subject = *Al,* verbs = *swam, rowed*)

Notice that some of the clauses have two subjects and some have two verbs, but each expresses one main idea. Here are a few examples of sentences with more than one clause:

SENTENCE: Michael struggled out from under the blankets, and then he dashed after the enemy agent.

CLAUSE 1: Michael struggled out from under the blankets (subject = *Michael,* verb = *struggled*)

CLAUSE 2: then he dashed after the enemy agent (subject = *he,* verb = *dashed*)

SENTENCE: After Cedric had developed the secret microfilm, Barbara sent it to whatever federal agency catches spies.

CLAUSE 1: After Cedric had developed the secret microfilm (subject = *Cedric,* verb = *had developed*)

CLAUSE 2: Barbara sent it to whatever federal agency catches spies (subject = *Barbara,* verb = *sent*)

CLAUSE 3: whatever federal agency catches spies (subject = *agency,* verb = *catches*)

With your sharp eyes, I'm sure you noticed something odd about the last example: Clause #3 is actually part of Clause #2. It's not a misprint. Sometimes one clause is entangled in another. (This topic is deep in the pathless forests of grammar. Get out now, while you still can!)

Here's one more example that's complicated:

SENTENCE: Whoever ate the secret microfilm is in big trouble.

CLAUSE 1: Whoever ate the secret microfilm (subject = *whoever,* verb = *ate*)

CLAUSE 2: Whoever ate the secret microfilm is in big trouble. (subject = *whoever ate the secret microfilm,* verb = *is*)

Yes, one clause is the subject of another clause. Good grief! What a system. For those who truly love grammar: The subject clause is a noun clause. See "Defining the Three Legal Jobs for Subordinate Clauses," later in this chapter, for more information.

EXAMPLE

Q. Examine the underlined words and decide whether they are a clause (C) or not a clause (NC).

Oh boy. Ella agreed to attend her fifteenth high school reunion! She resolved to get a promotion, a new wardrobe, and at least one impressive hobby before the class dinner.

A. **Oh boy = NC, Ella agreed to attend her fifteenth high-school reunion = C, to get a promotion = NC, before the class dinner = NC** The first underlined portion (*Oh boy*) has neither a subject nor a verb, so it isn't a clause. The second underlined portion has a subject and a verb (*Ella agreed*), which makes it a clause. *To get a promotion* has no subject, and strictly speaking, the infinitive *to get* isn't a verb in this sentence. Therefore, it's not a clause. *Before the class dinner* lacks a subject-verb pair. It's actually a prepositional phrase.

YOUR TURN

Examine the underlined elements and label them clause (C) or not a clause (NC).

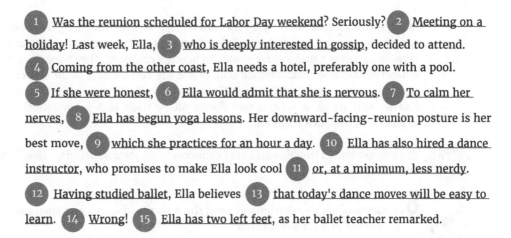

1. Was the reunion scheduled for Labor Day weekend? Seriously? 2. Meeting on a holiday! Last week, Ella, 3. who is deeply interested in gossip, decided to attend. 4. Coming from the other coast, Ella needs a hotel, preferably one with a pool. 5. If she were honest, 6. Ella would admit that she is nervous. 7. To calm her nerves, 8. Ella has begun yoga lessons. Her downward-facing-reunion posture is her best move, 9. which she practices for an hour a day. 10. Ella has also hired a dance instructor, who promises to make Ella look cool 11. or, at a minimum, less nerdy. 12. Having studied ballet, Ella believes 13. that today's dance moves will be easy to learn. 14. Wrong! 15. Ella has two left feet, as her ballet teacher remarked.

Sorting Subordinate and Independent Clauses

Some clauses are like mature grown-ups. They have their own house or apartment, pay their own expenses, and wash the dishes frequently enough to ward off a visit from the health inspector. These clauses have made a success of life; they're *independent*.

Other clauses are like the brother-in-law character in a million jokes. They crash on someone's couch, mooch free meals, and never visit a Parental Unit without a bag of dirty laundry. These clauses are not mature; they can't support themselves. They're *dependent*. These clauses may be called *dependent clauses* or *subordinate clauses*. (The terms are interchangeable.)

Following are two sets of clauses. Both have subject-verb pairs, but the first set makes sense alone and the second doesn't. The first set consists of independent clauses, and the second of subordinate, or dependent, clauses.

Independent clauses:

Elena blasted Bobby with a radar gun.

Bobby was going 50 mph.

The cheetah could not keep up.

Did the judge award the trophy?

Subordinate clauses:

After she had complained to the race officials

Because Bobby had installed an illegal motor on his skateboard

Which Tom bought from an overcrowded zoo

Whoever ran the fastest

Independent clauses are okay by themselves, but writing too many in a row makes your paragraph choppy and monotonous. Subordinate clauses, however, are not okay by themselves, because they don't make sense alone. To become complete, they have to tack themselves onto independent clauses. Subordinate clauses add life and interest to the sentence (just as the guy crashing on your couch adds a little zip to the household). But don't leave them alone, because disaster will strike. A subordinate clause all by itself is a grammatical felony in Standard English — a sentence fragment.

TIP

The best sentences combine different elements in all sorts of patterns. (See Chapter 24 for more on this topic.)

EXAMPLE

Q. Independent or subordinate? Read the underlined words and label each one I for independent or S for subordinate.

Betsy stares at her phone <u>whenever she has a free moment</u>.

A. **Subordinate** The underlined words don't form a complete thought, so this clause is subordinate. Clauses that give information about time are often subordinate. This one explains when *Betsy stares*.

YOUR TURN

Q. Independent or subordinate? Read the underlined words and label each I for independent or S for subordinate.

16 <u>The pocket for Betsy's phone has never been used</u> because Betsy never puts her phone away.

17 The last time <u>that Betsy left the house without her phone</u> was traumatic for her.

18 Sal, <u>who is Betsy's best friend,</u> told her that she must face her phone addiction.

19 <u>Betsy strongly denies having phone problems</u>, but Sal is not convinced.

20 <u>While Betsy was looking at her phone,</u> Sal removed Betsy's shoes.

21 When Betsy stood up, <u>she finally noticed that her feet were bare</u>.

22 Furious, Betsy grabbed Sal's phone, <u>which he had left on the table</u>.

23 <u>Will Betsy and Sal's fight be resolved</u>, or will the phone feud continue?

Defining the Three Legal Jobs for Subordinate Clauses

It's true that subordinate clauses can't stand alone, but they still do valuable work. In this section, I describe the three roles allotted to this grammatical element.

Describing nouns and pronouns

A subordinate clause may give your listener or reader more information about a noun or pronoun. Here are some examples, with the subordinate clause underlined:

> The book <u>that Michael wrote</u> is on the best seller list. *(that Michael wrote* describes the noun *book)*

> Anyone <u>who knows Michael well</u> will read the book. *(who knows Michael well* describes the pronoun *anyone)*

> The book includes some information <u>that will prove embarrassing to Michael's friends</u>. *(that will prove embarrassing to Michael's friends* describes the noun *information)*

You don't need to know this fact, so skip to the next paragraph. Still here? Okay then. When a subordinate clause describes a noun or a pronoun, it's doing an adjective's job. Therefore, it's called an *adjective clause.*

Describing verbs, adjectives, or adverbs

Subordinate clauses can also describe verbs, adjectives, or adverbs. The subordinate clauses tell you *how, when, where,* or *why.* Here are some examples, with the subordinate underlined:

> <u>Because Michael censored himself,</u> the book contains nothing about the wiretap. *(Because Michael censored himself* describes the verb *contains)*

> We will probably find out more <u>when the movie version is released</u>. *(when the movie version is released* describes the verb *will find)*

> The government may prohibit sales of the book <u>wherever it may increase international tension</u>. *(wherever it may increase international tension* describes the verb *may prohibit)*

Michael is so stubborn <u>that he may sue the government</u>. *(that he may sue the government* describes the adverb *so)*

More grammar terminology, in case you're having a very dull day: Subordinate clauses that describe verbs are called *adverb clauses*. Subordinate clauses that describe adjectives or adverbs (mostly in comparisons) are also *adverb clauses*. Adverb clauses do the same job as single-word adverbs. They describe verbs, adjectives, or other adverbs.

TIP

The questions you "pop" to identify adjectives and adverbs (see Chapter 6) also identify adjective and adverb clauses.

WARNING

Adjective and adverb clauses should be near the words they describe. If you place them in the wrong spot, your meaning may be muddled. Chapter 15 explains what to watch out for when you're inserting a description into a sentence.

Acting as subjects, objects, or subject complements inside another clause

This topic is a bit more complicated: Subordinate clauses may do any job that a noun does in a sentence. Therefore, subordinate clauses sometimes act as subjects, objects, or subject complements inside other clauses. Here are some examples, with the subordinate clause underlined:

<u>When the book was written</u> is a real mystery. *(When the book was written* is the subject of the verb *is)*

No one knows <u>whom Michael hired to write his book</u>. *(whom Michael hired to write his book* is the object of the verb *knows)*

Michael signed copies for <u>whoever bought at least five books</u>. *(whoever bought at least five books* is the object of the preposition *for)*

The problem is <u>that your homework is late</u>. *(that your homework is late* is the subject complement)

The grammar terminology is obvious: *Noun clauses* are subordinate clauses that perform the same functions as nouns — subjects, objects, appositives, and so on.

TIP

When you "pop the question" to locate a subject, object, or complement, you may find a noun clause. For more information on these magic questions, see Chapters 8 and 9.

Untangling Subordinate and Independent Clauses

You have to untangle one clause from another only occasionally — when deciding which pronoun or verb you need or whether commas are appropriate. (See the next section, "Deciding When to Untangle Clauses," for more information.) When you do have to untangle them, follow these simple steps:

1. Find the subject-verb pairs.

2. Use your reading comprehension skills to determine whether the subject-verb pairs belong to the same thought or to different thoughts:

   If the pairs belong to different thoughts, they're probably in different clauses.

   If the pairs belong to the same thought, they're probably in the same clause.

Another method also relies on reading comprehension skills. Think about the ideas in the sentence and untangle the thoughts. By doing so, you've probably also untangled the clauses.

Check out these examples:

SENTENCE: The acting award that Lola received comes with a hefty check.

SUBJECT–VERB PAIRS: *award comes, Lola received*

UNTANGLED IDEAS: (1) The award comes with a hefty check. (2) Lola received the award.

CLAUSES: (1) *The acting award comes with a hefty check.* (independent clause) (2) *that Lola received* (subordinate clause)

SENTENCE: When Lulu tattoos clients, they stay tattooed.

SUBJECT–VERB PAIRS: *Lulu tattoos, they stay*

UNTANGLED IDEAS: (1) Lulu tattoos clients (2) they stay tattooed

CLAUSES: (1) *When Lulu tattoos clients* (subordinate clause) (2) *they stay tattooed* (independent clause)

Q. Untangle this sentence into separate clauses.

Lola's last motorcycle, which she bought secondhand, was once Elvis's property.

A. **(1) Lola's last motorcycle was once Elvis's property (2) which she bought secondhand.**

Untangle the following sentences into separate clauses.

24) Egbert posted a bad review of that restaurant because the chef added too much salt to every dish.

25) Before Egbert had finished eating, the waiter presented him with the check.

26) Whoever eats at that restaurant is going to regret it.

27) If Egbert eats there again, he may find a spider in his soup.

28) The spider, however, eats very little.

29) Watch out for the restaurant cat.

30) The cat, whose name is Melissa, pounces on the table when no one is looking and eats everything!

Deciding When to Untangle Clauses

Why would you want to untangle clauses? Not just because you have nothing better to do. (If you have that much free time, please stop by to clean out my closets.) You should untangle clauses when you're choosing pronouns, verbs, and punctuation. Read on for the whole story.

When you're picking a pronoun

When you're deciding whether you need a subject or an object pronoun, check the clause that contains the word. Don't worry about what the entire clause is doing in the sentence. Untangle the clause and ignore everything else. Then decide which pronoun you need for that particular clause.

Many of the decisions about pronouns concern *who* and *whom*. (For tricks to help you make the *who/whom* and other pronoun choices, see Chapter 14.)

Here's one untangling example, with the pronoun problem in parentheses:

> SENTENCE: Ella wasn't sure (who/whom) would want a used engagement ring.
>
> UNTANGLED INTO CLAUSES: Clause 1: *Ella wasn't sure.* Clause 2: *(who/whom) would want a used engagement ring.*
>
> RELEVANT CLAUSE: *(who/whom) would want a used engagement ring.*
>
> CORRECT PRONOUN: *who* (subject of *would want*)

When you're deciding on the correct verb

When you're deciding on subject-verb agreement in one clause, the other clauses are distractions. (By *agreement*, I mean the matching of singular subjects with singular verbs and plural subjects with plural verbs.) If you're writing (not speaking), I recommend that you cross out or cover the other clauses with your finger. Check the clause that worries you. Decide the subject-verb agreement issue, and then erase the crossing-out line or remove your hand. (For more information on subject-verb agreement, see Chapter 13.)

Here are two untangling examples, with the verb choices in parentheses:

> SENTENCE: Larry, whose brides are always thrilled to marry into the royal family, (needs/need) no introduction.
>
> UNTANGLED INTO CLAUSES: Clause #1= *Larry (needs/need) no introduction.* Clause #2= *whose brides are always thrilled to marry into the royal family.*
>
> RELEVANT CLAUSE: *Larry (needs/need) no introduction.*
>
> CORRECT VERB: *needs* (Larry = singular, *needs* = singular)
>
> SENTENCE: That ring, which Larry recovers after each divorce and reuses for each new engagement, *has/have* received a recycling award.

UNTANGLED INTO CLAUSES: Clause #1 = *That ring has/have received a recycling award.*
Clause #2 = *which Larry recovers after each divorce and reuses for each new engagement.*

RELEVANT CLAUSE: *The ring has/have received a recycling award.*

CORRECT VERB: *has* (*ring* = singular, *has* = singular)

When you're figuring out where to put commas

Sometimes you have to untangle clauses in order to decide whether you need commas. Repeat the same untangling steps that I discuss earlier in this chapter (see "Untangling Subordinate and Independent Clauses") and then flip to Chapter 19 to see how to use commas correctly.

Choosing Content for Subordinate Clauses

What to put in a clause depends on the writer's purpose. Generally, the most important idea belongs in the independent clause. Subordinate clauses are for less crucial information, as in this example:

IMPORTANT IDEA: Aga just won a trillion dollars.

LESS IMPORTANT IDEA: His name means "ancient gambler" in an obscure language.

GOOD SENTENCE: Aga, whose name means "ancient gambler" in an obscure language, just won a trillion dollars.

NOT-SO-GOOD SENTENCE: Aga, who just won a trillion dollars, says that his name means "ancient gambler" in an obscure language.

Of course, some writers stray from this pattern to make a comic point or to emphasize a character trait. Suppose you're writing about someone who, to put it mildly, tends to be self-absorbed. A sentence like the following one emphasizes that trait:

While the stock price tanked and sales plummeted, the CEO examined his photo on the company website.

The wreck of the company isn't a big deal for this negligent CEO, and its placement in the subordinate clause reinforces that fact.

TIP

Regardless of what you place in a subordinate clause, be sure to connect it to the sentence properly. For more discussion on joining independent and subordinate clauses, see Chapter 10.

EXAMPLE

Q. Combine these ideas into a single sentence containing one independent and one subordinate clause.

IDEA #1: the archaeologist made a major discovery

IDEA #2: she was listening to classic rock on the radio

A. Several combinations are possible. Here's one:

While listening to classic rock on the radio, the archaeologist made a major discovery.

The subordinate clause is *While listening to classic rock on the radio.* The independent clause is *the archaeologist made a major discovery.* This version emphasizes the discovery. The classic rock information is interesting but not particularly important.

Here's another possibility:

As she made a major discovery, the archaeologist listened to classic rock.

Now the subordinate clause is *As she made a major discovery.* The independent clause is *the archaeologist listened to classic rock.* Placing the musical information in the independent clauses raises its importance. This version might appear in an essay about the role of music in the workplace, archaeologists' daily routines, or the musical tastes of this particular archaeologist.

YOUR
TURN

Combine these ideas into a single sentence containing one independent and one subordinate clause. *Note:* I provide one possible answer in the answer key, but your response may vary and still be correct.

31 IDEA #1: the discovery was an ancient betting parlor IDEA #2: the betting parlor was filled with discarded lottery tickets

32 IDEA #1: no one had torn up a losing ticket IDEA #2: the tickets were made from stone slabs

33 IDEA #1: I wonder IDEA #2: What was the prize?

34 IDEA #1: near the betting parlor was a bar IDEA #2 winners probably celebrated there

35 IDEA #1: anyone participating in the archaeological dig celebrated IDEA #2 they also celebrated in a bar

Practice Questions Answers and Explanations

1. **Was the reunion scheduled for Labor Day weekend? = C** This is a clause because it has a matching subject-verb pair, *reunion was scheduled*. To understand the structure of a question, try turning it into a statement. The original becomes "The reunion was scheduled for Labor Day weekend." Now you can more easily pick out the subject-verb pair and see that you have a clause.

2. **Meeting on a holiday = NC** With no subject and no verb, this is not a clause.

3. **who is very interested in gossip = C** The subject is *who,* and the verb is *is.*

4. **Coming from the other coast = NC** The verb form *coming* isn't paired with a subject, so this is not a clause. It's a verbal, a description. (For more on verbals, turn to Chapter 8 for some examples and 24 for advice on how to use them effectively.)

5. **If she were honest = C** The subject-verb pair is *she were.*

6. **Ella would admit that she is nervous = C** This underlined portion of the sentence contains two clauses, one inside the other. *Ella would admit* is the subject-verb pair, completed by the direct object *that she is nervous,* which is a clause because it contains a subject-verb pair, *she is.*

7. **To calm her nerves = NC** There's no subject here, and technically there's no verb either, because the infinitive form, *to calm,* doesn't function as a verb. Therefore, this is not a clause.

8. **Ella has begun yoga lessons = C** The subject-verb pair is *Ella has begun,* so this is a clause.

9. **which she practices for an hour a day = C** The subject-verb pair is *she practices,* making this a clause.

10. **Ella has also hired a dance instructor = C** The subject-verb pair is *Ella has hired.* Verdict: clause.

11. **or, at a minimum, less nerdy = NC** No verb, no subject, no clause!

12. **Having studied ballet = NC** This verb form isn't matched by a subject, so this is not a clause. Also, *having studied ballet* is a verbal — a verb form that doesn't function as a verb. Here it's describing *Ella.* (For more information on verbals, see Chapters 8 and 24.)

13. **that today's dance moves will be easy to learn = C** The matching subject-verb pair is *moves will be.*

14. **Wrong = NC** Lacking a subject and a verb, this isn't a clause.

15. **Ella has two left feet = C** The subject-verb pair is *Ella has.*

16. **Independent** If you chop off the rest of the sentence, you still have a complete thought. The reason Betsy has an untouched pocket is interesting, but it doesn't have to appear in that sentence in order for the underlined words to make sense.

17. **Subordinate** When you start a clause with *that,* it's often subordinate, which is the case here. Say the underlined words. They're incomplete without the support of the rest of the sentence.

18. **Subordinate** The underlined words would form an independent clause if they were asking a question, but they aren't. They're making a statement — an incomplete one. Therefore, you're looking at a subordinate clause.

(19) **Independent** Read the underlined words aloud. Do you hear the complete thought? This is an independent clause.

(20) **Subordinate** You have a time statement beginning with *while*, but that statement, all by itself, leaves you wondering. No doubt about it: This is a subordinate clause.

(21) **Independent** The underlined words make sense, so you have an independent clause.

(22) **Subordinate** The word *which*, when it isn't part of a question, generally signals a subordinate clause.

(23) **Independent** This one is a little tricky. You have only one question mark, but bring out your reading comprehension skills. Do you see that the sentence asks two separate questions? Question 1 is *Will Betsy and Sal's fight be resolved?* Question 2 is *will the phone feud continue?* Both parts of the sentence are independent clauses.

(24) **(1) Egbert posted a bad review of that restaurant (2) because the chef added too much salt to every dish**

(25) **(1) Before Egbert had finished eating (2) the waiter presented him with the check**

(26) **(1) Whoever eats at that restaurant is going to regret it (2) Whoever eats at that restaurant** One clause is the subject of another.

(27) **(1) If Egbert eats there again (2) he may find a spider in his soup**

(28) **(1) The spider, however, eats very little** (one clause only)

(29) **(1) Watch out for the restaurant cat** (one clause only)

(30) **(1) The cat pounces on the table when no one is looking and eats everything (2) whose name is Melissa** Did I catch you with the first clause? Because one subject, *cat*, pairs with two verbs, *pounces* and *eats*, there's only one clause.

(31) **The discovery was an ancient betting parlor that was filled with discarded lottery tickets.** The independent clause is *The discovery was an ancient betting parlor*. The subordinate clause — *that was filled with discarded lottery tickets* — adds information about the betting parlor. Your answer may vary.

(32) **No one had torn up a losing ticket because the tickets were made from stone slabs.** Other versions are possible. In this one, the independent clause is *no one had torn up a losing ticket* and the subordinate clause is *because the tickets were made from stone slabs*. The independent clause states the event, and the subordinate clause, a possible reason.

(33) **I wonder what the prize was.** The entire sentence is an independent clause; the direct object is the noun clause *what the prize was*.

(34) **Near the betting parlor was a bar where winners probably celebrated.** The first clause (*Near the betting parlor was a bar*) is independent; the second (*where winners probably celebrated*) is subordinate.

(35) **Whoever participated in the dig also celebrated in a bar.** In this sentence, the first idea is expressed in a noun clause (*whoever participated in the dig*) that functions as the subject of *celebrated*. The entire sentence is an independent clause.

If you're ready to test your skills a bit more, take the following chapter quiz that incorporates all the chapter topics.

Whaddya Know? Chapter 11 Quiz

Quiz time! Complete each problem to test your knowledge on the various topics covered in this chapter. You can then find the solutions and explanations in the next section.

Below is a true story about one of my granddaughters, who was 5 or 6 years old when it happened. Each sentence is numbered. Check the corresponding number for a question about the sentence.

(1) When my son and granddaughter were in the public library one day, my son spotted *English Grammar For Dummies* on the shelf. (2) "Look at this," he said to his daughter, who was engrossed in a picture book. (3) She took the book from his hand and flipped through the pages. (4) "Do you know what is special about this book?" (5) She shook her head; it looked like an ordinary book to her. (6) "Gran wrote it!"

(7) As he spoke, my granddaughter was watching him in disbelief. (8) "You mean that Gran came all the way across the country, wrote this book, and then *left* it here? (9) That can't be true!" (10) Although my son spent the next hour attempting to explain the publishing industry to her, she remained skeptical.

1 How many clauses are in sentence (1)?

2 Untangle the clauses in sentence (2).

3 Is there a subordinate clause in sentence (3)?

4 Untangle the clauses in sentence (4).

5 How many clauses are in sentence (5)?

6 Are the words enclosed in quotation marks in sentence (6) an independent clause?

7 Identify the subordinate clause in sentence (7).

8 How many clauses are in sentence (8)?

9 Identify the clause(s) in sentence (9).

10 Identify the adverb clause in sentence (10).

Answers to Chapter 11 Quiz

1. **2** The independent clause is *my son spotted* English Grammar For Dummies *on the shelf*. The subordinate clause is *When my son and granddaughter were in the public library one day*.

2. **Clause #1 Look at this** (subordinate clause, acting as the direct object of the verb *said*), **Clause #2: he said to his daughter** (independent clause) **Clause #3 who was engrossed in a picture book** (subordinate clause, describing *daughter*)

3. **no** One subject (*she*) pairs with two verbs (*took, flipped*). The entire sentence is a single independent clause.

4. **Clause #1: the entire sentence** (subject = *you*, verb = *do know*, *what is special about this book* = direct object), **Clause #2: what is special about this book** (subordinate clause, functioning as a direct object)

5. **2** The semicolon separates two independent clauses in this sentence.

6. **yes** The entire sentence is a quotation. It has a subject–verb pair and a complete thought, so it's an independent clause.

7. **As he spoke** This subordinate clause functions as an adverb describing the verb *was watching*.

8. **2 Clause #1: entire sentence** (*you* = subject, *mean* = verb, *that Gran . . . here* = direct object) **Clause #2: that Gran . . . here** (noun clause, functioning as the direct object of the verb *mean*)

9. **That can't be true** Did I trick you? The sentence is a single independent clause.

10. **Although my son spent the next hour attempting to explain the publishing industry to her** (describes the verb *remained*)

4

Clearing Up Confusing Grammar Points

In This Unit . . .

Chapter **12**

Relax! Understanding Verb Tense, Voice, and Mood

Ah, verbs! You can't live without them, because they carry so much information to your reader or listener. Sometimes you can't live with them, at least in terms of Standard English, because verbs can trip you up in several ways: specifically, tense, voice, mood, and number. I focus on number (singular or plural) in Chapter 13. This chapter throws you a lifeline to grammatically correct decisions about tense, voice, and mood.

It's All in the Timing: Tense

Are you obsessed with time: how to save it, race against it, borrow it, or watch it fly? Most people are. Perhaps that's one reason verbs are so important in the English language. They place the information in the sentence on a timeline stretching from the past through the present and into the future. This quality of verbs is known as *tense*.

Simplifying matters: The simple tenses

Three of the six English tenses are called *simple*. (I discuss the other three, the *perfect* tenses, in the next section. Trust me: The perfect tenses are far from it.)

The three simple tenses are *present, past,* and *future.* Each of the simple tenses (just to make things even *more* fun) has two forms. One is the unadorned, no-frills, plain tense. This form has no special name; it's just called *present, past,* or *future.* It shows actions or states of being at a point in time, but it doesn't always pin down a specific moment. The other form is called *progressive.* It shows actions or a state of being *in progress.*

Present tense

Present tense shows action or a state of being that is occurring now, that is generally true, or that is always happening. The *present progressive* form is similar, but it often implies a process. (The difference between the two is subtle. I go into more detail about using these forms in a later section, "Using the simple tenses correctly.") For now, take a look at a couple of sentences in the no-frills, plain present tense:

> Reggie often *rolls* his eyes in annoyance. (*rolls* = present tense)

> George *plans* nothing for New Year's Eve because he never *has* a date. (*plans, has* = present tense)

Here are two sentences with present progressive verbs:

> Luciana *is axing* the proposal to cut down the national forest. (*is axing* = present progressive)

> Miguel and Lulu *are skiing* far too fast toward that cliff. (*are skiing* = present progressive)

The simple present tense for regular verbs changes at times, depending on who or what is doing the action or existing in the state of being expressed by the verb. In Table 12-1, you see the plain and progressive forms of the regular verb *walk,* paired with subjects. (Check out "The rebels: Dealing with irregular verbs," later in this chapter, for verbs that don't follow this pattern.) The pronouns *he, she, it,* and *they* represent every possible noun.

Table 12-1   Present Tense

Singular Subject	Plain Present	Present Progressive	Plural Subject	Plain Present	Present Progressive
I	Walk	am walking	we	walk	are walking
you	walk	are walking	you	walk	are walking
he, she, it, they	walks	is walking	they	walk	are walking

TIP

As you see, the pronouns *you* and *they* may be either singular or plural. For more information on *they,* see "A note about pronouns" in the book's Introduction.

Past tense

Past tense tells you what happened before the present time. This simple tense also has two forms, *past* and *past progressive.* Consider these two past-tense sentences:

When the elastic in Professor Belli's girdle *snapped,* the students *woke* up. (*snapped* and *woke* = past tense)

Despite the strong tape, the package *split* and *spilled* onto the conveyor belt. (*split* and *spilled* = past tense)

Here are two more examples, this time in the past progressive form:

While Buzz *was sleeping,* his cat, Nipper, *was destroying* the sofa. (*was sleeping* and *was destroying* = past progressive)

Lola's friends *were passing* tissues to Lulu at a rate of five per minute. (*were passing* = past progressive)

The plain past tense is super easy to remember, and the past progressive is only a little bit harder. Have a glance at Table 12-2, which shows the past tense of the regular verb *walk.* The pronouns *he, she, it,* and *they* represent every possible noun.

Table 12-2   Past Tense

Singular Subject	Plain Past	Past Progressive	Plural Subject	Plain Past	Past Progressive
I	walked	was walking	we	walked	were walking
you	walked	were walking	you	walked	were walking
he, she, it, they	walked	was walking	they	walked	were walking

Future tense

Future tense talks about what has not happened yet. This simple tense is the only one that always needs helping verbs to express meaning, even for the plain version.

TIP

Helping verbs (see Chapter 5) such as *will, shall, have, has, should,* and others change the meaning of the main verb.

Future tenses — this may shock you — come in two forms. One form of the future tense is called *future,* and the other is *future progressive.* The unadorned form of the future tense goes like this:

Nancy *will position* her campaign poster in the center of the bulletin board. (*will position* = future tense)

Lisa and I *will* never *part,* thanks to that bottle of glue. (*will part* = future tense)

A couple of examples of the future progressive:

During final exams, George *will be cramming* his campaign strategy. (*will be cramming* = future progressive)

This summer, Lola *will be weeding* her garden every day for two hours. (*will be weeding* = future progressive)

Table 12-3 shows the future and future progressive forms of the regular verb *walk*. The pronouns *he, she, it,* and *they* represent every possible noun.

Table 12-3   Future Tense

Singular Subject	Plain Future	Future Progressive	Plural Subject	Plain Future	Future Progressive
I	will walk	will be walking	we	will walk	will be walking
you	will walk	will be walking	you	will walk	will be walking
he, she, it, they	will walk	will be walking	they	will walk	will be walking

TIP

The helping verb *shall* also creates a future or future progressive verb. Traditionally, *shall* pairs with *I* and *we*, and *will* pairs with other subjects. These days, most people prefer *will* for all subjects.

EXAMPLE

Q. Find the verbs and label them into present, present progressive, past, past progressive, future, or future progressive.

When a tornado is whirling overhead, we snap selfies, which we will post online later.

A. **is whirling = present progressive, snap = present, will post = future**

YOUR TURN

Find the verbs and label them as present, present progressive, past, past progressive, future, and future progressive tenses.

1. Will Mark inflate the balloons?

2. Exactly 5,000 years ago, a dinosaur was living in that mud puddle.

3. Zeus and Apollo are establishing a union of mythological characters.

4. When you were four, you blew out all the candles on your birthday cake.

5. The pilot will be joining us as soon as the aircraft clears the rooftop.

Using the simple tenses correctly

You can often interchange plain and progressive forms without creating any problems, but shades of meaning do exist.

Present and present progressive

The single-word form of the present tense may be used for statements that are generally true at the present time but not necessarily happening right now. For example:

Ollie *attends* wrestling matches every Sunday. (*attends* = present)

If you try to reach Ollie on Sunday, you'll get an annoying voicemail message because he's at the arena. Now read this sentence:

> Ollie *is playing* hide-and-seek with his dog, Spot. (*is playing* = present progressive)

This sentence means that right now, as you write or say this sentence, Ollie is playing with his dog.

Past and past progressive

The difference between the plain past tense and the past progressive tense is pretty much the same as in the present tense. The single-word form often shows what happened in the past more generally. The progressive form may pinpoint action or a state of being at a specific time or occurring in the past on a regular basis.

> Greg *went* to the store and *bought* clothes for all his friends. (*went* and *bought* = past tense)

This sentence means that at some point in the past Greg whipped out his charge card and finished off his Christmas list.

> While Greg *was shopping,* his friends *were planning* their revenge. (*was shopping* and *were planning* = past progressive)

This sentence means that Greg shouldn't have bothered, because at the exact moment he was spending his allowance, his friends were deciding whether to pour ink into his lunch box or to rip up his homework.

> Greg *was shopping* until he *was drooping* with exhaustion, despite his mother's strict credit limit. (*was shopping* and *was drooping* = past progressive)

This sentence refers to one of Greg's bad habits, his tendency to go shopping every spare moment. The shopping was repeated on a daily basis, over and over again. (Hence, Greg's mom imposed the strict credit limit.)

Future and future progressive

You won't find much difference between these two. The progressive gives you slightly more of a sense of being in the middle of things. For example:

> The actor *will be playing* Hamlet with a great deal of emotion. (*will be playing* = future progressive tense)

The actor's actions in the preceding sentence may be a little more immediate than

> The actor *will play* Hamlet with a great deal of emotion. (*will play* = future)

TIP

Understanding the difference between the two forms of the simple tenses entitles you to wear an Official Grammarian hat. But if you don't catch on to the distinction, don't lose sleep over the issue. If you can't grasp the subtle differences in casual conversation, your listeners probably won't either.

TIP

When you're dealing with a pair (or more) of statements about the same time period, you probably need one of the simple tenses. Look at the italicized verbs in each of these sentences:

Maya *swiped* a handkerchief and daintily *blew* her noise. (*swiped* and *blew* = two events happening at almost the same moment; both verbs are in past tense)

Maya *will be* in court tomorrow, and the judge *will rule* on her case. (*will be* and *will rule* = two events happening at the same time; both verbs are in future tense)

Maya *is* extremely sad about the possibility of a criminal record, but she *remains* hopeful. (*is* and *remains* = states of being existing at the same time; both verbs are in present tense)

If two actions take place at the same time (or nearly the same time), use the same tense for each verb.

Q. Fill in the blank with the correct form and tense of the verb in parentheses.

EXAMPLE

Yesterday, overreacting to a tiny taste of arsenic, Mike _____ his evil twin brother of murder. (accuse)

A. **accused** The clue here is *yesterday*, which tells you that you're in the past.

Fill in the blank with the correct form and tense of the verb in parentheses.

YOUR TURN

6 Fashion is important to David, so he always _____ the latest and most popular style. (select)

7 Last year's tight, slim lines _____ David, who, it must be admitted, does not have a tiny waist. (challenge)

8 While David _____ new clothes, his fashion consultant is busy on the sidelines, recommending stripes and understated plaids to minimize the bulge factor. (buy)

9 David hopes that the next fashion fad _____ a more mature, rounded figure like his own. (flatter)

10 Right now, Diane _____ an article for the fashion press stating that supertight leather is best. (write)

11 She once _____ a purple suede pantsuit, which clashed with her orange "I Love Motorcycles" tattoo. (purchase)

12 While she _____ the pantsuit, the salesperson urged her to "go for it." (model)

13. Two days after Diane's shopping spree, Grace _____ about show-offs who "spend more time on their wardrobes than on their spark plugs." (mutter)

14. However, Diane knows that Grace, as soon as she raises enough cash, _____ in a suede outfit of her own. (invest)

15. David, as always, _____ in with the last word when he gave Grace and Diane the "Fashion Train Wreck of the Year" award. (chime)

16. Two minutes after receiving the award, Diane _____ it on a shelf next to her "Best Dressed, Considering" medal. (place)

17. Every time I see the medal, I _____ what "considering" means. (wonder)

18. Grace _____ it to me in detail yesterday. (explain)

19. "We earned the medal for considering many fashion options," she _____. (state)

20. David, who _____ Diane tomorrow, says that the medal acknowledges the fact that Grace is fashion-challenged but tries hard anyway. (visit)

Not picture-perfect: Understanding the perfect tenses

Now for the perfect tenses, which, I must tell you, are not always used perfectly. In fact, these three tenses — present perfect, past perfect, and future perfect — may give you gray hair, even if you're only 12 years old. And they have progressive forms, too! As with the simple tenses, each tense has a no-frills version called by the name of the tense: present perfect, past perfect, and future perfect. The progressive form adds -ing to the mix. The progressive is a little more immediate than the other form, expressing an action or state of being in progress. In this section, I give you some examples of these tenses so that you can identify each. In a later section, "Employing the perfect tenses correctly," I go into detail about when and how to use each tense.

Present perfect and present perfect progressive

The two present perfect forms show actions or states of being that began in the past but are still going on in the present. These forms are used whenever any action or state of being spans two time zones — past and present.

First, check out examples with plain present perfect tense:

Roger and his friends *have spent* almost every penny of the inheritance. (*have spent* = present perfect)

For years, Lulu's best friend, Roger, *has pleaded* with her to stop robbing banks. (*has pleaded* = present perfect)

Now glance at these progressive examples:

> Roger *has been studying* sculpture for 15 years without learning any worthwhile techniques. (*has been studying* = present perfect progressive)

> Lulu and Lola *have been counting* sheep all night. (*have been counting* = present perfect progressive)

Table 12-4 shows the correct form of the regular verb *walk* in the present perfect and present perfect progressive. The pronouns *he, she, it,* and *they* represent every possible noun.

Table 12-4 Present Perfect Tense

Singular Subject	Plain Present Perfect	Present Perfect Progressive	Plural Subject	Plain Present Perfect	Present Perfect Progressive
I	have walked	have been walking	we	have walked	have been walking
you	have walked	have been walking	you	have walked	have been walking
he, she, it, they	has walked	has been walking	they	have walked	have been walking

As you see in the table, all present perfect verbs rely on the helping verb *have* — except for the one that pairs with *he, she,* and *it* (and the nouns those pronouns represent). For that sort of pairing, you need *has.* The singular *they* is generally paired with *have.*

Past perfect and past perfect progressive

Each of these forms places an action in the past in relation to another action in the past. In other words, these tenses create a timeline that begins some time ago and ends at some point before *now.* At least two events are on the timeline. Here are some examples of the past perfect tense:

> After she *had sewn* up the wound, Doctor Eliza Reed realized that her watch was missing. (*had sewn* = past perfect)

> The watch *had ticked* inside the patient for 10 minutes before the nurse discovered its whereabouts. (*had ticked* = past perfect)

Compare the preceding sentences with examples of the past perfect progressive:

> The patient, Jeb Smith, *had been considering* a malpractice lawsuit but changed his mind. (*had been considering* = past perfect progressive)

> Doctor Reed *had been worrying* about legal penalties until her patient dropped his case. (*had been worrying* = past perfect progressive)

Check out Table 12-5 for the past perfect tense, both plain and progressive. The pronouns *he, she, it,* and *they* represent every possible noun.

Table 12-5   Past Perfect Tense

Singular Subject	Plain Past Perfect	Past Perfect Progressive	Plural Subject	Plain Past Perfect	Past Perfect Progressive
I	had walked	had been walking	we	had walked	had been walking
you	had walked	had been walking	you	had walked	had been walking
he, she, it, they	had walked	had been walking	they	had walked	had been walking

Isn't this a lovely tense? Every subject pairs with the same plain or progressive verb. Little to learn and much to love — that's the past perfect tense when you're choosing a form. Lots to learn and much to dislike — that's the past perfect tense when you're deciding when it's needed. I tackle that topic in "Employing the perfect tenses correctly," later in this chapter.

Future perfect and future perfect progressive

These two forms talk about events or states of being that have not happened yet in relation to another event even further in the future. In other words, these forms create another timeline, with at least two events or states of being on it, all after the present moment.

First, take a look at the plain version of the future perfect:

> Appleby *will have eaten* the entire pie by the time recess ends. (*will have eaten* = future perfect.)

> When Appleby finally arrives at grammar class, the teacher *will have* already *outlined* at least 504 grammar rules. (*will have outlined* = future perfect)

Now take a look at the progressive form of the future perfect tense:

> When the clock strikes 4, Appleby *will have been chewing* for 29 straight minutes. (*will have been chewing* = future perfect progressive)

> By the time Appleby finishes dessert, his teacher *will have been explaining* the virtues of a healthy diet to her class for a very long time. (*will have been explaining* = future perfect progressive)

Ready for a table? Table 12-6 presents the future and future progressive forms of the regular verb *walk*. The pronouns *he, she, it,* and *they* represent every possible noun.

Table 12-6   Future Perfect Tense

Singular Subject	Plain Future Perfect	Future Perfect Progressive	Plural Subject	Plain Future Perfect	Future Perfect Progressive
I	will have walked	will have been walking	we	will have walked	will have been walking
you	will have walked	will have been walking	you	will have walked	will have been walking
he, she, it, they	will have walked	will have been walking	they	will have walked	will have been walking

As you probably noticed, all the plain future perfect forms are the same, and so are all the future progressive forms. You can relax when you're selecting the proper form to match a subject. Sadly, you can't relax when you're deciding when to use the future perfect. I tackle that issue in the next section, "Employing the perfect tenses correctly."

Employing the perfect tenses correctly

As anyone who watches crime dramas knows, figuring out when events happened isn't always an easy task. The perfect tenses are (sorry, I can't resist) a *perfect* example of this fact. But investigators do know how to put events in order. Read on, and you'll know too.

To clarify what's happening and when, timelines accompany some of the examples in this section. Match the events on the timeline to the verbs in the sentence to see where in time each tense places an action.

Case 1: Beginning in the past and continuing in the present

You started something, and you haven't stopped. What do you need for this situation? Present perfect tense. This tense mixes two words. One appears to be present (the helping verbs *has* and *have*) and the other past (*walked, told, been, smashed,* and so on). Take a look at these examples:

> I *have gone* to the school cafeteria every day for six years, and I *have* not yet *found* one tasty item.

This sentence means that at present I am still in school, still trying to find something to eat, and for the past six years I was in school also, trudging to the cafeteria every day, searching for a sandwich that doesn't taste like wallpaper paste.

> Bertha *has* frequently *texted* Charles, but Charles *has* not *texted* Bertha back.

This sentence means that in the present Bertha hasn't given up yet; she's still trying to reach Charles. In the past, Bertha also texted Charles. In the present and in the past, Charles hasn't bothered to check his phone, which now contains 604 messages from Bertha. Check out Bertha's activity on this timeline:

© *John Wiley & Sons, Inc.*

As with the simple present tense, the present perfect tense takes two forms. One is called *present perfect,* and the other, *present perfect progressive.* The progressive is a little more immediate, but nothing you need to worry about.

Q. Correct or incorrect? If you see an error in verb tense, correct it.

Isabel moved into that building in 2010 and lived there ever since.

A. **incorrect lived → has lived** This sentence makes a connection to the present. At one point in the past, *Isabel moved.* So far, so good. Because she began to live there in the past and continues to live there in the present, you need the present perfect verb *has lived.*

Case 2: Events at two different times in the past

Everything in the past happened at exactly the same moment, right? If this statement were true, history tests would be much easier, and so would grammar. To describe events in the past randomly, without worrying about when one occurred in relation to another, simple past tense is fine. To establish chronological order for more than one past event, you need past perfect tense. Check out the italicized verbs in this sentence:

Maya *had* already *swiped* the handkerchief when she *discovered* the joys of honesty.

This example has two events to think about, one taking place before the other. (Unfortunately for Maya, the joy of honesty came after the theft, for which she's doing two years in the penitentiary.) Note the timeline:

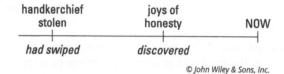

© John Wiley & Sons, Inc.

For two events in the past, write the earlier event with *had* and the more recent event in simple past tense (without *had*). Scan these examples:

Because of Lulu's skill with a needle, where a hole in the sock *had gaped,* a perfect heel now *enclosed* her tender foot. (Event 1: The hole in the sock gapes; Event 2: The mended sock covers the foot.)

After Roger *had inserted* the microfilm, he *sewed* the hole in the now illegal teddy bear. (Event 1: Roger inserts the microfilm; Event 2: Roger sews the bear.)

After the song *had* been *played* at least 12 times, Michael *shouted,* "Enough!" (Event 1: The song is played 12 times; Event 2: Michael loses it.)

A common error is using *had* for everything. Wrong! Don't use *had* unless you're consciously putting two events in order:

WRONG: Maya had dried her eyes and then she had gone to see the judge.

RIGHT: After Maya had dried her eyes, she went to see the judge.

Note: You may encounter one other use of *had,* the subjunctive, which I tackle later in this chapter.

EXAMPLE

Q. Which sentence tells you about events that happened at different times?

(A) When Maya slipped the judge a $50 bill, she hoped for mercy.

(B) Because Maya had slipped the judge a $50 bill, she hoped for mercy.

A. (B) Sentence (B) reports events at different times. Maya tried the bribe at 10 a.m. and spent the rest of the day planning a trip to Rio (canceled when her jail term was announced). In Sentence A, Maya bribes and hopes at the same time.

Case 3: More than two past events, all at different times

This rule, which also relies on past perfect tense, is similar to the one described in Case 2. Apply this rule when you talk about more than two events in the past if — and only if — the order matters:

> Maya *had baked* a cake and *had inserted* a sharp file under the icing before she *began* her stay in jail.

Now the timeline is as follows:

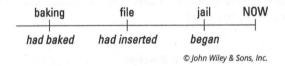

© *John Wiley & Sons, Inc.*

What do you notice? The most recent event (*began her stay in jail*) is written without *had*. In other words, the most recent event is in simple past tense. Everything that happened earlier is written with *had* — that is, in past perfect tense.

Here are some examples:

> Michael *had planned* the shower, and Lola *had* even *planned* the wedding by the time Ella *agreed* to marry Larry. (Events 1 and 2: Michael and Lola visit the wedding coordinator. Event 3: Ella makes the biggest mistake of her life.)

> Elizabeth *had composed* a sonata, *played* it for royalty, and *signed* a recording contract before she *reached* her tenth birthday. (Events 1, 2, and 3: Elizabeth writes the music, performs it, and makes big bucks. Event 4: Elizabeth's mom puts ten candles on the cake.)

In the last example, three verbs — *composed*, *played*, and *signed* — form a list of the actions that Elizabeth performed before her tenth birthday. They all have the same subject (*Elizabeth*). With your sharp eyes, you probably noticed that the word *had* precedes only *composed*, the first verb of the three. You may omit the word *had* in front of *played* and *signed* because they are part of the same list and they all have the same subject. The reader knows that the word *had* applies to all three of the verbs. In other words, the reader understands that *Elizabeth had composed, had played,* and *had signed.*

If you want to talk about events in the past without worrying about specific times, go for simple past tense. You *went* on vacation, *had* a great time, *sent* some postcards, *ate* a lot of junk food, and *came* home. You don't need *had* in this description because the order isn't the point. You're just making a general list. Use *had* when the timing matters. Don't overuse it.

Q. Which event in this sentence is most recent?

Where patriots had fought and wise founders had written a constitution, a fast-food restaurant stood.

A. **a fast-food restaurant stood** Here's a timeline for the whole sentence: People with a better idea fight the old government and write a plan for a new government. In the free and successful society that results, someone builds a restaurant after suing the land-marks preservation commission for the right to tear down a historic building.

Case 4: Two events in the future

Leaving the past behind, it's time to turn to the future. Read this sentence:

Nicky *will have completed* all 433 college applications before they are due.

Nicky's applications will be error-filled — he spelled his name *Niky* on at least three — but they will be done before the deadline. *Deadline* is the important word here, at least regarding verb tense. The *will have* form of the future, also called *future perfect tense*, involves a deadline. You don't necessarily see two verbs in the sentence, but you do learn about two events:

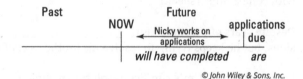

© John Wiley & Sons, Inc.

Use the future perfect tense to talk about the earlier of the two events.

Here are a few examples:

By 9 tonight, Egbert *will have* successfully *scrambled* the secret message. (The deadline in the sentence is 9 o'clock.)

Anna *will have left* for Mount Everest by the time the mountaineering supply company sends her gear. (The deadline in the sentence is the delivery of mountain-climbing supplies.)

Q. Which sentence is correct?

(A) Bernard will have tossed the salad tonight.

(B) Bernard will have tossed the ball out the window before anyone has a chance to catch it.

A. **(B)** Future perfect tense involves a deadline, and sentence (A) doesn't have one. In sentence (B), it's *before anyone has a chance to catch it.*

Write the correct perfect-tense form of the verb in parentheses in the blank.

21 Mike _____ on thin ice for 2 hours when he heard the first crack. (skate)

22 Diane _____ Mike for years about his skating habits, but he just won't listen. (warn)

23 After Mike _____ an hour in the emergency room, the doctor examined him and announced that the skater was healthy enough to go home. (wait)

24 By the time today's skating trip ends, David _____ a total of 32 hours for his friend and _____ countless outdated magazines in the hospital waiting room. (wait, read)

25 Grace _____ to speak to Mike ever since he declared that "a little thin ice" shouldn't scare anyone. (refuse)

26 Before the emergency room visit is over, Tim _____ quietly to both combatants. (speak)

27 Despite years of practice, Tim _____ success only on rare occasions, but he keeps trying to resolve his brother's conflicts anyway. (achieve)

28 Since childhood, Tim's conflict-resolution technique _____ of violent finger pokes in the fighters' ribs, but he is trying to become more diplomatic. (consist)

Speaking of the past and things that never change

Humans love to gossip, so I bet that right now you have a story to tell. Because you're telling (actually, retelling) something that already happened, your base of operations is past tense. Note the past-tense verbs in italics:

> She *caught* Arthur with Stella, but he *told* her that he was only tying Stella's bow tie and not nibbling her neck. Then she *said* that Arthur *brought* her a box of candy with a note saying that no one else *had* eyes like hers.

The verb tenses are all in the past because that's where a *summary of speech* usually resides. Therefore, even if Stella still *has* incomparable eyes, in this paragraph the verb *had* is better. However, if you're talking about something that will never change, that is forever true, present tense is the only one that makes sense, no matter what else is going on in the sentence. Take a look at this example:

WRONG: Marty told me that the earth was a planet.

WHY IT IS WRONG: What is the earth now, a bagel? The unchanging fact, that the earth is a planet, must be expressed in present tense, despite the fact that all other summarized speech should be in past tense.

RIGHT: Marty told me that the earth is a planet.

TIP

Another important exception to the rule that you must summarize speech in the past tense pops up when you're writing about a work of art or literature. See "Romeo lives! Writing about literature and art in present tense," later in this chapter, for more information.

WARNING

A common error is to switch from one tense to another with no valid reason. I often hear people say something like, "He finally texted me. He says that the big dance is a waste of time!" The writer begins in past tense *(texted)*, but the next two verbs *(says, is)* are in present tense. Penalty box. If you start in past tense, stay there, unless the content requires a change. The correct way to explain what went on is to say, "He finally texted me. He said the big dance was a waste of time!"

EXAMPLE

Q. Circle the verb that's correct in Standard English. The choices are in parentheses.

At yesterday's tryouts for a reality show, Roberta (tells/told/will tell) the producer that she (likes/liked/will like) dangling 20 feet above the ground.

A. **told, liked.** The first answer is easy. If the tryouts were yesterday, the fact that Roberta spoke to the producer has to be in past tense. *Told* is past tense. The second part is trickier. Roberta may continue to like dangling, but past tense is the way to go because a person's feelings can always change.

YOUR TURN

Circle the verb that's correct in Standard English. The choices are in parentheses.

29 The director, Arthur Marlow, explained to the candidates that he (has/had/will have) to select a maximum of 30 contestants.

30 Most of the contestants eagerly replied that they (want/wanted/would want) to make the final 30.

31 Those selected were set to compete against 14 other candidates, because the producers made two separate groups, and 15 (equals/equaled) half of 30.

32 Roberta, who (likes/like/had liked) to play hard to get, screamed at the director that he (doesn't/didn't) have the faintest idea how to select the best applicants.

33 One contestant who didn't make the cut, Michael Hooper, told me that Roberta (is/was/had been) the clear winner of the first two challenges.

34 For the first challenge, a tulip, which (is/was) a flower, (is/was) thrown into a container resembling a basketball hoop.

35 During the second contest, a statue resembling a watermelon, which (is/was) a fruit, (is/was) moved around the racetrack by contestants who (wear/wore) blindfolds.

(36) Michael whispered something surprising: Roberta (fails/failed/had failed) the psychological test.

(37) The test comes from Austria, which (is/was) in Europe.

(38) A month ago, when the psychologist (asks/asked) Roberta her feelings about television shows, Roberta said that the comedy shows (do/did) present a problem.

(39) "Why (don't/didn't) you like comedy shows?" (continues/continued) the psychologist.

(40) Roberta told me the psychologist (annoys/annoyed) her.

Romeo lives! Writing about literature and art in present tense

At the end of Shakespeare's *Romeo and Juliet* (spoiler alert!), the title characters die. Yet every time you open the book or go to the theater, they live again. Because the events in the book or play are always happening, present tense is generally the best choice when you're writing about literature. Not always, of course. At times, you want to explain that one event in the story occurred before another. In such a situation, past tense may be the only way to talk about the earlier event. Other types of art also rely on present tense. In Picasso's famous portrait of Gertrude Stein, for example, her massive form *looks* — not *looked* — like a monument carved from a block of stone.

TIP

If you write about the act of creating art, past tense is best, as in "Picasso *painted* Gertrude Stein's portrait." (*Painted* is a past-tense verb.)

Q. In the blank, write the correct form of the verb in parentheses.

In Jane Austen's *Sense and Sensibility*, Marianne _____ her ankle. (sprain)

EXAMPLE

A. **sprains** To write about this event in Austen's novel, present tense is best.

YOUR TURN

(41) The horizontal bands in Lola's paintings _____ random, but she _____ the width of each band using a complex formula involving the day's winning lottery number. (appear, calculate)

(42) Lola, who also _____ a mystery novel, _____ a character who _____ his lunch money every day and often _____. (write, create, bet, win)

(43) The character's name _____ William, and in every scene he _____ a hat. (be, wear)

44 William _____ the murder of a veterinarian; in one scene a parrot
_____ a vital clue, but William _____ the bird, perhaps because
earlier the parrot _____ William. (investigate, provide, ignore, bite)

45 When asked about her writing, Lola _____ that William
_____ loyalty, honor, and the need for a reliable birdseed pro-
vider. (maintain, represent)

The rebels: Dealing with irregular verbs

In earlier sections of this chapter, I provide charts showing you how regular verbs change in
each tense. If only all verbs were regular! But in grammar, as in life, some rebels don't follow
the rules. In Chapter 5, I show you the simple-tense forms of three irregular verbs you need
nearly every time you speak or write: *be, have,* and *do.* Here I show you some irregular *participles,*
including participles of those three verbs.

Don't let the name scare you. Participles are not mysterious; as you may guess from the spelling, a *part*iciple is simply a *part* of the verb. Each verb has two participles, a present participle
and a past participle. The present participle is the *-ing* form of the verb. Sometimes the spelling
changes a bit (an *e* may disappear or a letter may double), but other than spelling, present participles won't give you any trouble. Table 12-7 shows a selection of regular present participles.

Table 12-7   **Examples of Regular Present Participles**

Verb	Present Participle
ask	asking
beg	begging
call	calling
dally	dallying
empty	emptying
fill	filling
grease	greasing

Now for the irregulars. Dozens and dozens of English verbs have irregular participles, as well
as irregular past-tense forms. I won't list all the irregular verbs here, just a few you may find
useful in everyday writing. If you have questions about a particular verb, check your dictionary.

In Table 12-8, the first column is the infinitive form of the verb. (The infinitive is head of its
verb family and generally appears with *to* — *to laugh, to cry, to learn grammar,* and so on.) The
second column is the simple past tense. The third column is the past participle, which is combined with *has* (singular) or *have* (plural) to form the present perfect tense. The past participle
is also used with *had* to form the past perfect tense.

Table 12-8   Forms of Irregular Participles

Verb	Past	Past Participle
be	was/were	been
bear	bore	borne
become	became	become
begin	began	begun
bite	bit	bitten
break	broke	broken
bring	brought	brought
catch	caught	caught
choose	chose	chosen
come	came	come
do	did	done
drink	drank	drunk
drive	drove	driven
eat	ate	eaten
fall	fell	fallen
feel	felt	felt
fly	flew	flown
freeze	froze	frozen
get	got	got or gotten
go	went	gone
have	had	had
know	knew	known
lay	laid	laid
lead	led	led
lend	lent	lent
lie	lay	lain
lose	lost	lost
ride	rode	ridden
ring	rang	rung
rise	rose	risen
run	ran	run
say	said	said
see	saw	seen
set	set	set
shake	shook	shaken
sing	sang	sung
sink	sank or sunk	sunk
sit	sat	sat
sleep	slept	slept
speak	spoke	spoken

Verb	Past	Past Participle
steal	stole	stolen
swim	swam	swum
take	took	taken
throw	threw	thrown
wear	wore	worn
win	won	won
write	wrote	written

Q. Fill in the blanks with the correct irregular form, working from the verb and the tense in parentheses.

EXAMPLE

With one leg 3 inches shorter than the other, Natalie seldom _____ into first base, even when the team was desperate for a base hit. (slide, past)

A. **slid** No -ed for this past tense! *Slid* is the irregular past form of the verb *slide*.

Fill in the blanks with the correct irregular form, working from the verb and the tense in parentheses.

YOUR
TURN

46. If you discover a piece of pottery on the floor, look for Natalie, who _____ many vases because of her tendency to dust far too emotionally. (break, present perfect)

47. Once Natalie _____ with sadness at her first glimpse of a dusty armchair. (shake, past)

48. David, a duster himself, _____ a manual of daily furniture maintenance. (write, past)

49. The manual, titled *Dust or Die*, _____ to the top of the bestseller list. (rise, past)

50. Nearly all the copies _____ by fanatical cleaners. (buy, past perfect)

51. David once dusted the fire alarm so forcefully that it went off; the firefighters weren't amused because David _____ the fire alarm a little too often. (ring, past perfect)

52. The fire chief promptly _____ to speak with the mayor about David's false alarm. (go, past)

53. The mayor _____ an investigation into a new category of offenses, "False Dust Alarms." (begin, present perfect)

54. "I _____ to a new low," sighed David. "I hear that Arthur _____ a new hobby. Maybe Natalie and I can get one, too." (sink, present perfect; find, present perfect)

55. Natalie and David _____ origami, a paper-folding art. (choose, past)

56. One day they _____ miniature houses out of paper that they _____ out. (build, past; throw, past perfect)

Giving Voice to Verbs

Verbs can have two voices. Not the growl you hear in questions like "What do you think you're doing, young lady?" or the honey that flows through romantic exchanges like "You're beautiful!" but *active* or *passive*. Take a look at these two examples:

> "The cookies *were eaten* before the party began," reported Ben, quietly brushing some crumbs off his mouth.

> "I *ate* the cookies," reported Ben, regretfully handing the empty plate to his mother.

How do the two versions differ? Grammatically, Ben's statement in the first sentence focuses on the receiver of the action, the *cookies*, which received the action of *eating*. The verb is *passive* because the subject is not the person or thing doing the action. Instead, it's the person or thing receiving the action. In Sentence 2, the verb is in active voice because the subject (*I*) performed the action (*ate*). When the subject is acting or being, the verb is *active*.

TIP

To find the subject of a sentence, locate the verb and ask *who?* or *what?* before the verb. For more information on subjects, see Chapter 8.

Here are some active and passive verbs:

> Lulu *gives* a free-tattoo coupon to Lola. (active)

> Lola *is convinced* by Lulu to get a tattoo. (passive)

> Roger *urges* Lulu to visit the tattoo parlor, too. (active)

> Lulu *is tattooed* by Lola. (passive)

EXAMPLE

Q. Label the verbs in these sentences as active or passive.

The omelet <u>was made</u> with egg whites, and the yolks <u>were discarded</u>.

Egbert <u>slobbers</u> when he <u>eats</u>.

A. **was made, were discarded = passive, slobbers, eats = active**

YOUR TURN

Label the verbs in these sentences as active or passive.

57. The job opening <u>was posted</u> on a networking site.

58. About a thousand resumes <u>were emailed</u> within an hour.

59 When Pete <u>heard</u> about the position the day after it <u>was announced</u>, he <u>was</u> already too late.

60 The job <u>had been given</u> to someone else.

61 Pete <u>set</u> an alert on his computer. Now, when resumes <u>are requested</u> for someone with a degree in philosophy, Pete <u>is informed</u> immediately.

62 Philosophers <u>have</u> a high unemployment rate, and Pete <u>must apply</u> for every position he <u>can find</u>.

63 "Only so many burgers <u>can be flipped</u> before boredom <u>sets</u> in," <u>explained</u> Pete.

64 Pete <u>has been given</u> free room and board by friends and relatives for the past year, but they <u>are losing</u> patience with him.

65 Lola <u>offered</u> free tattoo training, but Pete <u>refused.</u>

66 "I <u>think</u> for a living," he <u>declared.</u>

Getting Your Verbs in the Proper Mood

Are you in the *mood* for more information about verbs? Or, to reword the question, what mood is your verb in? I can imagine your reaction: What? Verbs have moods? Yes, they do — three, to be exact. You probably don't have to worry about two of them, the *indicative* and the *imperative*, because most likely you use them correctly already. It's the third — the *subjunctive* — that causes problems. In this section, I run through the easy moods and then spend more time on the difficult one.

Stating the facts: Indicative

Almost all verbs are in indicative mood. *Indicative* is the everyday, this-is-what-I'm-saying mood, good for questions and statements. The verbs in the two sentences you just read, along with the verbs in the sentence you're reading right now, are in the indicative mood. So are the verbs italicized in these sentences:

Betsy *displayed* her musical range when she *played* a Bach concerto and a hip-hop song in the same concert.

Will Larry *be* the principal tenant of Honeymoon Hotel when Ella *agrees* to marry him?

Egbert often *dreams* about his family farm.

Commanding your attention: Imperative

Don't worry about imperatives. Just use them! The verbs in the first two sentences of this section are in the imperative mood. *Imperative verbs* give commands. Most imperative verbs have no written (or spoken) subject. Instead, the subject in an imperative (command) sentence is *you-understood.* The word *you* usually does not appear before the imperative verb. The reader or listener simply understands that *you* is implied.

Here's a command: Read these examples of imperative verbs, italicized in the following sentences:

> *Eat* a balanced diet.
>
> *Climb* every mountain.
>
> *Calculate* the odds.
>
> *Fake* a sincere smile to impress your boss.

There's almost nothing you can do wrong in creating an imperative sentence, so this topic is a free pass. *Go* fishing, or if you're in the mood to torture yourself, *move* on to the subjunctive. (The italicized verbs are in the imperative mood.)

Discovering the possibilities: Subjunctive

Headache time! The subjunctive mood is rare, but it draws errors the way honey attracts flies. The most common use of a subjunctive verb is to state something that is contrary to fact. The other, much less common situation is to express an indirect command.

Using subjunctives with "were"

Tevye, the main character in the musical *Fiddler On the Roof,* sings, "If I Were a Rich Man" with the sadness of a man who knows that he'll never be anything but poor. Tevye's song is about a *condition contrary to fact* — something that is not true. Take note of the verb in the title: *were.* Normally (that is to say, in an indicative sentence), the subject–verb pair would be *I was.* But Tevye sings *If I were* because he isn't a rich man. The verb *were* is in subjunctive mood.

TIP

Unless someone is going to quiz you on it, don't worry about the terminology. Just know that if you're expressing a condition contrary to fact, you need the verb *were* for present and future ideas. (Past tense is different. I discuss the past subjunctive form in "Forming subjunctives with 'had,'" later in this section.) Here are some examples of present and future tense:

> SUBJUNCTIVE: If Roger *were* an honorable spy, he would not reveal the secret computer code.
>
> WHY IT'S SUBJUNCTIVE: Roger is not an honorable spy, and he's going to blab the secret.
>
> WHAT THE NORMAL SUBJECT–VERB PAIR WOULD BE: Roger was.

> SUBJUNCTIVE: If Anna *were* less talented in mathematics, she would have taken fewer algebra courses.
>
> WHY IT'S SUBJUNCTIVE: Anna's a math genius, the kind of student who always says that the test was "totally hard" and then wrecks the curve with a 96.
>
> WHAT THE NORMAL SUBJECT–VERB PAIR WOULD BE: Anna was.

To sum up, in subjunctive sentences, *were* is usually all you need. Here are a few details about subjunctive for present or future statements of conditions contrary to fact:

» Use *were* for all subjects in the part of the sentence that expresses what is not true. (If she *were* entranced by Max's explanation.)

» Don't insert *were* in a sentence expressing a real possibility. (If it *is raining* this afternoon, we'll have the picnic tomorrow.)

» For the other part of the sentence, use the helping verb *would*. (Lola *would stare* at him in silence.)

» Never use the helping verb *would* in the untrue part of the sentence. For example:

WRONG: If I would have been president, I would ask the Martian colony to secede.

RIGHT: If I were president, I would ask the Martian colony to secede.

WRONG: Daniel acted as though he would have been grammarian-in-chief.

RIGHT: Daniel acted as though he were grammarian-in-chief.

EXAMPLE

Q. Which sentence is correct?

(A) Ella would be happier if she would have been in the Marines.

(B) Ella would be happier if she were in the Marines.

A. **B** The *if* part of sentence B contains a subjunctive verb *(were)* because it expresses something that is not true. The *if* part of the sentence should never contain the helping verb *would*.

TIP

As though may sometimes sub for *if* in a condition–contrary–to–fact sentence. Check out this example:

SUBJUNCTIVE: Egbert hurtled through the room *as though* a giant metal device were intent on scrambling him.

WHY IT'S SUBJUNCTIVE: Egbert isn't being pursued by giant egg-beaters. He is actually hurtling through the room because he is on a skateboard with one bad wheel.

WHAT THE NORMAL SUBJECT–VERB PAIR WOULD BE: *Giant metal device was.*

Forming subjunctives with "had"

Subjunctives also pop up from time to time with the helping verb *had.* For past-tense sentences, the *had* belongs in the part of the sentence that is contrary to fact. The contrary-to-fact (that is, the lie) part of the sentence may begin with *if,* or the *if* may be understood.

Just for comparison, in non-subjunctive sentences, the past tense is expressed by a single-word, past-tense verb. The *had* form, in a non-subjunctive sentence, is used only to show one action happening before another. (See "It's All in the Timing: Tense," earlier in this chapter, for more information.) Here are a few examples of the past subjunctive:

SUBJUNCTIVE WITH THE WORD *IF:* If Lola *had known* about the secret computer code, she would not have thrown away the flash drive.

SUBJUNCTIVE WITHOUT THE WORD *IF: Had* Lola *known* about the secret computer code, she would not have thrown away the flash drive.

WHY IT'S SUBJUNCTIVE: Lola knew nothing about the secret code; Roger told her he was working on a new video game.

WHAT THE NORMAL SUBJECT–VERB PAIR WOULD BE: *Lola knew.*

SUBJUNCTIVE WITH THE WORD *IF:* If Larry *had married* less often, he would have enjoyed this ceremony more.

SUBJUNCTIVE WITHOUT THE WORD *IF: Had* Larry *married* less often, he would have enjoyed this ceremony more.

WHY IT'S SUBJUNCTIVE: Larry has been married more times than he can count.

WHAT THE NORMAL SUBJECT–VERB PAIR WOULD BE: *Larry married.*

EXAMPLE

Q. Which sentence is correct?

(A) If Betsy would have played the tuba, the gang would have listened to her CD more often.

(B) If Betsy had played the tuba, the gang would have listened to her CD more often.

A. **B** Betsy played the piano, not the tuba, so subjunctive is appropriate. The word *would* is never part of an *if* statement.

Expressing an indirect command

I can tell you what to do:

Peel me a grape.

Peel is in the imperative mood, giving a direct command. But some command statements are indirect:

Woods decreed that all her grapes be peeled.

The verb *be* is in the subjunctive mood in that sentence. (The normal subject–verb pairing is *grapes are.*)

Insert the correct form of the verb in parentheses.

YOUR TURN

67 If the examiner _____ an appointment available in the late afternoon, Ellen would have signed up to take her road test then. (offer)

68 The test would have gone better if Ellen _____ a morning person. (be)

69 "If it _____," explained the instructor, "you will be required to take the test as soon as the roads are plowed." (snow)

70 If the snowplow _____ the entire route, Ellen would have passed. (complete)

71 Unfortunately, the supervisor of the snow removal crew ordered that the highways _____ cleaned first. (be)

72 If Ellen _____ her test on a dry, sunny afternoon, she would have passed. (take)

Practice Questions Answers and Explanations

1. **will inflate** = future

2. **was living** = past progressive

3. **are establishing** = present progressive

4. **were, blew** = past

5. **will be joining** = future progressive, clears = present

6. **selects** Notice the time clues? The first part of the sentence contains the present-tense verb *is*, and the second part includes the word *always*. You're in the present with a recurring action.

7. **challenged** Another time clue: *last year's* places you in the past.

8. **is buying** or **buys** The second verb in the sentence *(is)* takes you right into the store with David, watching the unfolding action. Present progressive tense gives a sense of immediacy, so *is buying* makes sense. The plain present tense *(buys)* works nicely also.

9. **will flatter** The key here is *next*, which puts the sentence in the future.

10. **is writing** The time clue *right now* indicates an ongoing action, so the present progressive form *is writing* works well here.

11. **purchased** Diane's bad-taste splurge happened *once*, which means it took place in the past.

12. **was modeling** or **modeled** The second part of the sentence includes the verb *urged*, which places the action in the past. I like the past progressive *(was modeling)* because the word *while* takes you into the process of modeling, which went on over a period of time. However, the sentence makes sense even when the process isn't emphasized, so *modeled* is also an option.

13. **muttered** or **was muttering** The clue to the past is *two days after*. The second answer gives more of a you-are-there feel, but either is correct.

14. **will invest** The time words here, *as soon as*, tell you that the action hasn't happened yet.

15. **chimed** If he *gave*, you're in past tense.

16. **placed** The expression *Two minutes after* tells you that you're in the past, so you know that the action of placing the award on the shelf is in past tense.

17. **wonder** The time clue here is *every time*, which tells you that this action is still happening at the present time and should be in present tense.

18. **explained** The word *yesterday* is a dead giveaway; go for past tense.

19. **stated** The saga of Grace and Diane's award is in past tense, and this sentence is no exception. Even without the story context, you see that the first verb *(earned)* is in past tense, which works nicely with the past-tense verb *stated*.

20. **will visit** The time clue is *tomorrow*, which places the verb in the future.

21. **had been skating** or **had skated** You have two actions in the past: the skating and the hearing. The two hours of skating came before the hearing, so you need past perfect tense. Either the plain or the progressive form works here.

22   **has been warning** or **has warned** The second half of the sentence indicates the present (*won't listen*), but you also have a hint of the past (*for years*). Present perfect is the best choice because it links past and present. I like the immediacy of progressive here (I can hear Diane's ranting), but plain present perfect is okay as well.

23   **had waited** or **had been waiting** The waiting preceded the doctor's announcement, so you should use past perfect. Progressive adds a you-are-there feel, but isn't necessary.

24   **will have waited, will have read** The deadline in the sentence (*the end of today's trip*) is your clue for future perfect tense.

25   **has refused** Notice the present-past link? Mike declared and Grace is acting now. Hence, you need present perfect tense.

26   **will have spoken** The future perfect needs an end point (in this sentence, the end of the hospital visit) before which the action occurs.

27   **has achieved** Because the sentence states that he keeps trying, you have a present-tense idea that's connected to the past (*despite years of practice* and *on rare occasions*). Present perfect connects the present and past.

28   **has consisted** This sentence has a past-tense clue (*since childhood*). The sentence tells you about the past (*at times*) and the present (*is trying*), so present perfect is the one you want.

29   **had** The tip-off is the verb *explained*, which tells you that you're summarizing speech. Go for the past tense *had*.

30   **wanted** *Replied* is a clue that you're summarizing speech, so *wanted*, the past tense, is best. The last choice, by the way, imposes a condition (they *would* do something under certain circumstances). Because the sentence doesn't impose a condition, that choice isn't appropriate.

31   **equals** Math doesn't change, so the verb must be in present tense.

32   **likes, didn't** The first choice has nothing to do with summary of speech and is a simple statement about Roberta. The present tense works nicely in this spot. The second choice is a speech summary (well, a *scream* summary, but the same rule applies), so the past-tense verb *didn't* fills the bill.

33   **was** The sentence tells you that *Michael Hooper told*. The past tense works here for summary of speech.

34   **is, was** A tulip is always a flower, so you need present tense for the first parenthesis. In the second, you're simply telling what happened on the show, so past tense rules.

35   **is, was, wore** A watermelon is always a fruit, and permanent conditions are best expressed by present tense, so *is* should be your choice in the first spot. The next two verb choices require past tense because they express actions that took place in the past.

36   **failed** You can arrive at the answer in two separate ways. If Michael *whispered*, the sentence is summarizing what he said. Another way to look at this sentence is to reason that Michael is telling you something that already happened, not something happening in the present moment. Either way, the past tense *failed* is best.

37   **is** Austria isn't going anywhere, so this sentence expresses an unchangeable condition. Go for present tense.

38   **asked, did** The first answer comes from the fact that the psychological test was in the past. The second is summary of speech (Roberta's words) and calls for past tense.

39. **don't, continued** Give yourself a pat on the back if you got this one. The quotation marks indicate that the words are exactly what the psychologist said. The speech isn't summarized; it's quoted. The present tense makes sense here because the tester is asking Roberta about her state of mind at the moment. The psychologist's action, however, took place in the past, so *continued*, a past-tense verb, is what you want for the speaker tag.

40. **annoyed** Straight summary of speech here, indicated by the verb *told*. Therefore, past tense is best.

41. **appear, calculated** The first part of the sentence describes a work of art, so the present tense verb *appear* is what you want. The second part of the sentence explains how the artwork was created, an event that took place in the past. Therefore, opt for the past-tense verb *calculated*.

42. **wrote, created, bets, wins** The first two verbs describe the process of making art, and because the process is over, past tense works well here. The second two verbs apply to the artwork (the novel), so you need present tense.

43. **is, wears** For these simple statements about a literary work, use present tense.

44. **investigates, provides, ignores, bit** The first three statements are in present tense, as comments about literature and art generally are. The last verb is a little tricky; the sentence explains why William ignores the bird by citing an earlier event. Because the order of events is important, the past-tense verb *bit* is best.

45. **maintained, represents** The verb *asked* tells you that Lola's comments also took place in the past, so the past-tense verb *maintained* is correct. The symbolic meaning, however, doesn't change and should be expressed in present tense.

46. **has broken**

47. **shook**

48. **wrote**

49. **rose**

50. **had been bought**

51. **had rung**

52. **went**

53. **has begun**

54. **have sunk, has found**

55. **chose**

56. **built, had thrown**

57. **was posted = passive** The *job opening* didn't do the posting. It received the action of the verb, *was posted*, so it's passive.

58. **were emailed = passive** The *resumes* (subject) didn't do the emailing. Whoever sent them did. *Were emailed* is a passive-voice verb.

(59) **heard = active, was announced = passive, was = active** The subject of *heard* is *Pete*, who performs the action. *Heard* is in active voice. *It* is the subject of *was announced*, but *it* didn't do any announcing. *It* receives the action and is a passive-voice verb. *He* is the subject of *was*, an active-voice verb.

(60) **had been given = passive** The subject is *job*, which didn't perform the action of giving. The verb is in passive voice.

(61) **set = active, are requested = passive, is informed = passive** *Pete* is the subject in the first sentence, and *Pete set*. Therefore, *set* is an active-voice verb. In the second sentence, the subject is *resumes* and the verb is *are requested*. The resumes don't perform the action, so the verb is passive. Next up, in the same sentence, is the subject-verb combo *Pete is informed*. Because the action happens to the subject, the verb *is informed* is passive, too.

(62) **have = active, must apply = active, can find = active** The first subject-verb pair is *Philosophers have*. *Philosophers* are the ones who *have*, so this is an active-voice verb. Next, you have *Pete must apply*. *Pete* is doing the applying, so the verb is in active voice. Finally, *he can find* creates another active-voice situation because *he* does the action expressed by *can find*.

(63) **can be flipped = passive, sets = active, explained = active** Three subject-verb pairs appear here: *burgers can be flipped*, *boredom sets*, and *explained Pete*. The first is passive because the flipping happens to the *burgers*. The next pair contains an active-voice verb because the *boredom* does the setting. The last pair reverses the usual subject-verb order, but that doesn't matter. This is an active-voice verb because the subject, *Pete*, does the action, *explained*.

(64) **has been given = passive, are losing = active** The subject, *Pete*, isn't giving. Instead, he's receiving, so *has been given* is in passive voice. The second pair has an active-voice verb because *they* are doing the action *(losing)*.

(65) **offered = active, refused = active** Two active-voice verbs here because Lola did the offering and Pete did the refusing.

(66) **think = active, declared = active** You may have a hard time thinking that *think* is in active voice, but it is because the subject, *I*, does the thinking. The subject of *declared*, *he*, also does the action, so *declared* is also an active-voice verb.

(67) **had offered** The subjunctive *had offered* is needed for this statement about available time slots because it's contrary to fact. No time slot was available in the afternoon.

(68) **were** Ellen likes to sleep until midafternoon. Because she's not a morning person, the subjunctive verb *were* expresses condition-contrary-to-fact. The verb *were* is better than *had been* because Ellen still *is* not a morning person, and *had been* implies that her grouchiness is in the past.

(69) **snows** Surprise! This one isn't subjunctive. The instructor is talking about a possibility, not a condition that didn't occur. The normal indicative form, *snows*, is what you want.

(70) **had completed** The plow didn't finish (the clue here is *would have passed*), so subjunctive is needed.

(71) **be** For this indirect command, *be* is the form you want.

(72) **had taken** This condition-contrary-to-fact sentence calls for subjunctive.

If you're ready to test your skills a bit more, take the following chapter quiz that incorporates all the chapter topics.

Whaddya Know? Chapter 12 Quiz

Quiz time! Complete each problem to test your knowledge on the various topics covered in this chapter. You can then find the solutions and explanations in the next section.

Correct or incorrect? Check the tense, mood, and voice of each underlined verb. Bonus points: Correct any errors you find.

To: All Employees

From: Sally

Subject: Paper clips

It (1) <u>had come</u> to my attention that some employees (2) <u>will be bending</u> paper clips nearly every day. Last week, a few managers also (3) <u>stealed</u> 12 boxes! The clips we (4) <u>use</u> these days (5) <u>were made</u> of steel. Steel (6) <u>was</u> a metal, and replacing broken metal items (7) <u>costed</u> us thousands of dollars last year! In my ten years as your boss, I (8) <u>gave</u> you a fair deal. If you (9) <u>would have been</u> respectful, I (10) <u>would have given</u> you all raises. I (11) <u>thinked</u> of you as responsible employees, but I (12) <u>had been</u> wrong. Therefore, I order that managers (13) <u>are locking</u> up paper clips from today onward. I (14) <u>inspecting</u> supply closets last week and (15) <u>have been found</u> bent clips. As of now, paper clip bending (16) <u>is prohibited</u>. (17) <u>Obeyed</u> the rules! If you (18) <u>do</u> not, you (19) <u>have been fired</u>. (20) <u>Think</u> about your future, please!

Answers to Chapter 12 Quiz

1. **incorrect** → *has come* or *came* The past perfect tense, *had come*, is appropriate only when you have two events in the past and you want to show that one is earlier than the other.

2. **incorrect** → *have been bending* The present perfect tense connects the present to the past. The employees were bending clips in the past and continue to do so in the present.

3. **incorrect** → *stole* The past-tense form of the irregular verb *steal* is *stole*.

4. **correct** *These days* tells you that you need the present tense verb *use*.

5. **incorrect** → *are made* The phrase *these days* indicates that you need present tense.

6. **incorrect** → *is* The fact that steel is a metal will not change, so present tense is appropriate here.

7. **incorrect** → *cost* This irregular verb does not form the past tense with *-ed.*

8. **Incorrect** → *have given* The writer is still the boss, so you need present perfect tense, which connects the past and present.

9. **incorrect** → *had been* The subjunctive is needed in this condition-contrary-to-fact statement.

10. **correct** The *would* form of the verb is appropriate in this subjunctive situation.

11. **incorrect** → *thought* This irregular verb does not add *-ed* to form the past tense.

12. **incorrect** → *was* Past tense works here; past perfect, which places two past events in order, does not.

13. **Incorrect** → *lock* This indirect command takes the subjunctive.

14. **Incorrect** → *was inspecting* or *inspected* Past and past progressive both work here.

15. **incorrect** → *found* You need an active verb here, not a passive one.

16. **correct** The word *now* tells you that you need present tense.

17. **incorrect** → *Obey* For this command, use the imperative form.

18. **correct** No subjunctive is required here, because there is a possibility, not a condition-contrary-to-fact.

19. **incorrect** → *will be fired* You need future tense and passive voice here. The subject, *you* (understood), will be on the receiving end of the firing.

20. **correct** The command is correctly expressed.

Chapter **13**

Agreement: Choosing Singular or Plural Verbs and Pronouns

bout a million Hollywood movies have tried to convince the public that opposites attract. Grammarians have clearly not gotten that message. Instead of opposites, the English language prefers matching pairs — singular with singular and plural with plural. Matching, in grammar terminology, is known as *agreement*.

In this chapter, I show you how to make subjects and verbs agree. I also discuss some of the trickier members of the pronoun family and the evolving rules of agreement that govern them.

Agreeing Not to Disagree

Agreement in the real world means that you share the same beliefs. In the world of grammar, the concept of agreement rests on these principles:

» Nouns (the part of speech that names people, places, things, and ideas) may be singular or plural.

- Pronouns (the part of speech that replaces or refers to nouns or other pronouns) may also be singular or plural. A few pronouns keep the same form for both singular and plural situations.

- When you're writing a sentence, you need a subject — a noun or a pronoun. A singular subject pairs with a singular verb. A plural subject pairs with a plural verb. For more information on subjects and verbs, turn to Chapter 8.

- A pronoun must agree with its *antecedent*, the word the pronoun refers to or replaces. Singular pronouns match up with singular nouns or other singular pronouns. Plural pronouns pair with plural nouns or other plural pronouns. A few pronouns (*you* and *who,* for example) do double duty, correctly referring to both singular and plural antecedents.

- Traditional rules call for a pronoun referring to a person to match the gender of the antecedent. As our understanding of gender has become more complex, so has pronoun usage. The underlying principles that should guide you are clarity and respect. I discuss pronoun-gender issues in detail in the Introduction and provide more information on gendered and nongendered pronouns in Chapter 4.

In most situations, making a match between a subject and a verb or a pronoun and an antecedent is simple. Once in a while, though, you face some complicated pairs. (Grammar resembles life in this regard, doesn't it?) In this chapter, you see how to deal with both easy and tough decisions about agreement.

Making Subjects and Verbs Agree: The Basics

The good news is that most of the time English verbs have only one form for both singular and plural. "I *burp*" and "the dinosaurs *burp*" are both correct, even though *I* is singular and *dinosaurs* is plural. You have to worry only in the few special circumstances I list here. I've italicized the subjects and verbs in the examples so that you can locate them quickly:

- **Talking about someone in the present tense requires different verb forms for singular and plural.** The singular verb ends in *s,* as in *he spits* (singular) and *babies spit* (plural).

- **Verbs that include *does/do* or *has/have* change forms for singular and plural.** Singular verbs use *does* or *has.* ("*John does paint* his toenails blue. *He has stated* that fact.") Plurals use *do* and *have.* ("*Do* the toenails *need* more polish? No, *they have* plenty already.")

- ***I* pairs with plural action verbs.** The pronoun *I* is always singular, but *I go* is correct, not *I goes.*

- ***You* and *they* may be either singular or plural, but these pronouns always pair with plural verbs.** *You catch* a robber, whether *you* refers to one person or ten, and *they go* to jail, whether you're talking about several robbers or a solo robber who uses gender-neutral pronouns.

- **The verb *be* changes form according to the noun or pronoun paired with it.** Chapter 5 introduces you to the entire "be" verb family.

Matching Subjects and Verbs in Some Tricky Situations

Most of the time the subject–verb match is obvious. Occasionally, you have to put on your thinking cap and analyze the sentence to come up with the proper form. In this section, I show you how to deal with compound subjects and subjects that may be tough to locate.

Compound subjects

Sentences with two subjects joined by *and* take a plural verb, even if each of the two subjects is singular. (Think of math: One subject + one subject = plural subject.)

Here are some sample sentences with subjects joined by the word *and:*

> The picture and its frame belong together. (*picture + frame* = plural subject, *belong* = plural verb)

> Romance and garlic do not mix. (*romance + garlic* = plural subject, *do mix* = plural verb)

TIP

When you join two subjects with *or*, however, you're not adding. You're offering two alternatives. Does that make your subject singular? Not necessarily. It depends on the two subjects. Check out "Either and neither, alone or with partners," later in this chapter, for more information.

Ignoring distracting descriptions

When you're checking agreement, focus on the subject–verb pair and ignore any descriptions that appear between them. Phrases such as "of the books" and "except for" and longer expressions such as "who golfs badly" and "which takes the cake" don't affect the subject–verb pair. Be especially wary of expressions that appear to create a plural (*as well as, in addition to*). Grammatically, these aren't part of the subject. Take a look at this sentence:

> The IRS agent, *fascinated by my last three tax returns,* is ruining my vacation plans. (*agent* = subject, *is ruining* = verb)

By ignoring the distracting phrase about my tax returns in this sentence, you can easily pick out the singular subject–verb pair. Here's another:

> The deductions, *not the tax rate,* are a problem. (*deductions* = subject, *are* = verb)

In this sentence, *deductions* is the plural subject. If you let yourself be distracted, you may incorrectly match your verb to *rate*, which is singular.

REMEMBER

Ignore all distracting phrases, and find the true subject–verb pair. Also, if any IRS employees are reading this book, please ignore my tax returns.

EXAMPLE

Q. Select the correct verb from the choices in parentheses.

The boy in the first row, along with all the kids posting on Instagram, (is ignoring, are ignoring) the teacher.

The girls in the last row, but not the football player in the hall, (is taking, are taking) selfies.

A. **is ignoring** The subject is *boy*. The boy *is ignoring. Along with all the kids posting on Instagram* is a distraction (in this case, a prepositional phrase).

are taking Ignore the distraction (in real life and in grammar) and match the plural subject *girls* with the plural verb *are taking.*

YOUR TURN

Select the correct verb from the choices in parentheses.

1. Hinting delicately that the teacher's attitude about his missing homework assignments (is, are) unfair, John (raises, raise) his eyebrows.

2. John, whose homework (has been, have been) late every day this year, says that he (suffers, suffer) from a toe condition that makes it impossible for him to study.

3. We (am, is, are) not buying his story.

4. You probably (believes, believe) John because you (gives, give) everyone the benefit of the doubt.

5. (Does, Do) you think that John's friends always (recognizes, recognize) the truth?

6. (Has, Have) his story fallen on disbelieving ears?

7. I never (knows, know) when John (is avoiding, are avoiding) reality.

8. Sometimes he (tells, tell) very odd tales.

9. Why (does, do) everyone listen to his stories?

10. Nadine, like most of John's closest friends, (was, were) completely dismayed by John's dishonest tendencies.

11. He, along with some other students, (cheats, cheat) on tests all the time.

12. The principal, in addition to everyone else on the faculty, (has wanted, have wanted) to expel John for years.

13. Recently, John (has, have) spent a lot of time in detention.

14. In the far corner of the cafeteria (is, are) six teachers taking turns as detention supervisors.

15. During today's detention, John and Dana (was texting, were texting) each other instead of studying math.

16. When he works on a math problem, John often (removes, remove) his cellphone from his pocket and (searches, search) for the correct answer.

17. "In my pocket (is, are) 15 math formulas," John once remarked.

18. John, as well as his friend Dana, (was caught, were caught) cheating on a midterm exam.

19. Only once (was, were) a guidance counselor and an assistant principal unjust in their punishment.

20. The counselor, in addition to John's parents, (wants, want) to set him on the path to success.

Each and every

Each and *every* are powerful words; they're strong enough to change any subject following them into a singular idea. Sneak a peek at these examples:

Each shoe and sock *is* in need of mending, but Larry refuses to pick up a needle and thread.

Every dress and skirt in that store *is* on sale, and Lulu's in a spending mood.

Do these sentences look wrong to you? Granted, they appear to have plural subjects: two things *(shoe and sock)* in Sentence 1, and another two items *(dress and skirt)* in Sentence 2. However, when *each* or *every* is placed in front of a group, you take the items in the group one at a time. In the first example, the subject consists of one *shoe*, one *sock*, another *shoe*, another *sock*, and so on. Therefore, the sentence needs a singular verb to match the singular subject. Ditto for the *dress and skirt* reference in the second example.

EXAMPLE

Q. Select the correct verb from the choices in parentheses.

Every knife and fork (has been, have been) snatched by that raccoon!

A. **has been** The word *every* creates a singular subject, which matches the singular verb *has been.*

Either and neither, alone or with partners

Two more pain-in-the-pick-your-body-part pronouns are *either* and *neither,* when they're without their partners *or* and *nor.* When they're alone, *either* and *neither* are always singular, even if you insert a huge group (or just a group of two) between them and their verbs. Take a look at these sentences:

Either of the two armies *is* strong enough to take over the entire planet.

Neither of the football captains *has shown* any willingness to accept Lola as quarterback.

Because the sample sentences mention *armies* and *captains*, you may be tempted to choose plural verbs. Resist the temptation! No matter what the sentence says, if the subject is *either* or *neither*, singular is the correct way to go. That last statement applies to pronouns also:

> *Each* of the armies follows *its* own leader.

> *Neither* of the men will change *his* strategy.

Note: In the last example, I used the masculine words *men* and *his.* When you don't know the gender of the antecedent or when more than one gender is represented, *their* is a good match. See "A Note about Pronouns" in the Introduction for more information.

When *either* and *neither* appear with their best pals, *or* and *nor*, two things happen. First, *either* and *neither* turn into conjunctions (joining words). Second, if they're joining two subjects, the subject that is closer to the verb determines whether the verb is singular or plural. Yes, that's right! This is a grammar problem you can solve with a ruler. The same ruler — er, I mean *rule* — applies when two subjects are joined by *or* alone. Check out these examples:

> Either *Ella* or *her bridesmaids have eaten* the icing on the cake. (*bridesmaids* = closer subject, a plural noun; *have eaten* = plural verb)

> Five *maids* of honor or *Ella has* an engraved cake knife. (*Ella* = closer subject, a singular noun; *has* = singular verb)

> Neither *the waiters* nor *Larry is planning* to eat the leftovers. (*Larry* = closer subject, a singular noun; *is planning* = singular verb)

If the *either/or* and *neither/nor* sentence is a question, the subject closer to the part of the verb that changes governs the singular/plural decision. Take a look at these examples:

> *Does* either *Ella* or *her cousins want* antacids? (*Ella* = subject closer to the helping verb *does*; *Ella* = singular subject, *does want* = singular verb)

> *Do* neither *her cousins* nor *Ella know* how to cook? (*cousins* = subject closer to the helping verb *do*; *cousins* = plural subject, *do know* = plural verb)

Q. Select the correct verb from the choices in parentheses.

EXAMPLE Either the window washers or the glassblower (is, are) responsible for the broken pane.

Neither the glassblower nor the window washers (admits, admit) to the crime.

(Does, Do) either the glassblower or the window washers have insurance?

A. **is** The subject closer to the verb is *glassblower*, a singular noun. Pair it with the singular verb *is.*

admit The subject closer to the verb is *washers*, a plural noun. Pair it with the plural verb *admit.*

Does The subject closer to the part of the verb that changes is *glassblower*, a singular noun. Pair it with the singular verb *does.*

Select the correct verb from the choices in parentheses.

21. Neither the fire marshal nor the police officers (was, were) aware of Lola's new production.

22. Either of the backup singers (has, have) enough talent to become a star.

23. Every orchestra seat and balcony box (has been, have been) reserved for Lola's family.

24. Neither her partners nor Lola (is, are) willing to speculate on the critical reception.

25. (Has, Have) either the director or the musicians agreed on a contract?

26. I don't understand Lola's interest in musical theater, because neither of Lola's parents (sings, sing) on key.

27. Perhaps every one of Lola's ten productions (is, are) a form of rebellion.

28. This show or the next two productions (is, are) sure to make a profit.

29. Every Tony and Oscar on Lola's shelf (is, are) a testament to her talent.

30. Neither of her Tony awards, however, (has, have) been polished for a long time.

Five puzzling pronouns

Earlier in this chapter, I told you to ignore descriptions when making subjects and verbs agree. Now I must confess that this rule has one small exception — actually, five small exceptions. Five pronouns — five little words that just have to stir up trouble — change from singular to plural because of the prepositional phrases that follow them. The five troublemaking pronouns are

>> any

>> all

>> most

>> none

>> some

Here they are with some prepositional phrases and verbs. Notice how the prepositional phrase affects the verb number.

Singular	Plural
any of the information is	*any* of the magazines are
all of the pie is	*all* of the shoes are
most of the city is	*most* of the pencils are
none of the pollution is	*none* of the toenails are
some of the speech is	*some* of the sleepwalkers are

See the pattern? For these five words, the prepositional phrase is the determining factor. If the phrase refers to a plural idea, the verb is plural. If the phrase refers to a singular idea, the verb is singular.

When you refer to one of these pronouns with another pronoun (in other words, if *any, all, most, none,* or *some* is an antecedent), follow the usual rule: Singular pairs with singular, and plural pairs with plural. Take a look at these examples:

> All of the pie is gone because I ate it. (*all* = singular, *it* = singular)

> None of the birds are in their nest. (*none* = plural, *their* = plural)

Q. Select the correct verb from the choices in parentheses.

EXAMPLE

All of the dancers in Lola's musical (is, are) required to get butterfly tattoos.

Most of the songs (has, have) been written already, but the out-of-town tryouts suggest that more work is needed.

A. **are** The pronoun *all* refers to *dancers*, a plural, so *are* is the correct verb.

have The pronoun *most* refers to *songs*, a plural, so the plural verb *have* is correct.

The ones, the things, and the bodies

Three pronoun "families" — the *ones*, the *things*, and the *bodies* — merit special attention. Take a peek at the family tree:

> The ones: *one, everyone, someone, anyone, no one*

> The things: *everything, something, anything, nothing*

> The bodies: *everybody, somebody, anybody, nobody*

These pronouns are always singular and match with singular verbs, even if they're surrounded by prepositional phrases that express plurals, as in these examples:

> Everybody *is* happy because *no one has caused* any trouble and *anything goes.*

> *Anyone* in the pool of candidates for mayor *speaks* better than Lulu.

> *One* of the million reasons to hate you *is* your tendency to argue about grammar.

> Not *one* out of a million spies *creates* as much distraction as George.

The rules for matching these pronouns to other pronouns have changed over the years. I discuss this topic in more depth in "A Note about Pronouns" in the Introduction. The operative principle now, for an increasing number of grammarians, is to match the "ones, the things, and the bodies" with *they, their, them,* and *theirs* if a pronoun is needed: Everyone was asked to bring *their* gum to the bubble-popping contest.

Q. Select the correct verb or pronoun from the choices in parentheses.

Why (does, do) no one understand that watching paint dry is boring?

Everybody has brought (his, her, their) brush, but I prefer spray paint.

A. **does** The pronoun *no one* is singular and pairs with the singular verb form *does*, part of the complete verb *does understand*.

their Many years ago, the correct answer in Standard English would have been *his*, regardless of the gender of the people included in the pronoun *everybody*. Some grammarians would insert *his or her* here, but these days, many prefer the pronoun *their*, understood in this context to be singular.

Select the correct verb or pronoun from the choices in parentheses.

31 Nobody (paints, paint) a room as fast as Ruthie.

32 Everyone (agrees, agree) that she tries hard, but not all of her work (is/was) neat.

33 Most of the walls in the library (has dried, have dried) already.

34 Much of the floor (seems, seem) dusty.

35 (Has, Have) someone sanded the shelves?

36 (Was, Were) any of the books wrapped in plastic?

37 I can't believe that nothing at all (has been done, have been done) to protect those treasures!

38 Someone (has, have) to confess to knocking over that paint can and staining Mom's favorite book.

39 Not one of the workers (wants, want) to admit guilt, because everybody (is/are) afraid of Mom's temper.

40 All of the sloppy painters (bears, bear) some responsibility.

Agreeing with Relative Pronouns

Who, which, and *that* are hardworking pronouns that often hold down two jobs: (1) representing or replacing a noun and (2) relating one idea to another. The second job is the reason their official grammar designation is *relative pronoun*. As usual, the grammatical term doesn't matter. What does matter is determining whether the relative pronoun is singular or plural in the context of the sentence. If the relative pronoun replaces or refers to a singular noun or pronoun, it's singular and pairs with a singular verb. If the relative pronoun replaces or refers to a plural pronoun, it magically turns into a plural pronoun and pairs with a plural verb.

When you match a verb or another pronoun to *who, which,* or *that,* think carefully about meaning. Then decide which verb or pronoun you need. Some examples:

> Elena, *who is* taking *her* first standardized test tomorrow, is nervous. (*who* = *Elena* = singular, *is* and *her* = singular)

> The students *who are taking* the test next week have to devote all *their* free time to studying. (*who* = *students* = plural, *are taking* and *their* = plural)

> The jug *that is falling* off the ledge is valuable, and I can't afford to replace *it.* (*that* = *jug* = singular, *is falling* and *it* = singular)

> The books *that interest* me are not in the library. I will have to buy *them.* (*that* = *books* = plural, *interest* and *them* = plural)

TIP

At times, locating the antecedent for *who, which,* or *that* can be tough, unless you apply your best reading comprehension skills. Compare these sentences, which are similar but not at all the same:

> Lindy is one of the nurses who love to dance. (*who* refers to *nurses,* a plural, because more than one nurse loves to dance)

> Lindy is the only one of the nurses who wears dancing shoes to work. (*who* refers to *one,* a singular, because no one but Lindy wears dancing shoes to work)

REMEMBER

Find the antecedent — the word that *who, which,* or *that* refers to — and match the pronoun and verb to the antecedent.

Q. Select the correct verb from the choices in parentheses.

Val, who (is, are) quite a comedian, will perform this evening.

Only the jokes that (gets, get) a big laugh will be posted on the Comics United website.

EXAMPLE

A. **is** The relative pronoun *who* stands in for *Val,* a singular subject, so you need a singular verb.

get The relative pronoun *that* refers to *jokes,* a plural subject, so you need a plural verb.

YOUR TURN

Guided by the conventions of Standard English, select the verb or pronoun from the choices in parentheses.

41 The microphone that (has broken, have broken) twice in the past three hours needs a permanent repair.

42 No one wants to hear a screech, which (harms, harm) eardrums.

43 Members of the audience who (sits, sit) near the stage are most at risk.

44 The microphone Val uses is the only one in the club that (does, do) not work.

45 She could easily select one of the mics that (functions, function) without a screech, but she thinks this one is good luck.

46 All my favorite comedians, who (performs, perform) here on special occasions, have worked with that microphone.

47 "That little piece of metal carries luck, which (is, are) what I need when I'm on stage," Val explained.

48 Val told three new jokes that (was, were) successful.

49 Social media websites, which (influences, influence) potential customers, lit up when Val posted the video.

50 One of the websites, which (has, have) 3 million followers, immediately crashed.

Politics and Other Irregular Subjects

The problem with politics is agreement — not the shouting that far too many people engage in these days, but rather subject–verb agreement. Specifically, *politics* looks plural because it ends in *s*. So do *mathematics, news, economics, civics, physics, athletics, measles, mumps,* and *analysis*. Surprise! All these words are singular and pair with singular verbs and, if these words are antecedents, with singular pronouns:

> *Politics is* never absent from Bob's conversation; he devotes most of his comment to *it*. (*politics, is, it* = singular)

> Roger thinks that *mathematics is* overrated, but he studies *it* anyway. (*mathematics, is, it* = singular)

> The *news* about the nutritional content of doughnuts *is* not encouraging. Did you hear *it*? (*news, is, it* = singular)

> "*Is measles* a serious disease?" asked Egbert. "I think I have *it*. (*Is, measles, it* = singular)

Another word — *statistics* — may be either singular or plural. If you're talking about numbers, you're in plural territory:

> Check the *statistics. They show* that grammar knowledge is declining. (*statistics, they, show* = plural)

If you're talking about a course or a field of study, *statistics* is singular:

> *Statistics is* a difficult course. I took *it* last year. (*Statistics, is, it* = singular)

The English language also has words that are always *plural*. Here are a few of them: *eyeglasses, pants, trousers, jeans, shorts,* and *scissors.* (Did you notice how many of those words refer to clothing? Strange.) Other common plural-only nouns are *credentials, acoustics, earnings, headquarters,* and *ceramics.* Plural verbs pair up with these words when they're subjects, and plural pronouns match them when they're antecedents:

> My *eyeglasses are broken.* I dropped *them* yesterday. (*eyeglasses, are broken, them* = plural)

When in doubt, check your dictionary and remember to match singular nouns with singular verbs and plural nouns with plural verbs.

Q. Select the appropriate verb or pronoun from the choices in parentheses.

The news (was/were) announced at noon yesterday.

A. **was** *News* is singular and takes the singular verb *is*.

Select the appropriate verb or pronoun from the choices in parentheses.

51 No matter how little studying Angie does, economics (is, are) an easy A+ for her.

52 The data (shows, show) that Angie never blows an economics test.

53 It's difficult to drag Angie away from the television, though she believes that the media (has, have) too much power.

54 Angie once screamed at a political rally, "My scissors (cuts, cut) your taxes."

55 The pair of scissors she waved (is, are) in a museum now.

Practice Questions Answers and Explanations

(1) **is, raises** You have two singular subjects here, which must match with singular verbs: *attitude is* and *John raises*.

(2) **has been, suffers** The verbs *has* and *suffers* are singular, as they should be, because the subject–verb pairs are *homework has* and *he suffers*.

(3) **are** The plural verb *are* matches the plural subject *we*.

(4) **believe, give** The pronoun *you* always takes a plural verb such as *believe* or *give*.

(5) **Do, recognize** Both verbs are plural, matching the plural subjects *you* and *friends*. In the first pair, the subject is tucked between the two parts of the verb because the sentence is a question.

(6) **Has** You need a singular verb here to pair with the singular subject, *story*.

(7) **know, is** The pronoun *I*, though singular, pairs with the plural form *know*. *John* is singular and matches the singular verb *is*.

(8) **tells** Because *he* is singular, the verb *tells* must also be singular.

(9) **does** The pronoun *everyone* is singular, so it matches the singular form *does*, which is part of the verb *does listen*.

(10) **was** The singular verb *was* matches the singular subject *Nadine*. Did you select *friends*? That's part of a description, which is a prepositional phrase, not a subject.

(11) **cheats** The singular subject is *He*, so you need *cheats*, a singular verb. The description, *along with some other students*, is irrelevant.

(12) **has** Pay no attention to the interrupter, *in addition to everyone else on the faculty*. The true subject, *principal*, is singular and takes the singular verb *has*.

(13) **has** This one's easy. *John* is a singular subject, which pairs nicely with the singular verb *has*.

(14) **are** The subject is *teachers*, a plural noun that matches the plural verb *are*.

(15) **were** *John and Dana* — two people, linked together by *and* (not to mention failing math grades) — equal a plural subject, so you need the plural verb *were*.

(16) **removes, searches** Because *John* is singular, the verbs *removes* and *searches* must also be singular.

(17) **are** *In my pocket* is a prepositional phrase. Ignore it! Identify the plural subject, *formulas*, and match it with the plural verb *are*.

(18) **was** Ignore the description (*as well as. . . Dana*) and zero in on the true subject, *John*, which matches the singular verb *was*.

(19) **were** You have a plural subject (*guidance counselor and assistant principal*), so you need the plural verb *were*.

(20) **wants** Ignore *in addition to John's parents* and match the verb to the singular subject, *counselor*.

(21) **were** The subject *police officers* is closer to the verb than *marshal*. Because *police officers* is plural, the verb must also be plural.

(22) **has** Without a partner, *either* is always singular and rates a singular verb, such as *has*.

(23) **has** The word *every* has the power to change *seat and balcony box* to a singular concept requiring the singular verb *has*.

(24) **is** The closest subject is *Lola*, so the singular verb *is* wins the prize, the only prize likely to be associated with Lola's musical.

(25) **Has** The sentence has two subjects, *director* and *musicians*. The subject *director* is closer to the part of the verb that changes, so the singular verb *Has* must match the singular subject *director*.

(26) **sings** When it's all alone, the pronoun *neither* is always singular and needs to be paired with the singular verb *sings*.

(27) **is** Did I catch you here? The expression *ten productions* suggests plural, but the subject is actually *one*, a singular.

(28) **are** The word *or* is alone in this sentence, but the rule is the same. The closer subject is plural, so you need the plural verb *are*.

(29) **is** The word *every* has the power to turn any subject to singular; *is* is a singular verb.

(30) **has** The pronoun *neither* is singular, so the singular verb *has* is needed here.

(31) **paints** The pronoun *nobody* is singular and pairs with the singular verb *paints*.

(32) **agrees, is** The pronoun *everyone* is singular, so you need the singular verb *agrees*. After the pronoun *all*, you see the prepositional phrase *of her work*. Because the phrase refers to *work*, which is singular, you want the singular verb *is*.

(33) **have dried** You have the plural *walls* in the phrase following the pronoun *most*, so you need the plural verb *have dried*.

(34) **seems** The object of the preposition is the singular noun *floor*, so the singular verb *seems* is correct.

(35) **Has** The pronoun *someone* is singular, so the singular verb *has* is correct here.

(36) **Were** After the pronoun *any*, you see the prepositional phrase *of the books*. The word *books* is plural, so *were* is the correct verb.

(37) **has been done** The singular pronoun *nothing* pairs with the singular verb *has been done*.

(38) **has** The singular pronoun *someone* takes the singular verb *has*.

(39) **wants, is** The pronoun *one* is singular, and a singular verb *(wants)* should pair with it. The singular verb *is* pairs with the singular pronoun *everybody*.

(40) **bear** The pronoun *all* is plural in this sentence, as it refers to *painters*, a plural, which matches the plural verb *bear*.

(41) **has broken** The pronoun *that* stands in for *microphone*, a singular noun, so the singular verb *has broken* fits here.

(42) **harms** The pronoun *which* stands in for *screech*, a singular noun, so you need the singular verb *harms*.

(43) **sit** The pronoun *who* stands in for *members*, a plural noun, so the plural verb *sit* is correct.

44. **does** The pronoun *that* refers to *the only one*, a singular expression, so the singular verb *does* fits here.

45. **function** The pronoun *that* refers to *mics*, a plural noun that should be paired with the plural verb *function*.

46. **perform** The pronoun *who* stands in for *comedians*, a plural noun that should be paired with the plural verb *perform*.

47. **is** The pronoun *which* stands in for *luck*, a singular noun, so the singular verb *is* fits here.

48. **were** The pronoun *that* stands in for *jokes*, a plural noun, so the plural verb *were* is correct.

49. **influence** The pronoun *which* stands in for *websites*, a plural noun, so you need the plural verb *influence*.

50. **has** You're talking about *one of the websites*, not all of them, so *which* is singular and needs the singular verb *has*.

51. **is** The noun *economics* is singular, so you need the singular verb *is*.

52. **show** The noun *data* is plural and pairs nicely with the plural verb *show*.

53. **have** You need the plural verb *have* to pair with the plural subject *media*.

54. **cut** *Scissors* is a plural subject and should match the plural verb *cut*.

55. **is** The subject (*pair*) is singular and takes the singular verb *is*.

If you're ready to test your skills a bit more, take the following chapter quiz that incorporates all the chapter topics.

Whaddya Know? Chapter 13 Quiz

Quiz time! Complete each problem to test your knowledge on the various topics covered in this chapter. You can then find the solutions and explanations in the next section.

Read this email from a store owner to an annoying customer. Following the rules of Standard English, mark the underlined words correct or incorrect and revise any incorrect expressions.

From: Johnson Jewelry

To: George Baker

Subject: Watch

The clerks at our store, who (1) <u>takes</u> pride in serving our customers' needs, (2) <u>have struggled</u> to meet your expectations. Your frequent visits to Johnson Jewelry, the best store in town, (3) <u>is</u> welcome, but each of the clerks (4) <u>have found</u> a problem after you leave. Yesterday evening, for example, Annie Leon noticed that one of the watches you examined (5) <u>were broken</u>. All of the watches (6) <u>was</u> in good condition in the morning. I am sure that either you or your friends (7) <u>were</u> misbehaving, and one of the group (8) <u>are</u> responsible for the missing minute hand. Furthermore, some of the gold on the back of the watch (9) <u>was</u> scraped off. Neither of the inscriptions on the watch (10) <u>were</u> legible. Everyone (11) <u>have</u> to take responsibility for (12) <u>their</u> actions. (13) <u>Does</u> either you or your friends intend to pay for repairs to the watch? Much work (14) <u>is</u> to be done before the watch is fit to sell. I also expect payment for the earring and toe ring that (15) <u>was damaged</u>.

Answers to Chapter 13 Quiz

1. **incorrect (take)** The pronoun *who* represents *clerks*, a plural, which pairs with the plural verb *take*.

2. **correct** The plural verb *have struggled* pairs correctly with the plural subject *clerks*.

3. **incorrect (are)** Ignore the distractions and pair the plural subject, *visits*, with the plural verb *are*.

4. **incorrect (has found)** The pronoun *each* takes a singular verb, which in this sentence is *has found*.

5. **incorrect (was broken)** Because the subject is *one*, the singular verb *was broken* is correct.

6. **incorrect (were)** The pronoun *all* is plural in this sentences because the object of the preposition is *watches*, a plural noun.

7. **correct** In an *either/or* sentence, match the verb to the closer subject, which is the plural *friends*, correctly paired with the plural verb *are*.

8. **incorrect (is)** The subject of the sentence is *one*, and *one* pairs with a singular verb.

9. **correct** The prepositional phrase following the pronoun *some* centers on *gold*, a singular noun, so you need a singular verb *was*.

10. **incorrect (was)** The pronoun *neither* is singular, so you must pair it with the singular verb *was*.

11. **incorrect (has)** The pronoun *everyone* is singular and correctly pairs with the singular verb *has*.

12. **correct** Most grammarians pair the gender-neutral pronoun *their* with the singular antecedent *everyone*.

13. **incorrect (Do)** The subject is *you*, which never pairs with a singular verb.

14. **correct** The subject is *work*, a singular noun, which matches the singular verb *is*.

15. **incorrect (were damaged)** The subject is *earring and toe ring*. That's two things, and therefore a plural. You need the plural verb *were damaged*.

IN THIS CHAPTER

» **Identifying the correct pronouns to act as subjects and objects**

» **Choosing between *who* and *whom***

» **Showing possession with pronouns**

» **Selecting the right pronoun for appositives and comparisons**

» **Attaching the appropriate pronoun to some nouns ending in *-ing***

Chapter **14**

Solving Pronoun Case

or *me? She* or *her? He* or *himself?* Or (gasp) *who* or *whom?* These are questions about pronoun case that millions of suffering grammar students have struggled to answer. The good news is that there's actually a logic to pronoun choice. Chapter 4 offers an overview of pronouns; Chapter 13 delves into pronoun number (singular or plural). In this chapter, I focus on helping you select the correct pronoun case.

While We're on the Subject: Choosing Pronouns to Act as Subjects

The subject is the person or thing doing the action or being talked about in the sentence. (For more on locating the subject, see Chapter 8.) You can't do much wrong when you have the actual name of a person, place, or thing as the subject — in other words, a noun — but pronouns are another story.

Legal subject pronouns for formal English include *I, you, he, she, it, we, they, who,* and *whoever.* If you want to avoid a grammatical felony, stay away from *me, him, her, us, them, whom,* and *whomever* when you're selecting a subject. Also avoid the *−self* pronouns (*myself, himself, herself, ourselves,* and so forth) when you're scouting out a subject, unless you insert one next to another subject for emphasis, as in *I myself will select the proper pronoun.*

TIP

A bunch of lovely pronouns are suitable as subjects and as objects: *either, neither, each, every, some, any, most, none, all, many, everyone, someone, no one, everybody, somebody, nobody, everything, something, nothing, few, both,* and *several.*

Here are some examples of pronouns as the subject of a sentence:

> *I* certainly did tell Lulu not to remove her nose ring in public! *(I* is the subject of the verb *did tell.)*

> *Nobody* knows the answer to that question about pronouns. *(Nobody* is the subject of the verb *knows.)*

> Alfred and *she* will bring their killer bees to the next meeting of the Unusual Pets Association. *(She* is one of the subjects of the verb *will bring.)*

> *Whoever* marries Larry should negotiate a good prenuptial agreement. *(Whoever* is the subject of the verb *marries.)*

Most people do okay choosing pronouns for one subject, but sentences with two subjects are a different story. For example, I often hear my otherwise grammatically correct students say such things as

> *Robert* and *me* are going to the supermarket for some chips.

See the problem? The verb is *are going.* To find the subject, ask your subject questions: *Who* or *what are going?* The answer right now is *Robert and me are going,* but in Standard English, *me* isn't acceptable as a subject pronoun. Here's the correct version:

> *Robert* and *I* are going to the supermarket for some carrots. (I couldn't resist correcting the nutritional content, too.)

One good way to check pronouns is to look at each one separately. If you've developed a fairly good "ear" for Standard English, isolating the pronoun helps you decide whether you've chosen correctly. You may have to adjust the verb a bit when you have one subject instead of two, but the principle is the same. If the pronoun doesn't sound right as a solo subject, it isn't right as part of a pair, either. Here's an example:

ORIGINAL SENTENCE: *Ella* and *her* went to the grammar rodeo yesterday.

CHECK 1: *Ella* went to the grammar rodeo yesterday. Verdict: sounds okay.

CHECK 2: *Her* went to the grammar rodeo yesterday. Verdict: sounds terrible. Substitute *she.*

CHECK 3: *She* went to the grammar rodeo yesterday. Verdict: much better.

RECOMBINED, CORRECTED SENTENCE: *Ella* and *she* went to the grammar rodeo yesterday.

Q. Which sentence is correct?

EXAMPLE

(A) Bud, you, and me appointed the judges for the grammar competition, so we have to live with their decisions, however wrong.

(B) Bud, you, and I appointed the judges for the grammar competition, so we have to live with their decisions, however wrong.

A. **B** *I* is a subject pronoun, and *me* is not. If you examine the parts of the subject separately, you can probably hear why: *me appointed* sounds wrong.

WARNING

In formal situations, don't "buddy up" a subject pronoun with a noun acting as subject.

WRONG: My friend he likes pronouns.

WHY IT'S WRONG: The subject is *friend,* so *he* is unnecessary.

RIGHT: My friend likes pronouns.

Subject pronouns may show up in another spot in the sentence — as a subject complement after a linking verb. Think of linking verbs as giant equal signs, equating two halves of the sentence. All forms of the verb *to be* are linking verbs, as are verbs such as *seem, appear, smell, sound,* and *taste.* A pronoun completing the equation is equivalent to the subject, so it must be a subject pronoun if you're speaking or writing formally. (Turn to Chapter 9 for more information about pronouns acting as complements.)

Q. Select the correct pronoun.

EXAMPLE

The person responsible for planting these beautiful trees is _____ (he, him, his).

A. **he** The linking verb *is* sets up an equation with the subject: *person = he.*

Q. Select the correct pronoun.

YOUR TURN

1. James and _____ (I, me) were hungry.

2. _____ (We, Us, Ourselves) raided the kitchen in search of food.

3. Mom _____ (she, her, no pronoun) had just gone to the supermarket, where _____ (she, her, herself) bought 17 bags of groceries.

4. "Thanks, Mom," said James politely, right before _____ (he, him, his, himself) gulped down an entire loaf of bread and two jars of peanut butter.

5. I _____ (me, myself) nibbled a bunch of grapes daintily, until _____ (it, its, itself) was completely gone.

6. "Those kids," Mom muttered as Aunt Agatha and _____ (she, her, herself) settled in front of the television.

7. Aunt Agatha _____ (she, her, no pronoun) said, "_____ (They, Them, Their, Themselves) eat up the entire month's food budget in one sitting."

8. Actually, the biggest eater in the family is _____ (she, her, hers).

Taking an Objective Viewpoint: Choosing Pronouns to Act as Objects

Up to this point in the chapter, I concentrate on subject pronouns, but now it's time to turn to the receiver of the sentence's action — the object. Specifically, it's time to turn to *object pronouns.* (For more information on finding the object, see Chapter 9.) Pronouns that may legally function as objects include *me, you, him, her, it, us, them, whom,* and *whomever.* (A few pronouns work as both subject and object pronouns. Check "While We're on the Subject: Choosing Pronouns to Act as Subjects," earlier in this chapter, for a list of those worry-free words.)

Dealing with direct and indirect objects

Here's some English teacher terminology for you, if you can stand it. (If not, don't worry. You don't need labels to use object pronouns correctly.) A *direct object* receives the action directly from the verb, answering the questions *whom?* or *what?* after the verb. An *indirect object* receives the action indirectly (clever, those grammar terms), answering the questions *to whom?* or *to what?* after the verb. Here are some examples of direct and indirect object pronouns, all in italics:

> Ticktock smashed *him* right on the nose for suggesting that "the mouse ran down the clock." (*smashed* is the verb; *him* is the object)

> Archie scolded *us* for ignoring his texts. (*scolded* is the verb; *us* is the object)

> Oliver, president of Grammarians 'R Us, sent *me* a horrifying *letter.* (*sent* is the verb; *letter* and *me* are objects)

In the last example, *letter* is the direct object and *me* is the indirect object. (For more information on direct and indirect objects, see Chapter 9.)

EXAMPLE

Q. Choose the correct pronoun.

The principal unjustly punished _____ (we, us, our, ours) for the food fight in the cafeteria yesterday.

A. **us** You need an object pronoun to serve as the object of the verb *punished.*

Are you talking to I? Prepositions and pronouns

Prepositions — words that express relationships such as *about, after, among, by, for, behind, since,* and others — always have objects, and some of those objects may be pronouns. Here are some examples of pronouns working as objects of prepositions, with both the preposition and the object pronoun italicized:

> Max, fearful for his pet tarantula, gave his dog *to us* yesterday. (*us* = object pronoun)

> Michael's latest play received a critical review *from them.* (*them* = object pronoun)

> Archie didn't like the window, so he simply plastered *over it.* (*it* = object pronoun)

The object of a preposition answers the usual object questions *(whom? what?)*, as in these examples:

> Max, fearful for his pet tarantula, gave his dog to *whom*? Answer: to *us*.
>
> Michael's latest play received a critical review from *whom*? Answer: from *them*.
>
> Archie didn't like the window, so he simply plastered over *what*? Answer: over *it*.

Also notice that all the pronouns — *us, him, her, them, it* — come from the set of object pronouns.

Q. Choose the correct pronoun.

According to Elton and _____ (she, her, hers, herself), the elephant's trunk is too long.

A. **her** The objects of the preposition are *Elton and her*. *Her* is an object pronoun. (*She* is a subject pronoun.)

WARNING

For some reason, the phrase *between you and I* has caught on. However, this usage isn't yet considered correct in Standard English. *Between* is a preposition, so object pronouns should follow it. The pronoun *I* is for subjects, and *me* is for objects. So, between you and me, *me* is the word you want.

Most of the tough pronoun choices pop up when the sentence has more than one object of the preposition (*Elton and her,* for example, in the preceding example). In this situation, try this rule of thumb — and I really mean thumb, at least when you're writing or looking for errors in someone else's writing. Take your thumb and cover one of the objects. Say the sentence. Does it sound right?

> According to Elton

Okay so far. Now take your thumb and cover the other object. Say the sentence. Does it sound right?

> According to she

Now do you hear the problem? Make the change:

> According to her

Now put the two back together:

> According to Elton and her

This method is not foolproof, but chances are good that you'll get a clue to the correct pronoun choices if you check the objects one by one.

Attaching objects to verbals

Isn't *verbal* a strange word? It sounds like something you keep in a little cage with an exercise wheel. But a *verbal* isn't a furry pet. It's a word derived from a verb (a word that expresses action or a state of being) that functions as a noun or as a description (in other words, as an adjective or an adverb). I discuss verbals in detail in Chapter 24. In this section, I show you how to select a pronoun for that coveted role, object of a verbal. (Everyone in Hollywood is auditioning for the part.) Later in this chapter, in the section "Dealing with Pronouns and *-ing* Nouns," I address another way that pronouns interact with verbals.

Take a look at these verbals and their objects, both of which are italicized. Also notice the true verb in each sentence, which I've underlined:

> Melanie <u>loves</u> *teasing him,* but Lulu favors nonviolence.
>
> Lola briefly <u>left</u> the meeting *to call them.*
>
> Oliver, *having heard us* at the party, <u>signed</u> up for singing lessons.

As you see, the verbals look like verbs. However, in the first sentence, *teasing* isn't acting as a verb. *Teasing* is a thing that Melanie loves. In other words, it functions as a noun. In the second example, *to call* provides a reason why Lola left the meeting. Therefore, *to call* describes the verb *left* (*left* why? *to call*), functioning as an adverb. In the third example, *having heard us* gives you more information about *Oliver,* a noun. Anything that describes a noun is functioning as an adjective.

When your writing includes a verbal, ask the object questions *whom? what?* after the verbal to locate its object. If the answer is a pronoun, be sure you've chosen an object pronoun.

Q. Choose the correct pronoun.

Oliver loves to show _____ (I, me, my, myself) and Melanie his new dance moves.

A. **me** *To show* is a verbal. *To show whom? To show me and Melanie. Me* is one of the objects of the verbal *to show.* (*Mel* is the other.) Did you select *myself?* Pronouns ending in *-self* have only two roles in Standard English: to double back to the subject (*she told herself that she was going to ace the test*) or to emphasize (*she herself had made the class review cards*).

Choose the correct pronoun.

9. Jessica sang songs to Mom and (he, him, himself) whenever the moon was full.

10. Her latest album is titled *Of Mom, (I, Me, Myself), and the Moon.*

11. Arthur offered _____ (we, us, our, ourselves) some songs he downloaded.

12. I said no, but Pedro accepted _____ (they, them, their).

13. Knowing _____ (she, her, hers), I'm guessing that Jessica copied someone else's songs, and I don't want to reward _____ (she, her, hers).

14 Once, she stole my dog Spike and asked for a reward when she returned Spike to (I, me, myself).

15 Showing loyalty to _____ (I, me, myself), Spike bit _____ (she, her, hers) right on the nose.

16 Spike likes to walk behind the letter carrier and (we, us, ourselves) when we approach the house, growling at _____ (she, her, herself) if the letter carrier comes too close.

17 "You have to run around _____ (he, him, himself)," I said to _____ (she, her, herself), and the letter carrier agreed.

18 I will also give _____ (he, him, himself) a treat when he behaves!

Knowing the Difference Between Who and Whom

Many grammarians believe that no one cares these days about the difference between *who/whoever* and *whom/whomever*. In their view, *whom* and *whomever* are fading away. They may be right, but many people (including me) still see a role for these pronouns. If your listeners or readers care about *who* and *whom*, you should know when each is appropriate. First, the rule:

>> *Who* and *whoever* are for subjects.

   Who and *whoever* also follow and complete the meaning of linking verbs. (In grammar terminology, *who* and *whoever* serve as subject complements.)

>> *Whom* and *whomever* are for objects — all kinds of objects (direct, indirect, of prepositions, of infinitives, and so on).

Check out these sample sentences:

   Whoever needs help from Roger is going to wait a long time. *(Whoever is the subject of the verb needs.)*

   Who is calling Lulu at this time of night? *(Who is the subject of the verb is calling.)*

   "Ask *whomever* you want to the prom," exclaimed Michael. *(Whomever is the direct object of the verb ask.)*

   To *whom* are you sending that email? *(Whom is the object of the preposition to.)*

TIP

Now that you know the rule and have seen the words in action, here's a trick for deciding between *who/whoever* and *whom/whomever*. Follow these steps:

1. Find all the verbs in the sentence.

2. Don't separate the helping verbs from the main verb. Count the main verb and its helpers as a single verb.

3. Now pair each verb with a subject.

4. If you have a verb flapping around with no subject, chances are *who* or *whoever* is the subject you're missing.

5. If all the verbs have subjects, check them one more time. Do you have any linking verbs without complements? (For more information on complements, see Chapter 9.) If you have a lonely linking verb with no complement in sight, you need *who* or *whoever*.

6. If all subjects are accounted for and you don't need a linking verb complement, you've reached a final answer: *whom* or *whomever*.

Here are two sample sentences, analyzed as just described:

SENTENCE 1: *Who/Whom* shall I say is calling?

The verbs = *shall say, is calling*.

The subject of *shall say = I*.

The subject of *is calling* = Okay, here you go. You need a subject for *is calling* but you're out of words. You have only one choice: *who*.

CORRECT SENTENCE: *Who* shall I say is calling?

SENTENCE 2: Jake is the ballplayer *who/whom* everyone thinks plays best.

The verbs = *is, thinks, plays*.

The subject of *is = Jake*.

The subject of *thinks = everyone*

The subject of *plays* = Umm. Once again, you're short a subject. Therefore, you need *who*.

CORRECT SENTENCE: Jake is the ballplayer *who* everyone thinks plays best.

Q. Which word is correct?

EXAMPLE

Agnes buys detergent in one-ton boxes for Roger, *who/whom* she adores in spite of his odor problem.

A. **whom** This pronoun is the direct object of the verb *adores*. You have two subject–verb pairs: *Agnes buys* and *she adores*. *Buys* and *adores* are action verbs, so no subject complement is needed. Therefore, you need an object pronoun, *whom*.

Select the correct pronoun.

YOUR
TURN

19 Does Peyton know _____ (who, whom) should get the secret message after Maria has decoded it?

20 Matt plans to sell the message to _____ (whoever, whomever) offers the most money.

21 _____ (Who, Whom) is his buyer?

22 Peyton says that _____ (whoever, whomever) believes Matt's sales pitch is foolish.

23 Peyton, _____ (who, whom) did a fair amount of research, thinks the message is a fake.

24 Do you know (who, whom) Peyton consulted?

25 Matt, (who, whom) I do not trust, has the most sincere face you can imagine.

Attracting Appositives

Do you want to say the same thing twice? Use an appositive. An *appositive* is a noun or a pronoun that is exactly the same as the noun or pronoun that precedes it in the sentence. Appositives fall naturally into most people's speech and writing, perhaps because human beings feel a great need to explain themselves. You probably won't make a mistake with an appositive unless a pronoun or a comma is involved. (See Chapter 19 for more information on appositives and commas.)

Pronouns show up as appositives mostly when you have two or more people or things to talk about. Here are some sentences with appositives and pronouns:

> The judges for the spitball contest, Sally and she, wear plastic raincoats. (Appositive — *Sally* and *she*)

> The director gave protective googles to the sloppiest contestants, Lulu and me. (Appositive = *Lulu* and *me*)

In the first sentence, the appositives are paired with the subject of the sentence (*judges, dancers*). In a sense, the appositives are potential substitutes for the subject. Therefore, you must use a subject pronoun. In the second sentence, the appositive matches *contestants*, the object of the preposition *to*, so you need the object pronoun *me*.

TIP

The appositive pronoun must always match its partner; if you pair it with a subject, the appositive must be a subject pronoun. If you pair it with an object, it must be an object pronoun.

EXAMPLE

Q. Select the correct pronoun.

The winners of the raffle, Ali and _____ (he, him) will appear on the *Tonight Show* tomorrow.

A. **he** You need a subject pronoun, *he*, as part of the appositive of the subject.

YOUR TURN

Select the correct pronoun.

26 The host praised the three contestants with the lowest scores — Bruce, Lola, and _____ (I, me).

27 During a commercial break, the director instructed some staff, the wardrobe manager, and _____ (they, them), to set up the next segment of the show.

28 Some actors promoting a new film, Bertha Lloyd and _____ (she, her), waited in the wings.

29 My favorite stars, Alix Rivo and _____ (he, him), weren't there.

Picking Pronouns for Comparisons

Lazy people that we are, we all tend to take shortcuts, chopping words out of our sentences and racing to the finish. This practice is evident in comparisons. Read this sentence:

> Lulu denies that she has as much facial hair as he.

That sentence really means

> Lulu denies that she has as much facial hair as he has.

If you say the entire comparison, as in the preceding example, the pronoun choice is a cinch. However, when you drop the verb *(has)*, you may be tempted to use the wrong pronoun, as in this sentence:

> Lulu denies that she has as much facial hair as him.

Sounds right, doesn't it? But in Standard English, the sentence is wrong. The words you say must fit with the words you don't say. Obviously, you aren't going to accept

> Lulu denies that she has as much facial hair as him has.

Him has sounds improper, and it is. The technical reason? *Him* is an object pronoun, so you can't use it as the subject of *has.*

TIP

Whenever you have an implied comparison — a comparison that the sentence suggests but doesn't state completely — finish the sentence in your head. The correct pronoun becomes obvious.

Implied comparisons don't always require subject pronouns. With an object pronoun, the meaning of the sentence changes. Check out these examples:

> IMPLIED: The dancers gave Michael more attention than she.
>
> MEANING: The dancers gave Michael more attention than she gave Michael.
>
> IMPLIED: The dancers gave Michael more attention than her.
>
> MEANING: The dancers gave Michael more attention than the dancers gave to her.

As you see in these examples, three little letters can add quite a bit of meaning to your sentence. Choose your pronouns wisely.

Q. Select the correct pronoun.

Tee Rex broke more claws than _____ (I, me) during the fight with Godzilla.

EXAMPLE

A. **I** Read the sentence this way: Tee Rex broke more claws than *I did* during the fight with Godzilla. In Standard English, *me did* is incorrect.

Select the correct pronoun.

YOUR TURN

30 Oscar is as careful as _____ (she, her) when he's weeding, but somehow he pulls out more plants than _____ (she, her).

31 The chipmunks consider Oscar their friend because he breaks as much garden fence as _____ (they, them).

32 With the fence down, the chipmunks munch more vegetables than _____ (we, us).

33 Oscar has planted fewer tomato plants than _____ (I, me).

34 Oscar gives more zucchini to the chipmunks than _____ (I, me) because I detest the taste of zucchini.

Dealing with Pronouns and -ing Nouns

Chapter 4 lists possessive pronouns and their most common uses. Here I focus on a topic that pops up more rarely: possessive pronouns and nouns ending in *-ing*. Choosing a pronoun to accompany these nouns is easy, once you think about what you're trying to say — specifically, what you want to emphasize. Compare these two sentences:

Mom, look at us riding our bikes!

Mom objects to our riding our bikes in traffic.

In both sentences, the pronoun precedes *riding* — a noun that ends in *-ing* and is created from a verb, *ride.* (In grammar terms, *riding* is a *gerund,* a member of the verbal family I discuss in "Attaching objects to verbals," earlier in this chapter.) In the first example, the speakers want their mother to look at them. Perhaps they've been struggling to learn how to ride, or perhaps they simply want attention. In either situation, the meaning is essentially complete after the pronoun:

Mom, look at us!

The phrase *riding our bikes* adds meaning, but it's not the point of the sentence. Now think about the second sentence. If you stop after the pronoun, the sentence is incomplete:

Mom objects to our.

Huh? *Our* what? You have to add the information about *riding our bikes in traffic* to end up with a statement that makes sense.

Consider for a moment what this sentence would mean:

> Mom objects to us.

Now the sentence makes sense, but the meaning is different. The mother objects to the speakers. Perhaps she's always despised them — in which case grammar is the least of their problems. This is not the most likely meaning.

Bottom line: A possessive pronoun in front of an *-ing* noun formed from a verb (a gerund, in grammar terms) emphasizes the action, not the person the pronoun represents. If that's your intention, use a possessive pronoun.

TIP

Some *-ing* words weren't created from verbs, and some *-ing* words aren't nouns. Don't worry about distinguishing between one and the other. Just consider what you're trying to say, and choose a pronoun that helps you express your meaning.

EXAMPLE

Q. Select the correct pronoun.

Although I'm not a literary critic, I think that _____ (he, him, his) writing a novel on his phone is a bad idea.

A. **his** The bad idea here is the writing, not *he* or *him*. The possessive pronoun shifts the attention to the task, which is the point of the sentence.

YOUR TURN

Select the correct pronoun.

(35) Peter Lincoln of the *Times* needs help with _____ (he, him, his) editing and must hire assistants.

(36) Lincoln looks forward to _____ (they, them, their) correcting his grammar.

(37) Lincoln said that he loved everything the employment agency did last week except _____ (they, them, their) sending him too many pronoun-obsessed editors.

(38) When Lori went for an interview, she saw _____ (he, him, his) reading a review of *The Pronoun Diet*; _____ (she/her) saying that the book was "trash" bothered Lincoln.

(39) When I applied, Lincoln looked favorably upon _____ (I, me, my) editing, but he loathed _____ (I, me, my) pronouncing his first name incorrectly.

Practice Questions Answers and Explanations

(1) **I**

(2) **We**

(3) **no pronoun, she**

(4) **he**

(5) **myself, it**

(6) **she**

(7) **no pronoun, They**

(8) **she**

(9) **him** (object of the preposition *to*)

(10) **Me** (object of the preposition *Of*)

(11) **us** (indirect object of the verb *offered*)

(12) **them** (direct object of the verb *accepted*)

(13) **her, her** (object of the verbals *Knowing* and *to reward*)

(14) **me** (object of the preposition *to*)

(15) **me** (object of the preposition *to*), **her** (direct object of the verb *bit*)

(16) **us** (object of the preposition *behind*), **her** (object of the verbal *growling*)

(17) **him** (object of the preposition *around*), **her** (direct object of the verb *said*)

(18) **him** (indirect object of the verb will *give*)

(19) **who** The subject–verb pairs are *Peyton does know, Maria has decoded,* and *who should get.*

(20) **whoever** The subject–verb pairs are *Matt plans* and *whoever offers.* Did the preposition *to* confuse you? It needs an object, but *whomever* isn't available, because it has to serve as the subject of *offers.* The whole statement, *whoever offers the most money,* is the object. (It's a clause, in case you were wondering. More on clauses appears in Chapter 11.)

(21) **Who** *Who* is the subject of *is.*

(22) **whoever** Sort out the subject–verb pairs: *Peyton says, whoever believes, pitch is.* **Note:** The last pair includes the linking verb *is.* Sometimes, *whoever* shows up in that role, but in this sentence, *foolish* completes the thought.

(23) **who** The subject–verb pairs are *Peyton thinks, who did,* and *message is.* The linking verb statement is completed by *fake.*

24. **whom** If you untangle the sentence and pair verbs with subjects, the answer is easy to find: *you do know, Peyton consulted.* Every verb has a subject, and neither is a linking verb. Therefore, you need *whom*, which is the direct object of *consulted*.

25. **whom** The verbs are *do trust, has,* and *can imagine.* Pair them up: *I do trust, Matt has, you can imagine.* You don't need a subject, so go for *whom*, the object of *do trust. Not*, by the way, is an adverb and not part of the verb.

26. **me** (appositive of *contestants*, a direct object)

27. **them** (appositive of *staff*, a direct object)

28. **she** (appositive of *actors*, a subject)

29. **he** (appositive of *stars*, a subject)

30. **she, she** Add the missing verbs: *Oscar is as careful as she is when he's weeding, but somehow he pulls out more plants than she does.*

31. **they** Add the missing verb: *The chipmunks consider Oscar their friend because he breaks as much garden fence as they do.*

32. **we** Finish the comparison: *than we do.*

33. **I** Complete the thought: *than I have.*

34. **me** Add the missing words: *Oscar gives more zucchini to the chipmunks than he gives me.*

35. **his** (focus on *editing*)

36. **their** (focus on *correcting*, not on *people*)

37. **their** (focus on *sending*)

38. **him, her** In the first portion of the sentence, the focus is on the person she saw *(him)*, with his action *(reading)* adding information about what he was doing. In the second portion of the sentence, the focus is on *saying*, so *her* is the appropriate pronoun.

39. **my, my** In both portions of the sentence, the focus is on the actions *(editing, pronouncing)*.

Whaddya Know? Chapter 14 Quiz

Quiz time! Complete each problem to test your knowledge on the various topics covered in this chapter. You can then find the solutions and explanations in the next section.

Check each underlined pronoun. Correct any errors you find.

Three chaperones and (1) <u>myself</u> left school at 10:03 A.M. with 45 fifth-graders, all of (2) <u>who</u> were excited about (3) <u>our</u> visiting Adventure Land. The day (4) <u>it</u> passed without incident. My friend Jim and (5) <u>me</u> sat in the Adventure Land Bar & Grill for five hours while the youngsters visited Space Control Center, Pirate Mountain, and other overpriced rides. The students sitting at my table, Arthur and (6) <u>him</u>, objected to (7) <u>me</u> eating while (8) <u>them</u> were hungry. I explained that (9) <u>whomever</u> forgot to bring lunch from home was out of luck. At the end of the day, students returned to the bus and were frightened by (10) <u>it</u> making a lot of noise. (11) "<u>Whom</u> is in charge of maintenance?" asked Arthur. "Joe and (12) <u>me</u> don't want to die!" Quieting Joe and (13) <u>he</u> with one glance, I told the driver to ignore (14) <u>they</u>, and everyone except for (15) <u>them</u> cheered.

Answers to Chapter 14 Quiz

(1) **I** Use *myself* only when the action doubles back or when you need strong emphasis. Here, neither situation exists, so the subject pronoun *I* is what you want.

(2) **whom** The pronoun *whom* is the object of the preposition *of.* (The subject of *were excited* is *all.*)

(3) **correct** The possessive pronoun *our* places the focus on *visiting.*

(4) **no pronoun** You already have a subject, *day*, so you don't need a pronoun to replace it.

(5) **I** This pronoun is the subject of *sat.*

(6) **he** You need a subject pronoun because *Arthur and he* are appositives of *students*, the subject.

(7) **my** The focus is on *eating*, so the possessive pronoun is what you want here.

(8) **they** This pronoun is the subject of the verb *were.*

(9) **whoever** This pronoun is the subject of the verb *forgot.*

(10) **its** The focus is on *making a lot of noise*, so the possessive pronoun is correct here.

(11) **Who** You need a subject pronoun to pair with the verb *is.*

(12) **I** You need a subject pronoun for the verb, *do want.*

(13) **him** You need an object pronoun to act as the object of the verbal *quieting.*

(14) **them** This object pronoun is the object of the verbal *to ignore.*

(15) **correct** The object pronoun *them* acts as object of the preposition *except for.*

Chapter 15

Getting Specific: The Power of Descriptions

With the right nouns (names of persons, places, things, or ideas) and verbs (action or *being* words), you can build a pretty solid foundation in a sentence. The key to expressing your precise thoughts, though, is to build on that foundation by adding descriptions. In Chapter 6, I go over the most basic descriptors — single-word adjectives and adverbs. In this chapter, I tackle comparisons and other, longer descriptive elements, explaining what they are and how to put them in their proper place.

Creating Comparisons with Adjectives and Adverbs

Are you happier than your friends? Which cantaloupe is juiciest? Will the final exam be harder than the midterm? If you've ever asked yourself questions like these, you're officially human, because our brains are hard-wired to make comparisons. (If you've never made a comparison, I hope you enjoy your visit to planet Earth.)

Standard English has two ways of creating comparisons, but you can't use them together, and they're not interchangeable. Both rely on adjectives and adverbs. *Adjectives* describe nouns and pronouns; *adverbs* attach to verbs, adjectives, and other adverbs. (See Chapter 6 for more information on these parts of speech.)

Ending it with -er or giving more to adjectives

Some adjectives form comparisons by adding *-er* or *-est* to the basic adjective. (To be clear: I'm using a hyphen here because the letters form a suffix, but don't insert a hyphen when you attach the suffix to a word.) Some rely on additional words. Take a close look at the italicized comparisons in these sentences:

> Roger's smile is *more evil* than Michael's, but Michael's giggle sounds *cuter*.

> Egbert searched for the *least expensive* car, believing that image is *less important* than having the *biggest* bank account.

> Betsy's *most recent* symphony was *less successful* than her *earlier* composition.

> Anna's *older* sister is an even *greater* mathematician than Anna herself, though Anna has the edge in geometry.

> Lulu's *latest* tattoo is *grosser* than her first, but Lulu, not the *shyest* girl in the class, is looking for the *most extreme* design for her next effort.

As you see, some comparisons rely on *-er* or *-est*, and some are expressed by adding *more*, *most*, *less*, or *least* to the quality being compared. How do you know which is correct? (Or, to use a comparison, how do you know which is *better*?) The dictionary is the final authority, and you should consult one if you're in doubt about a particular word. Here are some general guidelines:

>> Add *-er* and *-est* to most single-syllable adjectives when the comparison is positive (showing that the first item being compared is greater or more intense).

>> If the word already ends in the letter *e*, don't double the *e* by adding *-er* or *-est*. Just add *-r* or *-st*.

>> *-Er* and *-est* endings are not usually appropriate for words ending in *-ly*.

>> *-Er* and *-est* endings don't work for negative comparisons, when the second item being compared is greater or more intense.

Table 15-1 lists some adjectives that describe Lola with both the *-er* and *-est* forms. I include the context for each comparison.

Table 15-1   Single-Word Comparisons with Adjectives

Description of Lola	-ER Form	-EST Form
able	abler than Lulu	ablest of all the scientists in her lab
bald	balder than an eagle	baldest of the models
cute	cuter than an elf	cutest of all the assassins
edgy	edgier than a caffeine addict	edgiest of the atom splitters
friendly	friendlier than a grizzly bear	friendliest person on the block
glad	gladder than the loser	gladdest of all the lottery winners

TIP

Notice that when the last letter is *y*, you must often change the *y* to *i* before you tack on the ending.

Table 15-2 contains even more descriptions of Lola, this time with *more, less, most,* and *least* added to the adjective.

Table 15-2 Two-Word Adjective Comparisons

Description of Lola	More/Less Form	Most/Least Form
intelligent	more intelligent than her teacher	most intelligent of all the students
knock-kneed	less knock-kneed than an old sailor	least knock-kneed of all the beauty pageant contestants
magnificent	more magnificent than a sunset	most magnificent of all the ninjas
notorious	more notorious than a princess	most notorious of the florists
queenly	more queenly than Queen Elizabeth	most queenly of all the models
rigid	less rigid than a grammarian	least rigid of the traffic cops

TIP

These two tables give you a clue about another important comparison characteristic. Did you notice that the second column is always a comparison between Lola and *one other* person or thing? The addition of *-er* or *more* or *less* compares two things. This is the *comparative* form. In the last column of each chart, Lola is compared to a group with more than two members. When the group is larger than two, *-est* or *most* or *least* creates the comparison. This is the *superlative* form.

To sum up the rules:

>> Use *-er* or *more/less* when comparing only two things. (comparative form)

>> Use *-est* or *most/least* when singling out the extreme in a group that is larger than two. (superlative form)

>> Never combine two comparison methods, such as *-er* and *more*.

EXAMPLE

Q. Insert the correct form of the adjective in parentheses.

(A) Egbert's design for the new refrigerator is _____ than the one his competitor hatched. (simple)

A. **simpler** You're comparing two refrigerators in this sentence, so the *-er* form is the one you want.

YOUR TURN

1 Helen is the _____ of all the women living in Troy, New York. (beautiful)

2 Helen, who works for an auto parts company, is hoping for a transfer to the Paris office, where the salaries are _____ (low) than in New York but the nightlife is _____. (lively)

3   Helen's boss praises her work, claiming that she is the _____ (efficient) and _____ (valuable) of all his employees.

4   His secretary, however, has evaluated everyone's work and concluded that Helen is _____ (slow) and _____ (accurate) than Natalie. "Natalie is amazing," the secretary declared, "and Helen is not."

5   Natalie prefers to type her purchase orders because she thinks the result is _____ (neat) and _____ (professional) than handwritten work.

6   The Paris job went to Natalie, and Helen is now in the _____ (nasty) mood imaginable, even _____ (annoyed) than she was when her desk caught fire.

7   "Natalie takes one business course," commented Helen, "and she thinks she's _____ (qualified) than I am. How dare she!"

8   "I, on the other hand, am the _____ (professional) of the three clerks in my office," Helen continued, "and I am absent _____ (often) than everyone else."

Creating comparisons with adverbs

Placing the correct form of an adverb in a comparison is (mostly) simpler than figuring out how to select the proper adjective form for comparisons. Adverbs nearly always rely on two-word comparisons, employing *less*, *least*, *more*, and *most*. Exceptions to this pattern include a few irregular forms (explained in the next section) and some single-syllable adverbs such as *soon*, *fast*, and others. Have a look at these examples:

Ben's company markets its apps *more effectively* than Elena's firm.

Of all the coders in her group, Rebecca works *most rapidly*.

Did you know that the apps on your phone run *less reliably* than advertised?

That fuel, compared with all the others, burns *least efficiently*.

Check out Table 15-3 for some additional examples of adverb comparisons.

Table 15-3   Comparisons with Adverbs

Description of Tim's Actions	More/Less Form (Comparative)	Most/Least Form (Superlative)
[sings] beautifully	more beautifully than the opera star	of all the singers in the karaoke bar, [Tim sings] most beautifully
[punches] forcefully	less forcefully than a two-year-old	of all the boxers in the Olympics, [Tim punches] least forcefully
[gives] generously	more generously than his sister	of all the billionaires, [Tim gives] most generously
[speaks] carefully	less carefully than most philosophers	of all the philosophers, [Tim speaks] least carefully

As with adjectives, the comparative form compares two things by adding *more* or *less*. The superlative form singles out the *most* or *least* in a group of more than two.

Q. Insert the appropriate comparative or superlative form of the word in parentheses.

Of all the chefs, Angie prepares her dishes _____ (quickly). Diners never wait long when she's cooking.

Unfortunately, Angie has a nervous temperament. Of all the chefs, Angie cooks _____ (confidently).

A. **most quickly, least confidently** When comparing more than two actions, *most* or *least* is required.

Insert the appropriate comparative or superlative form of the word in parentheses.

9   Alonzo markets his spicy sauces _____ (effectively) now than in the past, when he didn't advertise.

10   George, on the other hand, posts recipes on social media _____ (frequently) than he used to. He says he's too busy these days.

11   Of all the students in the business school, Jenna spends her advertising budget _____ (intelligently); she reaches the maximum number of customers for very little money.

12   Alonzo flatters the professor _____ (obviously) than Jenna does. His compliments are subtle, and hers are not.

13   "Professor Jahn grades _____ (harshly) of all the teachers," Alonzo might say. "He is not as generous as you."

Breaking the rules: Irregular comparisons

Whenever English grammar gives you rules that make sense, you know it's time for the irregulars to show up. Not surprisingly, then, you have to create a few common comparisons without *-er*, *-est*, *more/less*, or *most/least* — the regular comparisons I explain in the preceding sections.

Good, bad, well

I think of these as the "report card" comparisons because they evaluate quality. The first word of each line provides a description. The second word shows you that description when two elements are being compared — the comparative form. The last word is for comparisons of three or more — the superlative form.

>> Good, better, best

>> Bad, worse, worst

>> Well, better, best

Time to visit *good*, *bad*, and *well* when they're on the job:

> Although Michael's trumpet solo is *good* and Roger's is *better*, Lulu's trumpet solo is the *best* of all. (adjectives)

> Lulu's habit of picking at her tattoo is *bad*, but Ralph's constant sneezing is *worse*. Egbert's tendency to crack jokes is the *worst* habit of all. (adjectives)

> Lola sings *well* in the shower, but Max sings *better* in the bathtub. Ralph croons *best* in the hot tub. (adverbs)

EXAMPLE

Q. Revise according to the rules of Standard English.

Who's the baddest kid in the playgroup?

Michael says that he is feeling more bad today than yesterday, but his statement must be considered in light of the fact that today is the algebra final.

A. baddest → worst

more bad → worse

Little, many, much

These are measuring comparisons, words that tell you about quantity. The first word on each line is the description, the second creates comparisons between two elements (the comparative form), and the last word applies to comparisons of three-plus elements (the superlative form).

> ➤ Little, less, least
> ➤ Many, more, most
> ➤ Much, more, most

Check out these words in action (actually, in sentences, but you know what I mean):

> Lulu likes a *little* grape jelly on her pizza, but Egbert prefers even *less* jelly because he doesn't like sweets. On that menu, Lulu likes chocolate pizza *least*. (*little, less* = adjectives, *least* = adverb)

> Roger spies on *many* occasions, but he seldom uncovers *more* secrets than his brother Alfred. Lola is the *most* successful spy of all. (adjectives)

> Anna has *much* interest in mathematics, though she's *more* devoted to her trumpet lessons. Of all the musical mathematicians I know, Anna is the *most* likely to succeed in both careers. (*much* = adjective, *more, most* = adverb)

Many or *much*? How do you decide which word is needed? Easy. *Many* precedes plurals of countable elements (*many crickets* or *shoes*, for example) and *much* precedes words that express qualities that can't be counted, though these qualities may sometimes be measured (*much noise* or *sugar*, for instance).

TIP

Q. Which sentence is correct?

(A) Anna and Michael studied together for the algebra final, but Michael is least prepared.

(B) Anna and Michael studied together for the algebra final, but Michael is less prepared.

A. **B** *Less* is the word you want when comparing two elements.

Insert the correct form of the word in parentheses.

14 Edgar's scrapbook, which contains souvenirs from his trip to watch-repair camp, is the _____ (good) example of a boring book that I have ever seen.

15 Edgar talks about his souvenirs in _____ (much) detail than anyone would ever want to hear.

16 Bored listeners believe that the _____ (bad) item in his scrapbook is a set of gears, each of which Edgar can discuss for hours.

17 On the bright side, everyone knows that Edgar's watch repair skills are _____ (good) than the jewelers' downtown.

18 Although he is only nine years old, Edgar has the _____ (many) timepieces of anyone in his fourth-grade class, including the teacher.

19 The classroom clock functions fairly well, but Ms. Appleby relies on Edgar to make it run even _____ (well).

20 Edgar's scrapbook also contains three samples of watch oil; Edgar thinks Time-Ola Oil is the _____ (good) choice.

21 Unfortunately, Edgar's mom cleaned his room and threw out a few things. Now Edgar has _____ (little) oil than he needs.

Resolving incomplete and illogical comparisons

Making a correct comparison involves more than selecting the correct form. You also have to place the comparison in the proper context and check that the underlying logic is sound.

Incomplete comparison

Check out this sentence:

Octavia screamed more chillingly.

Do you understand the meaning of this comparison? I doubt it. Take a look at these possible scenarios:

Octavia screamed more chillingly. "Uh-oh," thought Max. "Yesterday she nearly burst my eardrum. If she screams more chillingly today, I'd better get my earplugs out."

or

> Octavia screamed more chillingly. Max, rushing to aid Carmen, whose scream of terror had turned his blood to ice, stopped dead. "Octavia sounds even worse," he thought. "I'd better go to her first."

or

> Octavia screamed more chillingly. "Please," said the director, "I know you're tired after rehearsing for ten hours. But if you're going to star in my horror movie, you'll have to put a little more oomph into it. Try again!"

See the problem? Unless you complete the comparison, readers are left with as many possibilities as they can imagine.

Here's another comparison with a fatal error. Can you spot the problem?

> Lulu loved skydiving more than Lola.

Need another hint? Read on:

> Lulu loved skydiving more than Lola. Lola sobbed uncontrollably as she realized that Lulu, whom she had always considered her best friend, was on the way to the airport instead of on the way to Lola's birthday party. What a disappointment!

or

> Lulu loved skydiving more than Lola. Lola was fine for the first 409 jumps, but then her enthusiasm began to flag. Lulu, on the other hand, was climbing into the airplane eagerly, as if it were her first jump of the day.

Because the comparison is incomplete, your reader can understand the comparison in two different ways, as the two stories illustrate. The rule here is simple: Don't omit words that are necessary to the meaning of the comparison.

> WRONG: Lulu loved skydiving more than Lola.
>
> RIGHT: Lulu loved skydiving more than she loved Lola.
>
> ALSO RIGHT: Lulu loved skydiving more than Lola did.

In making a comparison, be clear and complete.

REMEMBER

EXAMPLE

Q. Which sentence is correct?

(A) My cat Agatha slapped her tail more quickly.

(B) My cat Agatha slapped her tail more quickly than Dorothy's cat.

A. **B** In sentence A, the reader is left asking *more quickly than what?* In sentence B, you know the two cats are being compared.

Illogical comparisons

What's wrong with the following sentence?

> Babe Ruth played better than any baseball player.

Before I continue, here's an explanation of that question for those of you who (gasp of pity) don't like baseball. Babe Ruth was one of the greatest baseball players of all time. The example removes Babe Ruth from the group of baseball players. To keep Babe Ruth in the sport, add *other:*

> Babe Ruth played better than any other baseball player.

The rule for comparisons here is simple: Use the word *other* or *else* when comparing someone or something to other members of the same group. Check out the following examples:

> WRONG: The star soprano of the Santa Lola Opera, Sarah Screema, sings louder than anyone in the cast.

> WHY IT'S WRONG: The sentence makes it clear that Sarah is in the cast, but the comparison implies that she's not in the cast. Illogical!

> RIGHT: The star soprano of the Santa Lola Opera, Sarah Screema, sings louder than anyone *else* in the cast.

Here's another problem. Can you find it?

> Max's nose is longer than Michael.

I should mention that Michael is tall — not skyscraper tall, but at least 6'2". Now do you see what's wrong with the sentence? Max's nose, a real tourist attraction for its length *and* width (not including the pimple at the end) is about four inches long. It is *not* longer than Michael. It is longer than Michael's *nose.*

> WRONG: Max's nose is longer than Michael.

> RIGHT: Max's nose is longer than Michael's nose.

> ALSO RIGHT: Max's nose is longer than Michael's.

Here's the bottom line:

>> Make sure your comparisons are logical.

>> Check to see that you have compared what you want to compare — two things that are at least remotely related.

>> If the first part of the comparison involves a possessive noun or pronoun (showing ownership), the second part of the comparison probably needs a possessive also. For more information on possessive nouns, see Chapter 17. For more information on possessive pronouns, see Chapter 4.

EXAMPLE

Q. Which sentence is correct?

(A) The beagle is cuter than any breed of dog.

(B) The beagle is cuter than any other breed of dog.

A. **B** The grammar in sentence B is correct, but feel free to cross out *beagle* and substitute your favorite dog breed. By definition, a beagle is a dog, and sentence A implies that beagles aren't. The word *other* in sentence B returns beagles to dogdom.

Another common error involves creating comparisons out of absolutes — characteristics that *can't* be compared. If I ask you whether this chapter is more unique than the previous chapter, the answer is definitely not. Nothing can be *more unique*. The word *unique* means "one of a kind." Something is either one of a kind or it's not. No halfway point, no degrees of uniqueness, no — well, you get the idea. You can't compare something that's unique to anything but itself. Check out the following examples:

> WRONG: The vase that Pete cracked was more unique than the Grecian urn.
>
> ALSO WRONG: The vase that Pete cracked was very unique.
>
> RIGHT: The vase that Pete cracked was unique.
>
> ALSO RIGHT: The vase that Pete cracked was unique, as was the Grecian urn.
>
> RIGHT AGAIN: The vase that Pete cracked was more unusual than the Grecian urn.
>
> WHY IT'S RIGHT: *Unusual* is not an absolute term, so you can use it in comparisons.

The word *unique* is not unique. Other words share its absolute quality: *perfect, circular, dead,* and *eternal,* for example. Before you sign off on a comparison, be sure it's logical. You can't compare absolute qualities, but you can compare how close people or things come to having those qualities.

TIP

One more word causes trouble in comparisons: *equally.* You hear the expression *equally as* quite frequently. You don't need the *as* because the word *equally* contains the idea of comparison. For example:

> WRONG: Roger got a lighter sentence than Lulu, but he is *equally as* guilty because he stole as many doughnuts as she did.
>
> RIGHT: Roger got a lighter sentence than Lulu, but he is *equally* guilty because he stole as many doughnuts as she did.
>
> ALSO RIGHT: Roger got a lighter sentence than Lulu, but he is as guilty as she is because he stole the same number of doughnuts.

EXAMPLE

Q. Find the correct sentence.

(A) Michael's recent drama is even more unique than his last play.

(B) Michael's recent drama is even more unusual than his last play.

A. **B** Sentence A incorrectly compares an absolute *(unique)*. In sentence B, *more unusual* expresses a correct comparison.

Find the correct sentence in each pair.

22 **(A)** "There are more fish in the sea," commented the shark as she searched for her posse.

(B) "There are more fish in the sea than on a restaurant menu," commented the shark as she searched for her posse.

23 **(A)** Mr. Trout, who is wealthier than a tech titan, spends a lot of money on waterproof smartphones.

(B) Mr. Trout, who is wealthier, spends a lot of money on waterproof smartphones.

24 **(A)** The octopus plays more video games, often opposing himself with different arms.

(B) The octopus plays more video games than any land animal, often opposing himself with different arms.

25 **(A)** The jokes in this exercise are more unique than the jokes in Chapter 18.

(B) However, the answers are more unusual in Chapter 18.

26 **(A)** The tip of a mermaid's tail is unique because it's circular.

(B) A mermaid's tail is equally as circular as a shark's fin.

27 **(A)** These marine jokes are so uninteresting that I may volunteer to be shark bait.

(B) These marine jokes are so uninteresting.

28 **(A)** The average pigeon is smarter than any animal.

(B) The average pigeon is smarter than any other animal.

29 **(A)** I once saw a woman on a New York street shampooing her hair in the rain, an experience that was weirder than anything I've seen in New York City.

(B) On a New York street, I once saw a woman shampooing her hair in the rain, an experience that was weirder than anything else I've seen in New York City.

30 **(A)** Singing a shower song with a thick New York accent, she appeared saner than city residents.

(B) Singing a shower song with a thick New York accent, she appeared saner than other city residents.

31 **(A)** A tourist gawking through the window of a sightseeing bus was more surprised than neighborhood residents on the street.

(B) A tourist gawking through the window of a sightseeing bus was more surprised than other neighborhood residents on the street.

On Location: Placing Descriptions Correctly

In some languages, word order isn't particularly important. You can write the equivalent of "cat dog bit" and the form of the word indicates which animal is the biter and which is the victim. English words have fewer forms (nice, right?), but location matters. To find out how to place every descriptive word and statement accurately, read on.

TIP

Descriptions can be a single word (an adjective or an adverb), but many are longer. In grammar terms, they can be *phrases* and *clauses.* You don't need to label a description in order to put it where it belongs. Logic is enough!

Troubling singles

A few single-word descriptions pack a huge punch when it comes to meaning. Specifically, when you see *even, almost, nearly, only,* or *just,* watch out! Errors pop up if they're in the wrong spot.

Placing "even"

Even is one of the sneaky descriptors that can land any place in a sentence — and change the meaning of what you're saying. Take a look at this example:

> It's two hours before the grand opening of the school show. Lulu and George have been rehearsing for weeks. They know all the dances, and Lulu has only one faint bruise left from George's tricky elbow maneuver. Suddenly, George's evil twin, Lester, mad with jealousy, "accidentally" places his foot in George's path. George is down! His ankle is sprained! What will happen to the show?

>> Possibility 1: Lulu shouts, "We can still go on! *Even Lester* knows the dances."

>> Possibility 2: Lulu shouts, "We can still go on! Lester knows *even the dances.*"

What's going on here? These two statements look almost the same, but they aren't. Here's what each one means:

>> Possibility 1: Lulu surveys the 15 boys gathered around George. She knows that any one of them could step in at a moment's notice. After all, the dances are easy. *Even Lester,* the clumsiest boy in the class, knows the dances. If *even Lester* can perform the role, it will be a piece of cake for everyone else.

>> Possibility 2: The whole group looks at Lester almost as soon as George hits the floor. Yes, Lester knows the words. He's been reciting George's lines for weeks now, helping George learn the part. Yes, Lester can sing; everyone's heard him. But what about the dances? There's no time to teach him. Just then, Lester begins to twirl around the stage. Lulu sighs with relief. Lester knows *even the dances.* The show will go on!

Got it? *Even* is a description and describes the words that follow it. To put it another way, *even* begins a comparison:

>> Possibility 1: *even* Lester (as well as everyone else)

>> Possibility 2: *even* the dances (as well as the songs and words)

So here's the rule. Put *even* at the beginning of the comparison implied in the sentence.

Placing "almost" and "nearly"

Almost and *nearly* are also tricky, as you see in these examples:

> Last night, Lulu wrote for *almost* (or *nearly*) an hour and then went rollerblading.

and

> Last night, Lulu *almost* (or *nearly*) wrote for an hour and then went rollerblading.

In the first sentence, Lulu wrote for 55 minutes and then stopped. In the second sentence, Lulu intended to write, but every time she sat down at the computer, she remembered that she hadn't watered the plants, called her best friend, Lola, made a sandwich, and so forth. After an hour of wasted time and without one word on the screen, she grabbed her rollerblades and left.

Almost and *nearly* begin the comparison. Lulu *almost wrote* (or *nearly wrote*), but she didn't. Or Lulu wrote for *almost an hour* (or *nearly an hour*), but not for a *whole hour.* In deciding where to put these words, add the missing ideas and see whether the position of the word makes sense.

Placing "only" and "just"

If only the word *only* were simpler to understand! If everyone thought about the word *just* for *just* a minute. Like the other descriptors in this section, *only* and *just* change the meaning of the sentence every time their positions are altered, as you see in these examples:

> *Only* (or *just*) Lex went to Iceland. (No one else went.)

> Lex *only* went to Iceland. (He didn't do anything else.)

> Lex *just* went to Iceland. (The ink on his passport is still wet. *Just* may mean *recently.*)

> Lex went *only* (or *just*) to Iceland. (He skipped Antarctica.)

Many people place *only* in front of a verb and assume that it applies to another idea in the sentence. I see T-shirts all the time with slogans like "My dad went to NYC and only bought me a lousy T-shirt." The *only* should be in front of *a lousy T-shirt* because the sentence implies that Dad should have bought more — the Empire State Building, perhaps. The original wording describes a terrible trip: Ride in from the airport, buy a T-shirt, and return home.

Q. Which sentence is correct?

(A) I only want one reindeer for my trip to the North Pole, not all of them.

(B) I want only one reindeer for my trip to the North Pole, not all of them.

A. **B** *Only* limits the number of reindeer, not the action *(want)*.

Which sentence is correct?

YOUR TURN

(32) (A) Just Allen attended the opera; he didn't have time for the party afterward.

(B) Allen attended just the opera; he didn't have time for the party afterward.

(33) (A) My Uncle Fred pays taxes only when he's in the mood or when the IRS serves an arrest warrant.

(B) My Uncle Fred only pays taxes when he's in the mood or when the IRS serves an arrest warrant.

(34) (A) Because she was celebrating an important birthday, Ms. Jonge gave us just 30 minutes of homework.

(B) Because she was celebrating an important birthday, just Ms. Jonge gave us 30 minutes of homework.

(35) (A) The first task nearly seemed impossible: to write an essay about the benefits of homework.

(B) The first task seemed nearly impossible: to write an essay about the benefits of homework.

(36) (A) After I'd almost written two pages, my phone beeped, and I put my pen down.

(B) After I'd written almost two pages, my phone beeped, and I put my pen down.

(37) (A) I figured that even Ms. Jonge, the meanest teacher on the planet, would understand the need to take a break.

(B) I even figured that Ms. Jonge, the meanest teacher on the planet, would understand the need to take a break.

Misplaced descriptions

One word to the left or two to the right can't matter much, right? Wrong. To see why, take a look at this sentence:

Lulu put a ring in her pierced nose that she bought last week.

The describing words *that she bought last week* follow the word *nose.* The way the sentence is now, *that she bought last week* describes *nose.* The internet sells plenty of unusual items, but no noses (yet), though I imagine a website for plastic surgeons offering discount nose jobs is out there somewhere.

Here's the correction:

In her pierced nose Lulu put a ring that she bought last week.

Now the description (*that she bought last week*) follows *ring*, which Lulu really did buy last week.

If you encounter a misplaced description in your writing, be sure that your revision doesn't create another error. Here's an example of a faulty revision, still working from the sentence about Lulu's nose:

Lulu put a ring that she had bought last week in her pierced nose.

In this version, Lulu's shopping took place inside her nose, which is rather large but not spacious enough to contain a jewelry store. The description *in her pierced nose* tells you where something happened. The sentence has two verbs: *put* and *bought*. The description describes the nearest action, which, in the faulty revision, is *bought*. In the true correction, *in her pierced nose* is at the beginning of the sentence, closer to *put* than to *bought*.

Here's another description that has wandered too far from home:

Lulu also bought a genuine, 1950-model, pink Hoopadoop toy with a credit card.

According to news reports, toddlers and dogs have received credit card applications, but toys have not. Yet the sentence says that the Hoopadoop toy comes with a credit card. How to fix it? Move the description:

With a credit card Lulu also bought a genuine, 1950-model, pink Hoopadoop toy.

Granted, people can often figure out the meaning of a sentence that has a poorly placed description. But chances are your reader or listener will pause a moment to unravel what you've said and then space out while reading the next couple of sentences.

The rule concerning description placement is simple: Place the description as close as possible to the word it describes.

Q. Which sentence is correct?

(A) Roger put the paper into his pocket with nuclear secrets written on it.

(B) Roger put the paper with nuclear secrets written on it into his pocket.

A. **B** The paper, not the pocket, has nuclear secrets written on it!

Which sentence is correct?

 (A) Anna pedaled to the mathematics contest on her ten-speed bicycle with a complete set of differential equations.

(B) With a complete set of differential equations, Anna pedaled on her ten-speed bicycle to the mathematics contest.

39 **(A)** Julie passed the eye examination administered by a very near-sighted clerk with flying colors.

   (B) With flying colors, Julie passed the eye examination administered by a very near-sighted clerk.

40 **(A)** The written test inquired about maneuvers for cars skidding on ice.

   (B) The written test for cars skidding on ice inquired about maneuvers.

41 **(A)** About a week after the written portion of the exam, the Department of Motor Vehicles sent a letter giving Julie an appointment for the road test lacking sufficient postage.

   (B) About a week after the written portion of the exam, the Department of Motor Vehicles sent a letter lacking sufficient postage and giving Julie an appointment for the road test.

Just hanging out: Danglers

Descriptions must have something to describe. This idea seems simple, and it *is* simple when the description is a single word. You're not likely to say

> I want to buy a red.

when you're putting together a Santa Claus outfit for a holiday party. Instead, you automatically declare:

> I want to buy a red suit.

In the preceding sentence, *red* describes *suit*. However, two types of descriptions tend to cause as many problems as a double date with your ex: participles and infinitives. These descriptions look like verbs, but they don't function as verbs. In grammar terms, they're known as *verbals*. (You can find out more about verbals in Chapter 24.)

In this section, I show you common mistakes with participles and infinitives. Don't worry about the names. Just place these descriptions properly.

First up is participles. Read this sentence:

> Munching a buttered sausage, the cholesterol really builds up.

As you see, the sentence begins with a verb form, *munching*, but *munching* isn't the verb in the sentence. It's a *participle* — a verb form that describes. (The true verb in the sentence is *builds*.) But participles have to describe something or someone. *Munching* must be tacked onto a muncher. So who is munching? You? Egbert? Everyone in the local diet club? In this sentence, no one is munching. Descriptive verb forms that have nothing appropriate to describe are called *danglers* or *dangling modifiers.* To correct the sentence, add a muncher:

> Munching a buttered sausage, Egbert smiled and waved to his cardiologist.

In sentences beginning with a descriptive verb form, such as a participle, the subject must perform the action mentioned in the descriptive verb form. In the sample sentence, *Egbert* is the subject of the sentence. The sentence begins with a descriptive verb form, *munching a buttered sausage.* Thus, *Egbert* is the one who is munching. (For more information on identifying the subject of a sentence, see Chapter 10.) If you want the cardiologist to munch, say

> Munching a buttered sausage, the cardiologist returned Egbert's wave.

Here's another example:

> Sitting on the park bench, the soaring space shuttle delighted the little boy.

Really? The space shuttle is sitting on a bench and soaring at the same time? Defies the laws of physics, don't you think? Try again:

> Sitting on the park bench, the little boy was delighted by the soaring space shuttle.

Now *little boy* is the subject of the sentence, so the introductory description applies to him, not to the *space shuttle.* Another correction may be

> The soaring space shuttle delighted the little boy who was sitting on the park bench.

Now the descriptive words *sitting on the park bench* are placed next to *little boy,* who is the one sitting and being delighted by the soaring space shuttle.

Q. Which sentence is correct?

EXAMPLE

    (A) Skidding over the icy pavement, the old oak tree couldn't escape the speeding sports car.

    (B) Skidding over the icy pavement, the speeding sports car slammed into the old oak tree.

A. **B** In choice A, the *old oak tree* is skidding. Problem! In choice B, the *speeding sports car* is skidding. No problem! Well, no grammar problem, anyway. The traffic cop sees the situation a little differently.

Which sentence is correct?

YOUR
TURN

  (42) **(A)** Sailing swiftly across the sea, Samantha's boat was a beautiful sight.

    (B) Sailing swiftly across the sea, the sight of the beautiful boat made Samantha sob.

  (43) **(A)** To enjoy a good cup of coffee, a clean coffeepot is essential.

    (B) To enjoy a good cup of coffee, you should use a clean coffeepot.

  (44) **(A)** While designing her latest tattoo, Lulu thought it would be a good idea to attach a small camera to the frames of her glasses.

    (B) While designing her latest tattoo, a small camera attached to the frames of her glasses seemed like a good idea.

45 **(A)** Covered in rhinestones, Lulu's glasses made a fashion statement.

(B) Covered in rhinestones, Lulu made a fashion statement with her glasses.

Avoiding confusing descriptions

Equal opportunity matters, but you don't want a description to have an equal opportunity to describe two things. Take a look at the following example:

The teacher that Roger annoyed often assigned detention to him.

What does the sentence mean? Did Roger *often annoy* the teacher? (I'm a teacher, and Roger would certainly annoy me. His burps alone . . . but back to grammar.) Perhaps the teacher *often assigned* detention to Roger. (Yup. Sounds like something Roger's teacher would do.)

Do you see the problem with the sample sentence? It has two distinct, possible meanings. Because *often* is between *annoying* and *assigning*, it may be linked to either of those two actions. The sentence violates a basic rule of description: All descriptions must be clear. Never place a description where it may have two possible meanings.

Fix the sentence by moving *often* so that it is closer to one of the verbs, thus showing the reader which of two words *often* describes. Here are two correct versions, each with a different meaning:

The teacher that Roger often annoyed assigned detention to him.

In this sentence, *often* is closer to *annoyed.* Thus, *often* describes *annoyed.* The sentence communicates to the reader that after 514 burps, the teacher lost her temper and assigned detention to Roger.

Here's a second possibility:

The teacher that Roger annoyed assigned detention to him often.

Now *often* is closer to *assigned.* The reader understands that *often* describes *assigned.* The sentence tells the reader that the teacher vowed "not to take anything from that little brat" and assigned detention to Roger every day of the school year, including winter break and Presidents' Day.

TIP

Sometimes you can clarify a confusing description by adding commas. Here's an unclear sentence:

The pig chewing on pig chow happily burped and made us all run for gas masks.

You don't know if the pig is *chewing happily* or *burping happily.* Commas make the meaning clear:

The pig, chewing on pig chow happily, burped and made us all run for gas masks.

I have to warn you about the comma correction. You can't always throw in a comma and fix a problem. In fact, sometimes you create an additional mistake by adding a comma! Check out Chapter 19 for comma advice, or fix the sentence by moving the description.

Q. Correct or incorrect? You decide.

The senator speaking last week voted against the Clarity Bill.

A. **Incorrect** The expression *last week* could apply to either *speaking* or *voted*.

Which sentence is correct?

46 **(A)** Running a red light once earned a stiff fine.

   (B) Running a red light earned a stiff fine at one time.

47 **(A)** Backing away from the traffic cop swiftly caused a reaction.

   (B) Backing swiftly away from the traffic cop caused a reaction.

48 **(A)** The punishment the judge imposed drew criticism from the press quickly.

   (B) The punishment the judge imposed quickly drew criticism from the press.

Practice Questions Answers and Explanations

1. **most beautiful** In choosing the top or bottom of a group of three or more, go for the superlative form. For long words, that means attaching *most* to the adjective.

2. **lower, livelier** The comparative form is the way to go because two cities, Paris and New York, are compared. One-syllable words such as *low* form comparatives with the addition of *-er*. Most two-syllable words rely on *more* or *less*, but *lively* is an exception.

3. **most efficient, most valuable** In choosing the top or bottom rank from a group of three or more, go for the superlative. *Efficient and valuable*, both long words, take *most* or *least*. In the context of this sentence, *most* makes sense.

4. **slower, less accurate** Comparing two elements — in this case, *Helen* and *Natalie* — calls for the comparative form. The one-syllable word takes *-er*, and the longer word relies on *less*.

5. **neater, more professional** Here the sentence compares typing to handwriting, two elements, so the comparative is correct. The one-syllable word becomes comparative with the addition of *-er*, and the two-syllable word turns into a two-word comparison.

6. **nastiest, more annoyed** In the world of imagined moods, Natalie's nasty mood is on top. Therefore, you need the superlative form. The second comparison compares two moods — her current mood and her mood when her desk burned. The comparative form of *annoyed* relies on *more*.

7. **more qualified** Two people are being compared here (Helen and Natalie), so go for the comparative form. Because *qualified* is a long word, attaching *more* is the way to go.

8. **most professional, less often** Choosing one out of three in the first part of the sentence calls for superlative. In the second part of the sentence, the speaker is comparing herself to every other employee, one at a time. Therefore, comparative is appropriate. Because the speaker is bragging, *less often* makes sense.

9. **more effectively** To compare two time periods, use *more*.

10. **less frequently** *Less* is what you need to compare actions in two time periods.

11. **most intelligently** Jenna is on top, so *most* is the word you need.

12. **less obviously** This is a comparison of two elements, so *less* is the appropriate choice.

13. **most harshly** The grading done by Professor Jahn is at the extreme, so *most* is correct.

14. **best** Once you mention the top or bottom experience of a lifetime, you're in the superlative column. *Best* is the word you want.

15. **more** Two elements are being compared here: the level of detail Edgar uses and the level of detail people want. When comparing two elements, the comparative form rules.

16. **worst** The superlative form singles out the extreme (in this case, the most boring) item in the scrapbook.

17. **better** The sentence pits Edgar's skills against the skills of one group (*the downtown jewelers*). Even though the group has several members, the comparison is between two elements — Edgar and the group — so comparative form is what you want.

(18) **most** The superlative form singles out the extreme — in this case, Edgar's timepiece collection, which included a raw-potato clock until it rotted.

(19) **better** The comparative deals with two states — how the clock runs before Edgar gets his hands on it and how it runs after.

(20) **best** To single out the top or bottom rank from a group of more than two, go for the superlative form.

(21) **less** The comparison is between what he has and what he needs — two items, so go for the comparative form.

(22) **B** The key here is to define the term *more*. *More than* what? Sentence A doesn't answer that question, so it's incomplete. Sentence B adds *than on a restaurant menu* to complete the comparison.

(23) **A** The problem with option B is that you can't tell what or who is being compared to Mr. Trout. The missing element of the comparison must be supplied, as it is in sentence A (*tech titan*).

(24) **B** Sentence A begins the comparison nicely (*more video games*) and then flubs the ending (*than what? than who?*). Sentence B supplies an ending — *than any land animal* — so the comparison is complete.

(25) **B** *Unique* can't be compared, because it's an absolute term. *Unusual*, which appears in sentence B, can be compared.

(26) **A** Two absolute words in sentence A (*unique, circular*) are treated as absolutes, so this sentence is correct. Sentence B contains *equally as*, which isn't correct in Standard English. The correct expression drops the *as*.

(27) **A** The word *so* begins a comparison, but only sentence A finishes it, adding *that I may volunteer to be shark bait*. **Note:** In informal situations, option B is acceptable, using *so* as an intensifier.

(28) **B** A pigeon is an animal, so sentence A doesn't make sense. Sentence B considers the pigeon in relation to other animals, so it's correct.

(29) **B** The *else* in option B creates a logical comparison between this (true!) event and other strange things I've seen in New York City. Because option A lacks *else*, it's illogical.

(30) **B** If she has a New York accent, she's probably a city resident. Without the word *other*, as in option A, you're saying that she's saner than herself. Not possible! Option B repairs the logic by inserting *other*.

(31) **A** The tourist isn't a *neighborhood resident* and therefore should be compared to one or more of them without the word *other*. In option B, the word *other* is unnecessary and illogical.

(32) **B** In this sentence, *the opera* and the *party* are the focus, so *just* should precede *the opera*, not *Allen*.

(33) **A** *Only* describes the conditions that prompt Fred to pay, so it should precede those conditions (*when he's in the mood or when the IRS serves an arrest warrant*).

(34) **A** *Just* limits the amount of homework, so choice A makes sense. Choice B lacks logic because the sentence mentions *she* (*Ms. Jonge*) and no other teachers.

(35) **B** In this sentence you're not limiting *seemed*. Instead, you're making a comment on how close to *impossible* the task seemed.

(36) **B** *Almost* limits the number of pages, not the act of writing.

(37) **A** *Even* should attach to *Ms. Jonge* because the sentence evaluates her as one of a group of teachers.

(38) **B** In sentence A, the bicycle has ten speeds, two tires, and a set of equations — not very useful in climbing hills and swerving to avoid taxis! The description must be close to *pedaled*, as it is in choice B.

(39) **B** *With flying colors* means "easily," which describes *passed*, not *clerk*. Place it at the beginning of the sentence and that's exactly what it does.

(40) **A** The description (*for cars skidding on ice*) describes *maneuvers*, not *test*.

(41) **B** The *letter* is *lacking sufficient postage*, not the *road test*.

(42) **A** *Sailing swiftly across the sea* describes Samantha's boat. Samantha's boat is performing that action. Sentence B is wrong because in sentence B, *sight*, the subject, is sailing. (And, of course, a *sight* can't sail.)

(43) **B** Choice A sounds correct, but when you stop to think, no one is enjoying *a good cup of coffee*. Insert *you* or *caffeine addicts* or some other person.

(44) **A** *While designing her latest tattoo* describes *Lulu*, not *camera*.

(45) **A** The *glasses* are *covered in rhinestones*, not *Lulu*.

(46) **B** In sentence A, *once* could refer to a single traffic mistake or to a single time period when stiff fines were the punishment. Sentence B clearly expresses the second meaning.

(47) **B** In sentence A, *swiftly* could refer to either the *backing away* or the timing of the cop's reaction. Sentence B attaches *swiftly* to *backing away*.

(48) **A** In sentence B, *quickly* could refer to the judge's action or to the reaction of the press. Sentence A clearly attaches the descriptive word to the reaction of the press.

If you're ready to test your skills a bit more, take the following chapter quiz that incorporates all the chapter topics.

Whaddya Know? Chapter 15 Quiz

Quiz time! Complete each problem to test your knowledge of the various topics covered in this chapter. You can then find the solutions and explanations in the next section.

As you breathe deeply, check out this yoga instruction manual, which, my lawyer begs me to mention, does *not* describe real postures that a normal human body can achieve. Do *not* try these positions at home, but *do* check every underlined portion for unclear or misplaced descriptions and comparisons. Mark them correct or incorrect.

Deciding which yoga posture to learn, (1) <u>Greeting Turtle or the One-Legged Grammar Cross</u> should be considered. If you (2) <u>only</u> learn one yoga posture, Greeting Turtle should be it. (3) <u>Even</u> beginners can do it, sometimes (4) <u>more well</u> than experienced athletes. In fact, Greeting Turtle is the (5) <u>easiest</u>.

To form Greeting Turtle, (6) <u>the mat</u> should extend from knees to armpits (7) <u>freshly laundered and dried to fluffiness</u>. (8) <u>Bend</u> the right knee up to the nose, as you relax the left ankle (9) <u>more completely</u>. Bend the knee (10) <u>least sharply</u> and then straighten the leg again. Now, for the (11) <u>most unique</u> aspect of this yoga posture, raise both arms to the sky and bless the yoga posture (12) <u>that is blue</u>. Learning this posture (13) <u>well</u> prepares you for (14) <u>harder</u> movements in yoga, the (15) <u>better</u> of all exercises.

Answers to Chapter 15 Quiz

1. **incorrect** The description that begins the sentence *(Deciding which yoga posture to learn)* should attach to the person deciding, not to the postures *(Greeting Turtle and One-Legged Grammar Cross)*. Substitute *you should consider* or something similar.

2. **incorrect** *Only* should precede *one yoga posture* because it limits the number, not the activity *(learn)*.

3. **correct** The comparison is between *beginners* and *experienced athletes,* so *even* is properly placed.

4. **incorrect** The word you want is *better.*

5. **incorrect** *Easiest* in what context? The comparison is incomplete.

6. **incorrect** The description that begins the sentence is attached to *the mat,* but *the mat* isn't forming Greeting Turtle. Reword so that *you* or *the student* forms Greeting Turtle, not *the mat.*

7. **incorrect** The armpits aren't *freshly laundered and dried to fluffiness* — *the mat* is. Move the description to follow *the mat.*

8. **correct** Not every sentence that begins with a verb form is incorrect! This one is a command to *you* and is correct.

9. **incorrect** *Complete* is an absolute — no comparisons allowed!

10. **incorrect** *Least* is the word when you're comparing one thing to more than two others. Here, the instructions refer to only two knee positions, so *less sharply* is what you want.

11. **incorrect** *Unique* is an absolute and can't be compared.

12. **incorrect** The *sky* is blue, not the *posture.* Move the description to follow *sky.*

13. **incorrect** *Well* is located between two actions — *learning* and *prepares* — and thus could apply to either. *Well* should follow *you.*

14. **correct** Two things are being compared — Greeting Turtle and a group of other movements. The comparative form is correct.

15. **incorrect** Yoga is singled out from a group, so *best* is the word you want.

5

Spelling, Punctuation, and Capitalization

In This Unit . . .

Chapter **16**

Becoming a Better ~~Speler~~ Speller

I f you see a "missteak" *(mistake)* when you're reading, you may be so distracted that you miss the writer's message. That's why you should pay attention to proper spelling. Because it follows few rules — and breaks even those some of the time — English spelling is hard. Nevertheless, with a little practice and perhaps some help from a computer program or the dictionary, you can perfect your spelling.

In this chapter, I explain some spelling rules and review words that puzzle many writers. Finally, I tell you how computer programs, smartphone apps, and the dictionary can help you become a champion speller.

Following the Rules of English Spelling

In some wonderful languages, what you see is what you say. You see a pair of letters in many different words, and you say them the same way, every time, because the written form follows strict rules. Sadly, English is *not* one of those logical languages. Read these words aloud:

thought

dough

doubt

The letters *ou* appear in every word. In *thought,* the *ou* sounds like *aw.* In *dough,* the same letters sound like *oh.* In *doubt,* the pair sounds like *ow.* Crazy, right?

You often have to memorize words or look up their correct spelling. However, English does follow some patterns. Not many, but some! In this section, I explain a few rules that help you write correctly.

Changing Y to I

One spelling rule involves words ending in *y* when you're adding *s* or *es* to make a plural or when you're adding a suffix. (A *suffix* is one or more letters added to the end of a word to create a new word.) The key is the letter just before the *y.* If it's a vowel (*a, e, i, o, u*), attach the suffix and you're done. If the letter is not a vowel, change the *y* to *i* before attaching the suffix. Some examples:

monkey → monkeys (vowel precedes *y*)

city → cities (consonant precedes *y*)

happy → happiest (consonant precedes *y*)

comply → compliance (consonant precedes *y*)

try → tried (consonant precedes *y*)

joy → joyful (vowel precedes *y*)

EXAMPLE

Q. Write the plural of each word: turkey, sky, prayer, butterfly.

A. **turkeys, skies, prayers, butterflies**

Q. Add the letters in parentheses to the base word, changing the base word as needed.

bounty (ful)

terrify (ing)

baby (ish)

fly (er)

try (ed)

A. **bountiful, terrifying, babyish, flier, tried**

In this minitable, you find some correctly spelled words and a couple of mistakes. If you see a mistake, write the proper spelling in the second column.

YOUR TURN

Word	Correct? Proper Spelling?
1. bunnies	
2. dutys	
3. lonelyness	
4. donkeys	
5. prettier	
6. tinyest	

I before E

Do you know this little rhyme?

> *I* before *E*
>
> except after *C*
>
> unless sounded like *A*
>
> as in *neighbor* and *weigh*

The rhyme explains a spelling rule:

>> **The letter *i* comes before the letter *e* most of the time.**

>> **After the letter *c*, place the letter *e* before the letter *i*.**

>> **If the letters *e* and *i* combine to sound like the letter *a*, the *e* comes before the *i*.**

WARNING

Some words don't follow this rule. Here are a few: *ancient, weird, science, efficient, fancied.* If you're unsure how to spell a word, check the dictionary.

EXAMPLE

Q. Write the word defined as "your sister's daughter."

A. **niece** The letter *i* generally precedes the letter *e*.

Q. Write the word defined as "the opposite of *give*."

A. **receive** After the letter *c*, the letter *e* precedes the letter *i*.

Q. Write the word defined as "measure with a scale."

A. **weigh** When the letters *e* and *i* combine to sound like the letter *a*, the letter *e* precedes the letter *i*.

YOUR TURN

In this minitable, you find some correctly spelled words and a couple of mistakes. If you see a mistake, write the proper spelling in the second column.

Word	Correct? Proper Spelling?
7. acheive	
8. shield	
9. breif	
10. their	
11. thief	
12. nieghbor	

Double letters

When you add -*ed* or -*ing* to a one-syllable word with a short vowel that ends with a consonant, double the consonant. If you're adding these endings to a one-syllable word with a long vowel, don't double the final consonant.

EXAMPLE

Q. Add the suffix -*ing* to the word *dot.*

A. **dotting** The word *dot* is a one-syllable word that ends with a consonant, *t*. When you add -*ing*, you must double the consonant, *t*, because the *o* is short.

Q. Add the suffix -*ed* to the word *bag.*

A. **bagged** The word *bag* is a one-syllable word that ends with a consonant, *g*. When you add -*ed*, you must double the consonant, *g*, because the *a* is short.

Q. Add the suffix -*ing* to the word *say.*

A. **saying** The vowel *a* in *say* is long. Don't double the final consonant when you add -*ing*.

Sometimes you double the final consonant in longer words, too, when you add -*ed* or -*ing*. Read these words. Pay attention to the sound of the words in the first column:

Original	With -ed or -ing
begin	beginning
occur	occurred
commit	committing
control	controlled

When you say the original words aloud, you hear that the accent — the stress — is on the last part of the word. You say

"be-GIN," not "BE-gin"

In this situation, check the last vowel sound. If it's short, double the final consonant when you attach *ed* or *ing*.

EXAMPLE

Q. Add *ed* to the word *contain*.

A. **contained** The word is pronounced "con-TAIN," with the stress on the second syllable. The vowel sound there is long, so the consonant *n* isn't doubled when you add *ed*.

Q. Add *ing* to *recall*.

A. **recalling** The word is pronounced "re-CALL," with the stress on the second syllable. The vowel sound is short, so the consonant *l* is doubled when you add *ing*.

YOUR TURN

In this minitable, you find some correctly spelled words and a couple of mistakes. If you see a mistake, write the proper spelling in the second column.

Word	Correct? Proper Spelling?
13. claimmed	
14. planned	
15. spinning	
16. puting	
17. runing	
18. beged	

WARNING

Double letters cause trouble in other situations, too. See "Taming Spelling Demons," later in this chapter, for more information.

Dropping the silent E

Many English words end with a silent *e*. If you skip that last letter, you may end up with a completely different word. *Hate* becomes *hat*, and *hope* turns into *hop*. If you say those words aloud, you notice that the silent *e* is a signal that the vowel before it is long. (A *long* vowel is pronounced like the name of the letter.) Don't forget to place the silent *e* where it's needed! *Hope* has a long *o*, and *hop*, a short *o*.

The spelling rule for words ending with a silent *e* has two parts:

» Keep the silent *e* if you add letters to the end of the word and if the first added letter is a consonant (any letter except *a, e, i, o,* or *u*):

- hate → hate<u>ful</u>
- pale → pale<u>ness</u>
- manage → manage<u>ment</u>

» Drop the silent *e* if you add letters to the end of the word and if the first added letter is a vowel (*a, e, i, o,* or *u*):

- arrive → arriv<u>ing</u>

- pure → pur<u>ity</u>

- nerve → nerv<u>ous</u>

EXAMPLE

Q. Add *-ly* to *time.*

A. **timely** The *i* in *time* is long, and the first letter you're adding is a consonant, *l.* Don't drop the silent *e.*

Q. Add *-ing* to *time.*

A. **timing** The *i* in *time* is long, and the first letter you're adding is a vowel. Drop the silent *e.*

I doubt you'll be surprised to hear that the silent *e* rule has exceptions. Here's one:

dye (to change the color of cloth) — dyeing

As always, if you're unsure how to spell a word, check the dictionary.

YOUR TURN

See how well you know the silent *e.* If you see a misspelled word in the first column, write the correct spelling in the second column. To help you, the words you're looking at are in sentences and underlined.

Word	Correct? Proper Spelling?
19. A tiger's <u>bit</u> can kill you.	
20. Mary is <u>givving</u> a concert this evening.	
21. <u>Haveing</u> a cold is miserable.	
22. Andrew was <u>driving</u> when he <u>hite</u> that tree.	
23. If the soap is <u>pur</u>, it will float.	
24. Play <u>nicely</u> with the other children!	

Taming Spelling Demons

Spelling demons aren't supernatural monsters. They're words that often trick writers. With a little care, though, you will always spell these words correctly.

How does the word end?

Read this paragraph. Look closely at the underlined words:

> Sandy was absent from school because she went to see the <u>doctor</u>. She was not ready for the <u>grammar</u> test. Sandy's mom, a <u>professor</u>, wrote a note to the <u>teacher</u>. "Please excuse my <u>daughter</u> from this exam," she wrote.

Every underlined word ends in *ar, er,* or *or*. These ending letters are different, but when you say the words aloud, the endings sound the same. (Isn't English delightful? Three ways to spell the same sound! Three spelling problems!) When you write these words, be careful. Here's a minitable to help you remember.

AR Endings	ER Endings	OR Endings
grammar	lawyer	doctor
scholar	plumber	tutor
dollar	builder	actor
collar	better	mentor
polar	counter	bachelor
burglar	writer	author
circular	kinder	director
molar	anger	editor
similar	climber	creator
spectacular	gangster	favor

The word *kinder* is a comparison: "Mary is *kinder* than Tom." When you're making a comparison, the word usually ends with *er.*

Another type of spelling demon is a word that ends with either *ant* or *ent*. These three-letter groups sound the same, so they're easy to confuse. Check this minitable:

Words Ending with ANT	Words Ending with ENT
important	different
pleasant	commitment
constant	argument
elegant	requirement
assistant	accent
instant	adolescent
irrelevant	client
immigrant	department
protestant	employment
tenant	monument

One more pair of word endings — *ible* and *able* — also confuses people. Read the words in this minitable:

Words Ending with IBLE	Words Ending with ABLE
visible	dependable
possible	washable
incredible	affordable
horrible	acceptable
sensible	understandable
responsible	reasonable

TIP No rule guides you automatically to the right choice between *ible* and *able*. However, *able* generally attaches to complete words. If you cross out *able* in every word in the second column, you see a real word (*depend, wash*, and so on). If you cross out *ible*, you don't find a real word.

TIP If you read these lists aloud once a week, gradually you will remember how to spell the words. Of course, these lists could be much longer, because many English words end the same way. If you don't know how to spell an ending, the dictionary can help.

One or two?

Are you *dissapointed* or *disappointed* or *disapointed* in your spelling skills? Deciding when to double a letter is annoying. Most often, you have to memorize the spelling. (One rule can help you figure out whether you need to double a letter when you add *-ing* or *-ed* to a word. See "Following the Rules of English Spelling," earlier in this chapter, for more information.)

Here are some demons that give you double trouble. I underline the spots where many people make a spelling error (doubling when one letter is needed or placing one letter where two is correct):

enro<u>ll</u>	di<u>s</u>gust	we<u>dd</u>ing	usua<u>ll</u>y
emba<u>rr</u>a<u>ss</u>	ba<u>gg</u>age	rea<u>ll</u>y	su<u>dd</u>en
a<u>p</u>artment	o<u>cc</u>ur	co<u>mm</u>i<u>t</u>ment	exce<u>ll</u>ent
o<u>pp</u>osite	u<u>nn</u>atural	casua<u>ll</u>y	<u>lo</u>se (not be able to find)
a<u>pp</u>ear	special	i<u>mm</u>ediately	<u>loo</u>se (not tight)

TIP Two phrases are sometimes mistakenly written as one word, when two words are correct: *a lot* (many) and *all right* (fine, agreed).

Which vowel?

Vowels — *a, e, i, o, u* — can confuse spellers. *Long* vowels (those that sound like the name of the letter, like the *e* in *be*) are easier than *short* vowels (like the *e* in *wet*). Why? Short vowels often sound like each other. Also, sometimes their sound blends into the word, so you may not realize they're present. Here are some spelling demons that cause vowel problems. The trouble spots are underlined:

separate	definite	cause	among
persuade	recognize	despair	jewelry
obey	nursery	division	officer
extraordinary	February	category	disguise

Correct or misspelled? You decide. If you find a mistake, write the proper spelling in the second column of the following minitable.

YOUR TURN

Word	Correct? Proper Spelling?
25. carpentor	
26. speler	
27. independant	
28. catagory	
29. occurr	
30. calendar	

Checking the Dictionary for Spelling Help

Rules and memory provide wonderful help with spelling. Sometimes, though, no rule applies. That's the time to seek help from the dictionary — either a book or a website. A dictionary is the final authority on English spelling and much more.

Dictionaries list words in alphabetical order. It's difficult to look up a word if you have no clue how to spell it. Try turning to the section that seems to match the first couple of letters in the word you need. (If you're working with an online dictionary, type those letters.) Look around a bit until you see a word that matches the meaning you want.

WARNING

Be sure that the definition matches the meaning you want. Some smartphones come with a program that recognizes speech. If you say the word, it appears on the screen. Before you use that spelling, check the definition of that word in a dictionary. The phone cannot tell the difference between many common words, so *lead* (the metal) may turn into *led* (directed, ruled).

Dictionaries are helpful, but so are people. If a teacher or a friend who is a good speller is nearby, ask! Most people feel good about assisting others and will happily spell a word for you.

Each word in the dictionary is explained in an *entry*. Dictionary entries can be confusing because they throw in a lot of information. Here's a sample dictionary entry of the word *comfort*:

comfort ′kəm – fərt

v. 1. to ease someone's worry or pain. "The doctor will comfort the injured child." 2. to help someone deal with grief. "Mourners at the funeral comfort the family."

n. 1. the act of comforting. "Jane offered comfort to her friend." 2. the quality of ease. "In this car, you travel in comfort." 3. a physical feeling characterized by lack of pain or stress. "Bill valued comfort more than convenience."

Here's how to read this entry:

>> **First you see the word.** I placed *comfort* in bold type. You may see it that way or in a different color or typeface.

>> **Next is the pronunciation.** Online, you can listen to someone say the word. On paper, a set of special symbols tells you how to pronounce the word. The key to the symbols appears at the beginning or end of the dictionary.

>> **The part of speech appears next.** Usually, this information is abbreviated. You see *v.* for *verb* and *n.* for *noun.* Other words may be labeled as *adj.* (adjective) or *adv.* (adverb). You also find *p.* for *pronoun, prep.* for *preposition,* and *conj.* for *conjunction.* One abbreviation, *int.* for *(interjection),* is rare because not many words fall into this category.

>> **Definitions are numbered in the order of importance.** The most common definition comes first, followed by other meanings that appear less frequently.

>> **Most dictionaries include sample sentences.** These sentences show you how to use the word properly.

TIP

The dictionary may also tell you the origin of the word. *Comfort,* for example, comes from the Latin word meaning "with strength."

The format of your dictionary may be a little different. Don't worry! All the information you need should still be there.

Practice Questions Answers and Explanations

(1) **correct** A consonant, *n*, precedes the *y*, so you change the *y* to *i* and add *es*.

(2) **duties** A consonant, *t*, precedes the *y*, so you change the *y* to *i* and add *es*.

(3) **loneliness** A consonant, *l*, precedes the *y*, so you change the *y* to *i* and add *ness*.

(4) **correct** A vowel, *e*, precedes the *y*, so you do not change the *y* to *i*.

(5) **correct** A consonant, *t*, precedes the *y*, so you change the *y* to *i* and add *er*.

(6) **tiniest** A consonant, *n*, precedes the *y*, so you change the *y* to *i* and add *est*.

(7) **achieve** Generally, the letter *i* precedes the letter *e*.

(8) **correct** Generally, the letter *i* precedes the letter *e*.

(9) **brief** Generally, the letter *i* precedes the letter *e*.

(10) **correct** When the letters *e* and *i* sound like *A*, the letter *e* precedes the letter *i*.

(11) **correct** Generally, the letter *i* precedes the letter *e*.

(12) **neighbor** When the letters *e* and *i* sound like *a*, the letter *e* precedes the letter *i*.

(13) **claimed** The vowels *ai* sound like the long vowel *a*. Don't double the final consonant after a long vowel sound.

(14) **correct** The word *plan* has a short *a*, so the final consonant, *n*, is doubled when you add *ed*.

(15) **correct** The word *spin* has a short *i*, so the final consonant, *n*, is doubled when you add *ing*.

(16) **putting** The word *put* has a short *u*, so the final consonant, *t*, is doubled when you add *ing*.

(17) **running** The word *run* has a short *u*, so the final consonant, *n*, is doubled when you add *ing*.

(18) **begged** The word *beg* has a short *e*, so the final consonant, *g*, is doubled when you add *ed*.

(19) **bite** The word *bit* means "a small portion of." When a tiger uses its jaws, the word is *bite*, which has a long *i*.

(20) **giving** Because there is a short *i* in *give*, drop the *e* when you add *ing*. Don't double the consonant.

(21) **having** The *a* in *have* is short, so drop the silent *e* when you add *ing*.

(22) **correct, hit** Because there is a long vowel, *i*, in *drive*, you drop the silent *e* when you add *ing*. You want a short *i* sound in *hit*, so there is no silent *e*.

(23) **pure** The *u* in *pure* is long, so the word ends with a silent *e*.

(24) **correct** When you add *ly* to *nice*, you keep the silent *e* because *ly* begins with a consonant, *l*.

(25) **carpenter** This word ends with *er*.

(26) **speller** Place this word in the double *l* category.

(27) **independent** You need an *ent* at the end of this word.

(28) **category** You need only one *a* in this word.

(29) **occur** Double up the *c* here, not the *r*.

(30) **correct** No rules here, just memory: The vowels in this word are *a, e, a* — in that order.

If you're ready to test your skills a bit more, take the following chapter quiz that incorporates all the chapter topics.

Whaddya Know? Chapter 16 Quiz

Quiz time! Complete each problem to test your knowledge on the various topics covered in this chapter. You can then find the solutions and explanations in the next section.

1. Add *ful* to *plate.*

2. Which word is spelled correctly? *commitmant, occur, catagory*

3. Which word is spelled correctly? *receive, beleive, nieghbor*

4. Add *-ing* to *bite.*

5. Which word is spelled correctly? *dissappoint, disapointing, disappointed*

6. What does the abbreviation *n.* stand for in a dictionary definition?

7. Add *ing* to *permit.*

8. Which word is spelled correctly? *seperate, author, extrordinary*

9. List three types of information a dictionary provides.

10. Which word is spelled correctly? *naming, enrol, peice*

Answers to Chapter 16 Quiz

1. **plateful** The *a* in *plate* is long, and the first added letter is a consonant. Don't drop the silent *e*.

2. **occur** The other two words, correctly spelled, are *commitment* and *category*.

3. **receive** The other two words, correctly spelled, are *believe* and *neighbor*. The rule is *i* before *e*, except after *c* or when sounded like *a*. In *receive*, *ei* follows *c*. In *neighbor*, you hear an *a* sound. You have no *c* or *a* sound in *believe*, so the *i* comes before the *e*.

4. **biting** The one-syllable word *bite* has a long *i* and a silent *e*. The first added letter is a vowel, *i*, so you drop the silent *e* before adding the suffix *-ing*.

5. **disappointed** The rule for this word: one *s*, double *p*.

6. **noun** Dictionaries identify the part of speech. The abbreviation for *noun* is *n*.

7. **permitting** The stress in the word *permit* is on the second syllable, *mit*. That syllable has a short *i*, so you must double the final consonant when you add *-ing*.

8. **author** The other two words, correctly spelled, are *separate* and *extraordinary*.

9. **definition, part of speech, pronunciation** Some dictionaries include sample sentences and word origins. If you listed those, count yourself correct.

10. **naming** The *a* in *name* is long, so drop the silent *e* when you add *-ing*. The correct spelling of the other words is *enroll* and *piece*.

Chapter **17**

Little Hooks, Big Problems: Apostrophes

O n a recent walk, I noticed an odd sign:

GRANDMAS PUNCH

"Interesting," I thought. *Grandmas punch* whom? People who won't look at pictures of their grandchildren? Then I realized the sign was in front of a bar and probably referred to *Grandma's punch* — a drink made from a family recipe. An apostrophe makes a big difference, doesn't it?

Apostrophes are punctuation marks that look like hooks and hang near certain letters, or, occasionally, numbers. They're useful, but placed where they are not needed or omitted where they are, they can sabotage your writing. In this chapter, I show you how apostrophes indicate ownership and shorten words.

The Pen of My Aunt or My Aunt's Pen? Using Apostrophes to Show Possession

Most other languages are smarter than English. To show possession in French, for example, you say

> the pen of my aunt *(la plume du ma tante)*

You can say the same thing in English, too, but English has added another option — the apostrophe:

> my *aunt's* pen

Apostrophes may also show another kind of ownership — a relationship:

> Bob's uncle

The uncle doesn't actually belong to Bob the way a book or a pen may. However, these two people are in an uncle–nephew relationship. The apostrophe shows that the *uncle* belongs to *Bob*.

Things or places can also be in an "ownership" role that's expressed by an apostrophe:

> the book's cover
>
> Brazil's coastline

When you're deciding whether you need an apostrophe, consider whether the word *of* expresses what you're trying to say. With the *of* method, you note

> the sharp claw *of* the crocodile = the *crocodile's* sharp claw
>
> the peanut-stained trunk *of* the elephant = the *elephant's* peanut-stained trunk

and so on.

The *of* test works even when no clear owner appears in the phrase. Such a situation arises mostly when you're talking about time. Take a look at these phrases:

> one week's house cleaning = one week *of* house cleaning
>
> a year's lawn care = one year *of* lawn care

Here's the bottom line: When you're talking about time, give your sentence the *of* test. If it passes, insert an apostrophe.

TIP

Think of an apostrophe as a little hand holding on to something or someone. The "owner" — the person or thing that possesses — is the word with the apostrophe and the letter *s*.

Ownership for singles

No, I'm not talking about buying a home all by yourself, with your very own mortgage. I'm talking about using apostrophes to show ownership with singular nouns. To show possession by one owner, add an apostrophe and the letter *s* to the owner:

> the *dragon's* burnt fang (the burnt fang belongs to the dragon)
>
> *Lulu's* pierced eyebrow (the pierced eyebrow belongs to Lulu)
>
> *Michael's* gold bar (the gold bar belongs to Michael)

EXAMPLE

Q. Use an apostrophe to express the underlined idea: I borrowed the car <u>that belongs to Jill</u>.

A. I borrowed <u>Jill's car</u>.

Q. Use an apostrophe to express the underlined idea: You have the amount of homework <u>that can be completed in an hour</u>.

A. You have <u>an hour's homework</u>.

YOUR TURN

Use an apostrophe to express the underlined idea in each sentence.

1. The diploma <u>that belongs to Sam</u> hangs on the wall.

2. Did you bring the umbrella <u>that Aunt Jane owns</u>?

3. Trains <u>in Spain</u> are very fast.

4. The motorcycle needs <u>a year of</u> work before it will run properly.

Sharing the wealth: Plural possessives

Not everything belongs to one owner. Amazon is close, but even that company hasn't taken over everything (yet). For now, you need to deal with plural owners. Plurals nouns can be regular or irregular in form, and so can plural possessives. To make your life more complicated, English has compound plural possessives, too. In this section, I explain all three.

Regular plural possessives

The plurals of most English nouns — anything greater than one — already end with the letter *s*. To show ownership, all you do is add an apostrophe after the *s*. Take a look at these examples:

> police officers' union (the *union* belongs to *police officers*)
>
> police officers' uniforms (the *uniforms* belong to *police officers*)
>
> many *dinosaurs'* habitat (the habitat belongs to a number of *dinosaurs*)
>
> a thousand sword swallowers' sliced tonsils (the *tonsils* belong to *a thousand sword swallowers*)

Did you notice that the possessive form of *officers* is *officers'* whether they "own" one thing *(union)* or more than one *(uniforms)?* Only the owner, not the possession, matters.

TIP

The *of* test works for plurals, too: If you can rephrase the expression using the word *of*, you may need an apostrophe. Remember to add the apostrophe after the letter *s*.

three *days'* editing work on that chapter = three days *of* editing work

16 *years'* creativity from Lulu's tattoo artist = 16 years *of* creativity

2 *degrees'* increase in temperature = 2 degrees *of* increase in temperature

EXAMPLE

Q. Which sentence is correct if the coach gives attention to all players?

   (A) The coach has only one goal in life: to improve the Yankee's batting.

   (B) The coach has only one goal in life: to improve the Yankees' batting.

A. **B** If the coach works with more than one player, you need the plural possessive form, which adds an apostrophe after the *s*. The first sentence would be correct if the coach were working with only one player.

Q. Which sentence is correct?

   (A) The Halloween decorations are decaying, especially the pumpkins' teeth. Sam carved all ten jack-o'-lanterns, and he can't bear to throw them away.

   (B) The Halloween decorations are decaying, especially the pumpkin's teeth. Sam carved all ten jack-o'-lanterns, and he can't bear to throw them away.

A. **A** The context of the sentence (*all ten jack-o'-lanterns*) reveals that more than one pumpkin is rotting away. In sentence A, *pumpkins'* expresses a plural possessive. In sentence B, the apostrophe is placed before the *s*, the spot for a single pumpkin.

Irregular plural possessives

At the beginning of this chapter, I mention *grandchildren*. That word is plural, but *grandchildren* doesn't end with the letter *s*. In other words, it's an irregular plural. To show ownership for an irregular plural, add an apostrophe and then the letter *s* (*grandchildren's*). Check out these examples:

teeth's cavities (The cavities belong to the teeth.)

children's toys (The toys belong to the children.)

the three blind *mice's* eye doctor (The eye doctor belongs to the three blind mice.)

geese's beaks (The beaks belong to the geese.)

Q. What is the plural possessive form of each word?

feet

fruit

deer

A. **feet's, fruit's, deer's** These irregular plurals do not end in the letter *s*, so you add an apostrophe and an *s* to create the plural possessive.

Compound plural possessives

What happens when two single people own something? In real life, they often go to court and sue each other. In grammar, they (or you) add one or two apostrophes, depending on the type of ownership. If two people share possession, use only one apostrophe.

George and Martha *Washington's* home (The home belonged to the two of them.)

Larry and *Ella's* wedding (The wedding was for both the blushing groom and the frightful bride.)

Roger and the superspy's secret (Roger told the superspy, so now they're sharing the secret.)

If two people own things separately, as individuals, use two apostrophes:

George's and *Martha's* teeth (He has his set of teeth — false, by the way — and she has her own set.)

Lulu's and *Gary's* new shoes. (She wears size 2, and he wears size 12. Hers are lizard skin with 4-inch heels. His are plastic with 5-inch heels.)

Cedric's and *Lola's* fingernails. (He has his; she has her own; both sets are fake and quite long.)

Q. Rewrite these expressions using the possessive form.

the puppies of Fido and Spot (Fido and Spot are the parents)

ears of Mickey and Minnie

paintings made by Michelangelo and by Rembrandt

A. **Fido and Spot's puppies, Mickey's and Minnie's ears, Michelangelo's and Rembrandt's paintings** The puppies belong to both *Fido and Spot*, so only one apostrophe is inserted. *Mickey and Minnie* have separate sets of ears, so they need separate apostrophes. In the same way, each artist has a separate set of *paintings* and a separate apostrophe.

Remember that an apostrophe shows ownership. Don't use an apostrophe when you have a plural that is *not* expressing ownership.

> RIGHT: Labels stick to your shoes.
>
> WRONG: Label's stick to your shoes.
>
> ALSO WRONG: Labels' stick to your shoes.

To sum up the rule on plurals and apostrophes: If the plural noun is not showing ownership, *don't* use an apostrophe. If the plural noun shows ownership, *do* add an apostrophe after the *s* (for regular plurals). For irregular plurals showing ownership, add *'s*.

I have to admit that, in two special cases, apostrophes may show up in plurals. To form the plural of a lowercase letter, add an apostrophe and an *s*. To help the reader along, you should italicize the letter but not the apostrophe or the *s*. To write the plural of a word used as a word (not for what it means), italicize the word and add a nonitalicized s (with no apostrophe). If you're writing with a pen, not a computer, italics aren't possible. Pen-writers should place the plural of the word used as a word or the letter in quotation marks and add an apostrophe and an *s*. Take a peek at these examples:

> You have too many *g*'s in that word, young lady!
>
> The boss throws "impossible's" into every discussion of my raise.

Until a few years ago, the plurals of capital letters, numbers, and symbols were also formed with apostrophes (*F*'s, *1960*'s, and *&*'s, for example). Most writers now omit the apostrophe in these cases (*Fs, 1960s,* and *&s*).

A few special possessions

Most singular and plural possessive situations are obvious, but a couple of special situations may trip you up.

Possession with proper nouns

Companies, stores, and organizations also own things, so these proper nouns — singular or plural — also require apostrophes. Put the apostrophe at the end of the name:

> *Macy's* finest shoes
>
> *Microsoft's* finest operating system
>
> *McGillicuddy, Pinch, and Cinch's* finest lawsuit
>
> *Grammar, Inc.'s* finest apostrophe rule

Some stores have apostrophes in their names, even without a sense of possession:

> *Macy's* occupies an entire city block.

Macy's is always written with an apostrophe, even when no noun appears after the store name. *Macy's* implies a shortened version of a longer name (perhaps *Macy's department store*).

Ownership with hyphenated words

Other special cases of possession involve compound words — son-in-law, mother-of-pearl, and all the other words with *hyphens* (those little horizontal lines). The rule is simple: Place the apostrophe at the end of the word. Never put an apostrophe inside a word. Here are some examples of singular compound nouns:

the *secretary-treasurer's* report on the missing money (The report belongs to the secretary-treasurer.)

the *dogcatcher-in-chief's* cat video (The cat video belongs to the dogcatcher-in-chief.)

my *mother-in-law's* huge elbows (The elbows belong to my mother-in-law.)

The same rule applies to plural compound nouns that are hyphenated. Take a look at these examples:

the *doctors-of-philosophy's* study lounge (The study lounge is owned by all the doctors-of-philosophy.)

my *fathers-in-law's* wedding present (The wedding present was from both fathers-in-law.)

Possessive nouns that end in S

Singular nouns that end in *s* present special problems. Let me explain: My last name is Woods. My name is singular, because I am only one person. When students evaluate me, they may write:

Ms. Woods's grammar lessons can't be beat.

or

Ms. Woods' grammar lessons can't be beat.

(They say a lot of other things, too, but I like to focus on the positive.)

TIP

In informal speech and writing, both sample sentences are correct. Why are these two options — *Ms. Woods's* and *Ms. Woods'* — acceptable? The answer has to do with sound. If you say the first sentence, by the time you get to the word *grammar*, you're hissing and spitting all over your listener. Not a pleasant idea. The second sentence sounds better. So the grammar police have given in on this one, except in the most formal situations or when the word may be misunderstood. For example, if you don't know that my name is *Woods*, you may think that *Woods' grammar book* is a book belonging to more than one person named *Wood*. If you ignore the saliva factor, you can write *Woods's grammar book* and avoid any confusion, because that format clearly shows a singular, possessive noun, *Woods's*.

To sum up: If the name of a singular owner ends in the letter *s* and you're in an informal situation, you may add only an apostrophe, not an apostrophe and another *s*. But if you like hissing and spitting or if you have to be on your best grammatical behavior, add an apostrophe *and* an *s*.

Rewrite the underlined words or expressions to show possession.

EXAMPLE **Q.** Bloomingdales merchandise

A. **Bloomingdale's merchandise** The store name is generally written as a possessive, and in this expression, the store possesses *merchandise*.

Q. Davy Jones shoes (Davy Jones is the owner of the shoes.)

A. **Davy Jones's shoes** or **Davy Jones' shoes** The owner's name ends in *s*. In a formal situation, add an apostrophe and the letter *s*. To avoid saliva spray, many people simply add the apostrophe in informal situations.

Q. sister-in-laws gown (gown belongs to one woman)

A. **sister-in-law's** gown Add an apostrophe and an *s* to the end of a hyphenated word.

 Rewrite the underlined words or expressions to show possession.

YOUR TURN

5 mugs designs (several mugs with varied designs)

6 mices feet

7 mother-in-laws graduation from law school

8 Len and Gary hometown (one town where they both live)

9 Len and Gary houses (separate houses)

10 Apples spring sale (the computer company)

11 flowers roots (many flowers)

12 people's choice

13 Guinness best beer (brewing company)

14 secretaries duties

15 childrens toys

Shortened Words for Busy People: Contractions

Are you busy? Probably. Therefore, like just about everyone in our society, you probably use contractions when you speak. A *contraction* shortens a word by removing one or more letters and substituting an apostrophe in the same spot. For example, chop *wi* out of *I will*, throw in an apostrophe, and you have *I'll*. The resulting word is shorter and faster to say, with only one syllable (sound) instead of two.

Making short work of common contractions

No matter how busy you are, it's worth learning the most common contractions. Take a look at Table 17-1. Notice that a couple of contractions are irregular. *(Won't, for example, is short for will not.)*

Table 17-1   Contractions

Phrase	Contraction	Phrase	Contraction
are not	aren't	she is	she's
cannot	can't	that is	that's
could not	couldn't	they are	they're
do not	don't	they will	they'll
does not	doesn't	they would	they'd
did not	didn't	we are	we're
he will	he'll	we will	we'll
he would	he'd	we would	we'd
he is	he's	we have	we've
is not	isn't	what is	what's
it is	it's	who is	who's
I am	I'm	will not	won't
I will	I'll	would not	wouldn't
I would	I'd	you are	you're
I have	I've	you have	you've
she will	she'll	you will	you'll
she would	she'd	you would	you'd

If you'd like to make a contraction that isn't in Table 17-1, check your dictionary to make sure it's legal!

Apostrophes also shorten numbers, as in these examples:

> Martha graduated in '10, a year later than her brother. (short for 2010)
>
> Are you a member of the class of '99? (short for 1999)
>
> During the last battle, in '06, the king died. (short for 1206)
>
> The grape harvest in '55 produced delicious wine. (short for 1855)

WARNING

Do not drop numbers unless you're sure that your reader knows what is missing. A member of the class of 1910 is a lot older than a member of the class of 2010! Saving time is good. Being clear is better.

You coulda made a contraction mistake

Woulda, coulda, shoulda. These three "verbs" are potholes on the road to better grammar. Why? Because they don't exist in Standard English. Here's the recipe for a grammatical felony. Start with three real verb phrases: *would have, could have,* and *should have.* Now turn them into contractions: *would've, could've,* and *should've.* Now turn them back into words. But don't turn them back into the words they actually represent. Instead, let your ears be your guide. (It helps if you have a lot of wax in your ears, because the sounds don't quite match.) Now say the following: *would of, could of,* and *should of.*

Take a look at these examples:

> WRONG: If George had asked me to join the spy ring, I would of said, "No way."
>
> RIGHT: If George had asked me to join the spy ring, I would have said, "No way."
>
> ALSO RIGHT: If George had asked me to join the spy ring, I would've said, "No way."

Here's another set:

> WRONG: When I heard about the spy ring, I should of told the Central Intelligence Agency.
>
> RIGHT: When I heard about the spy ring, I should have told the Central Intelligence Agency.
>
> ALSO RIGHT: When I heard about the spy ring, I should've told the Central Intelligence Agency.

TIP

When you're texting, you may be tempted to drop apostrophes altogether. It's annoying to type on small screens, and there's little chance someone will misunderstand *dont* without the apostrophe (*don't*). Resist the temptation, at least when you're writing to someone who expects to read Standard English. Also, be careful when an app presents you with one or two possible words after you type a couple of letters and when you're using a speech-to-text app. Be sure the word you want is on the screen, with or without an apostrophe as required by the meaning of what you're writing.

Change the underlined words into contractions.

EXAMPLE

Q. Jane <u>would not</u> go to the laundromat even though her hamper was overflowing.

A. **wouldn't**

Q. <u>Do not</u> underestimate the power of a good appetizer.

A. **Don't**

YOUR TURN

Q. Change the underlined words into contractions, or, if they're already contractions, expand them into the words they represent.

16. "Peanuts <u>are not</u> the best choice for an appetizer, because of allergies," commented Pam.

17. "I know. <u>That is</u> why I <u>did not</u> bring any," answered Adam.

18. "<u>I am</u> sure that <u>Sam has</u> selected a better appetizer," he added.

19. "I <u>would've</u> bought caviar, but I <u>could not</u> pass the cheese counter without buying something," commented Linda.

20. "<u>Who is</u> bringing dessert?" asked Adam.

21. Adam has baked a fancy dessert every year since <u>1992</u>, but this year <u>he is</u> watching his weight.

22. "If <u>they had</u> served ice cream," he once said after dining at Pam's house, "<u>I would've</u> eaten only a spoonful or two."

23. "Yes, <u>that is</u> enough," agreed Pam.

24. Some people think that dessert <u>cannot</u> be part of a healthful diet.

25. <u>They are</u> wrong; an occasional treat <u>will not</u> hurt most people.

26. They will get together next week with other graduates of the class of <u>2020</u>.

Managing Tricky Contraction/Pronoun Pairs

To indicate ownership, English also supplies pronouns — words that take the place of a noun. Some possessive pronouns are *my, your, his, her, its, our,* and *their.* Here's a rule so basic — and so often broken — that you should consider taping it to your pinky finger: No possessive pronoun ever has an apostrophe. These are a few examples of possessive pronouns in action:

> *your* completely unruly child — not your' completely unruly child (also wrong: that completely unruly child of yours')
>
> *our* extremely well-behaved youngster — not our' extremely well-behaved youngster (also wrong: the extremely well-behaved youngster of ours')
>
> *their* tendency to fight — not their' tendency to fight (also wrong: the tendency of theirs' to fight)
>
> *his* call to the police — not his' call to the police

A few possessive pronouns sound the same as contractions. The possessive pronoun should not be written with an apostrophe, and the contraction should. Here are three word pairs — and one set of triplets — that confuse many people. This section helps you sort them out so that you can always select the correct form.

Its/it's

You also have to be careful not to confuse the pronoun *its* with the contraction *it's*:

> » *Its* is a pronoun that shows ownership or belonging:
>
> The book had a stain on <u>its</u> cover.
>
> <u>Its</u> short leg makes the table wobble.
>
> » *It's* is a shortened form of *it is*:
>
> <u>It's</u> a blood stain!
>
> The tourist went to London because <u>it's</u> an interesting place.

Whose/who's

The pronoun *whose* acts as a word-bridge between owners and possessions, as in these sentences:

> Bill, <u>whose</u> parakeets like lettuce, has just planted some in his garden.
>
> The parakeets, <u>whose</u> beaks are sharp, ate Bill's curtains yesterday.

Don't confuse *whose* with *who's*, the short form of *who is*. Check out these examples:

> I don't know <u>who's</u> responsible for the mess. *(who's = short form of who is)*
>
> <u>Whose</u> coat is on the floor? *(Whose = possessive pronoun)*
>
> <u>Who's</u> going to clean up? *(Who's = short form of who is)*

Your/you're

You're in trouble if *your* apostrophes are in the wrong place. *You're* means *you are*. *Your* shows possession. These two words are not interchangeable. Here are some examples:

> "<u>You're</u> not going to eat that rotten pumpkin," declared Rachel. *(You're = short form of you are)*
>
> "<u>Your</u> refusal to eat the pumpkin means that you will be given mystery meat instead," commented Dean. *(your = possessive pronoun)*
>
> "<u>You're</u> going to wear that pumpkin if you threaten me," said Lola. *(You're = short form of you are)*

Their/there/they're

The pronoun *their* is not the same as *there* or *they're*.

>> *Their* shows ownership:

Their clothing was wet when they came in from the rain.

Do the students have their umbrellas?

>> *There* refers to a place:

Put the book there.

Over there is my favorite piano.

>> *They're* is a shortened form of *they are*:

They're in the library now.

Nina and Oscar said that they're ready when you are.

TIP

When you're typing on a smartphone or computer, words you may want to use pop up after you've entered only a letter or two. Be especially careful to choose the correct word, because it's likely that the app will give you one version with an apostrophe and one without. If you're using a speech-to-text app, you may also find a missing or an unneeded apostrophe. Proofread! For more on electronic media, see Chapter 25.

EXAMPLE

Q. Choose the proper word from the parentheses and write it in the blank.

_____ (Its, It's) snowing today, so the Santos family, _____ (who's, whose) neighborhood is very icy, will stay in _____ (they're, there, their) home. _____ (You're, your) sheltering at home, too, or you should be!

A. **It's, whose, their, You're** In the first blank "it is" makes sense, so you want the contraction *it's*, not the possessive pronoun *its*. *Who's* is short for "who is," which doesn't fit the second blank. You need the pronoun *whose* in that spot. The pronoun *their* shows that the home belongs to the Santos family. *You're* is short for "you are" and fits the last sentence perfectly.

YOUR TURN

Choose the proper word from parentheses and write it in the blank.

The school's boiler is broken and the building is freezing, so no one will go (27) ____ (they're, there, their). The bus driver doesn't trust his vehicle, especially (28) ____ (its, it's) brakes. The driver, (29) ____ (who's, whose) always careful, inspected the streets and reported that (30) ____ (they're, there, their) snowy. (31) ____ (You're, Your) watching the television reports of the storm, right? No one should be out (32) ____ (they're, there, their) in the midst of such bad weather.

Practice Questions Answers and Explanations

1. **Sam's diploma**

2. **Aunt Jane's umbrella**

3. **Spain's trains**

4. **a year's work** This phrase is equivalent to "a year of work."

5. **mugs' designs** Add an *s* and an apostrophe to indicate plural owners.

6. **mice's feet** *Mice* is an irregular plural. Add an apostrophe and the letter *s* to make the word possessive.

7. **mother-in-law's graduation from law school** Add an apostrophe to the end of a hyphenated word to show possession.

8. **Len and Gary's hometown** Len and Gary share their hometown, so only one apostrophe is necessary.

9. **Len's and Gary's houses** Len and Gary have separate houses, so two apostrophes are needed.

10. **Apple's spring sale** Add an apostrophe and the letter *s* to the company name to show possession.

11. **flowers' roots** Add an *s* and an apostrophe to indicate plural owners.

12. **people's choice** *People* is an irregular plural. Add an apostrophe and the letter *s* to make the word possessive.

13. **Guinness' best beer** or **Guinness's best beer** If the company name ends in an *s*, you may add an apostrophe after the *s* to show ownership or, if you wish, add another *s* following the apostrophe.

14. **secretaries' duties** Add an *s* and an apostrophe to indicate plural owners.

15. **children's toys** *Children* is an irregular plural. Add an apostrophe and the letter *s* to make the word possessive.

16. **aren't**

17. **that's, didn't**

18. **I'm, Sam's** *Note:* Sam's can also be a possessive form, as in *Sam's* appetite. In this sentence, *Sam's* is short for *Sam has.*

19. **would have, couldn't**

20. **Who's**

21. **'92, he's**

22. **they'd, would have**

23. **that's**

(24) **can't**

(25) **they're, won't**

(26) **'20**

(27) **there** (place)

(28) **its** (possessive)

(29) **who's** (short for *who is*)

(30) **they're** (short for *they are*)

(31) **You're** (short for *You are*)

(32) **there** (place)

If you're ready to test your skills a bit more, take the following chapter quiz that incorporates all the chapter topics.

Whaddya Know? Chapter 17 Quiz

Quiz time! Complete each problem to test your knowledge on the various topics covered in this chapter. You can then find the solutions and explanations in the next section.

Read this thank–you note for a somewhat odd present. Check the underlined words. If you find an error, correct it.

Dear Helen,

(1) <u>Its</u> always nice to hear from a member of the class of (2) <u>'2013</u>. Thanks so much for the birthday present and for informing me about the (3) <u>colleges</u> fundraising appeal. You (4) <u>should of</u> donated to the school instead of spending (5) <u>you're</u> hard-earned money on my gift. The (6) <u>Homeowner's</u> Association of Greenbury Hills, where I live, (7) <u>doesn't</u> allow large animals on the property. Last week, the security guard confiscated my (8) <u>neighbors</u> cat. I think you met them — Ben and Anna, both animal lovers! The association (9) <u>wouldn't</u> return the cat until they promised to put him on a diet. With (10) <u>Ben's and Anna's</u> situation in mind, I believe the (11) <u>residents'</u> committee will surely object to the crocodile you sent me. The (12) <u>secretary-treasurers</u> fear of reptiles is also a problem. Plus, (13) <u>Hollingsworth's</u> Pet Supply (14) <u>wont</u> order crocodile chow. For my next birthday, please send a money order, which is what I chose for (15) <u>your</u> (16) <u>childrens'</u> graduation present.

Your friend,

Allie

Answers to Chapter 17 Quiz

(1) **It's** You need the contraction for *it is* in this sentence. Without the apostrophe, *its* is a possessive pronoun.

(2) **2013** An apostrophe takes the place of missing numbers in a date, and all the numbers are present. The shortened form, if you wish to use it, is '13.

(3) **college's** The singular possessive form adds an apostrophe and the letter *s*.

(4) **should have** The expression *should of* is never correct in Standard English.

(5) **your** *You're* is short for *you are*. In this sentence, you need the possessive pronoun *your*.

(6) **Homeowners'** The association belongs to more than one homeowner, so the plural possessive form, which adds an apostrophe after the *s*, is what you want here.

(7) **Correct** *Doesn't* is short for *does not*.

(8) **neighbors'** The context reveals that more than one person owns the cat, so here you need the plural possessive form, which tacks an apostrophe onto the plural noun.

(9) **Correct** The contraction *wouldn't* is short for *would not*.

(10) **Ben and Anna's** The couple shares the situation (and the cat), so only one apostrophe is needed.

(11) **Correct** Because *residents* is plural, the apostrophe follows the *s*.

(12) **secretary-treasurer's** The possessive form of a compound adds an apostrophe and an *s* after the final word.

(13) **correct** Business names often include an apostrophe.

(14) **won't** The contraction *won't* is short for *would not*.

(15) **Correct** *Your* is a possessive pronoun, which is what you need here.

(16) **children's** *Children* is an irregular plural, so you tack on an apostrophe and an *s* to make the possessive form.

Chapter **18**

Quotations: More Rules Than the Strictest Teacher

What's the most annoying answer in English or any other language? *Because I said so.* No logic, or very little, underlies that answer. It's an assertion of power:

KID: Why can't I go to Elena's party? (powerless)

PARENT: Because I said so. (powerful)

A related statement (first runner-up in the annoying-answer competition) is *because tradition says so.* Once again, that answer comes from a position of power — in this case, from grammarians and editors who decide where and when to insert quotation marks. Reason and common sense govern some of these rules, but not all. Either way, you have to follow them to produce writing that follows the rules of Standard English. This chapter explains how.

And I Quote

A *quotation* is a written repetition of someone else's words — just one word or a whole statement or passage. *Quotation marks* are small curves — usually a pair but sometimes a single curve — that hang above the line, before and after the quoted words. In Britain, these punctuation marks are known as *inverted commas*, an accurate description of their appearance.

Quotations pop up in almost all writing online or on paper: in articles, novels, essays, blog posts, comment threads, and so on. To get an idea how to identify a quotation, take a look at the following story:

One day, while Betsy was on her way to a music lesson, she gazed through a shop window of a musical-instrument showroom. Suddenly, a piano whizzed by her ear. One of the movers had taken a bite of his tuna fish sandwich, allowing the piano to break loose from the ropes hoisting it to the third floor. The piano landed a mere inch away from Betsy. What did Betsy say?

She said that she was relieved.

This sentence tells you about Betsy and her feelings, but it doesn't give her exact words. It's a general report, or *paraphrase*, not an exact record of the words actually spoken or written. You can write that sentence if you heard Betsy say, "I am relieved." You can also write the same sentence if you heard Betsy say, "Thank goodness it missed me. My knees are shaking! I could have been killed."

As an observer, you can also record Betsy's reaction by writing

She said that she was "relieved."

This account of Betsy's reaction is a little more exact. Some of the sentence is general, but the reader knows that Betsy actually said the word *relieved*, because it's in quotation marks. The quotation marks are signs for the reader; they mean that the material inside the marks is exactly what was said.

Betsy said, "I am so relieved that I could cry."

"I am so relieved that I could cry," Betsy said.

These two sentences quote Betsy. The words enclosed by quotation marks are exactly what Betsy said. The only thing added is a tag identifying the speaker who said the words (in this case, Betsy). As you see in the example, you can place the tag at the beginning of the sentence or at the end. (You can also identify the speaker in the middle of the sentence. I talk about that situation later in this chapter.) The quotation marks enclose the words that were said or written.

Q. Which sentences are quotations? Which sentences are paraphrases?

(A) Bob doesn't get along with the conductor of the school orchestra, according to Lulu.

(B) "I refuse to play anything composed in the 21st century," declared Bob.

(C) The conductor muttered something about people who lived in the past.

(D) "Tomorrow's Beethoven is composing today!" exclaimed the conductor, himself a composer.

A. **Quotations: B, D Paraphrases: A, C** The quotation marks alert you to (surprise!) a quotation. Paraphrases lack quotation marks.

In the academic world, omitting quotation marks can get you into trouble. Without this punctuation, you're not identifying the original source. Teachers call this practice *plagiarism* and consider it a serious crime. Even outside the school walls, you want to be an honest person. Hijacking someone else's words is *not* honest. Plus, when quoted material is identified, the reader knows whom to credit or criticize. Given the exact words, the reader may also decide the meaning and importance of the remarks and not simply form an opinion based on the writer's interpretation.

If you're quoting someone who's long-winded, you may want to leave out some extra words. No problem, as long as you don't change the meaning of the quotation. Simply replace the missing words with an *ellipsis* (three spaced dots). If you're omitting more than one sentence, insert four spaced dots — one for the period, and the other three for the ellipsis. If you need to add a word to a quotation to clarify meaning, put *brackets* — these symbols [ ] — around the addition. Here's what I mean:

ORIGINAL STATEMENT: "I must practice the piano, the whole piano, and nothing but the piano in order to keep my notes sharp."

STATEMENT WITH WORDS OMITTED: "I must practice . . . in order to keep my notes sharp." (The ellipsis takes the place of *the piano, the whole piano, and nothing but the piano.*)

ORIGINAL STATEMENT: "He doesn't like flat-screen televisions."

STATEMENT WITH CLARIFICATION: "He [Ollie] doesn't like flat-screen televisions."

The following short paragraph is from an imaginary news article. Following the story are sentences about something in the paragraph. Based on the paragraph and what you can infer from it, write *quotation* if all or part of the sentence is quoted and *paraphrase* if no quotation appears. Because this is a grammar exercise, I haven't inserted quotation marks. In real-world situations, the quotation marks would be present.

A stunningly positive annual report for Jump-Thru Hoops International is due tomorrow. According to inside sources who wish to remain anonymous, the company is doing well, and profits have nearly doubled in the last year. The increase is credited to the company's newest product, the Talking Hoop. Buyers swinging the hoop around their hips hear a drill sergeant screaming commands as they exercise. Company officials have high hopes for their next product, Streaming Music Hoops.

1. The Talking Hoop has been so successful that the company has made twice as much money this year as it did last year.

2. Jump-Thru Hoops International plans to market a hoop that streams music.

3. The company is doing well, and profits have nearly doubled in the last year.

4. Go faster, Private! is what you hear when you're playing with this hoop.

5. The annual report should give shareholders cause for celebration.

6. Our best-selling product is the Talking Hoop, said Max Hippo, the president.

7. The Talking Hoop is used for exercise.

Punctuating Quotations

If quotation marks were the only punctuation you had to worry about, this chapter would be very short. But quotation marks hang out with other punctuation, including commas, periods, question marks, and other members of the punctuation family. Can't you just picture their holiday dinner table? As in most families, who sits next to whom matters. This section explains where to put your annoying cousins — er, I mean punctuation — in a sentence containing a quotation.

TIP

The rules I explain in this section are those of Standard English in the United States. In other English-speaking countries, some punctuation rules may be different.

Quotations with speaker tags

A *speaker tag* is what I call the label — *he said, Mary posted, the warden denies,* and so forth — that identifies the speaker or writer of the quoted words. In this section, I show you how to handle quotations with speaker tags attached.

Speaker tags before or after the quotation

When the speaker tag comes first, put a comma after the speaker tag. The period at the end of the sentence, if there is one, goes *before* the closing quotation mark.

> Lulu remarked, "Lola's lottery ticket is sure to win."

> Lola replied, "I didn't buy a ticket this week."

When the speaker tag comes last, put a comma *before* the closing quotation mark and a period at the end of the sentence.

> "Lola can't win the lottery if she has no ticket," Lulu continued.

> "I don't like the odds," explained Lola.

Now you know the first two (of far too many) quotation rules. Keep in mind that it doesn't matter where you put the speaker tag as long as you punctuate the sentence correctly.

EXAMPLE

Q. Which sentences are correct?

(A) Alonzo muttered, "I don't want to practice the piano".

(B) Alonzo muttered, "I don't want to practice the piano."

(C) "The equation that Al wrote on the board is incorrect," trilled Anna.

(D) "The equation that Al wrote on the board is incorrect", trilled Anna.

A. **B, C** In sentences B and C, the period and the comma precede the closing quotation marks, as they should. In sentences A and D, they are incorrectly placed outside the closing quotation mark.

Interrupted quotations

Sometimes a speaker tag lands in the middle of a sentence. To give you an example of this sort of placement, I revisit Betsy, who narrowly missed being squashed by a falling piano. (Her story is in "And I Quote," at the beginning of this chapter.)

"I think I'll sue," Betsy explained, "for emotional distress."

"You can't imagine," she added, "what I felt."

"The brush of the piano against my nose," she sighed, "will be with me forever."

"The scent of tuna," she continued, "brings it all back."

In each of these examples, the speaker tag interrupts the quotation. It's time for more rules for sentences with interrupted quotations:

» Place a comma *before* the quotation mark at the end of the first half of the quotation.

» Insert a comma *after* the speaker tag but *before* the quotation mark that begins the second half of the quotation.

» If the sentence ends with a period, place the period *before* the closing quotation mark.

» The second half of a quotation does *not* begin with a capital letter unless the word is a proper name or the pronoun *I*.

EXAMPLE

Q. Which sentences are correct?

(A) "After the concert", said Lulu, "the piano player goes out to eat."

(B) "After the concert," said Lulu, "the piano player goes out to eat."

(C) "He likes French fries," she added, "Because they are long and narrow, like piano keys."

(D) "I once ordered key lime pie for dessert," the piano player remarked, "but it didn't look like a piano key."

A. **B, D** Sentences B and D place the comma before the quotation mark that ends the first part of the quotation and a period before the quotation mark at the end of the sentence. Both sentences correctly begin the second part of the quotation with a lowercase letter. Sentence A incorrectly places the comma after the quotation mark at the end of the first part of the quotation. Sentence C incorrectly capitalizes the word that begins the second part of the quotation.

TIP

Notice that in all the interrupted quotations I supply in this section, the quoted material adds up to only one sentence, even though that sentence is written in two separate parts.

Avoiding run-on sentences with interrupted quotations

When you plop a speaker tag right in the middle of someone's conversation, make sure that you don't create a run-on sentence. A *run-on sentence* is actually two sentences that have been stuck together (that is, *run* together) without a conjunction (a word that joins grammatical elements) or a semicolon. Just because you're quoting is no reason to ignore the rules about joining sentences. Check out this set of examples:

WRONG: "When you move a piano, you must be careful," squeaked Al, "Betsy could have been killed."

RIGHT: "When you move a piano, you must be careful," squeaked Al. "Betsy could have been killed."

The quoted material forms two complete sentences:

SENTENCE 1: When you move a piano, you must be careful.

SENTENCE 2: Betsy could have been killed.

Because the quoted material forms two complete sentences, you must write two separate sentences. If you cram this quoted material into one sentence, you have a run-on.

TIP

Remove the speaker tag and check the quoted material. What remains? Enough for half a sentence? That's okay. Quoted material doesn't need to express a complete thought. Enough material for one sentence? Also okay. Enough material for two sentences? Not okay, unless you write two sentences. (For more information on run-on sentences, see Chapter 10.)

EXAMPLE

Q. Which sentences are correct?

(A) "A piano hits the ground with tremendous force," explained the physicist. "I would move to the side if I were you."

(B) "A piano hits the ground with tremendous force," explained the physicist, "I would move to the side if I were you."

(C) "I insist that you repeal the laws of physics," demanded Lola, "Pianos should not kill people."

(D) "I insist that you repeal the laws of physics," demanded Lola. "Pianos should not kill people."

A. **A, D** In choices A and B, the quoted material forms two complete sentences: *A piano hits the ground with tremendous force* and *I would move to the side if I were you.* Choice A correctly quotes these as separate sentences. Similarly, the quoted material in choices C and D adds up to two complete sentences: *I insist that you repeal the laws of physics* and *Pianos should not kill people.* Choice D quotes in two separate sentences. Choice B and C incorrectly mash the quotations together, making each a run-on sentence.

The quotations are underlined in these sentences. Insert quotation marks, periods, and commas.

8. The annual company softball game is tomorrow declared Becky

9. I plan to pitch added Becky, who once tried out for the Olympics

10. Andy interrupted As usual, I will play third base

11. Gus said No one wants Andy at third base

12. The odds favor our opponents sighed Becky but I will not give up

13. Sue has been known to cork her bat commented Harry

14. The corking muttered Sue has never been proved

Quotations without speaker tags

Not all sentences with quotations include speaker tags. The punctuation and capitalization rules for these sentences are a little different. Check out these examples:

> According to the blurb on the book jacket, Anna's history of geometry is said to be "thrilling and unbelievable" by all who read it.

> Michael said that the book "wasn't as exciting as watching paint dry" but was "useful" as a paperweight. Anna threw a pie in his face.

> Michael's lawyer is planning a lawsuit for "serious injury to face and ego."

The rules for quotations without speaker tags actually make sense. The quotations in this sort of sentence aren't set apart. They're tucked into the sentence. Treat them accordingly:

> ➤➤ If the quotation has no speaker tag, the first word of the quotation is not capitalized. The exception, of course, is proper names or the pronoun *I.*

> ➤➤ No comma separates the quotation from the rest of the sentence if the quotation has no speaker tag, unless you need a comma for some other reason. (Chapter 19 explains when commas are appropriate.)

See what I mean about making sense? You don't want to plop a random capital letter in the middle of the sentence, which is where quotations without speaker tags usually end up. Also, omitting the comma preserves the flow of the sentence.

Notice that quotations without speaker tags tend to be short — a few words rather than an entire statement. If you're reporting a lengthy statement, you're probably better off with a speaker tag and the complete quotation. If you want to extract only a few relevant words from someone's speech, you can probably do without a speaker tag.

TIP

Q. Which is correct?

EXAMPLE

    (A) Egbert said that the latest nutritional research was "Suspect" because the laboratory was "Unfair."

    (B) Egbert said that the latest nutritional research was, "suspect" because the laboratory was, "unfair."

    (C) Egbert said that the latest nutritional research was "suspect" because the laboratory was "unfair."

A. **C** In sentence A, *suspect* and *unfair* should not be capitalized. In sentence B, no comma should be placed after *was*.

If you're quoting a lengthy conversation between two people, you may want to omit some speaker tags to avoid repetition. Take a look at this extremely mature discussion, with every speaker tagged:

> "You sat on my tuna fish sandwich," Michael said. "It's flatter than a pancake, and I hate pancakes."
>
> "No, I didn't sit on your sandwich," Ella said. "I sat ten feet away from your lunch bag."
>
> "Did too," Michael said.
>
> "Did not!" Ella said.

Notice that every time the speaker changes, a new paragraph begins. That signal allows you to omit the speaker tag. Here's a streamlined version of the tuna fight:

> "You sat on my tuna fish sandwich," Michael said. "It's flatter than a pancake, and I hate pancakes."
>
> "No, I didn't sit on your sandwich," Ella said. "I sat ten feet away from your lunch bag."
>
> "Did too."
>
> "Did not!"

Although the speaker tags are left out after the first exchange, you can still figure out who is speaking because of the paragraph breaks.

The new-speaker/new-paragraph rule applies even if the argument deteriorates into single-word statements such as *yes* or *no* or some other single-word statements.

TIP

Q. Who said what? Label each statement, using clues from the paragraph.

"Are you in favor of piano-tossing?" asked Roger curiously.

"Not really," replied Cedric. "I like my pianos to have all four feet on the floor."

"But there's something about music in the air that appeals to me."

"There's something about no broken bones, no concussions, and no flattened bodies that appeals to me."

"You really have no artistic instinct!"

A. *Note:* Your speaker tags may vary. Just be sure they are correct and correctly punctuated.

"Are you in favor of piano-tossing?" asked Roger curiously.

"Not really," replied Cedric. "I like my pianos to have all four feet on the floor."

Roger continued, "But there's something about music in the air that appeals to me."

Cedric countered, "There's something about no broken bones, no concussions, and no flattened bodies that appeals to me."

"You really have no artistic instinct!" shouted Roger.

Quotations with question marks

Remember Betsy's piano from the section "And I Quote," earlier in this chapter? When the piano nearly squashed Betsy, she said a few more things. (Not all of them are printable, but I'll ignore those remarks.) Here are her other comments:

"How can you eat a tuna sandwich while lifting a piano?" Betsy asked as she eyed his lunch.

"May I have a bite?" she continued.

Let me put it another way:

As she eyed his lunch, Betsy asked, "How can you eat a tuna sandwich while lifting a piano?"

She continued, "May I have a bite?"

What do you notice about these two sets of quotations? That's right! The quoted words are questions. (Okay, I didn't actually hear your answer, but I'm assuming that because you were smart enough to buy this book, you're smart enough to notice these things.) The rule is simple: If you quote a question, put the question mark *inside* the quotation marks.

This rule makes good sense; it distinguishes a quoted question from a quoted statement tucked inside a question. It's time to look at one more part of Betsy's encounter with the falling piano. The piano mover answered Betsy, but no one could understand his words. (He had a mouthful of tuna.) I wonder what he said.

> Did he say, "I can't give you a bite of my sandwich because I ate it all"?

> Did he really declare, "It was just a piano"?

The quoted words in these examples are not questions. However, each entire sentence is a question. When the quoted words aren't a question but the entire sentence is a question, the question mark goes *outside* the quotation marks.

To sum up the rules on question marks:

>> If the quoted words are a question, put the question mark *inside* the quotation marks.

>> If the entire sentence is a question, put the question mark *outside* the quotation marks.

Some of you detail-oriented (actually, picky) people may want to know what to do when the quotation and the sentence are both questions. In this case, put the question mark *before* the closing quotation mark.

Here's an example of this rule:

> Did the mover really ask, "Is that lady for real?"

When quoting a question within a question, two question marks are inappropriate:

> INCORRECT: Did Betsy ask, "What's the number of a good lawyer?"?

> CORRECT: Did Betsy ask, "What's the number of a good lawyer?"

 Q. Which sentence is correct?

EXAMPLE

(A) Did Lulu say, "I wish a piano would drop near me so that I could sue?"

(B) Did Lulu say, "I wish a piano would drop near me so that I could sue"?

A. **B** The quoted words are not a question, but the entire sentence is. Therefore, the question mark belongs outside the quotation marks.

Quotations with exclamation points

Exclamation points follow the same general rules as question marks. In other words, if the entire sentence is an exclamation but the quoted words aren't, place the exclamation point *outside* the quotation marks. If the quoted words are an exclamation, place the exclamation point *before* the closing quotation mark.

Here are some sample sentences with exclamation points:

> Gene said, "I can't believe you got a tattoo!" (The quoted words are an exclamation, but the entire sentence is not.)

> I simply cannot believe that Gene actually said, "No, thank you"! (Now the entire sentence is an exclamation, but the quoted words are not.)

For those of you who like to dot every *i* and cross every *t*: If both the sentence and the quotation are exclamations, place the exclamation point *before* the closing quotation mark.

Take a look at this example:

> I cannot believe that Gene actually said, "No way would I run for president!"

Don't use two exclamation points:

> INCORRECT: I refuse to believe that Gene said, "In your dreams!"!

> CORRECT: I refuse to believe that Gene said, "In your dreams!"

The quoted words are underlined in each sentence. Insert quotation marks, periods, commas, question marks, and exclamation points as needed.

15 <u>Who wants to win</u> asked the boss in a commanding, take-no-prisoners tone

16 Did she mean it when she said that we were <u>not hard-boiled enough to play decently</u>

17 Sarah screamed <u>You can't bench Andy</u> (The statement Sarah is making is an exclamation.)

18 The opposing team is <u>first in the league and last in our company's heart</u> (The whole statement about the opposing team is an exclamation.)

19 The league states that <u>all decisions regarding player placement are subject to the umpire's approval</u>

20 The umpire has been known to label us <u>out-of-shape players who think they belong in the Olympics</u>

21 <u>Do you think there will be a rain delay</u> inquired Harry

Quotations with semicolons

Every hundred years or so, you may write a sentence that has both a quotation and a semicolon. (In Chapter 10, I explain semicolons in detail.) When writing a sentence that includes a quotation and a semicolon, put the semicolon *outside* the quotation marks, as in this example:

> Cedric thinks that vending machine snacks are a food group; "I can't imagine eating anything else," he said.

and

> Cedric said, "I can't imagine eating anything but vending machine snacks"; he must have the IQ of a sea slug.

Okay, maybe that last sentence was a bit nasty. I apologize to sea slugs everywhere.

Quotations inside quotations

Sometimes you need to place a quotation inside a quotation. Consider this situation:

Alfred is hoping to make a billion dollars selling his app, QuoPro, which punctuates quotations automatically. He's angry at Archie, who coded some parts of QuoPro, because he thinks that Archie made some semicolon errors. Alfred wants Archie to rewrite the program. Archie is outraged by the demand because he believes that his semicolons are exactly where they should be. You're writing a story, quoting Archie, who is quoting Alfred. How do you punctuate this quotation?

> Archie says, "Alfred had the nerve to tell me, 'Your semicolon should go after the closing quotation mark.'"

A sentence like this has to be sorted out. Without any punctuation, here's what Alfred said:

> Your semicolon should go after the closing quotation mark.

Without any punctuation, here are all the words that Archie said:

> Alfred had the nerve to tell me your semicolon should go after the closing quotation mark.

Alfred's words are a quotation inside another quotation. So Alfred's words are enclosed in single quotation marks, and Archie's are enclosed (in the usual way) in double quotation marks. In other words, surround a quotation inside another quotation with single quotation marks.

Q. Punctuate this sentence:

EXAMPLE

Lulu declares As a strong opponent of piercing, I am sorry to report that Lola told me I'm thinking of piercing my tongue.

To help you, here are the words each person said:

Lola: I'm thinking of piercing my tongue.

Lulu (to Lola's mom): As a strong opponent of piercing, I am sorry to report that Lola told me I'm thinking of piercing my tongue.

A. **Lulu declares, "As a strong opponent of piercing, I am sorry to report that Lola told me, 'I'm thinking of piercing my tongue.'"** Lola's words are inside single quotation marks, and Lulu's complete statement is enclosed by double quotation marks.

Commas and periods follow the same rules in both double and single quotations.

The Revolutionary War ended more than a couple of centuries ago, but the United States and Great Britain have not stopped fighting about grammar rules. Everything I've told you already about quotation rules is true for punctuating American English. But the reverse is often true for British English. British writers frequently use single quotation marks when they're quoting, and use double marks for a quotation inside another quotation. Thus, a British book might punctuate Lulu's comment in this way:

> Lulu says, 'As a strong opponent of piercing, I am sorry to tell you that Lola told me, "I'm thinking of piercing my tongue."'

What should you, a puzzled grammarian, do when you're quoting? Follow the custom of the country you're in.

Look at these pairs of sentences. Which sentence is correct, following U.S. rules?

 22

1. Angel complained, "Henry said to me, 'You are a devil.'"
2. Angel complained, "Henry said to me, "You are a devil."

 23

1. Henry explained, "Angel had the nerve to say, "You let my dog Spot sit in a mud puddle!"
2. Henry explained, "Angel had the nerve to say, 'You let my dog Spot sit in a mud puddle!'"

 24

1. Henry continued, "Angel declared, 'I demand you bathe him,' but I refused."
2. Henry continued, "Angel declared, "I demand you bathe him," but I refused."

Germ-Free Quotations: Using Sanitizing Quotation Marks

Sanitizing quotation marks (also known as *distancing quotation marks*) tell the reader that you don't completely approve of the words inside the quotation marks. You often see sanitizing quotation marks enclosing slang, highly informal speech that falls outside Standard English. (For more information on slang, see Chapter 2.) Check out this example:

> Mack's friends considered his burritos "delish" and thought "ka-ching" when Mack submitted the recipe to the Best New Chef contest.

The writer knows that "delish" and "ka-ching" aren't correct, but those words show the ideas (but not the exact remarks) of Mack's friends.

Sanitizing quotation marks may also show that you don't believe what they enclose, as in this sentence:

> I'd like to burn George's guitar after listening to two hours of his "music."

Clearly, the speaker doesn't like the screeches and twangs George produces with his guitar.

WARNING

Don't overuse sanitizing quotation marks. Think of them as plutonium: A little goes a long way. Or, to sanitize that statement, a little goes a "long" way. Annoying, right?

TIP

A useful little word is *sic*. *Sic* (a Latin word that literally means "thus") indicates that you're quoting exactly what was said or written, even though you know something is wrong. In other words, you put a little distance between yourself and the error by showing the reader that the person you're quoting made the mistake, not you. For example, if you're quoting from the works of Dan Quayle, former vice president of the United States (and a *very* poor speller), you may write

> "I would like a potatoe [sic] for supper."

Potato, of course, is the correct spelling.

Punctuating Titles: When to Use Quotation Marks

In your writing, you may need to include the title of a magazine, the headline of a newspaper article, the title of a song or movie, and so on. When punctuating these magazine titles, headlines, and song or movie titles, follow these rules:

> » **Quotation marks enclose titles of smaller works or parts of a whole.**
>
> and
>
> » **Italics or underlining sets off titles of larger works or complete works.**

In other words, use quotation marks for the titles of

» Poems

» Stories

» Essays

» Songs

» Chapter titles

- » Individual episodes of a podcast
- » Magazine or newspaper articles
- » Individual episodes of a television series
- » Page of a website

Use italic or underlining for the titles of

- » Collections of poetry, stories, or essays
- » Titles of books
- » Titles of CDs or tapes or records (if you're into retro)
- » Magazines or newspapers
- » Television and radio shows
- » Podcasts (the series)
- » Plays
- » The name of an entire website

Here are some examples:

- » "A Thousand Excuses for Missing the Tax Deadline" (a newspaper article) in *The Ticker Tape Journal* (a newspaper)
- » "Ode to Taxes Uncalculated" (a poem) in *The Tax Poems* (a book of poetry)
- » "I Got the W-2 Blues" (a song title) on *Me and My Taxes* (a CD containing many songs)
- » "On the Art of Deductions" (a podcast) in *Getting Rich and Staying Rich* (a series of podcasts)
- » "Small Business Expenses" (an individual episode) on *The IRS Report* (a television series)
- » *April 15th* (a play)
- » "Deductions Unlimited" (a page in a website) in *Beat the IRS* (the name of a website)

TIP

You may be wondering which letters you should capitalize in a title. For information on capitalization, see Chapter 21.

EXAMPLE

Q. Add quotation marks and italics to the following paragraph.

Gloria slumped slowly into her chair as the teacher read The Homework Manifesto aloud in class. Gloria's essay, expressing her heartfelt dislike of any and all assignments, was never intended for her teacher's eyes. Gloria had hidden the essay inside the cover of her textbook, The Land and People of Continents You Never Heard Of. Sadly, the textbook company, which also publishes The Most Boring Mathematics Possible, had recently switched to thinner paper, and the essay was clearly visible. The teacher ripped the essay from Gloria's frightened hands. Gloria had not been so embarrassed since the publication of her poem I Hate Homework in the school magazine, Happy Thoughts.

A. "The Homework Manifesto" (title of an essay), *The Land and People of Continents You Never Heard Of* (book title), *The Most Boring Mathematics Possible* (book title), "I Hate Homework" (title of a poem), *Happy Thoughts* (magazine title)

WARNING

When a title is alone on a line — on a title page or simply at the top of the first page of a paper — don't use italics or quotation marks. Don't underline the title, either. The centering calls attention to the title. Nothing else is needed. One exception: If part of the title is the name of another work, treat that part as you would any other title. Suppose that you've written a brilliant essay about Gloria's poem, "I Hate Homework." The title page contains this line, centered:

Freudian Imagery in "I Hate Homework"

If your brilliant essay is about the magazine *Happy Thoughts*, the title page includes this line (also centered):

The Decline of the School Magazine: A Case Study of *Happy Thoughts*

YOUR TURN

Check out the titles in this series of sentences. Which should be in quotation marks and which should be italicized or underlined?

25. Sarah's poem will be published in a collection titled Tax Day Blues.

26. Mary's fifth bestseller, Publish Your Poetry Now, inspired Sarah.

27. Some of us wish that Sarah had read a recent newspaper article, Forget About Writing Poetry.

28. Julie has turned Sarah's poem into a song, although she changed the name to Sonata Taxiana.

29. She's including it on her next CD, Songs of April.

30. I may listen to it if I can bring myself to stop streaming my favorite series, Big Brother and Sister.

31. During a recent episode titled Sister Knows Everything, the main character broke into her brother's blog.

32. In the blog was a draft of a play, Who Will Be My First Love.

Practice Questions Answers and Explanations

(1) **paraphrase** The information is from the paragraph, but the wording is different.

(2) **paraphrase** Nothing in the sentence reflects the wording in the paragraph.

(3) **quotation** Part of the sentence is quoted. The statement "the company is doing well, and profits have nearly doubled in the past year" comes directly from the text and should be enclosed in quotation marks.

(4) **quotation** Although the paragraph doesn't tell you what the drill sergeant says, you can infer that "Go faster, Private!" is a quotation, which should be surrounded by quotation marks.

(5) **paraphrase** Comb through the paragraph, and you see that these words don't appear.

(6) **quotation** The first part of the sentence, as far as the word *said*, tells you Max Hippo's exact words.

(7) **paraphrase** The words in this sentence are reported, not lifted directly from the paragraph.

(8) **"The annual company softball game is tomorrow," declared Becky.** Note that the comma goes before the closing quotation mark.

(9) **"I plan to pitch," added Becky, who once tried out for the Olympics.** The directly quoted words, *I plan to pitch,* are enclosed in quotation marks. The comma that sets off the speaker tag *added Becky* goes before the closing quotation mark. A period ends the sentence.

(10) **Andy interrupted, "As usual, I will play third base."** The speaker tag comes first in this sentence, so the comma is placed before the opening quotation mark. The period that ends the sentence precedes the closing quotation mark.

(11) **Gus said, "No one wants Andy at third base."** The speaker tag is followed by a comma, and a period ends the sentence.

(12) **"The odds favor our opponents," sighed Becky, "but I will not give up."** Here's an interrupted quotation, with the speaker tag in the middle. This sort of interruption is perfectly proper. The quoted material makes up one sentence, so the second half begins with a lowercase letter.

(13) **"Sue has been known to cork her bat," commented Harry.** A straightforward statement with the speaker tag *commented Harry* calls for a comma before the closing quotation mark. The quotation is a complete sentence. In quoted material, the period that normally ends the sentence is replaced by a comma because the sentence continues on — in this case, with *commented Harry*. Periods don't belong in the middle of a sentence unless they're part of an abbreviation.

(14) **"The corking," muttered Sue, "has never been proved."** A speaker tag breaks into this quotation and is set off by commas. The one after *corking* precedes the closing quotation mark, its spot when you're ending a quotation or part of a quotation. Ditto at the end of the sentence: The period needs to come before the closing quotation mark.

(15) **"Who wants to win?" asked the boss in a commanding, take-no-prisoners tone.** Because the quoted words are a question, the question mark goes before the closing quotation mark.

(16) **Did she mean it when she said that we were "not hard-boiled enough to play decently"?** The quoted words aren't a question, but the entire sentence is. The question mark belongs after the closing quotation mark.

(17) **Sarah screamed, "You can't bench Andy!"** A comma separates the speaker tag (*Sarah screamed*) from the quotation and precedes the opening quotation mark. Because the quoted words are an exclamation, the exclamation point belongs before the closing quotation mark.

(18) **The opposing team is "first in the league and last in our company's heart"!** The hint in parentheses gives the rationale for the answer. Because the whole statement is an exclamation, the exclamation point belongs outside the closing quotation mark.

(19) **The league states that "all decisions regarding player placement are subject to the umpire's approval."** This little quotation is tucked into the sentence without a speaker tag, so it takes no comma or capital letter. The period at the end of the sentence goes before the closing quotation mark.

(20) **The umpire has been known to label us "out-of-shape players who think they belong in the Olympics."** Ah, yes — the joy of amateur sport! This quotation is plopped into the sentence without a speaker tag, so the first word takes no capital letter and isn't preceded by a comma. It ends with a period, placed before the closing quotation mark.

(21) **"Do you think there will be a rain delay?" inquired Harry.** Harry's words are a question, so the question mark goes before the closing quotation mark.

(22) **1** You must enclose *You are a devil* in single quotation marks and the larger statement *Henry said to me you are a devil* in double quotation marks. The period at the end of the sentence goes before both marks.

(23) **2** You must enclose *You let my dog Spot sit in a mud puddle!* in single quotation marks and the larger quotation in double quotation marks.

(24) **1** Enclose the quotation-within-a-quotation *I demand you bathe him* in single quotation marks. Enclose the entire quotation, *Angel declared, 'I demand you bathe him' but I refused* in double quotation marks.

(25) **Tax Day Blues** Underline or italicize the title of a full-length work.

(26) **Publish Your Poetry Now** Underline or italicize the title of a full-length work.

(27) **"Forget About Writing Poetry"** Enclose the title of a newspaper article in quotation marks.

(28) **"Sonata Taxiana"** Enclose the title of a song in quotation marks.

(29) **Songs of April** Underline or italicize the title of a CD.

(30) **Big Brother and Sister** Underline or italicize the title of a television series.

(31) **"Sister Knows Everything"** Enclose the title of an episode in quotation marks.

(32) **Who Will Be My First Love?** Italicize or underline the title of a play.

If you're ready to test your skills a bit more, take the following chapter quiz that incorporates all the chapter topics.

Whaddya Know? Chapter 18 Quiz

Quiz time! Complete each problem to test your knowledge of the various topics covered in this chapter. You can then find the solutions and explanations in the next section.

Tommy Brainfree's classic composition is reproduced in the following figure. Identify ten spots where a set of quotation marks needs to be inserted. Place the quotation marks correctly in relation to other punctuation in the sentence. Also, underline titles where appropriate.

What I Did during Summer Vacation

by Tommy Brainfree

This summer I went to Camp Waterbug, which was the setting for a famous poem by William Long titled Winnebago My Winnebago. At Camp Waterbug I learned to paddle a canoe without tipping it over more than twice a trip. My counselor even wrote an article about me in the camp newsletter, Waterbug Bites. The article was called How to Tip a Canoe. The counselor said, Brainfree is well named. I was not upset because I believed him (eventually) when he explained that the comment was an editing error.

   Are you sure? I asked him when I first read it.

   You know, he responded quickly, that I have a lot of respect for you. I nodded in agreement, but that night I placed a bunch of frogs under his sheets, just in case he thought about writing How to Fool a Camper. One of the frogs had a little label on his leg that read JUST KIDDING TOO.

   At the last campfire gathering I sang a song from the musical Fiddler on the Roof. The song was called If I Were a Rich Man. I changed the first line to If I were a counselor. I won't quote the rest of the song because I'm still serving the detention my counselor gave me, even though I'm back home now.

Answers to Chapter 18 Quiz

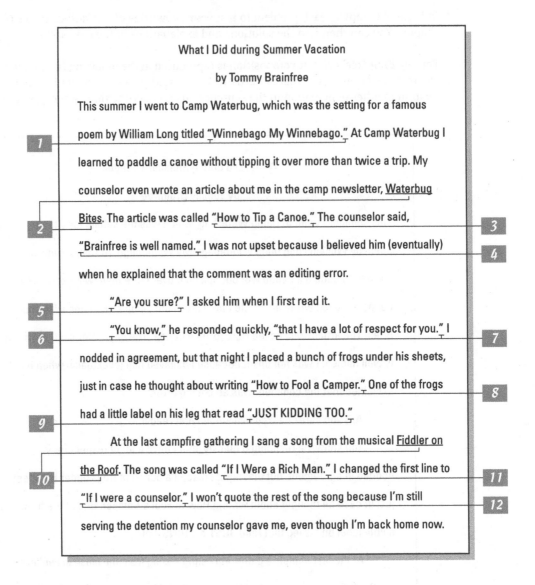

What I Did during Summer Vacation

by Tommy Brainfree

This summer I went to Camp Waterbug, which was the setting for a famous poem by William Long titled **1** "Winnebago My Winnebago." At Camp Waterbug I learned to paddle a canoe without tipping it over more than twice a trip. My counselor even wrote an article about me in the camp newsletter, Waterbug **2** Bites. The article was called "How to Tip a Canoe." **3** The counselor said, **4** "Brainfree is well named." I was not upset because I believed him (eventually) when he explained that the comment was an editing error.

5 "Are you sure?" I asked him when I first read it.

6 "You know," he responded quickly, "that I have a lot of respect for you." **7** I nodded in agreement, but that night I placed a bunch of frogs under his sheets, just in case he thought about writing "How to Fool a Camper." **8** One of the frogs had a little label on his leg that read "JUST KIDDING TOO." **9**

At the last campfire gathering I sang a song from the musical Fiddler on the Roof. **10** The song was called "If I Were a Rich Man." **11** I changed the first line to "If I were a counselor." **12** I won't quote the rest of the song because I'm still serving the detention my counselor gave me, even though I'm back home now.

1. Poem titles belong in quotation marks. The title of a collection of poems, on the other hand, needs to be underlined or italicized.

2. The newsletter title should be underlined or italicized.

3. An article title belongs in quotation marks. The period at the end of the sentence precedes the closing quotation mark.

4. Directly quoted speech belongs in quotation marks, with the period preceding the closing mark.

5. The quoted words are a question, so the question mark goes inside the quotation marks.

(6) The interrupted quotation with an inserted speaker tag needs two sets of marks. The comma at the end of the first part of the quotation precedes the closing mark.

(7) The period at the end of the quoted sentence goes before the closing mark.

(8) Another article title, another set of quotation marks. The period precedes the closing mark.

(9) This quotation reproduces the exact written words and thus calls for quotation marks. The period precedes the closing mark.

(10) The title of a play, a full-length work, needs to be underlined or italicized.

(11) The title of a song needs to be in quotation marks.

(12) Quoted lines from a song need to be in quotation marks.

Chapter **19**

The Pause That Refreshes: Commas

loud, commas are the sounds of silence — short pauses that contrast with the longer pause at the end of each sentence. Commas are signals for your reader. Stop here, they say, but not for too long. Commas also cut parts of your sentence away from the whole, separating something from whatever's around it in order to change the meaning of the sentence. When you're speaking, you do the same thing with your tone of voice and the timing of your breaths. In this chapter, I guide you through the underlying logic of commas so that you know where to place them in common situations.

Distinguishing Items: Commas in Series

Imagine that you text a shopping list to your roommate Charlie, who's at the store buying supplies for your birthday party. There are no commas or line breaks.

> flashlight batteries butter cookies ice cream cake

How many things does Charlie have to buy? Perhaps only three:

> flashlight batteries
>
> butter cookies
>
> ice cream cake

Or five:

> flashlight
>
> batteries
>
> butter cookies
>
> ice cream
>
> cake

How does Charlie know? He doesn't, unless you use commas. Here's what Charlie actually needs to buy — all four items:

> flashlight batteries, butter cookies, ice cream, cake

To put it in a sentence:

> Charlie has to buy flashlight batteries, butter cookies, ice cream, and cake.

The commas between these items are signals. When you read the list aloud, the commas emerge as breaths:

> Charlie has to buy flashlight batteries [breath] butter cookies [breath] ice cream [breath] and cake.

TIP You need commas between each item on the list, with one important exception: The comma in front of the word *and* is often optional. Why? Because when you say *and*, you've already separated the last two items. You must insert the comma if your reader may misunderstand the meaning. Suppose you see this sentence:

> Jenny made the podcast with her two sisters, Anne and Elizabeth.

How many people worked on the podcast with Jenny? Possibly two: Anne (Jenny's sister) and Elizabeth (Jenny's other sister). Possibly four: Jenny's sisters (Helen and Kelly) and Anne and Elizabeth. In this sort of sentence, that last comma makes all the difference:

> Jenny made the podcast with her two sisters, Anne, and Elizabeth.

Now the reader knows for sure that *Anne* and *Elizabeth* are part of a list that begins with *two sisters*, not the names of the *two sisters* added as extra information.

Never put a comma in front of the first item on the list.

WRONG: Charlie has to buy, flashlight batteries, butter cookies, ice cream and cake.

RIGHT: Charlie has to buy flashlight batteries, butter cookies, ice cream and cake.

ALSO RIGHT: Charlie has to buy flashlight batteries, butter cookies, ice cream, and cake.

ALSO RIGHT, BUT NOT A GOOD IDEA: Charlie has to buy flashlight batteries and butter cookies and ice cream and cake.

You don't need commas at all in the last sentence because the word *and* does the job. Grammatically, that sentence is fine. In reality, if you write a sentence with three *and*s, your reader will think you sound like a little kid.

If any item in a list has a comma *within* it, semicolons are used to separate the list items. Imagine that you're inserting this list into a sentence:

>> Peter McKinney, the mayor

>> Agnes Hutton

>> Jeannie Battle, magic expert

In a sentence using only commas, the reader wouldn't know that Peter McKinney is the mayor and may instead think that Peter and the mayor are two separate people. Here's the properly punctuated sentence:

> Because he has only one extra ticket to the magic show, Daniel will invite Peter McKinney, the mayor; Agnes Hutton; or Jeannie Battle, magic expert.

When you're texting, commas can be a pain to insert because you sometimes have to switch screens to find one. You can skip the commas if you want and instead separate the items, line by line, by pressing Enter after each. Be warned, though, that some apps send the text when you press Enter. Apps may also remove extra spaces automatically. Your job is to make sure the person reading the text will not misunderstand what you mean. For more about electronic media, turn to Chapter 25.

Q. Punctuate the following sentence.

Belle requested a jelly doughnut a corner office four sports cars and a racehorse in exchange for the rights to the computer code she had written.

A. **Belle requested a jelly doughnut, a corner office, four sports cars, and a racehorse in exchange for the rights to the computer code she had written.** You may omit the comma before the *and* because the meaning of the sentence is clear.

Insert the list from each question into a sentence and punctuate it properly. I supply the beginning of the sentence. *Note:* I use numbers to separate items on the list. Don't use numbers in your answer sentence.

1   List: (1) deodorant (2) shoe polish (3) earwax remover

Getting ready for his big date, Rob went to the pharmacy to purchase

_____

2   List: (1) pitted dates (2) chocolate-covered mushrooms (3) anchovies (4) pickles

Rob planned to serve a tasteful selection of _____

3   List: (1) Helen Ogee, state senator (2) Natasha Smith, childhood friend (3) Blair Berry, auto salesperson (4) Hannah Bridge, punctuation expert (5) Jane Fine, veterinarian

Rob's guest list is heavily tilted toward women he would like to date: _____

4   List: (1) get three phone numbers (2) arrange at least one future date (3) avoid police interference

Rob will consider his party a success if he can _____

Using "Comma Sense" to Add Information to Your Sentence

Your writing relies on nouns and verbs to get your point across. But if you're like most people, you also enrich your sentences with descriptions. In grammar terminology, you add adjectives and adverbs, participles and clauses, and an occasional appositive. Before you panic, let me explain that you don't have to know any of those terms in order to write — and punctuate — a good sentence. You just have to keep a couple of key ideas in your head. In this section, I explain how to place commas so that your writing expresses what you mean.

List of descriptions

Writers often string together a bunch of single-word descriptions — *adjectives*, in grammar lingo. (For more information on adjectives, turn to Chapter 6.) If you have a set of descriptions, you probably have a set of commas also. Take a look at the following sentences:

> "What do you think of me?" Belle asked Jill in an idle moment.

> Jill took a deep breath, "I think you are a sniffling, smelly, pimply monster."

> "Thank you," said Belle, who was trying out for the part of the witch in the school carnival. "Do you think I should paint my teeth black, too?"

Notice the commas in Jill's answer. Three descriptions are listed: *sniffling, smelly, pimply.*

A comma separates each of the descriptions from the next, but there is no comma between the last description (*pimply*) and the word it's describing (*monster*).

Here's a little more of Belle and Jill's conversation:

> "Do I get the part?" asked Belle.

> "Maybe," answered Jill. "I have four sniffling, smelly, pimply monsters waiting to audition. I'll let you know."

Now look closely at Jill's answer. This time, there are four descriptions of the word *monster: four, sniffling, smelly, pimply.*

There are commas after *sniffling* and *smelly*. As previously stated, no comma follows *pimply,* because you shouldn't place a comma between the last description and the word it describes. But why is there no comma after *four?* Here's why: *sniffling, smelly,* and *pimply* are more or less of equal importance in the sentence. They have different meanings, but they all do the same job — tell you how disgusting Belle's costume is. *Four* is in a different category. It gives you different information, telling you how many monsters are waiting, not how they look. Therefore, it's not jumbled into the rest of the list.

TIP

Numbers aren't separated from other descriptions or from the word(s) they describe. Don't put a comma after a number. Also, don't use commas to separate other descriptions from words that indicate number or amount — *many, more, few, less,* and so forth. More descriptive words that you shouldn't separate from other descriptions or from the words they describe include *other, another, this, that, these, those.* Examine these correctly punctuated sentences:

> Sixteen ugly, bedraggled, stained hats were lined up on the shelf marked, "WITCH COSTUME.

> No drippy, disgusting, artificial wounds were in stock.

> This green, glossy, licorice-flavored lipstick belongs in the witch's makeup kit.

Q. Punctuate this sentence.

Jill was worried about some items she must have for a musical number: 100 scraggly fluorescent flowing beards.

A. **Jill was worried about some items she must have for a musical number: 100 scraggly, fluorescent, flowing beards.** *Note:* Don't put a comma after a number *(one hundred)* or after the last description *(flowing)*.

Punctuate these descriptions.

5 some blue ribbons

6 fifteen complicated innovative sets

7 a few huge green lights

8 three charming little tattoos

Essential or extra? Commas tell the tale

The descriptions in a sentence may be longer than one word. You may have a subject-verb expression (which grammarians call a *clause*) or a verb form (in technical terms, a *participle*). No matter what they're called, these longer descriptions follow two simple rules: If a description is essential to the meaning of the sentence, don't put commas around it. If the description provides extra, nonessential information, set it off with commas.

Consider this pair of sentences:

> At Champion Floral Design, the florists, who are allergic to greenery, take frequent sneeze breaks.

> At Champion Floral Design, the florists who are allergic to greenery take frequent sneeze breaks.

Do the commas really matter? Yes. If the description *who are allergic to greenery* is set off from the rest of the sentence by commas, the description is extra — not essential to the meaning of the sentence. You can cross it out and the sentence still means the same thing. Therefore, the first example means

> At Champion Floral Design, the florists take frequent sneeze breaks.

It also means shoppers may have to wait for their bouquets because all *the florists* are on break, ah-chooing into their handkerchiefs.

If commas do not set off the description, the description is essential to the meaning of the sentence. The description *who are allergic to greenery* identifies which florists take sneeze breaks. In other words, some florists are sneezing, but others are creating bouquets for their customers.

TIP

The pronouns *which* and *that* may help you decide whether you need commas. *That* generally introduces information the sentence can't do without — essential information that isn't set off by commas. The pronoun *which*, on the other hand, often introduces nonessential information that may be surrounded by commas. Keep in mind, however, that these distinctions are not true 100 percent of the time. Sometimes *which* introduces a description that is essential and therefore needs no commas. On rare occasions, the pronoun *that* introduces nonessential material.

Here's another example, with the description in italics:

SENTENCE: The students *who are planning a sit-in tomorrow* want to be paid for doing homework.

PUNCTUATION ANALYSIS: The description is not set off by commas, so you may not omit it.

WHAT THE SENTENCE MEANS: Some students — those planning a sit-in — want to be paid for doing homework. Not all the students want to be paid. The rest are perfectly content to do math problems for free.

TIP

The word *because* generally introduces a reason. At the beginning of a sentence, the "because statement" acts as an introductory remark and is always set off by a comma.

Because the tattoo was on sale, Lulu whipped out her credit card and rolled up her sleeve.

At the end of a sentence, the "because statement" is sometimes set off by commas, in which case it may be lifted out of the sentence without changing the meaning. Without commas, it's essential to the meaning. Take a look at these two statements:

WITH COMMAS: Lulu didn't get that tattoo, because it was in bad taste.

MEANING: No tattoos for Lulu! The "because" information is extra, explaining why Lulu passed on the design.

WITHOUT COMMAS: Lulu didn't get that tattoo because it was in bad taste.

MEANING: Lulu got the tattoo, but not because it was in bad taste. She got it for another reason (perhaps a sale). The fact that the tattoo grossed out everyone who saw it was just an extra added attraction to Lulu, who enjoys looking strange.

EXAMPLE

Q. Which sentence means that you can't fly to Cincinnati for your cousin's wedding?

(A) The pilots who are going on strike demand that organic snacks be served in the cockpit.

(B) The pilots, who are going on strike, demand that organic snacks be served in the cockpit.

A. **B** The commas in the second sentence tell you that you can remove the words they enclose without changing the meaning. Therefore, *all* the pilots are going on strike. In the first sentence, the description is an identifier. Only the pilots who like organic snacks are going on strike.

Commas with appositive influence

If you're seeing double when you read a sentence, you've probably encountered an appositive. Strictly speaking, appositives aren't descriptions, though they do give you information about something else in the sentence. *Appositives* are nouns or pronouns that are the equivalent of the noun or pronoun preceding them in the sentence. Some appositives are set off by commas, and some aren't. The rule concerning commas and appositives: If you're sure that readers will know what you're talking about before they get to the appositive, set off the appositive with commas. If you're not sure readers will know exactly what you're talking about by the time they arrive at the appositive, don't use commas. (This rule is a variation of the rule that I explain in the preceding section.)

Note the difference between these two sentences:

> Michael's play *Dinner at the Diner* won the drama critics' Most Boring Plot award.
>
> *Dinner at the Diner,* Michael's play, won the drama critics' Most Boring Plot award.

In the first example, *Dinner at the Diner* is the appositive of *Michael's play*. When you get to *play,* you don't know which of Michael's plays is being discussed. The appositive supplies the name. Hence, the appositive is essential and isn't set off by commas. In the second example, *Michael's play* is the appositive of *Dinner at the Diner*. Because *Dinner at the Diner* comes first, readers already know the name of the play. The fact that Michael wrote the play is extra information and must therefore be surrounded by commas.

Here are two more examples. In each sentence, *Mary* is the appositive of *sister:*

> Lulu has five sisters, but her sister Mary is definitely her favorite.

Because Lulu has five sisters, you don't know which sister is being discussed until you have the name. *Mary* identifies the sister and shouldn't be placed between commas.

> Roger has only one sibling. His sister, Mary, does not approve of Roger's wife.

Because Roger has only one sibling, the reader knows that he has only one sister. Thus, the words *his sister* pinpoint the person being discussed. The name is extra information and is set off by commas.

Q. Which sentence is correct?

(A) Lola's spouse, Lou, doesn't approve of Lola's pierced eyebrow.

(B) Lola's spouse Lou doesn't approve of Lola's pierced eyebrow.

A. A Lola has only one spouse, so the name is extra, not identifying information.

9 Which sentence includes every senior?

(A) The seniors, planning to revolt, have given the network exclusive streaming rights to their demonstration.

(B) The seniors planning to revolt have given the network exclusive streaming rights to their demonstration.

10 Which sentence praises only some of the artwork?

(A) The posters, painted in bright colors, photographed well.

(B) The posters painted in bright colors photographed well.

11 Which sentence means the best speeches did not get streamed?

(A) Camera crew members, on lunch break, missed the demonstrators' best speeches.

(B) Camera crew members on lunch break missed the demonstrators' best speeches.

12 Which sentence means that all the raw footage shows students eating and sleeping?

(A) The raw footage, which will be destroyed after the film is released, shows students eating junk food and napping.

(B) The raw footage which will be destroyed after the film is released shows students eating junk food and napping.

13 Punctuate this sentence.

Jana's fourth play *How I Broke My Homework Habit* was a smash hit.

14 Punctuate this sentence.

The arm resting on a pillow was broken in a playground accident.

You Talkin' to Me? Direct Address

When writing a message to someone, you need to separate the person's name from the rest of the sentence with a comma. Otherwise, your reader may misread the intention of the message. Take a look at the following note that Michael left on the door:

Roger wants to kill Wendy. I locked him in this room.

You think: Wendy is in danger. That's a shame. Oh, well. I guess I'm safe. However, when you unlock the door and sit down for a cup of tea, Roger jumps up and starts chasing you around the room. You escape and run screaming to Michael. "Why didn't you tell me Roger was violent!" Michael pleads guilty to a grammatical crime. He forgot to put in the comma in his note to Wendy. Here's what he meant:

Roger wants to kill, Wendy. I locked him in this room.

It was your bad luck to read a note intended for Wendy. In grammatical terms, *Wendy* is in a *direct-address* sentence. Because the writer was directing his comments to Wendy, her name should be cut off from the rest of the sentence with a comma. Direct address is also possible at the beginning or in the middle of a sentence:

Wendy, Roger wants to kill, so I locked him in this room.

Roger wants to kill, Wendy, so I locked him in this room.

Q. Which sentence is correct?

(A) The teacher called, Emma, but I answered.

(B) The teacher called Emma, but I answered.

EXAMPLE

A. **A or B** Either sentence may be correct, depending on what you're trying to say. If you're talking to Emma, telling her that Mr. Mean phoned your house to report missing homework but you, not your mom, picked up the phone, then sentence A is correct. However, if you're explaining that the teacher screamed to Emma, "Bring your homework up here *this minute!*" and instead you replied, "Mr. Mean, Emma asked me to tell you that the computer crashed and erased her homework," sentence B is correct.

When you're emailing or texting, you don't need to type the name of the person who will read your message, because your words will pop up only on that person's phone or computer. Some people like to begin with "Hi, Wendy" or similar wording, to create a softer tone. Formal grammar requires a comma between the greeting *(Hi)* and the name *(Wendy)*. Increasingly, though, people don't bother inserting one. No one is likely to misunderstand *Hi Wendy*. Unless the reader loves punctuation rules, you can safely do without a comma.

TIP

Using Commas in Addresses and Dates

Commas are good, all-purpose separators. They won't keep you and your worst enemy apart, but they do a fine job on addresses and dates — especially when items that are usually placed on individual lines are placed next to each other on the same line.

Addressing addresses

Where are you from? Jill is from Mars. Belle is from a small town called Venus. Here's Belle's (fictional) address, the way you see it on an envelope:

> Ms. Belle Planet
>
> 223 Center Street
>
> Venus, NY 10001

In the body of a letter, you can insert an address in "envelope form" like this:

> Please send a dozen rockets to the following address:
>
> Ms. Belle Planet
>
> 223 Center Street
>
> Venus, NY 10001

The introductory words *(Please send a dozen rockets to the following address)* end with a colon (:) if they express a complete unit of thought. If the introductory words leave you hanging *(Please send a dozen rockets to,* for example), don't use a colon.

TIP

If you put Belle's address into a sentence, you have to separate each item of the address, as you see here:

Belle Planet lives at 223 Center Street, Venus, NY 10001.

Here's the address (envelope style) for her best friend, Jill:

Jill Willis

53 Asimov Court

Mars, CA 90210

And now the sentence version:

Jill Willis lives at 53 Asimov Court, Mars, CA 90210.

TIP

Notice that the house number and street are not separated by a comma, nor are the state and zip code.

If the sentence continues, you must separate the last item in the address from the rest of the sentence with another comma:

Belle Planet lives at 223 Center Street, Venus, New York 10001, but she is thinking of moving to Mars in order to be closer to her friend Jill.

If there is no street address — just a city and a state — put a comma between the city and the state. If the sentence continues after the state name, place a comma after the state:

Belle Planet lives in Venus, New York, but she is thinking of moving to Mars.

Commas also separate countries from the city/state/province:

Roger lives in Edinburgh, Scotland, near a large body of water. His brother Michael just built a house in Zilda, Wisconsin.

Q. Punctuate the following sentence.

EXAMPLE

Police believe that Scott ran away from his home at 77 Main Street Zilda Wisconsin because his parents reduced his screen time to 45 hours per week.

A. **Police believe that Scott ran away from his home at 77 Main Street, Zilda, Wisconsin, because his parents reduced his screen time to 45 hours per week.**

Punctuating dates

Confession time: The rules for placing commas in dates aren't exactly stable these days. What was once carved into stone (and I mean that literally) is now sometimes viewed as old-fashioned. To make matters even more complicated, writers from different areas (science, literature, and the like) favor different systems. In this section, I show you the traditional form and some variations. If you're writing for business or school, the traditional form should get you through. If you're anticipating publication, check with your editor about the publisher's preferred style.

If the date is alone on a line (perhaps at the top of a letter), these formats are fine:

September 28, 2060 or Sept. 28, 2060 (traditional)

9/28/60 (informal)

28 September 2060 (modern in the United States, traditional in many other countries)

TIP

In the United States, date order is generally month–day–year. In many other countries, the order is day–month–year. Therefore, 4/10/2060 is April 10, 2060, in the United States and October 4, 2060 elsewhere. Be sure the person reading your work will decode it correctly.

When dates appear in a sentence, the format changes depending upon (a) how traditional you want to be and (b) how much information you want to give. Take a look at the commas — or the lack of commas — in these sentences:

On September 28, 2060, Lulu ate far too much candy. (Traditional: Commas separate the day and year and the year from the rest of the sentence.)

In October, 2060, Lulu gave up sugary snacks. (Traditional: A comma separates the month from the year and the year from the rest of the sentence.)

Lulu pigs out every October 31. (Timeless: Both the traditional and modern camps omit commas in this format.)

In October 2060 Lulu suffered from severe indigestion. (Modern: No commas appear.)

Lulu visited a nutritionist on 20 October 2060. (Modern: No commas appear.)

Q. Punctuate this sentence, rearranging parts of the date as needed:

EXAMPLE

Lola testified under oath that on December 18 2022 she saw Lulu place a carton of gummy bears under the counter without paying for it.

A. **Lola testified under oath that on December 18, 2022, she saw Lulu place a carton of gummy bears under the counter without paying for it.** (traditional)

Lola testified under oath that on 18 December 2022 she saw Lulu place a carton of gummy bears under the counter without paying for it. (modern)

YOUR TURN

Insert commas where needed.

 15   Ladies and gentlemen I present the Fifth Annual Elbox Championships.

16   I know Mort that you are an undefeated Elbox competitor. Would you tell our audience about the sport?

(17) Elboxing is about 5,000 years old Chester. It originated in ancient Egypt.

(18) Excuse me a moment. The reigning champion has decided to pay us a visit. Miss William could you tell us how you feel about the upcoming match?

(19) Certainly sir. I am confident that my new training routine will pay off.

Which dates are correctly punctuated if they are placed in the specified location?

(20) in the middle of a sentence

(A) 20 July 1940

(B) July 20, 1940,

(C) July, 20, 1940

(21) alone, not part of a sentence

(A) Milton Smith

　　55 Oak Avenue

　　Floral Gardens, WA 98100

(B) Milton Smith

　　55 Oak Avenue

　　Floral Gardens WA, 98100

(C) Milton Smith

　　55 Oak Avenue

　　Floral Gardens WA 98100

Getting Started: The Introductory Comma

Some sentences plunge into the main idea immediately, and others take a moment (actually, one or more words) to kick into gear. Commas help readers figure out what's going on by separating introductory words from the rest of the sentence. This section explains the guidelines.

Words not connected to the meaning of the sentence

Yes, this section introduces a comma rule. No, it's not optional. Hey, have you figured out the rule yet? Reread the first three sentences of this paragraph. A comma separates words that aren't part of the sentence but instead comment on the meaning of the sentence. That's the rule. If you omit these words, the sentence still means the same thing. Common introductory words include *yes, no, well, oh,* and *okay.* Read these examples twice, once with the introductory words and once without. See how the meaning stays the same?

> Yes, you are allowed to chew hard candy during class, but don't complain to me if you break a tooth.

> Oh, I didn't know that you needed your intestines today.

To sum up the rule on introductory words, use commas to separate them from the rest of the sentence, or omit them entirely.

Phrases and clauses

Longer descriptions, what grammarians call *phrases* and *clauses*, sometimes serve as introductory elements. Don't worry about the terminology. Just think about the meaning. In these examples, the introductory element is italicized:

> *Scrolling through her newsfeed,* Lola stopped only when she glimpsed a motorcycle.

> *Whenever she can,* Lola works on her Harley.

> *At midnight last Wednesday,* Lola went out for a ride.

As you see, commas separate the introductory words and help the reader "hear" the sentence in the right way by adding a pause before the main idea. If the introductory element is very short, though, you can usually skip the comma:

> *At midnight* Lola is seldom at home.

 Punctuate these sentences.

EXAMPLE **Q.** Well Ella plays the piano forcefully when she is in the mood.

A. **Well, Ella plays the piano forcefully when she is in the mood.** Place a comma after the introductory word *(well).*

Q. When she is in the mood Ella plays the piano forcefully.

A. **When she is in the mood, Ella plays the piano forcefully.** Place a comma after the introductory element, *When she is in the mood.*

Punctuating Independently

When you join two complete sentences with the conjunctions (joining words) *and, or, but, nor, yet, so,* or *for,* place a comma before the conjunction. Some examples include the following:

Agnes robbed the bank, and then she went out for a hamburger.

James spies, but apart from that lapse he is not a bad fellow.

Sam bribed the judges, for he is determined to qualify for the national tournament.

If the two complete sentences are short, you may omit the comma:

Max won and you lost.

For more information on conjunctions and complete sentences, see Chapter 10.

WARNING

If you're joining two elements that aren't complete sentences — two descriptions or actions or people, for example — don't place a comma in front of the conjunction. Take a look at this example:

WRONG: Ella wrote a statement for the media, and then screamed at her press agent for an hour.

WHY IT IS WRONG: The sentence has one subject *(Ella)* and two verbs *(wrote, screamed)*. You aren't joining two complete sentences, so you shouldn't place a comma before *and*. Either way, Ella should learn to control her temper.

RIGHT: Ella wrote a statement for the media and then screamed at her press agent for an hour.

EXAMPLE

Q. Insert commas as needed in these sentences.

Alfred slits envelopes with his teeth but Dorothy opens the mail with a knife.

A. **Alfred slits envelopes with his teeth, but Dorothy opens the mail with a knife.**
The conjunction *but* joins two complete sentences. A comma must precede the conjunction *but*.

Q. Alfred answers every letter on the day he receives it but doesn't pay any bills.

A. No commas are needed because the conjunction *but* joins two verbs *(answers, does pay)*.

YOUR TURN

Insert commas as needed in these sentences about an unusual wedding venue.

22 The groom skated to the center of the rink and waited for his shivering bride.

23 The best man rode in a Zamboni for he was afraid of slipping on the ice.

24 The flowers and the colorful spotlights impressed the guests.

25 One of the bridesmaids whispered that her own wedding would be on a beach or in a sunny climate with absolutely no ice.

26 Do you know who is in charge of the gifts or who is paying the orchestra?

Practice Questions Answers and Explanations

1. **Getting ready for his big date, Rob went to the pharmacy to purchase deodorant, shoe polish, and earwax remover.** You have three items and two commas; no comma is needed before the first item on the list.

2. **Rob planned to serve a tasteful selection of pitted dates, chocolate-covered mushrooms, anchovies, and pickles.** Each item on Rob's list is separated from the next by a comma. No comma comes before the first item, *pitted dates.* The comma before the *and* is optional.

3. **Rob's guest list is heavily tilted toward women he would like to date: Helen Ogee, state senator; Natasha Smith, childhood friend; Blair Berry, auto salesperson; Hannah Bridge, punctuation expert; and Jane Fine, veterinarian.** Did you remember the semicolons? The commas within each item of Rob's dream-date list make it impossible to distinguish between one dream date and another with a simple comma. Semicolons do the trick. Also, I hope you noticed that this rather long list begins with a colon.

4. **Rob will consider his party a success if he can get three phone numbers, arrange at least one future date, and avoid police interference.** All you have to do is plop a comma between each item. Add a comma before the *and* if you wish.

5. **some blue ribbons** No commas are needed here because words that indicate quantity (*some*) aren't set off from the rest of the description by a comma. No comma separates the last description (*blue*) from the word it describes.

6. **fifteen complicated, expensive sets** No comma separates a quantity (*fifteen*) from the rest of the description. Nor should you place a comma between the last description and the word it describes.

7. **a few huge, green lights** *A few* is a quantity, so no comma sets it apart. The comma between *huge* and *green* separates the descriptions. No comma separates the final description, *green,* from the word it describes.

8. **three charming, little tattoos** The quantity indicator, *three,* isn't set off by commas. A comma properly separates two descriptions (*charming* and *little*). No comma ever separates the description and the word described.

9. **A** The commas indicate that the description is extra, nonessential information. Take it out, and you see that all the seniors are involved.

10. **B** Without commas, the description *painted in bright colors* is essential. It identifies which posters photographed well and implies that other posters did not photograph well.

11. **A** The commas that enclose *on lunch break* tell you that you can remove those words without changing the essential meaning of the sentence. Therefore, the camera crew missed the best speeches entirely.

12. **A** Lift out the description that's surrounded by commas and you see that *all the raw footage shows students eating junk food and napping* — not just the footage that will be destroyed.

13. **Jana's fourth play, *How I Broke My Homework Habit,* was a smash hit.** The sentence identifies the hit as *Jana's fourth play.* The name is extra information, not identification, so it should be surrounded by commas.

(14) **The arm resting on a pillow was broken in a playground accident.** Which arm was broken? You don't know much, but you do know it's the one *resting on a pillow.* Because it's an identifier, it's not surrounded by commas.

(15) **Ladies and gentlemen, I present the Fifth Annual Elbox Championships.** Even though *Ladies and gentlemen* doesn't name the members of the audience, they're still being addressed, so a comma sets off the expression from the rest of the sentence.

(16) **I know, Mort, that you are an undefeated Elbox competitor. Would you tell our audience about the sport?** Here you see the benefit of the direct-address comma. Without it, the reader thinks *I know Mort* is the beginning of the sentence and then lapses into confusion. *Mort* is cut away with two commas, and the reader understands that *I know that you are . . .* is the real meaning.

(17) **Elboxing is about 5,000 years old, Chester. It originated in ancient Egypt.** You're talking to *Chester,* so his name needs to be set off with a comma.

(18) **Excuse me a moment. The reigning champion has decided to pay us a visit. Miss William, could you tell us how you feel about the upcoming match?** Here the person being addressed is *Miss William.*

(19) **Certainly, sir. I am confident that my new training routine will pay off.** The very polite *Miss William* talks to *sir* in this sentence, so that term is set off by a comma.

(20) **A, B** In the first correct answer, commas disappear. In the second, commas separate the day from the year and the year from the rest of the sentence.

(21) **A** A comma separates the city and state and nothing else in this envelope-style address.

(22) **no comma** The words in front of the conjunction (*The groom skated to the center of the rink*) are a complete sentence, but the words after the conjunction (*waited for his shivering bride*) aren't. Because the conjunction *and* links two verbs (*skated* and *waited*) and words that describe those verbs, no comma is called for. In case you're wondering, *groom* is the subject of *skated* and *waited.*

(23) **The best man rode in a Zamboni, for he was afraid of slipping on the ice.** The conjunction (*for*) joins two complete sentences, so a comma precedes it.

(24) **No comma.** In this sentence, *and* joins two items (*flowers, spotlights*). Because they aren't complete sentences, you don't need a comma before *and.*

(25) **No comma.** The conjunction (*or*) joins two descriptions (*on a beach* and *in a sunny climate with absolutely no ice*). Because you're not linking complete sentences, you don't need a comma before *or.*

(26) **No comma.** This one is a little tricky. The conjunction *or* joins *who is in charge of the gifts* and *who is paying the orchestra.* These two questions sound like complete sentences. However, the real question here is *Do you know.* The *who* statements in this sentence are just that: statements. No complete sentence = no comma.

If you're ready to test your skills a bit more, take the following chapter quiz that incorporates all the chapter topics.

Whaddya Know? Chapter 19 Quiz

Quiz time! Complete each problem to test your knowledge on the various topics covered in this chapter. You can then find the solutions and explanations in the next section.

The following figure shows an employee self-evaluation with some serious problems, a few of which concern commas. See whether you can find five commas that appear where they shouldn't and ten spots that should have commas but don't. Circle the commas you're deleting and insert commas where they're needed.

Annual Self-Evaluation — October 1, 2019

Well Ms. Ehrlich that time of year has arrived again. I, must think about my strengths and weaknesses as an employee, of Toe-Ring International. First and foremost let me say that I love working for Toe-Ring. When I applied for the job I never dreamed how much fun I would have taking two, long lunches a day. Sneaking out the back door, is not my idea of fun. Because no one ever watches what I am doing at Toe-Ring I can leave by the front door without worrying. Also Ms. Ehrlich I confess that I do almost no work at all. Upon transferring to the plant in Idaho I immediately claimed a privilege given only to the most experienced most skilled, employees and started to take two, extra weeks of vacation. I have only one more thing to say. May I have a raise?

Answers to Chapter 19 Quiz

Annual Self-Evaluation — October 1, 2019

Well, Ms. Ehrlich, that time of year has arrived again. I/ must think about

my strengths and weaknesses as an employee/ of Toe-Ring International.

First and foremost, let me say that I love working for Toe-Ring.

When I applied for the job, I never dreamed how much fun I would have

taking two/ long lunches a day. Sneaking out the back door/ is not my idea

of fun. Because no one ever watches what I am doing at Toe-Ring, I can

leave by the front door without worrying. Also, Ms. Ehrlich, I confess that I

do almost no work at all. Upon transferring to the plant in Idaho, I

immediately claimed a privilege given only to the most experienced, most

skilled/ employees and started to take two/ extra weeks of vacation. I have

only one more thing to say. May I have a raise?

---

(1) Commas surround *Ms. Ehrlich* because she's being directly addressed in this sentence. Also, *well* is an introductory word, so even without *Ms. Ehrlich*, you'd still need a comma after *well*.

(2) See the preceding answer.

(3) The pronoun *I* is part of the main idea of the sentence, not an introductory expression. No comma should separate it from the rest of the sentence.

(4) The phrase *of Toe-Ring International* is an essential identifier of the type of employee being discussed. No comma should separate it from the word it describes (*employee*).

(5) A comma follows the introductory expression, *First and most important.*

(6) The introductory expression *When I applied for the job* should be separated from the rest of the sentence by a comma.

(7) Two descriptions are attached to *lunches: two* and *long.* These descriptions aren't of the same type. *Two* is a number, and *long* is a measure of time. Also, numbers are never separated from other descriptions by a comma. The verdict: Delete the comma after *two.*

(8) In this sentence the expression *Sneaking out the back door* isn't an introductory element. It's the subject of the sentence, and it shouldn't be separated from its verb *(is)* by a comma.

(9) The introductory expression *Because no one ever watches what I am doing at Toe-Ring* should be separated from the rest of the sentence by a comma.

(10) *Also* is an introduction to the sentence. Slice it off with a comma.

(11) A comma follows *Idaho* because it is the last word of an introductory element.

(12) Two descriptions are attached to *employees: most experienced* and *most skilled.* Because these descriptions are more or less interchangeable, a comma separates them from each other.

(13) No comma ever separates the last description from what it describes, so the comma before *employees* has to go.

(14) Two descriptions (in this case, *two* and *extra*) aren't separated by commas when one of the descriptions is a number.

Chapter **20**

Useful Little Marks: Dashes, Hyphens, and Colons

I n a classic episode of an old detective show, the hero's sidekick writes a book with no punctuation whatsoever. The author explains that he will put in "all that stuff" later. Many writers sympathize with the sidekick. Who has time to worry about punctuation when the fire of creativity burns? But the truth is that the three little marks I explain in this chapter — dashes, hyphens, and colons — go a long way toward getting your point across.

Inserting Information with Dashes

Long dashes — what grammarians call *em dashes* — are dramatic. Those long straight lines draw your eye and hold your attention. But long dashes aren't just show-offs. They insert information into a sentence and introduce lists. Short dashes — technically, *en dashes* — aren't as showy as their wider cousins, but they're still useful. Short dashes show a range or connect words when the word *to* or *and* is implied.

Long dashes

A long dash's primary job is to tell the reader that you've jumped tracks onto a new (though related) subject, just for a moment. Here are some examples:

> After we buy toenail clippers — the dinosaur in that exhibit could use a trim, you know — we'll stop at the cafe.

> With a tail as long as a basketball court, the dinosaur — delivered to the museum only an hour before the grand opening — is the star of the exhibit.

The information inside the dashes is slightly off-topic. Take it out, and the sentence makes sense. The material inside the dashes relates to the information in the rest of the sentence, but it acts as an interruption to the main point you're making.

A dash's second job is to move the reader from general to specific, often by supplying a definition. Check out the following examples:

> I think I have everything I need for the first day of camp — bug spray, hair spray, sunblock, and cellphone.

Everything I need is general; *bug spray, hair spray, sunblock,* and *cellphone* are the specifics.

> Louie said that he would perform the *chew-chew* — this ritual is the unwrapping of the season's first piece of chewing gum.

The definition of *chew-chew* follows the dash.

Long dashes may be fun to write, but they're not always fun to read. For a little change of pace, dash a new idea into your sentence. Just don't dash in too often or else your reader will be tempted to dash away.

Short dashes

If you master this punctuation mark, you deserve an official grammarian's badge — sure to improve your profile on dating apps! Short dashes show a range:

> From May–September, the editors prune commas from literature written over the winter.

Short dashes also show up when you're omitting the word *to* between two elements:

> The New York–Philadelphia train is always on time.

Finally, a short dash links two or more equal elements when *and* is implied:

> The pitcher–catcher relationship is crucial to the success of the Yankees. (Sorry, can't resist rooting for my favorite team.)

Don't confuse short dashes with hyphens, an even shorter punctuation mark that I cover in the next section. Also, don't send a short dash to do a long dash's job. One common mistake is to join two complete sentences with a short dash, as in this example:

> Don't worry about Lola–she'll impress your friends.

Here's the corrected sentence:

> Don't worry about Lola — she'll impress your friends.

EXAMPLE

Q. Insert long dashes (em dashes) or short dashes (en dashes) where appropriate in these sentences.

> While she was waiting for a bus, Melanie took out her lunch almonds, steamed broccoli, and a hard-boiled egg.
>
> The Bronx Manhattan express bus was late.

A. **While she was waiting for a bus, Melanie took out her lunch — almonds, steamed broccoli, and a hard-boiled egg.** The long dash moves the reader from general *(lunch)* to specific *(almonds, steamed broccoli, and a hard-boiled egg).*

The Bronx–Manhattan express bus was late. The short dash connects two locations.

Insert long and short dashes where they are needed.

YOUR TURN

1. Suddenly Melanie realized that two animals to be specific, a squirrel and a pigeon were staring at her.

2. "Well," thought Melanie, "I'll wait for two four minutes and then leave if it doesn't show up."

3. While thinking about the bus Melanie has always been good at multitasking and eating the egg, she continued to stare at the squirrel and the pigeon.

4. The human animal bond is amazing.

5. Who can imagine what questions go through the mind of a squirrel where's the food supply, how's my tail doing, why is that human looking at me, or something else?

6. Xander Hicksom (1802 1888) theorized that squirrels spend most of the day sleeping, not thinking.

7. Will an actual descendent of Xander Hicksom Melanie prove him right or wrong?

H-y-p-h-e-n-a-t-i-n-g Made Easy

Think of a hyphen as a dash that's been on a diet. Occasionally — perhaps when you're writing with a pen or pencil — you may need a hyphen to show that a word continues on a different line. You also need these short, horizontal lines to separate parts of compound words, to write certain numbers, and to create one description from two words. This section provides you with a guide to the care and feeding of the humble hyphen.

Understanding the great divide

If you're writing on an electronic device, you seldom have to worry about hyphens that break a word at the end of a line. Most of the time, the word processing program moves the entire word to a new line if it doesn't fit within the margins. But when you're writing by hand, you may need to divide a word at the end of a line to avoid a long blank space along the right margin. If you have to divide a word, follow these simple rules:

>> Place the hyphen between the *syllables*, or sounds, of a word. (If you're unsure where the syllable breaks are in a word, check the dictionary.)

>> Don't leave only one letter of a divided word on a line. If you have a choice, divide the word more or less in the middle.

>> Don't divide words that have only one syllable.

TIP

Web addresses can be very long. Don't divide them with a hyphen. Either place the web address on its own line or, if you absolutely have to divide, chop the address at a period or a slash mark.

Using hyphens for compound words

Hyphens also separate parts of compound words, such as *ex-wife*, *pro-choice*, and *mother-in-law*. When you type or write these words, don't put a space before or after the hyphen.

THE BRITISH SYSTEM

The practice of dividing a word between syllables is American. In Britain, words are often divided according to the derivation (family tree) of the word, not according to sound. For example, in the American system, *democracy* is divided into four parts — de-moc-ra-cy — because that's how it sounds. In the British system, the same word is divided into two parts — demo-cracy — because the word is derived from two ancient Greek forms, *demos (people)* and *kratia (power)*. Let the dictionary of the country you're in be the final authority on dividing words.

For some time, the trend (yes, language follows fads) has been toward fewer punctuation marks, and that trend has accelerated. Thus, many words that used to be hyphenated compounds are now written as single words. *Semi-colon,* for instance, has morphed into *semicolon.* Years ago I sent *e-mails,* but now I write *emails.* As always, the dictionary is your friend when you're figuring out whether a particular expression is a compound, a single word, or two separate words.

TIP

One cap or two? The answer is complicated. All the parts of a person's title are capitalized, except for prepositions and articles *(Secretary-Treasurer)).* Don't capitalize the prefix *ex-* (as in *ex-President Johnson).* Words that are capitalized for some other reason (perhaps because they're part of a book title or a headline) follow a different rule. Always capitalize the first half. Capitalize the second half of the compound if it's a noun, or if the second half of the compound is equal in importance to the first half: *Secretary-General Lola, President-elect Lulu.* (For more information on capitalization, see Chapter 21.)

Hyphens also show up when a single word might be misunderstood. I once received an email from a student. "I resent the draft," she wrote. I spent ten minutes worrying about her feelings before I realized that she sent the draft of a paper twice because the email didn't go through the first time. To avoid misinterpretation, she should have written *re-sent.* Similarly, a hyphen-free statement can provide two different interpretations — never a good idea. Imagine that you're writing about baseball and use the phrase "first base coach." You may be talking about the first person to coach at a base during a baseball game — the "first base-coach," who probably rode a horse to the ball field. Or, you may be discussing the person who's standing next to first base now, giving advice to players — the "first-base coach." The hyphen clarifies your intended meaning.

Placing hyphens in numbers

Decisions about whether to write a numeral or a word are questions of style, not of grammar. The authority figure in your life — teacher, boss, parole officer, whatever — will tell you what they prefer. In general, larger numbers are represented by numerals:

> Roger has been arrested 683 times, counting last night.

However, on various occasions you may need to write the word, not the numeral. If the number falls at the beginning of a sentence, for example, you must use words if you're writing in Standard English. You may also need to write about a fractional amount. Here's how to hyphenate:

>> Hyphenate all numbers from twenty-one to ninety-nine.

>> Hyphenate all fractions used as descriptions (*three-quarters full,* for example).

>> Don't hyphenate fractions used as nouns (*three quarters of the money; one third of all registered voters*).

Utilizing the well-placed hyphen

If two words create a single description, put a hyphen between them if the description comes before the word it's describing. For example:

> a *well-placed* hyphen BUT The hyphen is *well placed.*

WARNING

Don't hyphenate two-word descriptions if the first word ends in *-ly*:

nicely drawn rectangle

completely ridiculous grammar rule

EXAMPLE

Q. Place hyphens where they're needed.

Lulu was recently elected secretary treasurer of her club, the All Star Athletes of Antarctica. Lulu ran on an anti ice platform that was accepted by two thirds of the members.

A. Here's the paragraph with the hyphens inserted, along with explanations in parentheses:

Lulu was recently elected secretary-treasurer (hyphen needed for compound title) of her club, the **All-Star** (hyphen needed for two-word description) Athletes of Antarctica. Lulu ran on an **anti-ice** (hyphen needed for two-word description) platform that was accepted by **two thirds** (no hyphen for fractions not used as descriptions) of the members.

YOUR TURN

Check the hyphens and mark them as correct or incorrect.

8 well-planned plot

9 line 1: com-

line 2: plicated

10 writer director (refers to one person doing two jobs)

11 top-of-the-line

12 top-of-the-line car

13 sixty six

14 star studded cast

15 my great-grandmother, my mother's grandmother

16 three quarters of a cup

Creating a Stopping Point: Colons

A colon is one dot on top of another (:). It appears when a simple comma isn't strong enough. (It also shows up in the typed emoticons that people write in their emails.) In this section, I look at the colon in a few of its natural habitats: business communications, lists, and quotations.

Addressing a business letter or an email

Colons appear in business letters, memos, and emails, as you see in the following examples:

From: I. M. Incharj

Re: Employment status

Mr. Ganglia:

You're getting on my nerves. You're fired.

Sincerely,

I.M. Incharj

To Whom It May Concern:

Everyone in the division is fired also.

Sincerely,

I.M. Incharj

TIP

The colon makes a business communication more formal. The opposite of a business letter is what English teachers call a *friendly letter*, even if it says something like "I despise you." When you write a friendly letter, place a comma after the name of the person who will receive the letter.

Introducing lists

When you insert a short list of items into a sentence, you don't need a colon. (For more information on how to use commas in lists, see Chapter 19.) When you're inserting a long list into a sentence, however, you may sometimes introduce the list with a colon. Think of the colon as a gulp of air that readies the reader for a good-sized list. The colon precedes the first item. Here are some sentences using colons to introduce lists:

General Parker needed quite a few things: a horse, an army, a suit of armor, a few million arrows, a map, and a battle plan.

Roger sent each spy away with several items: printouts from an espionage website, the Wikipedia entry on Mata Hari, a burner cellphone, and a poison pill.

WARNING

If you place a colon in front of a list, check the beginning of the sentence — the part before the colon. Can it stand alone? If so, no problem. If not, problem — maybe. Here's the deal. Many *style manuals* (lists of rules for particular publications) frown on colons following an incomplete introductory thought. If your list begins with something like "Buy what you need for," the list elements complete that thought and a colon gets in the way. To be on the safe side, be sure you have a complete sentence before a colon that comes before a list. Take a look at these examples:

PUNCTUATION PROBLEM: The drawbacks of Parker's battle plan are: no understanding of enemy troop movements, a lack of shelter and food for the troops, and a faulty trigger for the retreat signal. (The words before the colon — *The problems with Parker's battle plan are* — don't form a complete thought.)

BETTER PUNCTUATION: The problems with Parker's battle plan are numerous: no understanding of enemy troop movements, a lack of shelter and food for the troops, and a faulty trigger for the retreat signal. (Now the words before the colon — *The problems with Parker's battle plan are numerous* — form a complete thought.)

For more information on complete sentences, see Chapter 10.

Introducing long quotations

The rule concerning colons with quotations is fairly easy. If the quotation is short, introduce it with a comma. If the quotation is long, introduce it with a colon. Take a look at the following two examples for comparison:

What did Lola say at the meeting? Not much, so a comma does the job.

> Lola stated, "I have no comment on the squirrel incident."

What did General Parker say at the press conference? Too much, so a colon is better.

> Parker explained: "The media has been entirely too critical of my preparations for war. Despite the fact that I have spent the past ten years and two million gold coins perfecting new and improved armor, I have been told that I am unready to fight."

TIP

When you write a paper for school, you may insert some short quotations (up to three lines) into the text. If a quotation is longer than three lines, you should double-indent and single-space the quoted material so that it looks like a separate block of print. Such quotations are called *block quotations*. Introduce the block quotation with a colon, and don't use quotation marks. (The blocking shows that you're quoting, so you don't need the marks.) Here's an example:

In his essay entitled, "Why Homework Is Useless," Smith makes the following point:

> Studies show that students who have no time to rest are not as efficient as those who do. When a thousand teens were surveyed, they all indicated that sleeping, listening to music, talking on the phone, and playing Minecraft were more valuable than schoolwork.

If you're writing about poetry, you may use the same block format:

> The postmodern imagery of this stanza is in stark contrast to the imagery of the Romantic period:
>
> > Roses are red,
> >
> > Violets are blue,
> >
> > Alfred is sweet,
> >
> > And stupid, too.

Colons sometimes show up inside sentences, joining one complete sentence to another. A colon may be used this way only when the second sentence explains the meaning of the first sentence, as in this example:

> Lola has refused to accept the nomination: She believes the media will investigate every aspect of her life.

The second half of the sentence explains why Lola doesn't want to run for president. Actually, it explains why very few Americans want to run for president. Notice that I've capitalized the first word after the colon. Some writers prefer lowercase for that spot. This decision is a matter of style, not grammar. Check with the authority figure in charge of your writing (teacher, boss, warden, and so on) about the preferred style.

Q. Correct or incorrect? You decide.

To Whom It May Concern,

A. **Incorrect.** This extremely formal and somewhat old-fashioned greeting is always followed by a colon.

Correct or incorrect? You decide.

17   Last week Joe campaigned in ten states, Maine, Vermont, New Hampshire, Massachusetts, Connecticut, Rhode Island, New York, New Jersey, Pennsylvania, and Ohio.

18   Joe stated: "I like states."

19   Quotations from Joe's essay, "A Statement about States: My Position," were widely tweeted.

20   Joe's campaign head remarked: "Joe is very qualified for the position of Regional Transportation Director. He drives. He takes trains and planes. Sometimes he bikes. If he can't avoid it, he walks. He knows a lot about transportation. True, he has never worked in the field, but he does use transportation."

21   Joe's energy level is low: He plans to run for Regional Transportation Secretary if he doesn't win the directorship.

SLASHING YOUR SENTENCES

A forward slanting line — the *virgule,* in grammar lingo, and the *slash* to ordinary people — shows up in URL addresses. It's also useful to present two alternatives, but if you insert slashes into your sentences, consider them the hottest chili peppers imaginable. How many chili peppers do you want in your meal? That's the number of slashes you should place in your writing. Very, very few.

Here's an example of the slash in action:

Job applicants must bring photos/examples of their work to the interview.

What should you bring to impress your potential boss? Either a photo of the mural you painted on the side of your house or the house itself. The slash shows the two possible choices.

Slashes also separate lines of poetry when you're quoting them inside a paragraph:

The effort of mountain climbing contributes to the imagery in Lulu's poem, "Everest or Nothing": "and then the harsh/breath of the mountain/meets the harsh/breath of the climber/I am/the climber."

The slashes tell you that Lulu's poem looks like this:

and then the harsh

breath of the mountain

meets the harsh

breath of the climber

I am

the climber.

Practice Questions Answers and Explanations

1. **Suddenly Melanie realized that two animals — to be specific, a squirrel and a pigeon — were staring at her.** You're better off with long dashes than simple commas here because *to be specific, a squirrel and a pigeon* already has a comma. Parentheses, however, would also be fine in this sentence.

2. **"Well," thought Melanie, "I'll wait for two–four minutes and then leave if it doesn't show up."** The short dash in this sentence shows a range of time.

3. **While thinking about the bus — Melanie has always been good at multitasking — and eating the egg, she continued to stare at the squirrel and the pigeon.** Here, the comment about Melanie's ability to do more than one thing at a time interrupts the statement *While thinking about the bus and eating the egg.* Two long dashes show the interruption.

4. **The human–animal bond is amazing.** A short dash shows a relationship between two categories, *human* and *animal*.

5. **Who can imagine what questions go through the mind of a squirrel — where's the food supply, how's my tail doing, why is that human looking at me, or something else?** The long dash signals the shift from general (*questions*) to specific (the content of those questions). A colon would also serve to introduce the list of possible questions.

6. **Xander Hicksom (1802–1888) theorized that squirrels spend most of the day sleeping, not thinking.** The short dash connects two dates here, the years of birth and death.

7. **Will an actual descendent of Xander Hicksom — Melanie — prove him right or wrong?** Simple commas would also do the job here, much less dramatically.

8. **Correct** The two words, *well* and *planned*, function as one description, so a hyphen should link them. If the same two words appear after the word they refer to (*plot*), the grammar changes. If you write, "The plot was well planned," *well* describes *planned*, which is part of the verb *was planned*.

9. **Correct** *Complicated* breaks into four syllables: com pli ca ted. The hyphen properly separates the first syllable from the next three.

10. **Incorrect** This title, like many others that identify one person doing two jobs, is hyphenated. If you're not sure about a particular title, check your dictionary.

11. **Incorrect** Creating one description such as *top-of-the-line* is correct only when you're describing something. In this expression, you're not.

12. **Correct** Now *top-of-the-line* does describe something (*car*).

13. **Incorrect** Numbers from twenty-one to ninety-nine should be hyphenated, so the correct form is *sixty-six*.

14. **Incorrect** Two words, *star* and *studded*, combine to describe *cast*, so you want a *star-studded cast*.

15. **Correct** The hyphen tells you that this word refers to a relative, not to a quality (greatness) that a grandmother may possess.

16. **Correct** Surprised? Used this way, *quarters* is a noun. *Three* is a description, telling you how many quarters you have.

(17) **Incorrect** A colon, not a comma, should introduce the list of states.

(18) **Incorrect** The quotation is short, so a comma, not a colon, should follow stated.

(19) **Correct** A colon properly separates the subtitle from the title.

(20) **Correct** This long quotation is properly introduced by a colon.

(21) **Incorrect** The second statement does not explain the meaning of the first statement, so a colon doesn't work here.

If you're ready to test your skills a bit more, take the following chapter quiz that incorporates all the chapter topics.

Whaddya Know? Chapter 20 Quiz

Quiz time! Complete each problem to test your knowledge on the various topics covered in this chapter. You can then find the solutions and explanations in the next section.

Ten portions of this letter from a florist to a client are underlined. Decide whether the underlined material properly employs dashes, hyphens, or colons. If you find a mistake, correct it. If everything is fine, leave it alone.

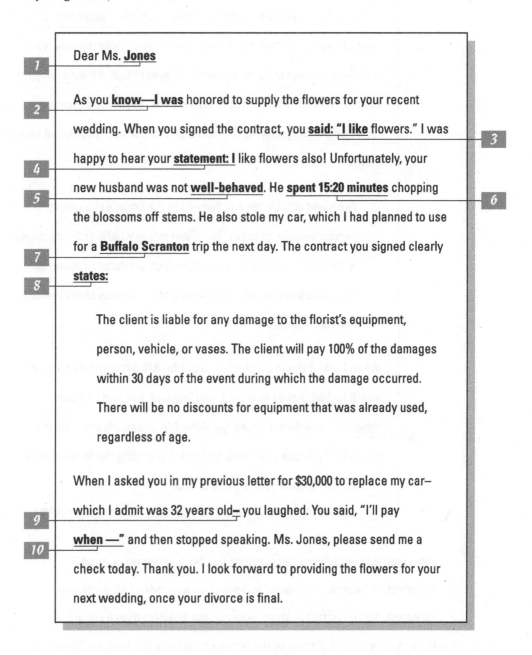

1 Dear Ms. **Jones**

2 As you **know—I was** honored to supply the flowers for your recent

wedding. When you signed the contract, you **said: "I like** flowers." I was **3**

4 happy to hear your **statement: I** like flowers also! Unfortunately, your

5 new husband was not **well-behaved**. He **spent 15:20 minutes** chopping **6**

the blossoms off stems. He also stole my car, which I had planned to use

7 for a **Buffalo Scranton** trip the next day. The contract you signed clearly

8 **states:**

> The client is liable for any damage to the florist's equipment,
>
> person, vehicle, or vases. The client will pay 100% of the damages
>
> within 30 days of the event during which the damage occurred.
>
> There will be no discounts for equipment that was already used,
>
> regardless of age.

When I asked you in my previous letter for $30,000 to replace my car—

9 which I admit was 32 years old— you laughed. You said, "I'll pay

10 **when —"** and then stopped speaking. Ms. Jones, please send me a

check today. Thank you. I look forward to providing the flowers for your

next wedding, once your divorce is final.

Answers to Chapter 20 Quiz

Dear Ms. **<u>Jones:</u>**   **1**

  2 As you **<u>know, I was</u>** honored to supply the flowers for your recent wedding. When you signed the contract, you **<u>said, "I like</u>** flowers." I was   **3**
happy to hear your **<u>statement:</u> I** like flowers also! Unfortunately, your   **4**
new husband was not **<u>well behaved</u>**. He **<u>spent 15–20 minutes</u>** chopping   **5**   **6**
the blossoms off stems. He also stole my car, which I had planned to use
for a **<u>Buffalo–Scranton</u>** trip the next day. The contract you signed clearly   **7**
<u>states:</u>   **8**

> The client is liable for any damage to the florist's equipment,
> person, vehicle, or vases. The client will pay 100% of the damages
> within 30 days of the event during which the damage occurred.
> There will be no discounts for equipment that was already used,
> regardless of age.

When I asked you in my previous letter for $30,000 to replace my car,
which I admit was 32 years **old,** you laughed. You said, "I'll pay   **9**
<u>when — "</u> and then stopped speaking. Ms. Jones, please send me a   **10**
check today. Thank you. I look forward to providing the flowers for your
next wedding, once your divorce is final.

(1) **Incorrect.** A colon follows the greeting in a business letter or email.

(2) **Incorrect.** A comma, not a dash, follows this short introductory phrase.

(3) **Incorrect.** The quotation is short, so a comma is better than a colon.

(4) **Correct.** The second portion of the sentence explains the first, so the colon is correct.

5. **Incorrect.** The description, *well behaved*, is not hyphenated when it appears after the word it describes, which in this sentence is *husband*.

6. **Incorrect.** A short dash shows the time range.

7. **Incorrect.** A short dash shows the path of the trip, from Buffalo to Scranton.

8. **Correct.** To introduce a blocked quotation, a colon is appropriate.

9. **Incorrect.** A short dash shows a range, not what you need in this sentence. Here, information is inserted into the main idea of the sentence, so commas work well. The long dash would add a touch of drama and would also be correct here.

10. **Correct.** The long dash shows an incomplete thought.

IN THIS CHAPTER

» Grasping the basics of capital letters

» Capitalizing names, places, and things

» Knowing when capital letters are needed in everyday writing

Chapter **21**

Capital Letters

Pads are popular, but not always with English teachers, because, well, take a look at the first letter of this sentence. It's in *lowercase* — what kindergarteners call "small letters." In Standard English, every sentence must begin with a capital letter. Why? Partly to help the reader separate sentences, but also because it's a tradition, and capitalization is bound by tradition. That said, I should mention that the major style-setters in the world of grammar sometimes disagree about what should be capitalized and what shouldn't. In this chapter, I explain commonly accepted practices for employing capital letters, and I point out some areas of disagreement. *Note:* Texting and some other electronic media have their own rules for capitalization, which I discuss in Chapter 25.

Knowing What's Up with Uppercase

The rules for *uppercase*, or capital letters, are easy. You already know one:

» **Begin every sentence with a capital letter.** Yes, the iPad (and the iMac and the *i* everything) break the rule, but a company has the power to name its products, and Apple picked a lowercase *i* for these items. Unless your sentence begins with a similar name (*eBay*, for example), start with a capital letter. If you're writing a sentence that begins with a number, write the word, not the numeral, or reword the sentence so that the number isn't first.

TIP

Traditionally, the first letter of each line of a poem is capitalized, even if it isn't the beginning of a sentence. However, poets, like computer companies, enjoy trashing (sorry, I meant *reinterpreting*) rules. In poetry, anything goes — including capitalization rules:

» **Capitalize *I*.** The personal pronoun *I* — the word you use to refer to yourself — must be capitalized.

>> **Capitalize names.** This rule applies when you're using an actual name, not a category. Write about *Elizabeth*, not *elizabeth*, when you're discussing one of the cutest kids ever (my granddaughter). She's a *girl*, not a *Girl*, because *girl* is a category, not a name. Elizabeth lives in *Washington*, not *washington* (her *state*, not *State,* because *state* is a general category, not a name). Also capitalize brand names (*Sony*, for example) unless the company itself uses lowercase letters.

>> **Begin most quotations with a capital letter.** When quotation marks appear, so do capitals — most of the time. (For exceptions to this rule, turn to Chapter 18.)

That's it for the basics. For the picky stuff, keep reading.

Capitalizing (or Not) References to People

If human beings were called only by their names, life would be much simpler, at least in terms of capital letters. But most people pick up a few titles and some relatives as they journey through life. In this section, I tell you what to capitalize when you're referring to people.

Sorting out job titles

Allow me to introduce my friend Egbert. He's *Mr.* Egbert Henhuff, *director of poultry* at a nearby farm. Next year, *Director of Poultry* Henhuff plans to run for *state senator,* unless he cracks under the pressure of a major campaign, in which case he'll run for *sheriff.*

Notice what's going on with the capitals in this introduction. The title *Mr.* always appears with a last name and is always capitalized because it's considered part of the name. *Director of Poultry* is capitalized when it precedes Egbert's last name but lowercased when it follows Egbert's name. Why? *Director of Poultry Henhuff* functions as a unit, a name, so it's capitalized. (Unimportant words in a title, such as *of,* are lowercased. See "Capitalizing Titles," later in this chapter, for more guidance.) When the title follows the name or appears elsewhere in the sentence, it functions as a description, not a name, and isn't capitalized. That accounts for the lowercased *director of poultry, state senator,* and *sheriff.*

WARNING

Some style manuals, but not all, tell you to capitalize very important titles — President of the United States and Prime Minister of Great Britain, for example — even when they appear without the name of the person who holds them. Because there's some leeway with this rule on titles, ask the preference of the authority figure (boss or teacher) who will read your work.

TIP

When capitalizing a hyphenated title, capitalize both words (*Chief Justice*) or neither (*assistant secretary*). One exception to the rule (you knew there had to be one!) is for *exes* and *elects:*

>> ex-President

>> President-elect

Q. Insert capitals where needed.

yesterday mayor victoria johnson ordered all public servants in her town to conserve sticky tape.

A. **Yesterday Mayor Victoria Johnson ordered all public servants in her town to conserve sticky tape.** Capitalize the first word of a sentence *(Yesterday)*, a title attached to a name *(Mayor)*, and a person's name *(Victoria Johnson)*.

Q. Insert capitals where needed.

herman harris, chief city engineer, has promised to hold the line on tape spending.

A. **Herman Harris, chief city engineer, has promised to hold the line on tape spending.** Capitalize the name of a person *(Herman Harris)* but not a title that appears after a name.

Writing about family relationships

It's not true that Elizabeth's *grandma* was imprisoned for illegal sentence structure. I know for a fact that *Uncle Bart* took the blame, although his *brother* Alfred tried desperately to convince *Grandma* to make a full confession. "My *son* deserves to do time," said *Grandma*, "because he dropped a verb when he was little and got away with it."

What do you notice about the family titles in the preceding paragraph? Some of them are capitalized, and some are not. The rules for capitalizing the titles of family members are simple. If you're labeling a relative, don't capitalize. (I'm talking about kinship — *aunt, sister, son,* and so on — not appearance or personality flaws — *chubby, sweet, dishonest,* and so on.) If the titles take the place of names (as in *Uncle Bart and Grandma*), capitalize them. For example:

Lulu's *stepsister* Sarah poured a cup of ink into every load of wash that Lulu did. *(stepsister* = label)

Sarah told *Mother* about the gallon of paint thinner that Lulu had dripped over Sarah's favorite rose bush. *(Mother* = name)

I was surprised when my *father* took no action; fortunately, *Aunt Aggie* stepped in with a pail of bleach for Lulu. *(father* — label; *Aunt Aggie* — name)

If you can substitute a real name — Mabel or Jonas, for example — in the sentence, you probably need a capital letter:

I told *Father* that he needed to shave off his handlebar mustache and put it on his bicycle. (original sentence)

I told *Jonas* that he needed to shave off his handlebar mustache and put it on his bicycle. (The substitution sounds fine, so capitalize *Father*.)

If the substitution sounds strange, you probably need lowercase:

> I told my *grandmother* not to shave off her mustache. (original sentence)

> I told my *Mabel* not to shave off her mustache. (The substitution doesn't work because you don't generally say *my Mabel.* Use lowercase for *grandmother.*)

The word *my* and other possessive pronouns (*your, his, her, our, their*) often indicate that you should lowercase the title. (For more information on possessive pronouns, see Chapter 4.)

Q. Which sentence is correct?

1. Archie helped mother tape signs to every tree in the neighborhood.

2. Archie helped Mother tape signs to every tree in the neighborhood.

A. **2** *Mother* is used as a name, not a label, so you must capitalize it. (Try the *Mabel* test; it works!)

Correct any capitalization errors you find in these sentences.

1. The Municipal Dogcatcher, Agnes e. Bark, insists on taping reward signs to every tree.

2. My Sister says that the signs placed by dogcatcher Bark seldom fall far from the tree.

3. Did you ask mom whether ms. Bark's paper signs will freeze in December?

4. Few Dogcatchers care as much as agnes about rounding up lost dogs.

5. The recent dog show champion, BooBoo, bit uncle Lou last week.

6. My Brother thinks that no one would have been hurt if Agnes had found BooBoo first.

7. The Mayor's Cousin, who owns a thumbtack company, has an interest in substituting tacks for tape.

8. Until the issue is resolved, Agnes, herself the chief executive of Sticking, Inc., will continue to tape.

Tackling race and ethnicity

The conventions for capitalizing words that refer to race and ethnicity, as well as the words themselves, have changed in recent years. Like everyone else, grammarians are struggling to overcome the legacy of a racist society and its language. Various style guides have chosen different paths and then recalibrated as editors' understanding deepens. So, what should you capitalize, and what should you lowercase? If you're writing for a specific authority figure, you can ask about the preferred style. If you're on your own, here are some guidelines:

>> *White* and *Black* are generally capitalized when the words refer to race or ethnicity — what the culture views as a shared historical or cultural identity. References to color (*a white dress,*

black piano keys), are lowercased. *Latino/Latina/Latinx* and *Hispanic* are always capitalized. The term *people of color* is usually lowercased, though some style guides capitalize the short form, *POC*.

» *European, Asian, African, South American, North American,* and *Central American* are always capitalized, because they refer to continents or regions. So are combination forms like *European American* and *African American.*

» All words that describe national origin are capitalized (*French, Pakistani, Kenyan,* and so forth). So are combination forms such as *Mexican American* and *Polish American.*

TIP

Combination forms normally appear without hyphens, though some style guides insert a hyphen when the words function as an adjective. (See Chapter 6 for more information on adjectives.)

EXAMPLE

Insert capital letters where they're needed in these sentences.

Q. my friend jules is studying african american history this year.

A. **My friend Jules is studying African American history this year.** The first word of a sentence *(My)* is capitalized, as is the name *Jules. African American* is always capitalized. Some style guides omit the hyphen; others insert it if the expression is used as an adjective, as it is in this sentence.

Q. my cousin gave me a book of poetry by japanese writers.

A. **My cousin gave me a book of poetry by Japanese writers.** Capitalize the first word in the sentence *(My)* and *Japanese,* a word referring to national origin.

Capitalizing Geography: Directions and Places

Even if nothing more than your imagination leaves the living room, you still need to know the rules for capitalizing the names of places, languages, geographical features, regions, and directions. Here's a complete guide to capitalizing geography.

My pet parakeets don't migrate for the winter, but if they did, where would they go — south or South? It depends. The direction of flight is *south* (lowercase). The area of the country where it's easy to find warmth is the *South* (uppercase). Got it? From New York City, you drive *west* to visit the *West* (or the *Midwest*).

The names of other, smaller areas are often capitalized, too. Plopped in the center of *New York City* is *Central Park. Chicago* has a *South Side* and *London* has *Bloomsbury.* Note the capital letters for the names of these areas.

Capitalize geographic features when the proper name is given (*Mississippi River, the Himalayas, the Great Plains*). The word *the* is generally lowercased, even when it appears with a name. Use lowercase for geographical features that are not named (*mountain, valley, gorge,* or *beach,* for instance).

TIP

Nearly always, the names of countries and words derived from them are capitalized. One exception to this rule: common objects with a country, area, or nationality as part of the name (*french fries, scotch whiskey, venetian blinds,* and so forth). By attaching itself to a common object, the name takes on a new meaning. It no longer refers to the country or language. Instead, the reader simply thinks of an everyday object. If you're unsure whether to capitalize the geographical part of a common item, check the dictionary.

EXAMPLE

Q. Correct the capitalization in this paragraph.

When Alex sent his little brother Abner to Italy, Abner vowed to visit mount Vesuvius. Alex asked Abner to bring back some venetian blinds, but Abner returned empty-handed. "Let's go out for chinese food," said Abner when he returned. "Some sesame noodles will cheer me up."

A. Here is the answer, with explanations in parentheses:

When Alex sent his little brother Abner to Italy (correct — country name), **Abner vowed to visit Mount Vesuvius** (capitalize the entire name of the mountain). **Alex asked Abner to bring back some venetian blinds** (correct — lowercase for the name of a common object), **but Abner returned empty-handed. "Let's go out for Chinese food** (because this isn't the name of one specific item, such as french fries, capitals are better)," **said Abner when he returned. "Some sesame noodles will cheer me up."**

Marking Seasons and Other Times

Read this paragraph, paying special attention to the italicized words and letters:

Lou hates the *summer* because of all the tourists who invade his coastal town. He's been known to roar something about *"winter's* peaceful *mornings,"* even though he seldom wakes up before *3 P.M.* and never before *noon.* He starts his day by reading about the *Renaissance.*

After reading the preceding example, you can probably figure out this rule without me. Write the seasons of the year in lowercase, as well as the times of day. Words referring to historical eras or important events, such as *Elizabethan* and *Great Depression,* are also capitalized.

TIP

Some books tell you to capitalize the abbreviations for morning and afternoon (*A.M.* and *P.M.*) and some specify lowercase (*a.m.* and *p.m.*). Therefore, no matter what you do, half your readers will think you're right (the good news) and half will think you're wrong (the bad news). Your best bet is to check with the authority overseeing your writing. If you're the authority, do what you want. Just be careful not to confuse the reader with *am* (a form of the verb *be*) and the abbreviation for morning (*a.m.*).

Correct any errors in capitalization.

9 On a Westward voyage, Sindy hoped to reach Europe and visit places associated with world war II.

10 During the Summer, Sindy has about a month off and usually looks for Lakes with cabins nearby.

11 Last monday Sindy spent several hours reading history books about the War.

12 She immediately called a travel agent and tried to book an Eastbound flight to Amsterdam.

13 The fare was too high, so she chose to cross the atlantic on a ship instead.

14 "I love Oceans," remarked Sindy as she searched the horizon, looking for islands.

15 When the ship neared Iceland, Sindy sighed. "A Volcano erupted there last year," she remarked.

16 Sindy planned to continue her trip, moving west across the Continent until she reached the Middle East.

17 The suez canal had been at the top of her must-see list since December, when she saw a documentary on its construction.

18 Sindy plans to spend some time in old Cairo, a neighborhood rich in history.

Capitalizing Work and School Terms

On Monday mornings, work often feels like WORK, but that's not how the word is written in Standard English. In the business world, company names are capitalized, and general terms are not. (For titles, see "Sorting out job titles," earlier in this chapter.) At school, capitalize the name of the institution (*Hunter College, Marian Anderson High School*). Don't capitalize subjects and subject areas (*history, science, physics, phys ed*) unless the name refers to a language (*Spanish, Latin, English*). Capitalize the titles of courses (*Economics 101, Math for People Who Can't Count, Paper Clips in American History*). The years in school, though interminable and incredibly important, aren't capitalized (*seventh grader, freshman,* or *sophomore,* for instance).

 Q. Correct the capitalization in this paragraph.

Hurrying to Chemistry class, Jack slipped on the stairs on the very first day of his Senior year. He wanted to see his sweetheart, a Freshman named Lila Jones, who had enrolled in history of the ancient world with Professor Krater. Lila, deep in the study of history, didn't see Jack's accident.

A. Here's the correct version, with the reasons in parentheses:

Hurrying to chemistry (don't capitalize subjects) **class, Jack slipped on the stairs on the very first day of his senior year** (never capitalize years in school). **He wanted to see his sweetheart, a freshman** (never capitalize years in school) **named Lila Jones, who had enrolled in History of the Ancient World** (capitalize course titles) **with Professor Krater. Lila, deep in the study of history** (this one is correct — lowercase for subject areas), **didn't see Jack's accident.**

Correct the capitalization errors.

YOUR TURN

19 After extensive research, the united nose ring company has determined that freshmen prefer silver rings, except Psychology majors.

20 The spokesperson for the Company commented that "gold rocks the world" of future Psychologists.

21 "I wore a gold ring to the curriculum committee during the Spring Semester," explained Fred Stileless, who is the student representative to that committee.

22 "My gold earring was a turnoff for juniors," explained Fred, who hasn't had a date since he was a senior at Smith And Youngtown United high school. "I hope they like my new nose ring."

23 The Spokesperson surveyed competing Products, including a silver-gold combination manufactured by in style or else, inc., a division of Nosy Industrials, where every worker has a College Degree.

Capitalizing Titles

Titles of articles, books, websites, blog posts, and other writings require capital letters. Two systems of capitalization are acceptable, roughly divided by content. If the work falls into the general interest or humanities slot (literature, art, history, and so forth), you probably want *headline style*. Scientists opt for *sentence style*, which also sometimes pops up in publications devoted to other types of content. If you're not sure where your work belongs, check with the relevant authority figure. No supervisor? Pick the system you like the best. In this section, I explain both.

Headline style

Most newspaper and magazine articles, as well as creative works, employ headline style. You can find examples by looking at — how surprising — headlines. Here are the rules, which I illustrate with a title of a book, *I Am Not a Monster*. (This isn't a real book, by the way.)

>> Capitalize *I* and *Monster*. *I* is always uppercase, and *Monster* is an important word. Also, *I* is the first word of the title, and the first word of the title is always capitalized.

>> Capitalize *Am* because it's a verb, and verbs are at the heart of the title's meaning.

>> Capitalize *Not* because it changes the meaning of the verb and thus has an important job to do in the sentence.

>> Lowercase the only word remaining — *a*. Never capitalize articles (*a, an,* and *the*) unless they're the first words in the title.

Do you see the general principles I've applied? Here's a summary of the rules for all sorts of titles:

>> Capitalize the first word in the title.

>> Capitalize verbs and other important words.

>> Lowercase unimportant words — articles *(a, an, the),* conjunctions (words that connect, such as *and, or, nor,* and the like), and prepositions (*of, with, by,* and other words that express a relationship between two elements in the sentence).

TIP

Some grammarians capitalize long prepositions — those with more than four letters. Others tell you to lowercase all prepositions, even the huge ones — *concerning, according to,* and so on. (See Chapter 7 for a list of common prepositions.) Your best bet is to check with your immediate authority — editor, boss, teacher — to make sure that you write in the preferred style.

WARNING

When writing the title of a magazine or newspaper, should you capitalize the word *the?* Probably not. Modern style manuals generally lowercase *the,* even when the publication itself uses a capital *T,* unless the title is alone on the line or is the first word of a sentence.

EXAMPLE

Q. Use headline style to capitalize these titles.

the importance of being prepared

romeo and lulu

slouching toward homework

A.

The Importance of Being Prepared *The* is the first word of the title. *Importance, Being,* and *Prepared* are important words. Lowercase *of* because it's not an important word.

Romeo and Lulu *Romeo* is the first word of the title and is also a name. Similarly, *Lulu* is a name. Lowercase *and* because it's not an important word.

Slouching Toward Homework *Slouching* is the first word of the title. *Homework* is important. *Toward* can go either way. It's a preposition — a relationship word — and thus may be lowercased, at least according to some grammarians. It's also a long word, which makes it suitable for capitalization in the opinion of other grammarians.

Sentence style

Scientists are practical people, don't you think? They've simplified the rules of capitalization for works in their field, such as this article (which doesn't actually exist):

Oxygen saturation in freshwater: A comparative study of Kelton Lake and Walden Pond

Can you figure out the rules? Here they are, in all their glory:

>> **Capitalize the first word of the title.** In this article, that's *Oxygen.*

>> **Capitalize the first word of the subtitle.** Here, that word is *A.*

>> **Capitalize proper names.** *Kelton Lake* and *Walden Pond* name specific places and are therefore capitalized.

>> **Lowercase everything else.**

Don't you love science? At least when you're capitalizing?

Q. Capitalize these titles using sentence style.

EXAMPLE

congo river flora: a study of algae growth

copper pipe erosion and its effect on water purity

the arm effect: a psychological study of hand gestures

A. **Congo River flora: A study of algae growth** The name of the river is capitalized, as is the first word of the subtitle.

Copper pipe erosion and its effect on water purity The first word is capitalized, and everything else is in lowercase.

The arm effect: A psychological study of hand gestures The first word of the title and the first word of the subtitle are in caps. Everything else is in lowercase.

Capitalize these titles according to the rules of the style in parentheses.

YOUR TURN

24 moby duck: a tale of obsessive bird–watching *(headline)*

25 "an analysis of the *duckensis mobyous*: the consequences of habitat shrinkage on population" *(sentence)*

26 "call me izzy smell: my life as a duck hunter" *(headline)*

27 the duck and i: essays on the relationship between human beings and feathered species *(sentence)*

28   duck and cover: a cookbook *(headline)*

29   "the duck stops here: political wisdom from the environmental movement" *(sentence)*

30   duck up: how the duck triumphed over the hunter *(headline)*

?4U: Cn U AbbreV8?

Do you like the shortened title of this section? At 18 characters, it's half the length of the full version: *Question for You: Can You Abbreviate?* With this abbreviation, you save time and space.

But abbreviations have a downside. The first time you saw *e.g.*, did you know that it meant *for example?* If so, fine. If not, you probably didn't understand what the author was trying to say. Second, abbreviations clash with formal writing. Formal writing implies thought and care, not haste. (Things are different when you're thumbing a message, a post, or a tweet. Check out Chapter 25 for more on electronic media and grammar.)

Sometimes, however, you do want to abbreviate. Here's how to do so correctly:

>> Capitalize abbreviations for titles and end the abbreviation with a period. For example, *Mrs.* Snodgrass, *Rev.* Tawkalot, *Sen.* Veto, Jeremiah Jones, *Jr.*, and *St.* Lucy.

>> Capitalize geographic abbreviations when they're part of a name but not when they're a general category. Place a period at the end of the abbreviation: Appalachian *Mts.* or Amazon *R.*, for example. On a map, you may write *mt.* (mountain).

>> The United States Postal Service has standard, two-letter state abbreviations. Don't put periods in these abbreviations. Examples: *AZ* (Arizona), *CO* (Colorado), *WY* (Wyoming), and so on.

>> Write most measurements in lowercase and end the abbreviation with a period *(yds.* for *yards* or *lbs.* for *pounds).* Metric abbreviations are written without periods *(km* for *kilometer* or *g* for *gram).*

WARNING

Don't confuse abbreviations with acronyms. Abbreviations chop some letters out of a single word. Acronyms are new words made from the first letters of each word in a multiword title. Some common acronyms include the following:

NATO: North Atlantic Treaty Organization

OPEC: Organization of Petroleum Exporting Countries

WHO: World Health Organization

WARNING

Want to drive your teacher crazy? Write a formal essay with &, *w/*, *w/o*, or *b/c*. (For the abbreviation-deprived, & means "and," *w/* means "with," *w/o* means "without," *b/c* means "because.") These symbols are fine for your notes but not for your finished product. Similarly, save *brb (be right back)*, *lol (laugh out loud)*, and other texting abbreviations for your friends, not for authority figures. (For more on texting and electronic media, turn to Chapter 25.)

Q. Correct Legghorn's homework.

EXAMPLE

Yesterday (Tues.) I went in the a.m. to CO. I saw Mr. Dean, who told me that the EPA had outlawed his favorite pesticide. I have three gal. in the basement, & I'll have to discard them.

A. **Yesterday (Tuesday) I went in the morning to Colorado. I saw Mr. Dean, who told me that the EPA had outlawed his favorite pesticide. I have three gallons in the basement, and I'll have to discard them.**

Don't abbreviate in homework assignments except for titles *(Mr. Dean)* and easily understood acronyms *(EPA,* or *Environmental Protection Agency).* If you're writing about an acronym that your reader may not understand, write the whole thing out the first time you use it and place the acronym in parentheses. Thereafter, the acronym alone is fine. Also, if this had been a note to a friend, the abbreviations would have been perfectly acceptable.

YOUR TURN

Write the proper abbreviation or acronym for the following words, taking care to capitalize where necessary.

(31) figure

(32) before common era

(33) mister Burns

(34) united states president

(35) national aeronautics and space administration

(36) reverend Smith

(37) new york

(38) Adams boulevard

(39) irregular

(40) incorporated

Practice Questions Answers and Explanations

1. **municipal dogcatcher, E.** The title in this sentence isn't attached to the name; in fact, it's separated from the name by a comma. It should be in lowercase. Initials take capitals and periods.

2. **sister, Dogcatcher** Family relationships aren't capitalized unless the relationship is used as a name. The title *Dogcatcher* is attached to the name, and thus it's capitalized.

3. **Mom, Ms.** The word *Mom* substitutes for the name here, so it's capitalized. The title *Ms.* is always capitalized, but the period is optional.

4. **dogcatchers, Agnes** The common noun *dogcatchers* doesn't need a capital letter, but the proper name *Agnes* does.

5. **Uncle** The title *uncle* is capitalized if it precedes or substitutes for the name. Did I catch you on *BooBoo?* People can spell their own names (and the names of their pets) how they want.

6. **brother** Family titles aren't capitalized unless they substitute for the name.

7. **mayor's, cousin** These titles aren't attached to or used as names, so they take lowercase.

8. **Correct** Names are in caps, but the title isn't, except when it precedes the name.

9. **westward, World War II** Directions aren't capitalized. Names referring to historical eras and important events should be capitalized.

10. **summer, lakes** Use lowercase for seasons and general geographical terms.

11. **Monday, war** Days of the week should appear in caps, but the general term *war* should not. Did I catch you with *history?* That's a general term, so it appears in lowercase.

12. **eastbound** Directions aren't capitalized. *Amsterdam*, the name of a city, is correctly capitalized.

13. **Atlantic** The name of the ocean (or any geographical feature) should be capitalized.

14. **oceans** General geographical terms, such as oceans and islands, take lowercase.

15. **volcano** *Volcano* is a general term, so write it in lowercase. *Iceland*, the name of a country, is properly capitalized.

16. **continent** Another general term, another lowercase letter. *Middle East*, the name of a region, is capitalized.

17. **Suez Canal** This one is a specific place, so capitals letters do the job. *December*, like all months, is capitalized.

18. **Old** The sentence tells you that *Old Cairo* is a neighborhood, an area, so capital letters are needed.

19. **United Nose Ring Company, psychology** Although college freshmen think they're important (and, of course, they are), they rate only lowercase. The name of the company should be in uppercase. Don't capitalize subject areas.

(20) **company, psychologists** Common nouns such as *company* and *psychologists* aren't capitalized.

(21) **spring semester** The name of the committee is generic and generally would not take capitals, though you have some elbow room here for style. Seasons, both natural and academic, should be lowercased.

(22) **and, High School** Years in school and school levels aren't capitalized. The name of the school is (and the name includes *High School*), but an unimportant word such as *and* is written in lowercase.

(23) **spokesperson; products; In Style or Else, Inc.; college degree** A common noun such as *spokesperson* or *college degree* isn't capitalized. The names of companies are capitalized according to the preference of the company itself. Most companies follow headline style, which is explained in "Capitalizing Titles," earlier in this chapter.

(24) **Moby Duck: A Tale of Obsessive Bird-Watching** In headline style, the first word of the title (*Moby*) and subtitle (*A*) are in caps. Nouns (*Duck*, *Tale*, and *Watching*) and descriptive words (*Obsessive*, *Bird*) are also uppercased. The short preposition *of* merits only lowercase.

(25) **"An analysis of the *Duckensis mobyous*: The consequences of habitat shrinkage on population"** In sentence-style capitalization, the first words of the title and subtitle are in caps, but everything else is in lowercase, with the exception of proper names. In this title, following preferred scientific style, the names of the genus (a scientific category) and species are in italics with only the genus name in caps.

(26) **"Call Me Izzy Smell: My Life As a Duck Hunter"** Per headline style, the article (*a*) is in lowercase. I caught you on *As*, didn't I? It's short, but it's not an article or a preposition, so it rates a capital letter.

(27) **The duck and I: Essays on the relationship between human beings and feathered species** Sentence style titles take caps for the first word of the title and subtitle. The personal pronoun *I* is always capitalized.

(28) **Duck and Cover: A Cookbook** Headline style calls for capitals for the first word of the title and subtitle and all other nouns. The joining word *and* is lowercased in headline style, unless it begins a title or subtitle.

(29) **"The duck stops here: Political wisdom from the environmental movement"** Sentence style gives you two capitals in this title — the first word of the title and subtitle.

(30) **Duck Up: How the Duck Triumphed over the Hunter** Because this title is in headline style, everything is in caps except articles (the) and prepositions (over).

(31) **fig.**

(32) **BCE** (The Latin expression *Anno Domini* — abbreviated *AD* — means "in the year of our Lord" and is used with dates that aren't *BC*, or *before Christ*. To make this term more universal, historians often substitute *CE* or *Common Era* for *AD* and *BCE* or *Before the Common Era* for *BC*.)

(33) **Mr. Burns**

(34) **US Pres.**

(35) **NASA** (an acronym)

(36) **Rev. Smith**

(37) **NY** (postal abbreviation) or **N.Y.** (traditional form)

(38) **Adams Blvd.**

(39) **irreg.**

(40) **Inc.**

If you're ready to test your skills a bit more, take the following chapter quiz that incorporates all the chapter topics.

Whaddya Know? Chapter 21 Quiz

Quiz time! Complete each problem to test your knowledge on the various topics covered in this chapter. You can then find the solutions and explanations in the next section.

Find ten capitalization mistakes in the following figure, which is an excerpt from possibly the worst book report ever written.

Moby, the Life Of a Duck: A Book Report

If you are ever given a book about Ducks, take my advice and burn it. When i had to read *Moby Duck*, the Teacher promised me that it was good. She said that "Excitement was on every page." I don't think so! A duckling with special powers is raised by his Grandpa. Moby actually goes to school and earns a Doctorate in bird Science! After a really boring account of Moby's Freshman year, the book turns to his career as a Flight Instructor. I was very happy to see him fly away at the end of the book.

Answers to Chapter 21 Quiz

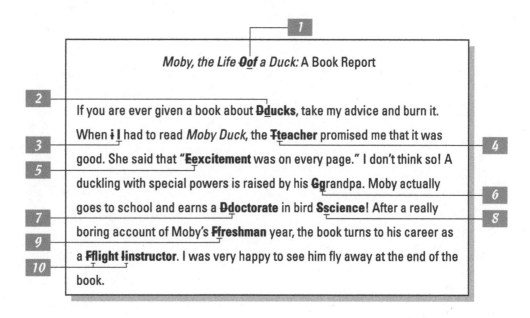

Moby, the Life ~~O~~of a Duck: A Book Report

If you are ever given a book about ~~D~~ducks, take my advice and burn it. When ~~i~~ I had to read *Moby Duck*, the ~~T~~teacher promised me that it was good. She said that "~~E~~excitement was on every page." I don't think so! A duckling with special powers is raised by his ~~G~~grandpa. Moby actually goes to school and earns a ~~D~~doctorate in bird ~~S~~science! After a really boring account of Moby's ~~F~~freshman year, the book turns to his career as a ~~F~~flight ~~I~~instructor. I was very happy to see him fly away at the end of the book.

(1) In a headline-style title, prepositions aren't capitalized.

(2) An ordinary term for animals — in this case, *ducks* — is lowercased.

(3) The personal pronoun *I* is always capitalized.

(4) The name of the teacher isn't given, just the term *teacher*, which should be lowercased.

(5) When a quotation is written without a speaker tag, the first word isn't capitalized.

(6) Family relationships are capitalized only when they serve as a name.

(7) Most academic degrees take lowercase.

(8) Most school subjects are written in lowercase. (I must point out that *English* is in caps because it's important. Okay, I'm lying. It's in caps because it's the name of a language.)

(9) School years are in lowercase, too.

(10) Job titles, when they aren't attached to the beginning of a name, are in lowercase.

6
Developing Style

In This Unit . . .

Chapter **22**

Adding Meaning with Well-Chosen Words

You're reading this book. That much I know is true. What I don't know is whether you're *skimming* or *scrutinizing* my words. Nor do I know whether you're holding a *paperback* or an *e-reader*. You may argue that precise language isn't necessary, and most of the time you'd be right. But how much extra meaning can be packed into a sentence if you choose your words carefully! That's the skill this chapter addresses.

Going Vivid with Verbs

Blah, general verbs are like dim light bulbs. They allow you to see what's happening, barely. Vivid verbs turn up the wattage, adding detail and shades of meaning. In this section, I show you how to select verbs that outshine neon lights.

"There is" a problem with boring verbs

When I ask students in my writing class to describe a standard school chair, I get sentences like these:

There is a curved seat.

There are five slats on the back.

There is a school identification mark on the bottom of the chair.

Nothing's wrong with these sentences. They're all grammatically correct, and they're all accurate. But I bet they made you yawn. *There is* and *there are,* as well as their cousins — *there was, there will be, there has been,* and others — are standard (and therefore boring) expressions. Swap them for something more precise:

> The seat *curves* to fit your bottom.
>
> Five slats *support* your back.
>
> The school *stamps* an identification mark on the bottom of each chair.

Don't you think the second set of sentences is more interesting? You get more information, and the verbs — *curves, support,* and *stamps* — catch the reader's eye.

EXAMPLE

Q. Revise this sentence without using the underlined words. Add words if you want.

There was a storm.

A. **A storm raged.** I've supplied one possible revision, but your answer may differ. As long as you have a verb that makes sense, count yourself correct.

Does your writing "have" a problem?

If they're overused, forms of the verb *have* can put your reader to sleep faster than a sedative. Sometimes you need these verbs to indicate *tense* — situating the action or state of being on a timeline. But too often *has, had,* or *have* ends up in a sentence because the writer isn't thinking creatively. Try changing

> The chair has a shiny surface.
>
> The slats have rounded edges as big as my finger.

to

> The chair shone under the fluorescent light.
>
> The rounded edges fit my finger perfectly.

Okay, I added some information to the second set, but you see my point. *Shone* and *fit* are more interesting than *has* and *have.* Plus, after you insert a good verb, other ideas follow, and the whole sentence improves.

EXAMPLE

Q. Revise this sentence without using the underlined words. Add words if you want.

This area has many storms.

A. **Many storms plague this area.** Other verbs that may take the place of *has* include *hit, oppress,* and *invigorate* (for those who like wet, windy weather). If you have a verb that makes sense, count yourself correct.

Don't just "say" and "walk" away

Say and *walk* are fine, upstanding members of the verb community, but they don't give you much information. Why *say* when you can *declare, scream, whisper, hint, bellow, assert, remark,* or do any one of the zillions of alternatives available to you when you're describing communication? For movement, consider *stroll, saunter, plod, strut, rush, speed, zigzag,* and — well, you get the point by now. Look for verbs that go beyond the basics, that add shades of meaning to your sentence. Check out these before-and-after sentence sets:

> BEFORE: Heidi said that she was tired of climbing mountains.
>
> AFTER: Heidi contended that she was tired of climbing mountains. (Now you know that she's speaking with someone who may not believe her.)
>
> ANOTHER AFTER: Heidi murmured that she was tired of climbing mountains. (Here, Heidi's a bit shy or perhaps fearful.)
>
> ONE MORE AFTER: Heidi roared that she was tired of climbing mountains. (In this sentence, no one is going to mess with Heidi — not without a struggle!)
>
> BEFORE: Heidi's hiking partner walked away from her.
>
> AFTER: Heidi's hiking partner edged away from her. (The partner knows that Heidi's in one of her moods and trouble is on the way.)
>
> ALSO AFTER: Heidi's hiking partner stomped away from her. (Now the partner is angry.)
>
> THE LAST AFTER: Heidi's hiking partner wandered away from her. (The partner isn't paying attention.)

TIP

Your word processor probably has a built-in *thesaurus* — a reference app that lists synonyms for most verbs. You can also buy a thesaurus in book form. If you're looking over your writing and need some spicier verbs, a thesaurus can suggest some alternatives. Be cautious: Verbs, like all words, may be similar but not exactly the same. The list for *stroll,* for example, includes *ramble* and *promenade.* You may *ramble* (or *amble,* another verb on this list) without a fixed destination or purpose. If you *promenade,* you're probably also in recreational mode, but this time you have an audience.

REMEMBER

Never insert a verb or any other verb into your sentence unless you're sure you know what it means.

Q. Choose any verbs that could substitute for the underlined word(s) in the original. Be sure that your choice fits the context of the sentence.

Max was angry when he <u>walked</u> into the store.

   I. strolled

   II. ambled

   III. charged

A. **III** If Max was angry, he wouldn't "move slowly without purpose," which is the definition of *stroll* and *amble*. *Charge* means "to move quickly and aggressively," so choice III fits best here.

What can substitute for the underlined word(s)? You may find more than one answer. Be sure that your choice(s) will fit the context of the sentence.

1. "I want my money back," <u>said</u> Max, his temper rising by the minute.

    I. screamed

    II. declared

    III. whispered

2. <u>There was an empty chair</u> by the information desk.

    I. An empty chair sat

    II. An empty chair abutted

    III. an empty chair waited

3. The chair <u>had</u> a red cushion.

    I. sported

    II. showed

    III. revealed

4. Max defiantly <u>sat in</u> the chair.

    I. plopped on

    II. eased into

    III. sank into

5. With menace in his eyes, Max <u>looked</u> at the clerk.

    I. glanced

    II. glared

    III. smiled

6. The clerk <u>was nervous</u>.

    I. trembled

    II. tensed

    III. quivered

7. Max <u>looked at</u> the clerk for two minutes.

    I. examined

    II. visualized

    III. scrutinized

8 Finally, ashamed of his tantrum, Max <u>said</u>, "I'm sorry I scared you."

   I. mentioned

   II. commented

   III. whispered

9 "That's all right, sir," the clerk <u>said to</u> Max.

   I. commanded

   II. directed

   III. reassured

10 A police officer <u>walked</u> toward the clerk, radiating authority.

   I. strode

   II. plodded

   III. hobbled

11 Max <u>went</u> to the other end of the counter, hoping the officer would not notice him.

   I. leapt

   II. slithered

   III. bounced

12 The clerk <u>gestured to</u> the officer, grateful the situation was no longer her problem.

   I. high-fived

   II. slapped

   III. pinched

Pinpointing Meaning with Nouns and Descriptions

Here's a sentence about a character in a novel:

Juan picks up a pen but can't find anything to write on.

Picture the scene. Now read these sentences:

Juan picks up a quill but can't find any parchment.

Juan picks up a stylus but can't find a laptop.

Did your imagination come up with a match? I doubt it! How could you possibly move accurately from the general statement about writing materials to something as specific as *quill* and *parchment* or *stylus* and *laptop*? Nouns that pinpoint meaning add information and interest.

So do descriptions. Picture Juan's *unusual* stylus. Now adjust your image as you read these:

fluorescent blue stylus

thought-controlled stylus

ten-pound stylus

One more example: Juan appeared *upset*. Was he *irate? Apprehensive? Mournful?* These words all qualify as *upset*, but they carry extra meaning:

irate → anger

apprehensive → worry

grief-stricken → sorrow

Of course, sometimes a general noun or description is all you need, and you don't want to over-load your readers or listeners with insignificant details. Keep in mind, though, that just the right word can pack a punch.

EXAMPLE

Q. Choose any nouns or descriptions that could substitute for the underlined word(s) in the original. More than one answer may be correct, but be sure that your choice fits the context of the sentence.

Juan made a decision that could lead to <u>problems</u>, including loss of life.

    I. catastrophe

    II. issues

    III. worries

A. **I** *Loss of life* is a clue that the problems might be horrible, enough to qualify as a *catastrophe*. The other options are too general.

YOUR TURN

Choose any nouns or descriptions that could substitute for the underlined word(s) in the original. More than one answer may be correct, but be sure that your choice fits the context of the sentence.

13 Juan got into his <u>vehicle</u> and set a course for Mars.

    I. car

    II. interstellar transporter

    III. spaceship

14 Halfway there, he discovered a <u>problem</u> in his sleeping quarters.

    I. poisonous snake

    II. comfy quilt

    III. candy apple

15 His facial expression was <u>interesting</u>. Nothing would stop his journey!

    I. determined

    II. joyful

    III. different

16 He retrieved <u>a book</u> from his personal locker and found the answer he needed.

    I. a manual

    II. Atlas of the Stars

    III. Pest Control in Outer Space

17 From a different locker, he extracted <u>an item</u>.

    I. a thing

    II. a solution

    III. a long cage, complete with bait.

18 That done, Juan turned his attention to the atmosphere on Mars, which was <u>not good</u>.

    I. gentle

    II. toxic

    III. inviting

19 Juan wasn't discouraged; <u>a special</u> helmet and spacesuit would protect him.

    I. a colorful

    II. an airtight

    III. a free

20 So off Juan soared, on his way to rescue <u>someone important</u>.

    I. his mother

    II. the emperor

    III. a fellow astronaut

21 Juan's success brought about <u>change</u>.

    I. a promotion

    II. alterations

    III. difference

Saving Time: Cutting Unnecessary Words

Have you ever endured an hour-long meeting that contained five minutes' worth of information? Remember that "Just say it already!" feeling when you're writing. No one appreciates repetition and wordiness. In this section I show you how to avoid both.

Repetition

I think of repetition as the "road-highway-expressway" error, as in

> Tom drove on roads, highways, and expressways during his trip from New York City to Seattle.

Granted, each word names a slightly different sort of thoroughfare, and if you're writing a technical discussion of transportation alternatives, you may need these three terms. But if you're discussing a cross-country trip, all you've done is waste your readers' time. Another example:

> Alfred loved to keep his house neat and tidy.

Neat and *tidy* are synonyms, so you don't need both words.

 Q. Identify repetitive words or phrases.

EXAMPLE

Elizabeth constructed a dollhouse from three-sided magnetic triangular blocks.

 A. **three-sided, triangular** Triangles, by definition, have three sides.

Identify repetitive words or phrases.

YOUR
TURN

22 Agnes was entirely and completely devoted to her pot-bellied pig.

23 The most carefree and unworried vacation awaits you at Pine Tree Estates!

24 The one-acre lot was covered with weeds and undesirable plants.

25 Herb has a nonfatal illness that never leads to death.

26 It's my opinion that eight hours' sleep is essential to one's well-being and overall health.

Wordiness

This is the first line of an autobiography I don't want to read:

> It was on the fourth of March of the year 1899 that my mother gave birth to me in a town known as Ballygreen in the country of Ireland.

Here's another first line. It isn't great, but at least I can get through it in a glance:

I was born on March 4, 1899, in Ballygreen, Ireland.

The first example takes 29 words to say what the second example says in 10 — 8 if you count the date as a unit. Chopping out two thirds of the words doesn't change the information, but it does respect the audience by treating their time as valuable.

To avoid wordiness, watch out for

>> **padding** If you're writing a report and have too little information, find out more or say what you *do* know and then stop. Teachers and supervisors have built-in fluff detectors.

>> **insecurity** Worried that their message isn't clear, writers sometimes overexplain or say the same thing in two different ways to be sure the reader understands. Trust yourself! Say it clearly and then move on to a new topic.

>> **showing and telling** Writing teachers often preach "show, don't tell" as a guiding principle. That's good advice, because examples, sensory details, and facts enlighten the reader. Too many writers, though, show *and* tell. Gasping, sweating runners with their hands on their knees don't have to be labeled as "tired." Nor do you have to state that they "tried as hard as they could."

>> **stating the obvious** Similar to the preceding bullet point, assume that your audience can figure out the obvious. I often read essays about literary works that include phrases such as "in the book" or "in the poem." Unless you're comparing the same topic or character in two different media, delete those words. Similarly, don't bother writing "I think" unless you're contrasting your point of view with someone else's. The reader assumes you're expressing what you think. Why else would you write it?

>> **overly complicated sentences** Tucking a couple of ideas into one sentence can make your writing sound more mature — if you do so skillfully. (See Chapter 24 for tips.) Meandering sentences that leave readers confused, however, muddle your message.

**YOUR
TURN**

How should the original sentence be revised, if at all, to avoid wordiness? *Note:* Be sure the revision you choose is grammatically correct and faithful to the meaning of the original sentence.

27 Original sentence: The title character in *Macbeth* is ambitious, and it is this ambition that leads him to crime.

    I. The title character, Macbeth, has ambition and leads him to crime.

    II. Leading to crime, the title character in *Macbeth* is ambitious.

    III. Ambition leads to crime in Shakespeare's Macbeth.

    IV. The ambition of the title character of *Macbeth* leads him to crime.

28. Original sentence: Jill was always fair and reasonable, and she saw the advantages and disadvantages of both sides in every argument.

    I. Fair and reasonable, Jill saw the advantages and disadvantages of both sides in every argument.

    II. Jill was always fair and reasonable, and she saw each side's advantages and disadvantages.

    III. Jill seeing the advantages and disadvantages of both sides in every argument fairly.

    IV. Jill's fairness and reasonableness led her to see both sides.

29. Original sentence: Smith Publishing, which publishes some books that deal with science and math, employs many experts in science and math to check its publications and eliminate any errors.

    I. Smith Publishing, which publishes some books about science and math, employs many experts in science and math to check its publications and eliminate any errors.

    II. Smith Publishing employs many experts to eliminate errors in its science and math publications.

    III. Smith Publishing, publishing some books about science and math, employs many experts in science and math to check its publications.

    IV. Smith Publishing, which publishes some books about science and math, employs many experts to check its publications and eliminate any errors.

30. Original sentence: We were already sitting in seats when the orchestra, all musicians, began to play at the direction of the conductor, who raised his baton to start the performance.

    I. We were already seated when the conductor raised his baton and the orchestra began to play.

    II. We were already sitting when the orchestra, all musicians, began to play as the conductor, he raised his baton to start the performance.

    III. The conductor raised his baton and the orchestra began to play and we were sitting in seats then.

    IV. We were already sitting in seats when all musicians began playing at the direction of the conductor, who raised his baton to start the performance.

Practice Questions Answers and Explanations

(1) **I, II** You know Max is angry, so *whispered*, option III, doesn't fit. The other two choices add an edge to Max's voice. The first *(screamed)* is angrier. The second, *declared*, is firm and powerful but less aggressive.

(2) **I, II** The chair wasn't doing anything, so it *sat*. It was *by the information desk*, so the verb *abutted* also works. With a bit of a stretch, option III fits, because it anticipates Max's use of the chair.

(3) **I** Red is a lively color, so *sported* — "wore with flair" — fits well here.

(4) **I** If there's defiance, you don't want options II or III, which are somewhat timid synonyms for *sat. Plopped* can show physical exhaustion, but it also has an element of force in it, so it's a good fit.

(5) **II** You have *menace*, so *glared* works well here. *Smiled* is the opposite of what you want, and *glanced* is too casual.

(6) **I, II, III** To show fear, you can select *trembled* or *quivered* because both indicate that the clerk is shaking. *Tensed* also fits.

(7) **I, III** Max doesn't have to *visualize* (see with his imagination) the clerk because he's actually looking at the clerk for two minutes. That's a long time, so options I and III, which both mean "analyze," are good substitutes.

(8) **III** Max is ashamed, so *whispered* is the best choice. *Mentioned* is too casual, as is *commented*.

(9) **III** The clerk has just told Max not to worry about the tantrum, so option III works best here.

(10) **I** *Strode* means "walked with authority and purpose," an excellent fit for this sentence.

(11) **II** *Slithered* means "move like a snake," and snakes have a low profile. *Leapt* and *bounced* would call attention, the opposite of Max's purpose.

(12) **I** To celebrate, two people can each raise one arm and slap their palms together. In other words, they *high-five*. The other actions imply anger, not celebration.

(13) **II, III** To reach another planet, Juan can't travel in a car, so option I is out. The other two, while still in the realm of fantasy, are a good fit for this sentence.

(14) **I** Only a *poisonous snake* qualifies as a problem!

(15) **I** *Determined* fits because *nothing would stop* Juan.

(16) **III** Any of the options would be better than *book*, but III is the most appropriate for a snake problem.

(17) **III** The most specific choice gives the reader information about how Juan handled the snake.

(18) **II** Only *toxic* fits with *not good*.

(19) **II** To protect Juan from the Martian atmosphere, he needs an *airtight* helmet.

(20) **I, II, III** We can argue about this one, but my view is that all three qualify as *someone important*.

(21) **I** Options II and III are general. Only option I gives specific information.

(22) **entirely, completely**

(23) **carefree, unworried**

(24) **weeds, undesirable plants**

(25) **nonfatal, never leads to death**

(26) **well-being, overall health**

(27) **IV** The original sentence repeats *ambitious* and *ambition*. Option IV includes all the information of the original but drops five words. Options I, II, and III are shorter than IV, but something is lacking or amiss in each. In different ways, options I and II state that the *title character leads to crime.* Option III drops an important reference to the title character. Only option IV does the job.

(28) **I** Option I cuts four words from the original without sacrificing meaning. If it's *every argument, always* is implied. By turning *was always fair and reasonable* into an introductory description, you also save words. Option II is longer than option I and omits the idea of *argument.* Without that word, the sentence may discuss political or social advantages of siding with one or another group. Option III is a fragment, not a complete sentence. Option IV may refer to a visit with two sides, not an evaluation of each argument.

(29) **II** Once you read *Smith Publishing* in the original sentence, you know that the company *publishes.* If *experts eliminate errors in its science and math publications,* that they are *experts in science and math* and that they *check* are implied. Option II supplies all the information in half the space. All the other options contain unnecessary words.

(30) **I** The original sentence includes *sitting in seats.* Where else can you sit? Okay, you can sit on the grass or on an exercise ball, but those are the exceptions. Also, *the orchestra* is made up of *all musicians* — another common fact you don't have to mention. Finally, *began to play* and *start the performance* provide the same information.

Whaddya Know? Chapter 22 Quiz

The following excerpt is from a holiday letter sent to friends and family. Answer the questions that follow.

(a) Hi to all and everyone! (b) I'm devoting my New Year's letter to an amazing trip, a truly remarkable journey, that I took in late October. (c) It was on the morning of October 20th around 9 A.M. that I set out from my home. (d) I didn't know my destination at that point in time. (e) My priority was to experience new places, locations I had never been to before. (f) Traveling without a plan has advantages and disadvantages, I believe, because there are some good and some bad aspects of spontaneous unplanned action. (g) My first stop was Lake Ponke, where I looked at the world's largest giant ball of rubber bands. (h) There is a fence around the ball. (i) "It's the biggest rubber ball I have ever seen," said a tourist. (j) She moved to the ball, not looking at the fence and not looking at the sign that said, "Do Not Enter." (k) There was a security guard in front of the ball. (l) "Don't try to bounce it," he said.

1 How should sentence (a) be revised?

   I. Hi, everyone!

   II. Hi, all, and that includes everyone!

2 How should sentence (b) be revised?

   I. I'm devoting my New Year's letter to an amazing trip I took in late October.

   II. In late October I took an amazing trip that I want to tell you about in this, my New Year's letter.

3 How should sentence (c) be revised?

   I. It was around 9 a.m. on October 20 that I set out from my home.

   II. I left my home around 9 a.m. on October 20.

4 How should sentences (d) and (e) be revised?

   I. I didn't know my destination at that point in time because my priority was to experience new places.

   II. With no planned destination, my priority was to experience new places.

5 How should sentence (f) be revised?

   I. There are good and bad aspects of spontaneous action.

   II. Delete the entire sentence.

6. How should sentence (g) be revised?

    I. My first stop was Lake Ponke, where I looked at the world's largest giant ball of rubber bands.

    II. First I stopped at Lake Ponke to marvel at the world's largest giant ball of rubber bands.

7. How should sentence (h) be revised?

    I. A fence surrounds the ball.

    II. There is a surrounding fence at the ball.

8. How should sentence (i) be revised?

    I. "It's the biggest rubber ball I have ever seen," exclaimed a tourist.

    II. "It's the biggest rubber ball I have ever seen," said a tourist.

9. How should sentence (j) be revised?

    I. She paced to the ball, not looking at the fence and not looking at the sign that declared, "Do Not Enter."

    II. She strode to the ball, ignoring the fence and the sign that proclaimed, "Do Not Enter."

10. How should sentences (k) and (l) be revised?

    I. "Don't try to bounce it," ordered a security guard.

    II. There was a security guard in front of the ball who said, "Don't try to bounce it."

Answers to Chapter 22 Quiz

(1) **I** Repeating *all* and *everyone* serves no purpose.

(2) **I** Option II is unnecessarily wordy. Why include *this?*

(3) **II** The construction *it was . . . that* is generally an open door to wordiness. The simpler sentence works well.

(4) **II** Option II is shorter and gets the job done.

(5) **II** Everything has good and bad aspects. I'd delete this sentence and move on to the specifics of what worked and what didn't.

(6) **II** *Marvel* is more interesting than *looked*, and *I stopped* more concise than *My first stop was.*

(7) **I** *There is* and similar expressions add little to your writing. Opt for the more interesting verb, *surrounds.*

(8) **I** *Exclaimed* adds a sense of the tourist's emotion.

(9) **II** Stronger verbs (*strode, ignoring*) and fewer words make this sentence the better option.

(10) **I** Option I is shorter and includes all the information.

Chapter **23**

Grammar Gremlins

G*remlins* are fictional creatures blamed for unexpected problems. The good news about grammar gremlins is that once you learn to recognize them, you can rid your writing of the problems they cause. From double negatives to sound-alikes to expressions that are common but not correct in Standard English, this chapter explains everything you need to know.

Deleting Double Negatives

In some languages, the more negatives, the better. In English, however, two negatives are a no-no. (By the way, no-no is *not* a double negative! It's just slang for something that's prohibited.) Two negative words logically create a positive statement. Take a look at these examples:

WHAT LENNY SAID: I didn't kill nobody.

WHAT LENNY THINKS THAT MEANS: I am not a murderer. I have killed no one.

WHAT IT REALLY MEANS: I am a murderer. I didn't kill *nobody,* but I did kill *somebody.*

CORRECTED SENTENCE: I didn't kill anybody.

You can argue, and in part you'd be right, that most listeners or readers will understand that Lenny is trying to say he's innocent. In Standard English, though, Lenny's confessing. Why take a chance on being misunderstood?

One of the most common double negatives is *cannot help but*, as in

> Egbert *cannot help but* act in that dramatic style; he was trained by a real ham.

Unfortunately, this sentence states a double negative with the word *not* (inside the word *cannot*) and *but*. One or the other gives you a negative, but not both. Here's the correct version:

> Egbert *cannot help acting* in that dramatic style; he was trained by a real ham.

If you think this is one in a long list of useless grammar rules, think again. When you say *cannot help but*, you actually express the opposite of what you imagine you're saying (or writing). For example:

> WHAT MAX SAID TO THE BOSS: I cannot help but ask for a raise.
>
> WHAT HE THINKS HE SAID: I have to ask for a raise.
>
> WHAT HE REALLY SAID: I can't ask for a raise.

> WHAT THE BOSS SAID TO MAX: I cannot help but say no.
>
> WHAT THE BOSS THINKS SHE SAID: No.
>
> WHAT THE BOSS ACTUALLY SAID: Yes.

EXAMPLE

Q. Which sentence is free of double negatives?

(A) I cannot help but think that this double-negative rule is ridiculous.

(B) I ain't got nobody.

(C) I cannot help thinking that this double-negative rule is ridiculous.

A. **(C)** Sentence (a) contains *cannot help but*, and sentence (b) has *ain't* (a slang form of *don't*) and *nobody*. Only sentence (c) is free of double negatives.

Another common double negative is *can't hardly.* That's a phrase in wide use in many areas, and it's fine in informal, friendly situations. When you're using Standard English, though, stay away from this expression. *Can't* is short for *cannot*, which contains the negative *not. Hardly* is another negative word. If you combine them, by the logic of grammar, you've said the opposite of what you intended — the positive instead of the negative. Here are a few examples:

> WHAT ROGER SAID: Lulu can't hardly count her tattoos.
>
> WHAT ROGER THINKS HE SAID: Lulu can't count her tattoos.
>
> WHAT ROGER ACTUALLY SAID: Lulu can count her tattoos.

> WHAT EUGENE WROTE: Ella can't hardly wait until her divorce becomes final.
>
> WHAT EUGENE THINKS THE SENTENCE MEANS: Ella is eager for her divorce to become final.
>
> WHAT THE SENTENCE ACTUALLY MEANS: Ella can wait.

TIP

A variation of this double negative is *can't scarcely*, *aren't scarcely*, or *isn't scarcely*. Once again, *can't* is short for *cannot*, clearly a negative. *Aren't* and *isn't* are the negative forms of *are* and *is*. *Scarcely* is also negative. Use them together and you end up with a positive, not an emphatic negative.

Here's one more double negative, in a couple of forms: *hadn't only*, *haven't only*, *hasn't only*, *hadn't but*, *haven't but*, and *hasn't but*. All express positive ideas because the *not* (*n't*) part of the verb and the *only* or *but* are both negatives:

WRONG: Alfred *hadn't but* ten seconds to defuse the bomb before civilization as we know it ended.

WHY IT'S WRONG: As it reads now, the sentence says that Alfred had more than ten seconds to defuse the bomb, but the little red numbers on the trigger were at seven and decreasing rapidly.

RIGHT: Alfred *had but* ten seconds to defuse the bomb before civilization as we know it ended.

ALSO RIGHT: Alfred *had* only ten seconds to defuse the bomb before civilization as we know it ended.

WRONG: Roger *hasn't only* ten nuclear secrets.

WHY IT'S WRONG: The sentence now says that Roger has more than ten secrets, but he just counted them and he has only ten.

RIGHT: Roger *has only* ten nuclear secrets.

EXAMPLE

Q. Which sentence is correct in Standard English?

(A) Ella can't hardly understand those pesky grammar rules.

(B) Ella can't help but be confused by those pesky grammar rules.

(C) neither

A. (C) In sentence (A), *can't hardly* is a double negative. In sentence (B), *cannot help but* is a double negative.

YOUR TURN

Which sentence is correct in Standard English?

1 (A) Vincent is humming so loud that I can't hardly think.

(B) Vincent is humming so loud that I can hardly think.

(C) neither

2 (A) Candice hasn't got a problem with Vincent's noisy behavior.

(B) Candice ain't got no problem with Vincent's noisy behavior.

(C) neither

3   **(A)**   The teacher looked at Vincent and declared, "I allow no singing here."

       (B)   The teacher looked at Vincent and declared, "I do not allow no singing here."

       (C)   neither

4   **(A)**   Vincent hadn't but five minutes to finish the math section of the test.

       (B)   Vincent had but five minutes to finish the math section of the test.

       (C)   neither

5   **(A)**   "I can't help but believe that your rule is unfair to musicians," said Benny.

       (B)   "I can't hardly believe that your rule is unfair to musicians," said Benny.

       (C)   neither

Sounding Incorrect

Many people speak quickly, often dropping letters. Most listeners can guess the intended meaning. But if you reproduce those sounds when you're writing, you may end up with a misspelled word. This section explains how to avoid grammatically illegal sound effects.

Scoring D minus

Judging from the signs I often see on my walks around New York City, the letter *D* stands for "dropped." Stores sell *grill cheese* (not *grilled*, as it should be) and *ice tea* (which is actually *iced*). You may find these sentences familiar, too:

> Lola *was suppose* to take out the garbage, but she refused to do so.

> Ralph *use* to take out the trash, but after an unfortunate encounter with a raccoon, he is reluctant to go anywhere near the cans.

Check out the italicized verbs: *was suppose* and *use*. Both represent what people hear but not what the speaker is actually trying to say. The correct words are *supposed* and *used* — past-tense forms.

I can't leave this topic without mentioning the opposite error, which is far less common but can lead to some silly mistakes. A restaurant in my neighborhood posted a "Help Wanted" sign, asking *grilled men* to apply. I believe they wanted someone who could cook on a grill, not someone who'd sat on a barbecue. The added *D* makes quite a difference in meaning!

Q. Correct or incorrect in Standard English?

The boss is hiring experience applicants only.

A. **incorrect** The applicants should be *experienced*, not *experience*.

Three terrible twos

English has three words that sound like 2, and no, they don't add up to six. *To* may be part of an infinitive (*to speak, to dream*), or it may show movement toward someone or something (*to the store, to me*). *Two* is the number (*two eyes, two ears*). *Too* means "also" (*Are you going too?*) or "more than enough" (*too expensive, too wide*). In other words:

> If you *two* want *to* skip school and go *to* the ball game, today's a good day because the teacher will be *too* busy *to* check.

> The *two* basketballs that hit Larry in the head yesterday were *too* soft *to* do much damage, but Larry is suing anyway.

> *Two* things you should always remember before you decide *to* break a grammar rule: It's never *too* late *to* learn proper English, and you're never *too* old *to* get in trouble with your teacher.

TIP

In Chapter 17, I discuss *whose/who's, its/it's, their/there/they're*, and *your/you're* — words that sound alike but have different meanings.

EXAMPLE

Q. Select the word that is correct in Standard English.

(To, Two, Too) hours is (to, two, too) much time (to, two, too) waste on homework.

A. **Two, too, to** The first blank calls for quantity and the second for intensity. The third blank is part of an infinitive.

You gotta problem with grammar?

If you speak proper English all the time — and few people do — you don't say *gotta, gonna,* or *gotcha.* These words sound like *got to, going to,* and *got you,* which are correct in Standard English. Although saying *gotta* when you're chatting with a friend is perfectly okay, it isn't okay when you're speaking to a teacher, a boss, a television interviewer, the supreme ruler of the universe, or anyone else in authority. Thus,

> NONSTANDARD: You *gonna* wait for Cedric? He bought a new car, and he might give us a ride.

> STANDARD: *Are* you *going* to wait for Cedric? He bought a new car, and he might give us a ride.

> NONSTANDARD: No, I *gotta* go.

> STANDARD: No, I *have to* go.

> NONSTANDARD: *Gotcha.* Next week we'll go bowling.

> STANDARD: *I understand.* Next week we'll go bowling.

I'd add another sample conversation, but it's almost time for lunch. I gotta go.

Q. Identify the sentences written in Standard English. You may find one, more than one, or none.

(A) When you're in trouble, remember that you have a friend.

(B) When you're in trouble, remember that you gotta friend.

(C) When you're in trouble, remember that you've gotta friend.

A. **(A)** *Gotta* is not Standard English. Only option (a) eliminates that expression and substitutes *have.*

Almost twins

Some word pairs that sound almost the same sometimes trespass on each other's territory. Sort them out, and you'll avoid errors in your writing.

Continual/continually; continuous/continuously

Continual and *continually* refer to events that happen over and over again, but with breaks between each instance. (*Continual* describes nouns, and *continually* describes verbs.) *Continuous* and *continuously* are for situations without gaps. (As you've probably guessed, *continuous* attaches to nouns, and *continuously* to verbs.) *Continuous* noise is steady, uninterrupted, like the drone of the electric generator in your local power plant. *Continual* noise is what you hear when I go bowling. You hear silence (when I stare at the pins), a little noise (when the ball rolls down the alley), and silence again (when the ball slides into the gutter without hitting anything). After an hour, you hear noise (when I finally hit something and begin to cheer). In case you're wondering, I'm a very bad bowler.

Here are a couple of examples of these two descriptions in action:

NONSTANDARD: Jim screams *continually* until Lola stuffs rags in his mouth.

WHY IT'S NOT STANDARD: Jim's screams don't come and go. When he's upset, he's really upset, and nothing shuts him up except a gag.

STANDARD: Jim screams *continuously* until Lola stuffs rags in his mouth.

WHY IT'S STANDARD: In this version, Jim takes no breaks.

NONSTANDARD: Ella's *continuous* attempts to impress Larry were unsuccessful. Despite the fact that she sent him a fruit basket on Monday and flowers on Tuesday, Larry ignored her.

WHY IT'S NOT STANDARD: Ella's attempts stop and start. She does one thing on Monday, rests up, and then does another on Tuesday.

STANDARD: Ella's *continual* attempts to impress Larry were unsuccessful.

WHY IT'S STANDARD: Now the sentence talks about a recurring action.

Q. Select the word that is correct in Standard English.

If you (continually, continuously) interrupt me, I'll never finish my novel.

A. **continually** An interruption happens, stops, and happens again. Therefore, *continually* fits here.

Farther/further

Farther refers to distance. If you need to travel *farther*, you have more miles to cover. *Further* also has a sense of "more" in it, but not more distance. Instead, *further* means "additional." *Further* is for time, ideas, activities, and so forth. Some examples:

> Abe's online profile requires *further* work, but he's too lazy to update it.
>
> Mimi flew *farther* than anyone else in the club, even though she's afraid of heights.
>
> They believe *further* discussion is silly, because everyone's mind is already made up.
>
> The *farther* Jim walks, the more his shoes hurt.

Select the word that is correct in Standard English.

Q. Fueled by the caffeine in two double espressos, Jake drove (farther/further) than anyone else.

A. **farther** If you're dealing with distance, *farther* is the one you want.

Accept/except

Accept is "to say yes to, to agree, to receive." *Except* means "everything but." *Except* excludes, and *accepts* welcomes. Therefore,

> Please *accept* my apology. I cleaned everything in the kitchen *except* for the oven. I ran out of time.
>
> Marge *accepted* all her in-laws *except* for Larry. She despised him!

Q. Select the word that is correct in Standard English.

Everyone in the motorcycle gang, (accept, except) for Lola, graciously (accepted, excepted) a new muffler from the Society for the Prevention of Road Noise.

A. **except, accepted** The first blank calls for a word that excludes, and the second for one that willingly receives.

Affect/effect

Affect is a verb meaning "to influence." *Effect* is a noun meaning "a change that is the result of an action." Hence

> Sunlight affects Pete's appetite; he never eats during the day.
>
> Lola thinks that pizza will positively affect her diet, but I think the effect will be disastrous.

Special note: Affect may also be a noun meaning "the way one relates to and shows emotions." *Effect* may act as a verb meaning "to cause a complete change." You rarely need these secondary meanings.

EXAMPLE

Q. Select the word that is correct in Standard English.

The roar of Lola's motorcycle always (affects, effects) my concentration.

A. **affects** You need a verb here, because the sentence means that the noise influences focus.

YOUR TURN

Select the word that is correct in Standard English.

6　I (accept, except) the nomination for president.

7　That donation to my campaign has no (affect, effect) on my political views.

8　The (continual, continuous) sound from that machine is driving me crazy! It never stops!

9　The judge insisted on (farther/further) proof that the cop's speed gun was broken.

10　I gave the judge tons of proof, which he refused to (accept/except).

11　Waving my wallet vigorously at the judge, I tried to (affect/effect) the verdict by hinting at a large bribe.

12　Judge Crater stubbornly refused to hear my side of the story and (continually/continuously) interrupted me.

13　"Don't go any (farther/further) with your testimony," he snarled.

14　The judge's words, unfortunately, are (gonna, going to) be drowned out by the (continual/continuous) hammering from the construction next door, which never stopped.

15　"It's (to, too, two) loud and the (affect/effect) of this noise is disastrous," said the defendant.

16　"We're (suppose, supposed) to meet in a quiet room," added the defense attorney.

17　Nothing they said (affected/effected) the judge's ruling, and we eventually became (use, used) to the sound level.

18 (To, Too, Two) portraits of the judge (use, used) to be on the wall behind the bench, but they were (to, too, two) distracting.

19 "My romantic partner is not (gonna, going to) spend (farther/further) time with me if the judge imposes a large fine," whispered the defendant.

20 He thinks his beloved is (use, used) to high-priced food and will not (accept/except) a date to a cheap restaurant.

Pairs of Trouble: Complicated Verbs

Whenever I'm trying to set up a new piece of technology, I think about the person who wrote the manual. In my imagination, the writer is sitting in a windowless room, laughing at the trouble the complicated instructions cause buyers. The same sort of person, I think, also created a few pairs of verbs that are guaranteed to give you a headache — unless you read this section.

Sit/set

Sit (as well as *sat*) is a verb describing what you do when you plop yourself down on a chair, the floor, or anywhere. *Set* means "to put something else down, to place something in a particular spot." Thus,

Ron seldom sits for more than two minutes.

I'd like to sit down while I speak, but only if you promise not to set that plate of pickled fish in front of me.

Q. Select the word that is correct in Standard English.

EXAMPLE

"I (sat, set) the diamonds on the shelf!" cried Maria as she (sat, set) in the witness chair. "There was a guard (sitting, setting) right next to them!"

A. **set, sat, sitting** The first spot calls for a word meaning "to put down an object," and the next two require words that convey the action of moving the body into a chair.

Hanged/hung

To hang is a verb meaning "to suspend." In the present tense, the same verb does double duty. You *hang* a picture and you also *hang* a murderer, at least in countries with that form of capital punishment. Past tense is different; in general, people are *hanged* and objects are *hung*. Therefore,

In Michael's new movie, Lulu stars as the righteous rebel leader *hanged* by the opposition.

After the stirring execution scene, the rebels gain strength, inspired by a picture of Lulu that someone *hung* on the wall of their headquarters.

Q. Select the word that is correct in Standard English.

EXAMPLE

The decorator (hanged, hung) the painting on the wall.

A. **hung** The painting was "suspended," not "executed."

Rise/raise

Rise means "to stand," "to get out of bed," or "to move to a higher rank" under one's own power. *Raise* means "to lift something or someone else" or "to bring up children or animals." Check out these verbs in action:

> Egbert *rises* when a poultry expert enters the room.
>
> Egbert is an apprentice, but he hopes to *rise* to the rank of master poultry-breeder someday.
>
> He *raises* roosters on his farm, delighting the neighbors every morning at sunrise.
>
> When a nest is too low, Egbert *raises* it to a higher shelf.

Here's another way to think about this pair: *Rise* is a self-contained action. *Raise* is an action that begins with one person (or thing) and moves to another person or thing. You *rise* by yourself; you *raise* something else.

Q. Which word is correct in Standard English?

EXAMPLE

Roberta claims it wasn't hard to (rise, raise) 16 children.

A. **raise** The action here begins with one person (Roberta) and moves to others (the children).

Lie/lay

Whoever invented the verbs *lie* and *lay* had an evil sense of humor. Besides meaning "not to tell the truth," *lie* also means "to rest or to plop yourself down, ready for a snooze" or "to remain." *Lay* means "to put something down, to place something." Here are some examples:

> Sheila likes to *lie* down for an hour after lunch. Before she hits the couch, she *lays* a soft sheet over the upholstery.
>
> Roger *lies* in wait behind those bushes. When unsuspecting tourists *lay* down their picnic blankets, he swoops in and steals their lunches.

So far, this topic isn't too complicated. The problem — and the truly devilish part — comes in the past tense. The past tense of *lie* (to rest, to recline, to remain) is *lay*. The past tense of *lay* (to put or place) is *laid*. Check out these examples:

> Sheila *lay* down yesterday, but a car alarm disturbed her rest. She immediately went to the street and *laid* a carpet of nails in front of the offending vehicle.

Yesterday, while Roger *lay* in wait, a police officer *laid* a hand on Roger's shoulder. "You are under arrest," intoned the cop.

One more complication: When you add *has, had,* or *have* to the verb *lie* (to rest, to recline, to remain), you say *has lain, had lain, have lain.* When you add *has, had,* or *have* to the verb *lay* (to put or place), you say *has laid, had laid, have laid.* In other words:

Sheila *has lain* in the hammock all morning, and her brothers *have laid* a basket of red ants on the ground beneath her. When Sheila gets up, she'll be surprised!

Roger *has lain* in the lumpy bunk all night, but no one *has laid* a blanket over him.

Q. Select the word that is correct in Standard English.

EXAMPLE

Yesterday Alice was so tired that she (lie/lay/lied/laid/lain) down for a nap even though her favorite true-crime show was on television.

A. **lay** The past tense of *lie* (to rest) is *lay.*

Lose/loose

To lose is "not to win, to come up short." *Lose* also means that you can't find something or have had to give something up. *Loose* is nearly always used as a description meaning "roomy, not tight." As a verb, *to loose* is "to set free." Read these examples:

If you *lose* the game, your team will ask for a rematch.

That uniform is too *loose;* tighten your belt!

Loose the giant hound, Sherlock. He's been tied up too long.

Jim often *loses* when he plays that video game.

Q. Which word is correct in Standard English?

EXAMPLE

The (lose, loose) belt shows that Roger does not need to (loose, lose) more weight.

A. **loose, lose** The belt is not tight, so it's *loose.* Thus, Roger doesn't have to get rid of, or *lose,* excess weight.

Which word is correct in Standard English?

YOUR TURN

21　The main character in Alice's favorite show (lies/lays) in bed, comatose.

22　As in all soap operas, the handsome doctor (sits/sets) by the bed every day with a look of concern and love on his face.

23 In yesterday's episode, the doctor (sit/sat/set) a bouquet of flowers on the nightstand. By the end of the show, he would (lose, loose) his temper and smash the vase.

24 When the nurse told the doctor to go home and (lie/lay) down, the doctor replied that she would "(sit/set) down for a while."

25 Last week the doctor (hanged/hung) a wreath on a mysterious tomb. A dog got (lose, loose) and snatched the wreath.

26 Viewers think the tomb belongs to the doctor's long-lost lover, who will (rise, raise) a fuss when she returns from an extended vacation to hear everyone say she (raised, rose) from the dead.

27 In a special episode, someone was (hanged, hung) for the crime of killing the long-lost lover!

28 In a dramatic scene, the lover will (sit/set) next to the doctor in the cafeteria and confess that she doesn't want to (lose, loose) him.

29 The final show will reveal that her evil twin was the one (lying/laying) in bed, comatose.

30 The evil twin will (rise, raise) to her feet and explain how she was injured.

One Word or Two?

Here's a spelling tip: The following words are often written as one, but that's incorrect in Standard English: *a lot, all right, each other.*

> Ella has *a lot* of trouble distinguishing between the sounds of "l" and "r," so she tries to avoid the expression *"all right"* whenever possible.

> Ella and Larry (who also has pronunciation trouble) help *each other* prepare state-of-the-union speeches every January.

Here's another tip: You can write the following words as one or two words, but with two different meanings: *altogether* means "extremely, entirely." *All together* means "as one."

> Daniel was *altogether* disgusted with the way the flock of dodo birds sang *all together.*

Another set of tricky words: *Sometime* means "at a certain point in time," and *some time* means "a period of time." *Sometimes* (with an *s*) means "from time to time, occasionally."

> Lex said he would visit Lulu *sometime,* but not now, because he has to spend *some time* in jail for murdering the English language.

> *Sometimes* Peter and Rebecca go to the gym on Friday, but Monday is their usual day.

Still more: *Someplace* means "an unspecified place." The word functions as an adverb, describing an action. The expression *some place* means "a place" and refers to a physical space.

> Lex screamed, "I have to go *someplace* now!"
>
> Lulu thinks he headed for *some place* near the railroad station where the pizza is hot and no one asks any questions.

And another pair: *Everyday* means "ordinary, common." *Every day* means "occurring daily."

> Larry loves *everyday* activities such as cooking, cleaning, and sewing.
>
> He has the palace staff perform all those duties *every day*.

Last set, I promise: *Anyway* means "in any event." *Any way* means "a way, some sort of way."

> *"Anyway,"* added Roy, "I don't think there is *any way* to avoid jail for grammar crimes."

Q. Select the word or words that create a sentence that is correct in Standard English.

EXAMPLE

This fork belongs to Lola's (everyday, every day) set of silverware.

A. **everyday** This sentence isn't about time; you need a word that means "ordinary."

Select the word or words that create a sentence that is correct in Standard English.

YOUR TURN

31 Do you have (sometime, sometimes, some time) to help Roger with his algebra homework?

32 He hasn't done homework all year, so he will need (alot, a lot) of help.

33 If it's (alright, all right) with you, have the chorus sing (altogether, all together).

34 Vince told his brothers that he wanted them (already, all ready) to go before he came home from work.

35 When he called them at 11, he discovered that they had spoken with (eachother, each other) and had (already, all ready) left.

36 "I need (sometime, sometimes, some time) alone," cried Jane.

37 Henry promised to visit his friends (sometime, some time) next year.

38 (Sometime, Sometimes, Some time) Henry ignores his own promises, but he usually follows through.

39 Carl was busy and would not allow Roger (anytime, any time) to speak.

40. Bill said Roger could phone him (anytime, any time).

41. (Everyday, Every day), Glen washes the dishes.

42. Your approach to chores is (altogether, all together) unacceptable.

Three for the Road: Other Common Errors

If you made it this far into the chapter, you've cleared up (I hope!) a few confusing grammar points. Time to hit you with a few last mistakes that appear often — and that are super easy to correct.

Between/among

Between and *among* are two tricky prepositions that are often used incorrectly. To choose the appropriate preposition, decide how many people or things you're talking about. If the answer is two, you want *between*, as in this sentence:

> Lola was completely unable to choose *between* the biker magazine and *Poetry for Weightlifters*. (two magazines only)

If you're talking about more than two, *among* is the appropriate word:

> Lola strolled *among* the parked motorcycles, reading poetry aloud. (more than two motorcycles)

One exception: Treaties are made *between* nations, even if more than two countries sign:

> The treaty to outlaw bubblegum was negotiated *between* Libya, the United States, Russia, and Ecuador.

Being that

Many people say *being that* to introduce a reason, but this expression is not correct in Standard English. Try *because* or *given that*. For example:

> NONSTANDARD: *Being that* it was Thanksgiving, Mel bought a turkey.

> STANDARD: *Because* it was Thanksgiving, Mel bought a turkey.

> ALSO STANDARD: *Given that* it was Thanksgiving, Mel bought a turkey.

> NONSTANDARD: The turkey shed a tear or two, *being that* it was Thanksgiving.

> STANDARD: The turkey shed a tear or two, *because* it was Thanksgiving.

> ALSO STANDARD: The turkey shed a tear or two, *given that* it was Thanksgiving.

WARNING

Irregardless is in the same category as *being that* — a word many people say that is not correct in Standard English. If you want to be sure that everyone views your language as proper, try *regardless* or *nevertheless*.

Try and/try to

Should you *try and* or *try to* figure out a grammar problem? *Try and* means that you're going to do two different things: *try* (first task) and *figure out* (second task). People using this expression don't really have two tasks in mind. What they mean is *try to figure this one out*. *Try to* follows the normal English pattern of a verb and an infinitive. *Try to remember* the verb-infinitive rule and *try to forget* about *try and*. Some examples:

> Try to remember where you parked the car.
>
> Jack tried to tie the car to a tree, but someone stole the Mercedes anyway.

EXAMPLE

Q. Select the word or words that are correct in Standard English.

(Because, Being that) I'm the most determined person on the planet, I have only one message for you: (Try and, Try to) stop me! I bet you can't!

A. **Because, Try to** *Being that* and *try and* are nonstandard.

YOUR TURN

Select the word or expression that is correct in Standard English.

43 (Between, Among) the 15 club members there was little agreement.

44 (Because, Being that) the club has a tight budget, club members should not plan an expensive field trip.

45 The club members will (try and, try to) find a local company willing to sponsor their activities.

46 (Between, Among) you and me, I doubt anyone will be interested in helping them.

Practice Questions Answers and Explanations

1. **(B)** *Can't hardly* is a double negative, so (A) is out. Sentence (B) correctly changes the expression to *can hardly*.

2. **(A)** Option (B), *ain't got no problem*, sounds wonderfully emphatic, but logically it means "have got problems." Sentence (A) is correct.

3. **(A)** Sentence (A) has only one negative, *no singing*. Sentence (B) has a double (*not, no*).

4. **(B)** *Hadn't but* is a double negative, so (A) isn't Standard English. Sentence (B) includes only one negative word, *but*, so it's correct.

5. **(C)** *Can't help but* and *can't hardly* are both double negatives, so neither sentence is correct in Standard English.

6. **accept** In this sentence you need a verb meaning "to receive willingly."

7. **effect** This sentence calls for a noun meaning "a change that is the result of an action."

8. **continuous** If it never stops, it's *continuous*.

9. **further** In this sentence you're not talking about distance, so *further*, which means "additional," fits.

10. **accept** The judge did not "receive willingly," or *accept*, the proof.

11. **affect** The sentence calls for a verb meaning "influence."

12. **continually** The sentence is about an action (interrupting) that starts and stops.

13. **further** The word *further* means "additional" and applies to everything but distance.

14. **going to, continuous** *Gonna* isn't standard. The hammering didn't stop, so it's *continuous*.

15. **too, effect** The first spot calls for an intensifier, *too*. The second requires a noun meaning "result."

16. **supposed** If you drop the *d*, you're in nonstandard territory.

17. **affected, used** The first spot calls for a verb meaning "influence." The second requires an expression meaning "accustomed to," *used*.

18. **Two, used, too** In the first spot you need a number; in the second, a verb meaning "accustomed"; and in the third, an intensifier.

19. **going to, further** *Gonna* isn't standard, and *further* is required to express "additional" time.

20. **used, accept** In the first spot you need a word meaning "accustomed," and in the second a verb meaning "willingly accept."

21. **lies** This sentence needs a verb meaning "rest or recline."

22. **sits** The doctor is in a chair, so he *sits*.

(23) **set, lose** The first spot calls for a verb meaning "to put"; in the second spot, you need a verb showing that the doctor couldn't hold onto his temper.

(24) **lie, sit** Both spots require body positions — the first reclining and the second remaining in a chair.

(25) **hung, loose** The tomb wasn't executed, so *hung* is the verb for the first spot. The dog gained freedom and thus got *loose.*

(26) **raise, rose** In the first spot, the lover will lift something (*raise* her voice); in the second spot, people are saying she lifted herself (*rose*).

(27) **hanged** This verb means "executed."

(28) **sit, lose** The first is a body position, the second an expression about giving up something or having it taken away.

(29) **lying** The evil twin is reclining, or *lying.*

(30) **rise** This verb expresses body position or movement.

(31) **some time** The correct expression refers to a period of time.

(32) **a lot** These words should always be separated if you're writing in Standard English.

(33) **all right, all together** The word *alright* is nonstandard. The chorus should sing as one, *altogether.*

(34) **all ready** Vince has more than one brother, and he wants them *all* [to be] *ready.*

(35) **each other, already** *Eachother* as one word is nonstandard. For the second spot, you need a word meaning "prior to, before."

(36) **some time** The meaning needed here is "a period of time."

(37) **sometime** The meaning needed here is "at some point in time."

(38) **Sometimes** The sentence calls for a word meaning "from time to time."

(39) **any time** Here you need an expression meaning "an unspecified period of time."

(40) **anytime** The sentence suggests that "at an unspecified point in time" is the meaning.

(41) **Every day** Glen washes the dishes seven days a week, every week. That's *every day.*

(42) **altogether** In this sentence you need a word that means "completely."

(43) **Among** Because you're talking about more than two, *among* is the word you need here.

(44) **Because** *Being that* is nonstandard.

(45) **try to** *Try and* implies two tasks, but that's not logical in this sentence.

(46) **Between** In a group of two, *between* is the word you want. Also, the grammatically correct expression is *between you and me,* not *between you and I.* Why? *Between* is a preposition and requires an object pronoun, *me,* not a subject pronoun, *I.* (For more on object pronouns, see Chapter 14.)

Whaddya Know? Chapter 23 Quiz

Which word is correct in Standard English?

1. (Sometime, Sometimes, Some time) the teacher's views on having (alot, a lot) of technology in the classroom bother Mark, such as when he texts his brother Jim.

2. Jim doesn't usually answer immediately, (because, being that) he is very busy.

3. When Mark (raises, rises) the issue, he and Jim talk to (eachother, each other) about whether texting takes priority over homework.

4. The brothers are (altogether, all together) committed to (setting, sitting) down for a good talk when (two, to, too) much tension exists between them.

5. "If you (sit, set) your phone on the top shelf (everyday, every day) at bedtime," said Mark, "you will sleep better.

6. "(Alright, All right)," replied Jim, "I will (try and, try to) do that, but I'm afraid I'll forget and (lose, loose) my phone.

7. "I (hanged, hung) a note over the bathroom mirror reminding me to take my phone with me when I go to school," commented Mark.

8. "You (use, used) to be more fun! Now you only do what you're (suppose, supposed) to do!" shouted Jim.

9. Mark and Jim's mom can't (accept, except) any phone use after 9 p.m. because she's sure their texting (affects, effects) their grades.

10. She explains her views daily, usually during dinner, but her (continual, continuous) nagging has little (affect, effect).

Answers to Chapter 23 Quiz

(1) **Sometimes, a lot** The word *sometimes* best describes an event that occurs occasionally. *A lot* is two words.

(2) **because** Being that isn't correct in Standard English.

(3) **raises, each other** The verb *raise* is appropriate for calling attention to or lifting an item. *Rise* is best for the act of lifting oneself. *Each other* is never written as a single word in Standard English.

(4) **altogether, sitting, too** The first spot calls for a word meaning "completely." The second refers to getting comfortable in a chair; the third spot requires an intensifier.

(5) **set, every day** *Set* is the verb you want when someone places an object somewhere. *Every day* as two words means "each day."

(6) **All right, try to, lose** *Alright* and *try and* aren't correct in Standard English. *Lose* is the verb you want when you can't find something.

(7) **hung** The note isn't being executed, or *hanged*. It's being suspended, or *hung*, over the mirror.

(8) **used, supposed** If you delete the *d* in these words, they're not standard.

(9) **accepts, affects** In the first spot you need a verb, not a preposition that excludes someone or something. In the second spot you need a verb meaning "influences."

(10) **continual, effect** The nagging stops and starts, so it's *continual.* The result, or *effect,* isn't what the mom hoped for. (Perhaps she should switch to *continuous* nagging! Without a pause, Mark and Jim may give in to her demands!)

Chapter **24**

Writing Stylish Sentences

Many television shows feature aspiring designers who cut patterns and sew, glue, or staple fashion-forward clothing. Why do so many people, including me, watch? To see something new, to be jolted out of the "same old, same old" pattern. Writing is no different. Chances are you have some basic sentence patterns that serve you well. But if you've ever longed for a change of pace, this chapter is for you. Here you find out how to add variety and style to your sentences by employing verbals and clauses, combining ideas artfully, changing word order, and adjusting sentence structure and length.

Speaking Verbally

Every family has some members who add zing to holiday dinners. *Verbals* are the grammatical equivalent of those relatives. As the name implies, verbals have a connection with verbs, and they also share traits of other parts of speech (nouns, adjectives, and adverbs). Verbals never act as the verb in a sentence, and they're never part of the matching subject-verb pair required for a complete sentence. They may anchor a *verbal phrase*, with an object or a subject complement and descriptions. Verbals also have *tense*, an expression of time. This section explains how to identify verbals and use them to enliven your sentences.

Identifying verbals

You've spent a lot of time with the verbal family, most likely without knowing their names — *infinitives*, *participles*, and *gerunds*.

Infinitives

Infinitives are what you get when you tack *to* in front of the most basic form of the verb. An infinitive may function as a description or as a noun, but never as the verb in a sentence. In these examples, the *infinitive phrase* (the infinitive plus its object or subject complement and descriptions) is in italics:

> *To protect herself against bad breath,* Alice packed a few hundred rolls of mints. *(to protect* = infinitive describing *packed)*

> *To win an Oscar* was Roger's goal. *(to win* = infinitive acting as the subject of the verb *was)*

TIP

Somewhere, sometime, someone came up with the idea that you shouldn't split an infinitive. That is, you shouldn't place any other word between *to* and the verb. This "rule," which many people still follow, may have arisen from the fact that in Latin (a language that has contributed much to English) the infinitive is a single word, which of course can't be split. In English, though, it's fine to insert a word between *to* and the verb:

> Greg tried to gently remove the bandage.

> To frequently wash the windshield is important in this dusty area.

WARNING

If you're writing for an authority figure who believes that split infinitives are wrong, you may be scolded for breaking the rule, despite the fact that the rule doesn't exist. In such a situation, arguing may not help you. Reword the sentence if you can:

> Greg tried to remove the bandage gently.

> Frequent windshield-washing is important in this dusty area.

Participles

Participles are the *-ing* or *-ed* or *-en* form of verbs, plus a few irregulars. Sometimes participles function as part of the verb in a sentence, attached to *has, have, had, is, are, was, were,* or *will be.* In this situation, participles aren't verbals. When participles act as descriptions, they're verbals. In these sentences, the *participial phrase* (the participle and its object or subject complement and descriptions) is in italics:

> *Inhaling sharply,* Elaine stepped away from the blast of peppermint that escaped from Alice's mouth. *(inhaling* = participle giving information about *Elaine)*

> The *dancing* statue is so famous that everyone *seeing it* takes a selfie. *(dancing* = participle describing the noun *statue, seeing* = participle describing the pronoun *everyone)*

Participles have to appear in the right spot or else the meaning you're trying to express doesn't come across. (For more information on where to place descriptions, turn to Chapter 15.)

Gerunds

Gerunds are the *-ing* form of verbs, functioning as nouns. In these examples, the *gerund phrase* (the gerund and its object or subject complement and descriptions) is in italics:

> *Riding a motorcycle around town* is Gina's favorite activity. *(Riding* = gerund acting as the subject of the verb *is)*

> Her father dislikes *Gina's riding a motorcycle,* because he's afraid she'll get hurt. *(riding* = gerund acting as the direct object of the verb *dislikes)*

TIP

Did you notice the possessive word, *Gina's,* in the preceding example? You need a possessive pronoun in front of a gerund when the action expressed by the gerund is the focus. Take a look:

> WRONG: Sheila loves him shopping for just the right present.

> WHY IT'S WRONG: In this sentence, the important idea — what Sheila loves — is the attempt to find the perfect gift. The emphasis should be on *shopping,* not on *him.*

> RIGHT: Sheila loves his shopping for just the right present.

> WHY IT'S RIGHT: The possessive pronoun *his* leads the reader or listener onward to the next idea — the *shopping.* The emphasis is on that activity, not on *him.*

Verbals can shorten your sentences and make your writing more sophisticated. I discuss this technique in "Sprucing Up Boring Sentences with Clauses and Verbals," later in this chapter.

EXAMPLE

Q. Label the underlined portions of each sentence I for *infinitive,* P for *participle,* or G for *gerund.* If none of these labels fit, write *N* for *none.*

Sam flew <u>to Phoenix</u> for a conference on "<u>Rebranding</u> Your Company."

A. **N, G** *Phoenix* is not a verb, so *to Phoenix* is not a verbal. (It's a prepositional phrase, in case you're curious.) *Rebranding* is a gerund. It's derived from a verb *(rebrand)* and functioning as a noun (object of the preposition *on*). *Rebranding Your Company* is the entire gerund phrase.

YOUR TURN

Label the underlined portions of each sentence I for *infinitive,* P for *participle,* or G for *gerund.* If none of these labels fit, write N for *none.*

(1) <u>Arriving</u> in the tropics, Sam was eager <u>to settle</u> in at his hotel.

(2) The hotel room, newly <u>redecorated</u>, was on the same floor as an <u>overflowing</u> ice machine.

(3) <u>To reach</u> his room, Sam had <u>to skate</u> across a miniature glacier.

(4) <u>Sliding</u> across a slippery floor <u>to his room</u> was not one of Sam's happiest moments.

(5) Sam, <u>easygoing</u> by nature, nevertheless decided <u>to complain</u>.

(6) "I want <u>to relax</u>, not <u>to practice</u> winter sports!" Sam stated <u>firmly</u>.

⑦ The manager, not <u>knowing</u> about the ice machine, found Sam's comment <u>confusing</u>.

⑧ <u>Reaching</u> 100 degrees is not unusual during summer in this part of the world.

⑨ <u>Choosing</u> his words carefully, the manager replied, "Of course, sir. I will cancel the bobsled <u>racing</u>."

⑩ Sam forgot about the ice machine and <u>protested</u>, because his lifelong dream was <u>to race</u> downhill on a fast sled.

Choosing the correct tense

Like verbs, verbals situate action on a timeline through their *tense.* In Chapter 12, I explain everything you need to know about tense as it applies to the verb of a sentence. Here I focus on verbals.

Simultaneous events

Verbals often show up when two events take place at the same time. In the following sentences, check out the italicized verbals. Also keep your eye on the main verb, which is underlined. Notice that the same verbal matches with present, past, and future verbs and places the two actions at the same time or close enough in time to make the difference irrelevant. Also notice that none of the verbals is formed with the words *have* or *had.* (*Have* and *had* help to express actions taking place at different times. I explain this point in detail later in this section.)

> *Selecting* a slender paintbrush, Maya lightly <u>dabs</u> the canvas. (The *selecting* and the *dabbing* take place at nearly the same time — in the present.)
>
> *Selecting* a slender paintbrush, Maya lightly <u>dabbed</u> the canvas. (The *selecting* and the *dabbing* took place at nearly the same time — in the past.)
>
> *Selecting* a slender paintbrush, Maya <u>will</u> lightly <u>dab</u> the canvas. (The *selecting* and the *dabbing* will take place at nearly the same time — in the future.)

Another variation:

> *To dab the canvas lightly,* Maya <u>selects</u> a slender paintbrush. (The *dabbing* and the *selecting* take place at nearly the same time — in the present.)
>
> *To dab the canvas lightly,* Maya <u>selected</u> a slender paintbrush. (The *dabbing* and the *selecting* took place at nearly the same time — in the past.)
>
> *To dab the canvas lightly,* Maya <u>will select</u> a slender paintbrush. (The *dabbing* and the *selecting* will take place at nearly the same time — in the future.)

Different times

When verbals express actions or states of being that occur at different times, a helping verb (*having* or *have)* is involved.

Check out this sentence:

> *Having sealed* the letter containing his job application, Nobrain *remembered* his name.

In other words, Nobrain's job application — unless he rips open the envelope — is anonymous because the *sealing* of the letter took place before the *remembering* of his name.

Here are additional examples:

> *Having finished* her homework, Elizabeth *turned* on the television to watch the algebra tournament. (Event 1: Elizabeth finishes her homework at 2 A.M. Event 2: The tournament begins at 3 A.M. The networks seem reluctant to broadcast the match during prime time. I'm not sure why.)

> *Having scored* five goals in the soccer match, Lucette was named Most Valuable Player. (Event 1: Lucette scores five goals. Event 2: Lucette gets a trophy.)

If you have a life, skip this paragraph. If you like grammar, read on to learn the technical terms. The *present participle* (*finishing*, for example) combines with present, past, and future verbs to show two events happening at the same time or at nearly the same time. The *present perfect* form of the participle (*having finished*) combines with present, past, and future verbs to show two events happening at different times.

Another one of the verb-forms-that-aren't-verbs, the *infinitive*, may also show events happening at two different times. The *present perfect infinitive* (*to have finished*, for example) is the one that does this job. Don't worry about the name; just look for the *have*. Here's an example:

> "How smart *to have packed snacks* for John's dinner party!" thought Greta. (Event 1: Preparty, Greta stuffs food into her backpack. Event 2: Greta takes one bite of John's Alfalfa-Stringbean Surprise and congratulates herself on bringing snacks.)

WARNING

The *have* form (the present perfect form) of the infinitive always places an event *before* another in the past. Don't use the *have* form unless you're putting events in order:

> WRONG: Nice to have met you.

> RIGHT: Nice to meet you.

> ALSO RIGHT: Nice to have met you before agreeing to marry you. I think I'll hold out for a better offer or the end of the world, whichever comes first.

EXAMPLE

Q. Select the correct form from the choices in parentheses.

(Perfecting/Having perfected) a new tooth-whitening product, the chemists asked the boss to conduct some market research.

A. **Having perfected** The two events occurred in the past, with the chemists' request closer to the present moment. The event expressed by the verbal (a participle, as you may have guessed) attributes another action to the chemists. The perfect form (created by *having*) places the act of *perfecting* prior to the action expressed by the main verb in the sentence, *asked.*

Select the correct form from the choices in parentheses.

11. (Peering/Having peered) at each interview subject, the researchers checked for discoloration.

12. One interview subject shrieked upon (hearing/having heard) the interviewer's comment about "teeth as yellow as sunflowers."

13. (Refusing/Having refused) to open her mouth, she glared silently at the interviewer.

14. With the market research on the tooth whitener (completed/having been completed), the team tabulated the results.

15. The tooth whitener (going/having gone) into production, no further market research is scheduled.

16. The researchers actually wanted (to interview/to have interviewed) 50 percent more subjects after the product's debut, but the legal department objected.

17. Not (securing/having secured) additional interviews, the legal department tore up the "will not sue" forms they'd hoped potential subjects would sign.

18. "(Sending/Having sent) this product to the stores means that I am sure it works," said the CEO.

19. (Deceived/Having been deceived) by this CEO several times, reporters were skeptical.

20. (Interviewing/Having interviewed) dissatisfied customers, one reporter was already planning an exposé.

Sprucing Up Boring Sentences with Clauses and Verbals

A *clause* is any expression containing a subject and a verb. (For tons more detail about clauses, read Chapter 11.) In this section, I show you how to manipulate clauses and verbals to make your writing more interesting and sophisticated.

Read these two paragraphs. Which one sounds better?

> Michael purchased a new spy camera. The camera was smaller than a grain of rice. Michael gave the camera to Lola. Lola is rather forgetful. She is especially forgetful now. Lola is planning a trip to Antarctica. Lola accidentally mixed the camera into her rice casserole along with bean sprouts and soy milk. The camera baked for 45 minutes. The camera became quite tender. Michael unknowingly ate the camera.

> Michael purchased a new spy camera that was smaller than a grain of rice. He gave the camera to Lola, who is rather forgetful, especially now that she is planning a trip to Antarctica. Accidentally mixed into Lola's rice casserole along with bean sprouts and soy milk, the camera baked for 45 minutes. Michael unknowingly ate the camera, which was quite tender.

The second paragraph is better, isn't it? The first is composed of short, choppy sentences. The second one flows. Grammatically, the difference between the two is simple. The second paragraph has more subordinate clauses and verbals than the first. (A *subordinate clause* is a subject-verb statement that can't stand alone; I discuss verbals earlier in this chapter.)

TIP

Don't let the names scare you. If you're allergic to grammar terms, just read your writing aloud and listen carefully. If your sentences sound like those in the first example, it's time to spruce them up with the techniques I describe in this section.

Clauses

Every sentence has to have a subject-verb pair expressing a complete thought. Fine, but you have lots of thoughts, don't you? Rather than plodding through them one by one, try tucking one thought inside another with subordinate clauses. Again, don't hyperventilate over the terminology. Just take a look at these before-and-after sentences and focus on the italicized bits, which are subordinate clauses:

> BORING "BEFORE" VERSION: Max sat on a tuffet. Max did not know that he was sitting on a tuffet. Max had never seen a tuffet. He was quite comfortable. Then Ms. Muffet came in and caused trouble.

> EXCITING "AFTER" VERSION: Max, *who was sitting on a tuffet,* did not know *what a tuffet was, because he had never seen one. Until Ms. Muffet came in and caused trouble,* Max was quite comfortable.

The "after" paragraph is two words shorter (32 instead of 34 words), but more important than length is the number of sentences. The "before" paragraph has five, and the "after" paragraph has two. The revised paragraph is less choppy.

One more example:

> BORING "BEFORE" PARAGRAPH: The taxi sounded its horn. The taxi was traveling south. The intersection was clogged with trucks. The trucks were heading west. The taxi could not move. The traffic police finally arrived. They cleared the intersection.

> EXCITING "AFTER" PARAGRAPH: The taxi, *which was traveling south,* sounded its horn. *Because the intersection was clogged with trucks heading west,* the taxi could not move. The traffic police cleared the intersection *when they arrived.*

By combining sentences, you create a smoother flow of ideas. The writing sounds more mature, and therefore so do you.

TIP

When you combine sentences, you often find that fewer words get your meaning across — a plus for both you and your audience. Everyone's busy, so repetition is seldom welcome! When you proofread, check for unnecessary expressions ("an island surrounded by water," for example) and eliminate them.

EXAMPLE

Q. Combine these sentences by creating subordinate clauses. You may change the wording of the original sentences as needed, but not the meaning.

The tea was very hot. The tea was not ready to drink. Catherine waited a few minutes.

A. You may combine these ideas in several different ways. Here are two possibilities, with the subordinate clauses italicized:

The tea, *which was very hot*, was not ready to drink, so Catherine waited a few minutes.

Because the tea, which was very hot, was not ready to drink, Catherine waited a few minutes.

In the second possible answer, one subordinate clause (*which was very hot*) is tucked into another (*Because the tea was not ready to drink*).

YOUR TURN

Combine these sentences by creating subordinate clauses. You may change the wording of the original sentences as needed, but not the meaning.

21 Carl was impatient. He was thirsty. He reached for the cup.

22 Catherine pulled Carl's hand away. His hand couldn't touch the cup.

23 Catherine wanted to help Carl. Her action jarred his hand. The table shook.

24 The cup was full. Catherine and Carl didn't notice.

25 The tea splashed. It was still extremely hot. It burned their hands.

26 Catherine will call her Uncle Larry. Uncle Larry is a burn specialist.

27 Carl will call his Uncle Andrew. Uncle Andrew is a personal-injury lawyer.

Verbals

Because verbals blend two parts of speech, they provide two perspectives in just one word. Look at this before-and-after example:

BORING "BEFORE" VERSION: Lulu smacked Larry. Larry had stolen the antique toe hoop from Lulu's parrot. The toe hoop was discovered 100 years ago. Lulu's parrot likes to sharpen his beak on it.

EXCITING "AFTER VERSION": *Smacking Larry* is Lulu's way of telling Larry that he should not have stolen the antique toe hoop from her parrot. *Discovered 100 years ago*, the toe hoop serves *to sharpen the parrot's beak*.

LABELS IN CASE YOU CARE: *Smacking Lulu* = gerund, *discovered 100 years ago* = participle, *to sharpen the parrot's beak* = infinitive.

Are you awake enough for another example? Take a look at this makeover. The verbal phrases are italicized:

BORING "BEFORE" VERSION: The sled slid down the hill. Luis was on the sled. He was excited. He forgot about the brake.

EXCITING "AFTER" VERSION: *Sliding down the hill on the sled*, Luis was *excited* and forgot *to brake*.

LABELS IN CASE YOU CARE: *Sliding down the hill on the sled* = participle, *excited* = participle, *to brake* = infinitive.

EXAMPLE

Q. Using verbals, combine these ideas into one or more sentences.

Larry bakes infrequently. He bakes with enthusiasm. His best recipe is for king cake. King-cake batter must be stirred for three hours. Larry orders his cook to stir the batter. The cook stirs, and Larry adds the raisins. Sometimes Larry throws in a spoonful of vanilla.

A. Many combinations are possible, including this one:

Larry's *baking* is infrequent but enthusiastic. His best recipe, king cake, requires three hours of *stirring*, which Larry orders his cook to do. *Adding* raisins and the occasional spoonful of vanilla is Larry's job. The italicized words are gerunds.

YOUR TURN

Using verbals, combine these ideas into one or more sentences. You may change the words but not the meaning.

28. Jesse is cleaning his teeth. He realizes the boss wants the memo immediately. He stops cleaning his teeth. He starts typing.

29. Jesse is considering retirement. Jesse discovers he still owes a lot of money on his mortgage. Jesse decides that he will work 50 more years.

30. Jesse desperately desires quality time on a tropical island. Jesse wants to keep his house.

31. The bank manager speaks in a firm voice. She points out that Jesse has $.02 in his savings account.

32. Jesse knows that he can rob the bank. Jesse is an honest man. He will not commit a crime.

33. The bank manager has a goal. She wants a luxurious life on a tropical island. She makes a decision. She robs the bank.

Mixing It Up: Changing Sentence Patterns and Length

To create interesting sentences, you can play around with clauses and verbals, as I explain in the preceding section. In this section I give you two other tools for "redecorating" your sentences: pattern (what's where in the sentence) and length. I also show you how to express yourself concisely.

Patterns

When you were little, you may have played the game duck-duck-goose. It's a simple contest. Kids sit in a circle and the one who's "it" walks around the outside, tapping each child and saying "duck" — until suddenly the "it" kid changes the pattern and says "goose." I mention this game because it relies on surprise — the establishment of a pattern and then a break from it.

Word order

When you write, you probably follow the most common sentence pattern automatically: subject, verb, complement (a direct object, an indirect object, or a subject complement). Scan these examples, in which the major sentence elements are identified:

> Ali wants the stars. (*Ali* = subject, *wants* = verb, *stars* = direct object)
>
> He built a rocket in less than a year. (*He* = subject, *built* = verb, *rocket* = direct object)
>
> Ali traveled out of Earth's atmosphere, across thousands of light-years, to the planet Jupiter. (*Ali* = subject, *traveled* = verb, no complement)
>
> Ali is a national hero. (*Ali* = subject, *is* = verb, *hero* = complement)

That structure dominates because it's sturdy; it supports a ton of ideas. It's comforting. Readers are used to it, and they know what to expect. A change in routine, though, goes a long way toward improving your writing. Take a look at what happens when you shake up the word order:

> The stars, Ali wants. (*Ali* = subject, *wants* = verb, *stars* = direct object)
>
> A rocket in less than a year built he! (*He* = subject, *built* = verb, *rocket* = direct object)
>
> Out of Earth's atmosphere, across thousands of light-years, to the planet Jupiter traveled Ali. (*Ali* = subject, *traveled* = verb, no complement)
>
> A national hero, Ali is. (*Ali* = subject, *is* = verb, *hero* = complement)

WARNING

I wrote these examples to show you some possibilities, but don't change the usual sentence order too often — certainly not four times in a row. You can't play duck-duck-goose unless you have some ducks — a lot of ducks! Placing too many unusual sentences in the same story would annoy your readers. Use scrambled word order for an occasional change of pace, not as a steady diet.

EXAMPLE

Q. Change the order of words in this sentence to make it more dramatic. Don't change the meaning.

Juan Gonzalez is a fine writer.

A. **A fine writer, Juan Gonzalez is.** This sentence places the complement first.

Parallelism

Taken any train trips recently? The tracks you see stretching before you are parallel — or they'd better be. If they aren't, your train goes offtrack and chaos quickly follows. In grammar, you should nearly always stay on track also by creating parallel constructions — sentences and expressions in which every part of the sentence performing the same job has the same grammatical identity. Take a look at these two sentences:

> Larry wanted with all his heart to find a bride who was smart, beautiful, and wealthy.

> Larry wanted with all his heart to find a bride who was smart, beautiful, and had millions of dollars.

Not counting Larry's matrimonial ideas, the first example has no problems: The qualities that Larry seeks are expressed as adjectives. Nothing stands out; they're more or less equal in importance. This is the version you should use when you're following the rules. The second example is not parallel, because the expression *had millions of dollars* contains a verb. Technically, this is a grammar error. That said, this construction calls attention to the last item on Larry's wish list. Because it's longer and doesn't fit, the economic status of the bride stands out. Readers would assume that item is more important than the other two.

WARNING

Don't break parallelism casually, and never when you're writing for someone who insists on grammatically correct expression or when the break makes no sense, as in this sentence with multiple verbs:

> Larry begs Ella to marry him, offers her a crown and a private room, and finally won her hand.

> Larry, as part of his pro-environment stance, presented Ella with the wedding ring his last bride had worn, because you recycle when you can.

The first example has two verbs in present tense (*begs, offers*), and one in past tense (*won*). The pattern break is illogical and comes across as sloppy, not creative. The second example veers from third person (talking about Larry) to second person (talking to *you*), another unnecessary break from parallelism.

In addition to lists and compound verbs, check the parallelism when you're making a comparison or employing a conjunction pair, such as *not only/but also, neither/nor, either/or, both/and,* or *whether/or.* (For more information on conjunctions, see Chapter 7.) To be parallel, the elements joined by these conjunctions should have the same identity:

> Both *because he stole the garter* and *because he lost the ring,* Roger is no longer welcome as best man. (This conjunction pair joins two subject–verb combinations.)

> Either you or I must break the news about the fake diamond to Larry. (The conjunction pair joins two pronouns, *you* and *I.*)

Q. Which sentences, if any, are parallel?

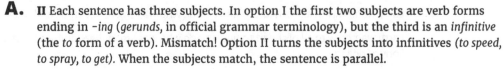

    I. Speeding down Thunder Mountain, spraying snow across his rival's face, and to get the best seat in the ski lodge were Robert's goals for the afternoon.

    II. To speed down Thunder Mountain, to spray snow across his rival's face, and to get the best seat in the ski lodge were Robert's goals for the afternoon.

A. **II** Each sentence has three subjects. In option I the first two subjects are verb forms ending in *-ing* (*gerunds*, in official grammar terminology), but the third is an *infinitive* (the *to* form of a verb). Mismatch! Option II turns the subjects into infinitives (*to speed, to spray, to get*). When the subjects match, the sentence is parallel.

Which sentences, if any, are parallel?

34   I. The ski pants that Robert favors are green, skintight, and stretchy.

    II. The ski pants that Robert favors are green, skintight, and made of stretch fabric.

35   I. When he eases into those pants and zips up with force, Robert feels cool.

    II. When he eases into those pants and zipping up with force, Robert feels cool.

36   I. In this ski outfit, Robert can not only breathe easily but also forcefully.

    II. In this ski outfit, Robert can breathe easily as well as forcefully.

37   I. The sacrifice for the sake of fashion is worth the trouble and how he feels uncomfortable, Robert says.

    II. The sacrifice for the sake of fashion is worth the trouble and discomfort, Robert says.

Going long or cutting it short

Pick up something you wrote recently and zero in on a random paragraph. Count the number of words in each sentence. What do you find? If your writing resembles most people's, you tend to place the same number of words in every sentence. Yet sentences can be as short as two words (I quit!) or go on for pages and pages. (Check out Virginia Woolf's or Charles Dickens's work to see some marathon statements.)

How do you mix it up when it comes to sentence length? Try these techniques:

>> Combine some sentences by making the less important idea into a subordinate clause. Read the section "Clauses," earlier in this chapter, to see some possible combination patterns.

>> Use a conjunction such as *and, but, or, nor,* or *for* to join two complete sentences that state ideas of equal importance. A bonus of this technique is that the conjunction may reveal the logic that leads from one sentence to the next.

>> Throw in a verbal to replace some less important ideas. "Speaking Verbally," earlier in this chapter, provides some examples.

If you have a very long sentence — perhaps the result of combining several shorter sentences — consider following it with a short, emphatic statement, as in this example:

> After the crowds left, when the remains of the meal had been cleared away, just before the band finished packing up its instruments, and while Katie was still opening her presents to see what she'd gotten for her birthday, the door opened. He'd arrived.

See what I mean? Doesn't that last sentence hit you right in the face? This long-short pattern doesn't work if you overuse it, but it's certainly a great choice for an occasional dramatic effect.

EXAMPLE

Q. Take a crack at this paragraph. Change the sentence length and patterns using some or all of the suggestions in this section.

Bill lit the candles. He bought flowers. He put the bank reports on the table. Tonight he would propose to Belle. Bill's company was very profitable. Belle's company was super-profitable. Bill was aware of her sales figures. Bill sought a merger. Bill hoped Belle would accept. Then their companies would combine. Bill and Belle would be very rich.

A. You can revise this paragraph in any one of about a million ways. Here's one, with an explanation in parentheses after each change:

Having lit the candles and bought flowers (participles), Bill put the bank report on the table. Tonight he would propose to Belle, *whose company was super-profitable,* (subordinate clause) *as was Bill's* (subordinate clause). *Knowing her sales figures* (gerund) led Bill *to seek a merger* (infinitive). Bill hoped Belle would accept *combining their companies and making Bill and Belle very rich.* (gerunds)

Practice Questions Answers and Explanations

1. **P, I** The participle *arriving* gives information about *Sam*, the subject of the sentence. The verb in the sentence is *was*. *To settle* is an infinitive.

2. **P, P** *Redecorated* (from the verb *redecorate*) describes *room*. *Overflowing* (from the verb *overflow*) describes *machine*.

3. **I, I** These infinitives perform different jobs in the sentence. *To reach* describes the verb *had; to skate* is the object of the verb *had*.

4. **G, N** *Sliding* is the subject of the verb *was*. *To his room* is a prepositional phrase, not a verb. (For more information on prepositional phrases, turn to Chapter 7.)

5. **N, I** *Easygoing* isn't a verbal, because the verb "easygo" doesn't exist. *To complain* is an infinitive acting as the object of the verb *decided*.

6. **I, I, N** *To relax* and *to practice* are both infinitives acting as objects. *Firmly* is an adverb, not a verbal. (For more information on adverbs, read Chapter 6.)

7. **P, P** Both *knowing* and *confusing* are participles. The first describes *manager*, and the second describes *comment*.

8. **G** *Reaching* is a gerund acting as the subject of the verb *is*.

9. **P, G** *Choosing* is something the manager is doing, but it's not the verb in the sentence. It's a description, what grammarians call an *introductory participle* because it sits at the beginning of the sentence. *Racing* is a gerund acting as an object.

10. **N, I** *Protested* isn't a verbal; it's a verb. *To go* is an infinitive acting as a subject complement.

11. **Peering** Here the two actions take place at the same time. The researchers check out the subjects' teeth and check for trouble. The perfect form (with *having*) is for actions at different times.

12. **hearing** Once again, two actions take place at the same time. Go for the plain form.

13. **Refusing** The "not in this universe will I open my mouth" moment is simultaneous with an "if looks could kill" glare, so the plain form is best.

14. **having been completed** The plain form *completed* would place two actions (the completing and the tabulating) at the same time. Yet common sense tells you that the tabulating follows the completion of the research. The perfect form (with *having*) places the completing before the tabulating.

15. **having gone** The decision to stop market research is based on the fact that it's too late; the tooth whitener, in all its glory, is already being manufactured. Because the timeline matters here and one action is clearly earlier, the perfect form is needed.

16. **to interview** The *have* form places the action of interviewing *before* the action expressed by the main verb in the sentence. With *have*, the timeline makes no sense.

17. **having secured** Three actions are expressed by this sentence: securing, tearing, and hoping. The earliest action is the hoping, as indicated by both logic and the past perfect verb, *had hoped*. Moving forward is the securing of additional interviews — actually, the failure to secure additional interviews! *Having secured* places this action before the tearing of the forms, the most recent action.

18 **Sending** The CEO's statement places two things, sending and being sure, at the same time. The plain form is best.

19 **Having been deceived** The point of the sentence is that one action (deceiving the reporters) precedes another (being skeptical). You need the perfect form to make the timeline work.

20 **Interviewing** The interviews and the planning of an exposé are simultaneous, so the plain form is best.

21 **Carl, who was impatient and thirsty, reached for the cup.** Another possibility: *Because he was impatient and thirsty, Carl reached for the cup.*

22 **Before it could touch the cup, Catherine pulled Carl's hand away.** Another possibility: *Catherine pulled Carl's hand away before it could touch the cup.* **Note:** In both possible answers, *it* clearly refers to *Carl's hand.* Your answer isn't correct if *it* might refer to the hand or the cup (*Before Carl's hand could touch the cup, Catherine pulled it away*).

23 **Although Catherine wanted to help Carl, her action jarred his hand, and the table shook.** Instead of *although,* you can substitute *even though* or *though.*

24 **Catherine and Carl didn't notice that the cup was full.** Another possibility is *Catherine and Carl didn't notice the level of liquid in the cup, which was full.* I like the first version better because it's shorter.

25 **The tea, which was still extremely hot, burned their hands.** This revised version flows smoothly.

26 **Catherine will call her Uncle Larry, who is a burn specialist.** Another possibility: Catherine will call her Uncle Larry because he is a burn specialist.

27 **Carl will call his Uncle Andrew, who is a personal-injury lawyer.** Notice how the clause beginning with *who* tightens up the sentence, eliminating repetition of *Uncle Andrew.*

28 **Realizing that the boss wants the memo immediately, Jesse stops cleaning his teeth and starts typing.** *Realizing . . . immediately* is a participial phrase describing Jesse. *Cleaning* and *typing* are gerunds. **Note:** Your answer may differ. If it's grammatically correct, count yourself right.

29 **Considering retirement but discovering that he still owes a lot of money on his mortgage, Jesse decides to work 50 more years.** Two participles (*considering* and *discovering*) and their objects and descriptions start this sentence off with a bang, and an infinitive phrase (*to work 50 more years*) brings it to a smooth finish.

30 **Despite desperately desiring quality time on a tropical island, Jesse wants to keep his house.** *Desiring* is a gerund acting as the object of the preposition *despite. To keep his house* is an infinitive phrase, acting as the object of the verb *wants.* **Note:** Your answer may differ. If it's grammatically correct, count yourself right.

31 **The bank manager, speaking in a firm voice, points out that Jesse has $.02 in his savings account.** *Speaking in a firm voice* is a participial phrase describing *manager.* **Note:** Your answer may differ. If it's grammatically correct, count yourself right.

32 **Jesse wants to rob a bank, but being an honest man, he will not.** The infinitive phrase *to rob a bank* is the object of the verb *wants. Being an honest man* is a participial phrase describing *he.* **Note:** Your answer may differ. If it's grammatically correct, count yourself right.

(33) **To achieve her goal of luxurious living on a tropical island, the bank manager decides to rob the bank.** *To achieve . . . living* is an infinitive phrase describing the verb *decides. Luxurious living on a tropical island* is a gerund phrase acting as the object of the preposition *of. To rob the bank* is an infinitive phrase acting as direct object of the verb *decides.* **Note:** Your answer may differ. If it's grammatically correct, count yourself right.

(34) **I** In option I, *Green, skintight,* and *stretchy* are all adjectives, single-word descriptions of the *ski pants.* They match, so the sentence is parallel. Option II has two adjectives and a participial phrase *(made of stretch fabric),* so it isn't parallel.

(35) **I** In option I, the compound verbs *(eases, zips)* match. Option II pairs *eases* with *zipping.* Not parallel!

(36) **II** In option II, *as well as* joins *easily* and *forcefully.* They match, and the sentence is parallel. Option I has a paired conjunction, *not only/but also,* which joins *breathe easily* with *forcefully.* One has a verb, *breathe,* and one doesn't, so the sentence isn't parallel.

(37) **II** *Trouble* and *discomfort* match in option II, but *trouble* and *how he feels uncomfortable* break parallel structure.

If you're ready to test your skills a bit more, take the following chapter quiz that incorporates all the chapter topics.

Whaddya Know? Chapter 24 Quiz

Quiz time! Complete each problem to test your knowledge on the various topics covered in this chapter. You can then find the solutions and explanations in the next section.

The questions for the quiz are based on this paragraph, which is full of boring sentences desperately in need of a makeover:

> (a) Darla fainted. (b) Darla lay on the floor. (c) She was in a heap. (d) Her legs were bent under her. (e) She breathed in quick pants at a rapid rate. (f) Henry came to her. (g) He ran as fast as he could. (h) He didn't stop running. (i) He took out his phone but didn't call an ambulance. (j) He checked the baseball score as he ran. (k) His favorite team was in the playoffs. (l) He reached Darla. (m) He gasped. (n) "My angel," he said. (o) His heart was beating fast. (p) He saw that his team was losing. (q) His heart was beating even faster. (r) Henry saw Darla. (s) She was unconscious. (t) She was the love of his life! (u) He grasped her hand. (v) Darla woke up. (w) Henry was overjoyed. (x) He could go home. (y) He could watch the game on his big-screen television. (z) He did not have to feel guilty about leaving Darla.

1 Which is a better revision of sentences (a), (b), and (c)?

I. Fainting, Darla lay on the floor, and she was in a heap.

II. Having fainted, Darla lay on the floor in a heap.

2 Which is a better revision of sentences (d) and (e)?

I. Her legs bent under her, she breathed in quick pants.

II. Her legs bent under her, she breathed quickly, at a rapid rate.

3 Which is a better revision of sentences (f) and (g)?

I. Henry ran to her as fast as he could.

II. Fastest, Henry ran to her.

4 Which is a better revision of sentences (h), (i), (j), and (k)?

I. Not stopping to call an ambulance, Henry took out his phone, checking the baseball score as he ran because he wanted to see how his favorite team was doing in the playoffs.

II. Running, Henry used his phone not to call an ambulance but to see how his favorite baseball team was doing in the playoffs.

5 Which is a better revision of sentences (l), (m), and (n)?

I. "My angel!" Henry gasped on reaching Darla.

II. Reaching Darla, Henry both gasped and he said, "My angel!"

6 Which is a better revision of sentences (o), (p), (q), and (r)?

    I. Henry's heart beat fast when he saw Darla, and his team losing made it even faster!

    II. Fast beat Henry's heart when he saw Darla — even faster when he saw that his team was losing!

7 Which is a better revision of sentences (s), (t), (u), and (v)?

    I. Darla, the love of Henry's life, woke up when he grasped her hand.

    II. When he grasped Darla's hand, the unconscious love of Henry's life woke up.

8 Which is a better revision of sentences (w), (x), (y), and (z)?

    I. Henry was overjoyed and without guilt to go home to watch the game on his big-screen television.

    II. Overjoyed, Henry could go home guiltlessly to watch the game on his big-screen television.

Answers to Chapter 24 Quiz

1 **II** If you read these sentences aloud, you hear that option II sounds more fluid. Also, it makes sense that the fainting happened before Darla lay on the floor. That situation calls for *having fainted,* which places one action before the other. With *fainting,* the actions happen at the same time.

2 **I** *Quick* and *at a rapid rate* are repetitive. Option I combines the ideas smoothly and drops the repetitive portion.

3 **I** Option II is shorter, but it's a little confusing. *Fastest* compared to what — Olympic competitors? Option I gets the point across: Henry is speeding to Darla.

4 **II** You can't check a phone unless you've taken it out, so option II gives the same information as option I, but with less fuss.

5 **I** Option II is wordier, but that's not the only reason option I is better. The paired conjunction *both/and* should connect parallel elements unless you're trying to emphasize a point. In option II, *both* is followed by *gasped* (a verb), but *he said* (a subject-verb pair) follows *and.* With no reason to stress that *he said* something, breaking parallelism doesn't make sense.

6 **II** Option II has an unusual word pattern that suits this dramatic situation. Option I has a grammar problem: Henry's upset about *his team's losing,* not *his team losing.* The original places the emphasis on *team,* but it should be on their performance.

7 **I** Option I gets the point across neatly. If she *woke up,* you know she was unconscious, so there's no need to state the obvious. Option II leaves open the possibility that *Darla* and *the unconscious love of Henry's life* are two different people.

8 **II** Option II is shorter than option I, but all the ideas are present.

7

Grammar in Action

In This Unit . . .

Chapter **25**

Adapting Your Style to Electronic Media

Written communication most likely began with a stick dragged across loose dirt and evolved to fingers tapping on keyboards and screens. Technology is not always a writer's friend, as anyone who's experienced a computer crash can testify. But technology does come with benefits — the ability to write and revise with very little effort and to reach your intended reader in milliseconds, to name just two.

The intersection of grammar and electronic communication can be tricky. Which rules of Standard English apply? Which are impractical or outmoded? Answers to these questions exist — too many answers! Grammarians have been known to fight about, say, punctuation in texts with the passion of soldiers defending their homeland. In this chapter I explain commonly accepted guidelines for writing via electronic media, including texts, tweets, social media posts, blog posts, and presentation slides.

Hitting the Screen with Formal or Informal Language

In Chapter 2, I discuss adapting language to suit your purpose, audience, and message. The same tiered structure applies to electronic media also, with a few added twists:

>> **Friendspeak** is my term for deliberately informal English. Friendspeak, in electronic media, includes abbreviations (*imho* = in my humble opinion, *g2g* = got to go, and so forth) and visuals (emoticons, emojis, stickers, and other picture-communications). Punctuation, in friendspeak, both decreases and increases. Messages often omit periods and commas but pile on exclamation points or question marks (or a combination of the two) to show strong feeling.

WARNING

Be careful with emoticons and emoji (stylized illustrations representing faces, animals, objects, and so forth). Not every reader understands how to decode them, and on a tiny screen, they may not be clear. Put a Thanksgiving turkey leg in your message, and your reader may picture your holiday dinner — or mistake the image for a "Rosie the Riveter" muscled, human arm. Imagine your reader's response to the accompanying message "I ate too much of this!" A sensible approach is to use emoticons to write to friends who are likely to enjoy and decode them accurately. For anything serious, opt for actual words.

>> **Conversational English** is somewhat informal, the casual language used between friends and acquaintances. In texts, tweets, and social media posts, conversational English drops words and various punctuation, and adds other punctuation to show enthusiasm, anger, and other feelings. Conversational English is usually the language of choice for captions or memes or other illustrations on social media sites, and for blogs with an informal tone.

>> **Standard English** takes formality to the max. It respects all the rules and conventions of grammar that educated people hold dear. In professional situations — tweets representing a company or a publication, for example — Standard English is the safest choice.

I've seen texts and tweets written in all three of these general categories, and under the right circumstances I think all of them work well. In deciding which level of formality is appropriate, apply these guidelines:

TIP

>> Consider the identity of the person receiving the message, as well as the medium you're using. If you're dealing with someone who can practically read your mind, Standard English isn't necessary in texts. Ditto for posts to websites that celebrate edginess or rebellion against the rules taught in school — or any sort of rebellion, for that matter.

Before you post, survey the website. Match your level of formality to what you read.

>> The less personal the relationship between writer and reader, the more closely your language and grammar should follow the conventions of Standard English. On social media you may be connected to a huge number of people. When you post, don't assume they'll all understand you as easily as the friends you spend time with in real life. Be careful with abbreviations or usage that only you and your buddies understand.

>> Anything connected with work and academics requires more formality than whatever you do to forget about work and academics. Avoid abbreviations, slang, and broken grammar rules, all of which signal a relaxed attitude.

» Power matters also. If you're the boss, you make the rules. Your subordinates won't point out that you lowercased a word that should be in caps — not if they want to keep working for you! But if your message is moving up the chain of command, bring out your most formal English.

» Think about the impression you're trying to make. If you're writing to a potential client, formal language may show respect and care. On the other hand, if you have an antsy client — the type who wants the work done yesterday, if not sooner — a few dropped words or characters may give the impression that you're speeding along on the client's behalf, too busy for such niceties as commas and periods.

EXAMPLE

Q. Which level of formality suits the situation described? Very informal (VI), somewhat informal (SI), or formal (F)?

email from parents to their children's teachers

text to electrician rewiring your house

post on a website called *Cuz Rock'nRoll Ain't Gone*

A. **F** In an academic situation, formal language signals respect.

SI You're the employer, so you set the tone. Go too casual and the electrician may think it's okay to raid your refrigerator. Opt for extreme formality and you may create an uncomfortable atmosphere.

VI Judging by its name, the website prizes informality.

YOUR TURN

Which level of formality suits the situation described? Very informal (VI), somewhat informal (SI), or formal (F)?

1 direct message to someone who follows you on social media

2 statement to a potential employer, sent via an app that alerts job-seekers to open positions

3 comment on an article in a newspaper, posted on the paper's website

4 email to a classmate you haven't seen recently

5 text from nephew to aunt

6 caption for a photo you posted on social media

Communicating Clearly in Texts, Tweets, and Posts

Short. Fast. Effortless. These are the qualities you want when you text or tweet, compose captions for photos, or post comments on social media. Rather than take your readers on a leisurely stroll through every aspect of a topic, you want to get your message out in as few words as possible.

No matter the medium, one quality must always be present in your work — clarity. Your readers must understand what you mean. If they don't, why bother writing at all? (Yes, I know that photos and videos communicate meaning also, but this is a book about grammar, so the focus is on written expression.)

The good news is that you can be crystal clear even when you're writing with a character limit. (A character, in this context, is a letter, number, symbol, or space.) How? Read on.

Dropping words

The most common shortcut is to drop some words, distilling your message to its essence. As long as your meaning remains intact, any word can be on the chopping block.

Omitting subjects and verbs

The easiest place to start is the subject, the *who* or *what* doing the action or in the state of being that the verb expresses, and the verb itself, especially if it consists of more than one word:

FULL SENTENCE: I will come by bus.

SHORTENED MESSAGE: Will come by bus. Or: Coming by bus.

FULL SENTENCE: I need a ride to the party.

SHORTENED MESSAGE: Need ride to party.

In both examples, the subject dropped from the sentence is *I*. Most readers assume that *I* is the subject in texts and messages. If the subject is not *I*, you probably need to include it to avoid confusion, as these examples illustrate:

FULL SENTENCE: Henry will come with me.

SHORTENED MESSAGE: Will come with me.

READER'S REACTION: *Who* will come with you?

FULL SENTENCE: Shane and Debby need a lift to the party.

SHORTENED MESSAGE: Need a lift to the party.

READER'S REACTION: I thought you were coming by bus. Have your plans changed?

FULL SENTENCE: Mark will bring soda.

SHORTENED MESSAGE: Will bring soda.

READER'S REACTION: You are bringing both wine and soda? That's too much!

Of course, your reader may understand that *Mark will bring soda* if the text is part of a longer exchange, such as this one between Sal and Wendy. Note the full version in parentheses:

SAL'S SHORTENED MESSAGE: Will bring wine. (I will bring wine.)

WENDY'S SHORTENED MESSAGE: Mark? (What will Mark bring?)

SAL'S SHORTENED MESSAGE: Bringing soda. (Mark will bring soda.)

WENDY: Good.

Because *Mark* shows up in the second message, the third line makes sense.

Dropping other words

One evening a friend of mine was worried about her daughter, who was traveling to a party all by herself for the first time. She told her daughter to text when she arrived. This is the message my friend received:

here

The single word communicates everything the parent wants to know, even though no subjects or verbs appear. (It also expresses the teenager's annoyance. Every parent understands that *here* contains an eye roll and this unwritten sentence: "Mom, I'm *fourteen*. Checking in is for *babies*.") A few more examples:

MESSAGE: On bus.

MEANING: I am on the bus.

WHAT IS LEFT OUT: The subject *(I)*, the verb *(am)*, and *the*.

MESSAGE: Traffic jam. Late.

MEANING: I am in a traffic jam. I will be late.

WHAT IS LEFT OUT: In the first sentence, the subject *(I)*, the verb *(am)*, and two other words, *in a*. In the second sentence, the subject *(I)* and verb *(will be)*.

MESSAGE: Meeting horrible.

MEANING: The meeting is (or was) horrible.

WHAT IS LEFT OUT: The verb *is* or *was*, and *the*.

In the last example, the person receiving the message probably knows which meeting you're writing about and whether that meeting is over *(was horrible)* or still going on *(is horrible)*.

Omissions work only when the person you are writing to understands the situation. Suppose that you send this text:

MESSAGE: Sandy sick.

MEANING: Sandy is not at work (or at school or somewhere else) because of illness.

WHAT IS LEFT OUT: The verb *(is)* and the place (work, school, wherever).

If the person reading the message doesn't know where Sandy is supposed to be (or who Sandy is), this message is too vague. A better message in that situation would explain more:

Lab partner out sick. Working alone today.

Articles *(a, an, the)* and conjunctions (words that join, such as *and, or, but,* and so forth) can often be omitted. Just be aware that the resulting message sounds rushed and at times strange. Can you imagine typing, "I went to bar"? Somehow, *the* makes a big difference.

Dropping punctuation and capital letters

In the preceding section, I inserted capital letters, but many people don't bother. If you type

saw helen after the meeting

civilization won't crumble. I like this version better, but I'm a grammarian:

Saw Helen after the meeting.

or

Saw Helen after the meeting

Did you notice that I didn't insert a period at the end of the preceding text? You can, but surveys show that periods at the end of a text are sometimes interpreted as anger. The "send message" button has become the new period, closing the door on a unit of communication. Inserting an actual period can come across as slamming the door.

Don't omit periods needed for clarity within a text message. Compare these two texts:

Come over all cleaned up

Come over. All cleaned up

If I send the first text, I may be asking someone to take a shower and put on freshly laundered clothing before visiting. It's also possible that I'm explaining that I've cleaned up a mess and it's safe to come over. The period clarifies the situation: I filled a dumpster with debris from my living room and vacuumed the floor that was suddenly visible.

End marks can make a difference, though, as you see here:

> TEXT: Walk at 4
>
> MEANING: I am going for a walk at 4.

> TEXT: walk at 4!
>
> MEANING: I'm really looking forward to taking a break and going for a walk at 4.

> TEXT: walk at 4?
>
> MEANING: Would you like to go for a walk at 4? OR Are you going for a walk at 4?

Inserting multiple end marks — two or three question marks and exclamation points to show strong emotion — is fine between friends, but not if you're texting a colleague, teacher, or boss.

Abbreviating

I often receive messages or read social media comments with abbreviations, such as *U* (for *you*) and *L8* (for *late*). *IMHO* (long form = *in my humble opinion*), these shortened forms are generally fine among friends and in informal situations. If you employ an uncommon abbreviation or if you're writing to someone who doesn't spend much time on the internet, the reader may not understand, and *TWBAS*. Confused? *TWBAS* is an abbreviation I just made up. It means "*that would be a shame.*" How could you know what I was *TTS*? (*TTS* is another abbreviation I dreamed up. It stands for *trying to say*.) Before you compose a comment or message, consider your audience and the effect you want to make. If you want to present yourself as an educated person, Standard English is the best choice. If no one's likely to care and everyone's likely to understand, abbreviate as you wish.

EXAMPLE

Q. Which shortened messages, if any, are clear? Assume that you're writing to a co-worker or friend and that your goals are accuracy, clarity, and brevity.

Intended meaning: I don't know what Lola thinks.

(a) Lola's thoughts?

(b) Lola?

(c) Lola thoughts?

A. **(a)** If you're writing to a close friend and you're talking about a comment you just heard or read, option (b) may be enough. I prefer option (a) because it's clear regardless of whether the person receiving the message has been paying strict attention. Option (c) may be understood as "What do you think about Lola?"

YOUR TURN

Which shortened messages, if any, are clear? Assume that you're writing to a co-worker or friend and that your goals are accuracy, brevity, and clarity.

7 Intended meaning: Lola is in jail and needs ten thousand dollars for bail money. She was arrested for driving without a license. She needs your help.

(a) 10K L in jail help

(b) Lola jail 10000! help!

(c) fyi: Lola in jail. Driving w/o license. Needs 10K bail. Help!

8 Intended meaning: Her lawyer is hopeful that Lola will be sentenced to probation and community service.

(a) Hope prob and cs

(b) Lawyer hopeful for probation + community service

(c) sentence probation and community serv fingers Xd lawyer

9 Intended meaning: Lulu will visit Lola as soon as possible. Lulu will probably arrive at the jail around noon.

(a) 12 L to L

(b) Lulu > Lola asap 12?

(c) Lulu to visit Lola asap, probably 12 p.m.

10 Intended meaning: The bad news for Lola is that the judge, Larry Saunders, was once flattened by a motorcycle. He's bitter and will probably give Lola the maximum penalty because she was riding a motorcycle when she was arrested.

(a) Judge Saunders bad news for Lola b/c bitter about motorcycles after his own accident. Top penalty probable

(b) JS = bad news bitter cycles top penalty

(c) Judge S not good motorcycle accident jail ∧

11 Intended meaning: Lola claimed that her license had been shredded when she washed her jeans.

(a) Lola claimed license shredded in wash

(b) License shredded wash

(c) Claimed license shredded in washing machine

12 Intended meaning: Will you attend the press conference when Lola is released?

(a) Press conference?

(b) Attend press conference on release?

(c) You going to press conference on L's release?

Emailing Your Way to Good Grammar

At least once a week someone informs me that email is "old-fashioned." Maybe so, but it's still a valuable and much-used method of communication. Therefore, you should know how to compose an acceptable email.

The heading

The *heading* is the little box that includes the From, To, and Subject lines. You don't have to worry about the proper format of the To and From boxes. The To line contains the name connected with the email address of the recipient, and the email program automatically slots your name into the From line.

The *subject line* is the title of the email — the line that tells the reader what you're writing about. Check out these key points about subject lines:

>> **Be sure to include a subject line in the email.** With no subject line, the person receiving your email may ignore it. The time you spent writing the email will then be wasted. Also, the subject line begins the conversation with the reader, establishing what the reader should expect.

>> **Make the subject line short and clear.** You want to get the point across, but you don't want the reader to turn away before checking the message. *Why You Should Hire Me to Manage Your Business* is too long. *Hiring* is too short. *Applying for Management Position* is clear and may spark interest.

>> **Capitalize the subject line as if it were a title.** This practice is not always necessary. Some people choose to capitalize the first word of the subject line and nothing else. If you do treat the subject line as a title, be sure to do so correctly. (Chapter 21 explains everything you need to know about capitalizing titles.)

>> **Update the subject line in later emails.** You can leave the same subject line in every reply, but sometimes an update is helpful. Suppose you're replying to an email asking about the repairs. The original subject line might be "Status of Repairs?" or similar wording. Changing the subject line to "Repairs Completed" gives immediate and important information.

The greeting

Time being a precious resource, many email writers skip the greeting and go directly to the message. No problem, unless you happen to be writing to traditionalists, who prefer the time-honored formats, or egotists, who love seeing their names in print. A message without a greeting may seem informal (okay for friends) or cold (not okay for potential customers). If you do include a greeting (in English-teacher terminology, a *salutation*), you have several choices. These are all acceptable greetings, complete with punctuation:

Dear Ms. Snodgrass, or **Dear Ms. Snodgrass:** The one with the comma is less formal. Begin the message on the following line.

Hi, Lola. or **Hi Lola.** Use these forms for friends and acquaintances. Begin the message right after the period, not on the next line. Most people omit the comma — a good example of how language standards evolve. Because technically you're addressing *Lola*, traditional punctuation rules specify that a comma separate her name from the rest of the sentence. In an email, either is acceptable.

Hi, Lola! or **Hi Lola!** This one is for friends only. Begin the message right after the exclamation point. The comma is optional, as I explain in the preceding point.

Lola, Informal messages need nothing more than the name. The message begins on the following line.

Snodgrass, This greeting can be a bit stern, as if you couldn't be bothered with the *Dear*. Start the message one line below this greeting.

Hi, everyone. or **Hi everyone!** Use these when you write to a group of friends or colleagues. Begin the message on the same line.

The body

The body contains what you want to communicate — words, links to websites, photos or videos, whatever. Don't try to mimic the indentations and line spacing of mailed-in-envelopes letters. What you're seeing on your screen isn't necessarily what readers see on theirs. Concentrate on complying with the conventions of Standard English, matching your level of formality to the identity of the person you're writing to. (See "Hitting the Screen with Formal or Informal Language," earlier in this chapter, for more information.)

TIP

If you truly care about how the document looks, you can attach the message as a PDF file — a "picture" of your document. I should point out that your recipient may not open the file for fear of unleashing a computer virus, so if you choose this option, call or text the recipient first.

The closing

If you haven't bothered with a greeting (which I explain a little earlier in this chapter), don't worry about a closing either, unless you want to "sign" your name at the end of the message. If you like a big send-off, try one of these:

Best, (short for "best regards" and good for formal and informal emails)

Sincerely, (formal)

See you soon, (informal)

Hope to hear from you, (somewhere between formal and informal)

Regards, (formal and a little old-fashioned)

TIP

All the preceding closings contain commas. You can also close your message by simply typing your name (*Lola* or *Ms. Snodgrass*) or with your initials (*LS* for "Lola Snodgrass"), in which case no commas are needed.

Q. Examine the underlined portion of this email and label it "correct" (C) or "incorrect" (I).

From: Mary Jones, Main Street Auto Repair

To: Carl Berger

CC: Alan Smith

Subject: <u>repairs Completed</u>

A. **I** The first word of the subject should be capitalized.

Examine the underlined portions of this email and label them "correct" (C) or "incorrect" (I).

13 <u>Dear Mr. Berger</u>

Your car repairs have been completed. Please call our service manager, Alan Smith, to arrange delivery. 14 <u>Thanx</u> for entrusting your business to 15 <u>Main Street Auto Repair</u>.

16 <u>best,</u>

17 <u>Mary Jones</u>

18 <u>assistant Manager</u>

PowerPoint to the People

When you present information to business colleagues or classmates, you may be a bit nervous. In the old days, you'd probably work from index cards and illustrations printed on actual pieces of paper. (That's one reason the "good old days" weren't always good, by the way.) Now you have presentation software to help you organize and illustrate your ideas and research. PowerPoint, Prezi, Keynote, and similar computer programs give you the ability to create a series of slides containing text and visuals — charts, graphs, diagrams, photos, and the like. The information is organized and accessible. All you have to do is speak a little about each slide as it flashes in front of the audience. Oh, and follow some simple grammar rules. (You knew there was a catch, right?) In this section, I tell you everything you need to know about proper presentation slides.

If you're not making an oral presentation, you may still find useful material in this section. The format for bullet points remains the same whether those points are on a ten-foot screen or a standard sheet of paper. Check out "Biting the bulleted list," later in this chapter, for more information.

Surveying presentation slides

Presentation slides come in many varieties, and a few elements appear in most. Here's a sample presentation slide in the most common format:

Title

Introduction

- Bullet point
- Bullet point
- Bullet point

As you see in the sample presentation slide, a list follows the introduction. A *bullet point* — punctuation that marks the beginning of every item on the list — is a key element of a presentation slide. Bullet points may be check marks, circles, arrows, or other designs.

The sample presentation slide has three bullet points. You may have two, four, or more. (You can't have just one bullet point, though.) In a real presentation, a slide may also feature links to video clips and other visual elements (charts, photos, drawings, graphs, and so on). Some individual slides have titles.

TIP

A title may take the place of an introduction. Then your slide looks like this.

Title

- Bullet point
- Bullet point
- Bullet point

I centered the title, but you may place the title elsewhere.

WARNING

Avoid slides with bullet points but no title or introductory phrase. The audience will wonder what the list is about. If people are wondering, they aren't listening! You want the audience to look at the slide *and* hear what you're saying.

In the following sections, I walk you through each element of a presentation slide.

Writing titles

Every presentation has a focus, the topic you're explaining. A phrase stating that focus is the *title* of the presentation. Within the presentation, the main topic divides into subtopics. Each subtopic may have a title also.

A good title fits like a tailored suit. It's not too big — something so general that it mystifies your audience. Nor should the title be too narrow, covering only a portion of your presentation.

A good title refers to everything you're going to say and nothing more. Here's an example of a presentation with good and not-so-good titles:

CONTENT: Information on Germany's industry and trade, including statistics about the auto industry and general manufacturing, estimates of economic growth, and possible trouble spots

TOO-BIG TITLE: Germany: Facts and Figures

WHY IT'S TOO BIG: A presentation with this title might be about population growth, land area, climate, education, and many other aspects.

TOO-NARROW TITLE: Germany's Auto Industry

WHY IT'S TOO NARROW: Part of the presentation concerns the auto industry, but not all.

JUST-RIGHT TITLE: Germany's Current and Future Economy

WHY IT'S JUST RIGHT: Industry and trade are part of the economy, as are the auto industry and general manufacturing. The "Current and Future" part of the title takes into account "economic growth" and "possible trouble spots."

Check out one more example:

CONTENT: Examination of the reign of Tutankhamun, a ruler in ancient Egypt, including his associates and family, the change in religion during his reign, his early death, theories about the cause of his death, the discovery of his tomb in the 1920s, and public interest in his life and times.

TOO-BIG TITLE: Ancient Egypt

WHY IT'S TOO BIG: The presentation deals with Tutankhamun, one ruler of ancient Egypt. The title "Ancient Egypt" could cover thousands of years and discuss the daily life of ordinary people, other rulers, foreign relations, art, and many other topics.

TOO-NARROW TITLE: How Tutankhamun Died

WHY IT'S TOO NARROW: This title ignores associates, family, religion, and the discovery of Tutankhamun's tomb.

JUST-RIGHT TITLE: Tutankhamun: Life and Legacy

WHY IT'S JUST RIGHT: Tutankhamun's "life" includes his associates and family, the change in religion, and his death. His "legacy" takes into account his tomb, its discovery, and public interest.

When you place the presentation title on a slide, follow these guidelines:

>> **The title appears on the first slide.** Usually, the title is alone or accompanied by photos or other types of illustration. It may be centered or placed so that it balances the visual material. Save the supporting text for other slides.

>> **Capitalize the important words in the title.** Important words are nouns, verbs, and descriptions. Unimportant words — such as *a, an, the, to, from,* and *by* — should not be capitalized. (For more information on capitalizing titles, turn to Chapter 21.)

>> **Don't enclose the title in quotation marks.** Because the title stands alone, it stands out! Quotation marks identify titles within a paragraph. You don't need them when the title is all by itself.

>> **Don't place a period at the end of a title.** If the title is a question, a question mark appears at the end of the title.

Individual slides may have titles also. The title of a slide, like the title of the presentation as a whole, should refer to all the information on the slide and follow the guidelines in the preceding bullet points.

EXAMPLE

Q. Correct any errors you see in this title.

"Learning two languages: benefits and challenges"

Q. **Learning Two Languages: Benefits and Challenges** Remove the quotation marks and capitalize the important words.

Correct any errors you see in these titles.

YOUR TURN

19 Our Class Trip to Peru.

20 The Care And Feeding Of Canaries And Parakeets

21 "Annual Budget for Springfield School System"

22 Advantages of Investing in Bonds

Biting the bulleted list

A bullet is an important punctuation mark that introduces each item in a list. A bulleted list has two parts, the introduction and the bullet texts.

Bullet introductions

If the introduction to your bulleted list is a complete thought, end it with a colon, as in these sample introductions:

Fleas divert themselves with many exercises:

Fleas' favorite pastimes are varied:

If the introduction to a bulleted list is not a complete thought, don't place any punctuation mark at the end of the introduction. Check out these examples:

Fleas love to play with

Fleas' pet peeves are

If the introduction line ends with a linking verb as in the second example, no punctuation follows the verb. See Chapter 5 for more information on linking verbs.

These guidelines make sense. If the introduction is not a complete sentence, the bullets finish the thought. So why would you interrupt with a period? If the introduction is a sentence, the colon indicates that more information is coming. (Turn to Chapter 20 for more about colons.)

If the introduction line leads to a series of quotations, place a comma at the end, as in these examples:

> Simon Flea always says,
>
> The flea trainer explains,

Q. Correct any errors you see in this introduction to a bulleted list.

Fundraising will be the responsibility of several organizations

A. **Fundraising will be the responsibility of several organizations:** This introduction is a complete sentence, so it should be followed by a colon.

Correct any errors you see in these introductions.

23 The fundraiser is:

24 The Marketing Campaign Will Appear In

25 Seven media outlets will participate.

26 Why do we need a fundraiser?:

27 Careers requiring college degrees include the following:

Bullet texts

The text for each bullet point is usually fairly short — sometimes just one or two words and sometimes a bit more. Follow these guidelines in writing bullet points:

>> If the text is a complete sentence, begin with a capital letter and end with a period. If the sentence is a question, end with a question mark. You may also end a bullet statement with an exclamation point, but in a business or academic setting, this punctuation may be too casual.

>> If the text isn't a complete sentence, don't use any end marks. You may capitalize the first word of each bullet point, but most people prefer lowercase, especially if the introduction line isn't a complete sentence. Whatever style you choose, be consistent. Don't write half of your bullet points with capital letters and half with lowercase.

>> Each bullet point on a slide or in a list should have the same grammatical identity. If the first bullet point is a complete sentence, all the bullet points should be complete sentences.

If you've begun one bullet point with a noun, begin all of them with nouns. Here's a before-and-after bullet list, illustrating a common mistake and its correction:

INCORRECT

o table tennis

o playing air guitar

o to swing from a trapeze

CORRECT

o table tennis

o air guitar

o trapeze swinging

This grammatical principle is called *parallelism*. (For more information on parallelism, check out Chapter 24.)

WARNING

Many presentations, especially in the academic world, require a slide listing sources (books, websites, articles, films, and so forth). Sources are formatted differently from just about everything else on the planet. You can find out more in *College Research Papers For Dummies*, by Joseph J. Giampalmi (Wiley), or you can check any of the many websites devoted to source citation, including www.mla.org and www.apa.org.

EXAMPLE

Q. The following sample "slide" is from a presentation without capital letters and punctuation. Underneath is a list of corrections. Select all the corrections needed to create a grammatically correct slide.

parakeet hobbies

- bowling

- they like to toss seeds

- hang-gliding

(A) Capitalize *Parakeet*.

(B) Capitalize *Hobbies*.

(C) Change the second bullet to *toss seeds*.

(D) Change the second bullet to *seed-tossing*.

A. **(A), (B), (D)** Capitalize both words of the title. The second bullet doesn't match the other two. Of the two possible changes, (D) is better because it matches the *-ing* verb form of the other two bullets.

Select all the corrections needed to create a grammatically correct slide.

---

parakeets need the following items for bowling

- three-toed bowling shoes

- beak-adapted bowling balls

- featherweight pins

(A) Capitalize *Parakeets*.

(B) Place a comma at the end of the first line of the slide.

(C) Place a colon at the end of the first line of the slide.

(D) Place a period at the end of each bullet point.

---

the best-selling bowling shoes for parakeets have

- they have room for overgrown claws

- most are in brightly colors

- many include a complimentary seed stick

- they have clips rather than laces

(A) Capitalize *The*.

(B) Place a colon at the end of the first line.

(C) Place a period at the end of each bullet point.

(D) Change bullet points to *overgrown claws, bright colors, complimentary seed stick,* and *clips rather than laces.*

> most prominent parakeet bowlers are
>
> - able to think on their feet (claws)
>
> - sponsored by well-known pet food companies
>
> - active only for five or six years

(A) Capitalize *Most.*

(B) Place a colon after *are.*

(C) Capitalize the first word of each bullet point.

(D) Place a period at the end of each bullet point.

31

> history of parakeet bowling
>
> - the sport began in the 15th century
>
> - early bowlers used apples to knock down corn stalks
>
> - first professional tour — 1932

(A) Capitalize every word in the title except for *of.*

(B) Capitalize the first word in each bullet point.

(C) Place a period at the end of each bullet point.

(D) Change the last bullet point to *The first professional tour took place in 1932.*

Autocorrect and Other Error Magnets

When you're writing with pen and paper, only your brain and hand are involved. When you're working on an electronic device, however, computer code enters the picture. You should proofread carefully before you hit Send when you're emailing or texting and before you display a presentation slide on a screen. Why? Read on.

Text prediction programs suggest the most likely word after you type one or two letters, based on what other people have written. Sometimes the device proposes an entire word before you hit even a single letter, because the computer program links that word with the one preceding it. If I type *loo*, for example, the screen offers *look, looking*, and *looks*. After I hit *looking*, the program suggests *forward*. These shortcuts are terrific, but it's far too easy to hit the wrong spot on the screen — what some people call "fat finger" mistakes.

Autocorrect — a program that is supposed to find errors and fix them without your input — can also be a problem. I once texted my husband that I was "heading home on CPW," referring to a street named Central Park West. The text he received was "heading home on a cow." He knew I was on a bus, not an animal, because not many herds of cattle roam around New York City, where I live. He didn't know where I was, though, because he couldn't make a logical connection between "cow" and "Central Park West." And at least that's an innocent substitution. Some autocorrects aren't. A quick internet search for **auto correct fails** will show you exactly how bad things can get. (*Hint:* Really, really bad. X-rated! Be careful!)

Speech-to-text programs, which convert what you say to your phone into written words on the screen, have improved quite a bit in recent years. Unfortunately, improvement isn't perfection. You may say, "I kneaded bread" and end up with "eye needed bread."

Practice Questions Answers and Explanations

1. **SI or F** You don't necessarily know your followers, so very informal writing is not a good idea. Choosing between the other two levels of formality depends on why you're being followed. If you write about serious topics, formal language emphasizes that your ideas deserve attention. If your followers love you because you post adorable videos of baby animals, somewhat informal writing may emphasize the relaxing, fun aspect of your web page.

2. **F** If it's a job, it's important enough to bring out your most formal language.

3. **F** A newspaper comment is public, and people who don't know you may read it. Present your most educated language if you want to be taken seriously.

4. **SI** If you haven't seen the classmate recently, a somewhat formal message is a safe bet.

5. **SI** To make the best choice, think about the closeness of the relationship. There's a power imbalance, but there's also a family tie. The middle ground seems appropriate, but if the aunt and nephew are comfortable joking around with each other, informal language is fine.

6. **SI** If you're too formal, people may stop reading, because they go to social media to relax. If only close friends will see the post, however, informal language is appropriate.

7. **(C)** Options (A) and (B) have cut out too much. Did Lola steal $10,000? Could be, the way these texts read. Option (C) clarifies the situation. The abbreviation *FYI* ("for your information") is standard, as is *w/o* ("without") and *K* ("thousand"). The last sentence is clearly a plea for bail money.

8. **(B)** Option (B) gets the job done. I wouldn't mind cutting the *for*, but with that word the message sounds a little more respectable (not like Lola). The plus sign could also be an ampersand (&) or the word *and*. Options (A) and (C) aren't clear. What's *cs? Prob?* I made up the abbreviations, so anyone receiving this message isn't likely to understand. In option (C), whose fingers are crossed — the texter's or the lawyer's?

9. **(C)** Option (C) is short, but not too short. The standard abbreviation for "as soon as possible" is *ASAP*, but you don't really need the capital letters here. You could also cut P.M. from the message, if you wish, as it's unlikely that a jail would allow visitors at midnight. Option (A) is vague, and (B) uses the greater-than (>) math symbol in an attempt to show that Lulu's going to visit Lola. Too far out for clarity!

10. **(A)** Option (A) is clear. The abbreviation *b/c* ("because") is standard, though you wouldn't use it for formal writing. Notice that I deleted the verbs because the meaning comes through without them. I also substituted *top penalty probable* for the longer *will probably give Lola the maximum penalty*. The other options need CIA code-breakers.

11. **(A)** In option (A), you have all the information you need at half the length. Option (B) has shed too many words. Option (C) is tempting, and if you know your reader well, it might be fine. Because three people are involved in the story (the judge, Lola, and the texter), I prefer option (A), which names Lola.

12. **(C)** The shorter options don't work, because three people (the judge, Lola, and the texter) are possibilities. Only (C) supplies enough words to clarify the situation.

13. **I** You need a comma or a colon at the end of this greeting line.

14. **I** The email has a formal tone, which is exactly what you want in a business communication. *Thanx* is nonstandard. Substitute *Thanks*.

(15) **C** The name of the business is properly presented here.

(16) **I** Capitalize *Best*.

(17) **C** The employee's name is appropriate here.

(18) **I** Capitalize *Assistant*.

(19) **Our Class Trip to Peru** Remove the period.

(20) **The Care and Feeding of Canaries and Parakeets** Place unimportant words within the title (*and, of, and*) in lowercase.

(21) **Annual Budget for Springfield School System** Don't enclose a title in quotation marks.

(22) **correct** Everything works here: no extra punctuation, and capital letters for the important words.

(23) **The fundraiser is** Remove the colon because the introduction ends with a linking verb.

(24) **The marketing campaign will appear in** Capitalize only the first letter of the first word.

(25) **Seven media outlets will participate:** Use a colon instead of a period.

(26) **Why do we need a fundraiser?** Remove the colon because the introduction ends with a question mark.

(27) **correct** The introductory statement is a complete sentence, so a colon is appropriate.

(28) **(A), (C)** Because the introductory statement is a complete sentence, it should begin with a capital letter (option A) and end with a colon, which indicates that a list follows (option C). A comma shouldn't introduce a bulleted list. The bullet points aren't complete sentences, so no periods are necessary.

(29) **(A), (D)** The first word of the introductory statement needs a capital letter (option A). No punctuation follows *have* because the statement isn't a complete sentence (options B and C). In the original list, each item is a complete sentence, so they don't combine well with the introductory statement. *The best bowling shoes for parakeets have they have room* — nope, I don't think so. The bullets should be *room for overgrown claws, bright colors, complimentary seed sticks,* and *clips rather than laces* (option D).

(30) **(A)** Did I catch you with this one? No punctuation is needed in the first line because *are* doesn't complete the introductory sentence. Nor should you capitalize any of the bullet points, as they complete the sentence begun by the introductory statement. Option (D) is tempting, but you have three half sentences, one in each bullet point, all connected to the introductory line. Placing three periods doesn't make sense. Some grammarians recommend a semicolon after each bullet point, with a period after the last. This is somewhat stuffy. My recommendation is no punctuation at all after the bullet points. The only change is a capital *M* for the first word in the introductory sentence (option A).

(31) **(A), (B), (C), (D)** This slide has a title, and titles need capital letters. The first two bullet points are complete sentences, so the third should match.

If you're ready to test your skills a bit more, take the following chapter quiz that incorporates all the chapter topics.

Whaddya Know? Chapter 25 Quiz

Correct or incorrect? Consider context and medium as you answer.

1 Subject line of an email sent by a soccer coach to a player's father:

less aggression more skill

2 Text response from player's father to soccer coach:

UR wrong!!!!! kids xtra skilled

3 line from a post on the website "Youth Soccer," written by the soccer coach:

Studies show that parents prioritize aggressive play over skill development.

4 Slide from a presentation given by a soccer referee at the end of the season to an audience of parents and players:

> **Season Statistics for Springfield Sockets**
>
> - 266 goals (average 13.3 per game)
> - 17 injuries (2 players, 6 parents, 4 coaches, 5 referees)
> - 4–16 won–lost record (interleague games)

5 Slide from a presentation given by a soccer mom to the Parents' Booster Club:

> **Benefits of Youth Soccer**
>
> - College admissions officers react positively.
> - Team spirit
> - Children are out of the house several times a week.

6 Line from an email from school principal to the Parents' Booster Club:

"Less fighting, more delighting" is the motto of our sports program, which I'm sure you'll agree does not benefit from negative press reports about spectators' attacks on the referees.

7 Text from one player to another:

my mom and urs fighting!!! ROFL!!!!

8 Comment on newspaper website about an article entitled "Local Woman Arrested in Soccer Brawl":

This is a non-story totally blown out of proportion by parents of players on the other team. One owns this newspaper. Just saying.

9 Caption for a photo of a fistfight, posted on social media:

parents :(

10 Email sent by the parent in the photo to the manager of the social media site:

My attorneys assure me that you are liable for any damage to my reputation caused by that photo.

Answers to Chapter 25 Quiz

1. **incorrect** The subject line should be capitalized. Also, the tone is a bit argumentative and the wording vague.

2. **incorrect** A parent writing to a professional (in this case, a coach) should write more formally. Abbreviations such as *UR* and *xtra* are out of place, as are four of the five exclamation points.

3. **correct** I don't know whether the study is correct (I made it up), but the sentence is correct in Standard English, a good choice for someone who wants to make a convincing argument.

4. **correct** Everything on this slide, except for the statistics (which would be appalling if they were real) is correct.

5. **incorrect** Bullet points should match grammatically. The first and third bullet points are complete sentences, but the second is not. Change it to "Team spirit builds character" or similar wording.

6. **correct** A school official should write in Standard English when communicating with parents. That's the case here, so this one is correct.

7. **correct** The language is correct (not necessarily the sentiment or the fight that provoked it). In peer-to-peer texts, there's no need for Standard English. *ROFL*, in case you didn't know, means "rolling on the floor laughing."

8. **incorrect** I won't address the question of whether the writer should make accusations in a comment thread. Instead, I focus on the language. The first sentence is formal, and the last isn't. Consistency matters!

9. **incorrect** The tone of this caption would be fine for a text or email between friends, but social media draws a wide audience and merits somewhat more formal language.

10. **correct** If you're threatening to sue, opt for Standard English.

Chapter 26

Writing at School and on the Job

U nless you're the ruler of the entire world, you have a boss. At school, your boss is a teacher or a professor. At work, your boss is, well, the boss! Writing done for an authority figure requires proper English. Plus, when you're writing at school or on the job, you must conform to additional standards — traditions built up over the years.

Chapter 25 focuses on the media you use for writing — specifically, electronic media (texts, tweets, email, and slide presentations). In this chapter, I turn the spotlight on content and form, showing you how to master the most common types of school and workplace writing. Mastering these will help you achieve better grades or perhaps a promotion and a higher salary.

A Is for Accomplished: Writing at School

It happens every school day, sometimes more than once a day. Your teacher assigns a report, an essay, a research paper, or a similar document. You sigh and wonder, "How long until vacation?" No one likes homework. But grasping the *conventions* — the basic format of assignments — can make writing them easier.

Essays and research papers

An *essay* is a written discussion of an idea. Usually, an essay expresses a point of view — your opinion on the topic or the conclusion you've drawn from the information you presented in the essay. A *research paper* generally includes information (ideas, opinions, statistics) that you gathered from books, articles, and websites. A research paper may express your own view on the subject or simply present a neutral overview of the topic. In this section are some guidelines for writing these works.

TIP

Businesspeople write research papers, too, but in the business world, these papers are generally called *reports*. Every guideline you see here applies to both academic papers and business reports.

Formal writing

Essays and research papers are formal. Slang words, a conversational tone, and most abbreviations have no place in these assignments. (You may use abbreviations attached to dates, such as *A.D.* or *C.E.* in formal papers. Both abbreviations refer to the modern or "common" era.) When you're writing an essay or a research paper, pretend that you're arguing a case before a judge or lecturing a group of scholars. The level of formality you'd use in a courtroom or lecture hall is your goal. Take a look at some acceptable and unacceptable sentences for this type of assignment:

> UNACCEPTABLE SENTENCE: The plot is kind of complicated, with too much stuff to keep track of.

> BETTER SENTENCE: With a complicated plot, the novel challenges the reader to keep track of events.

> WHY IT'S BETTER: In the first version, *kind of* and *stuff* are too informal. The wording in the second sentence is more mature.

> UNACCEPTABLE SENTENCE: The general ordered his troops to attack very late in the battle. Big mistake! Lots of soldiers died.

> BETTER SENTENCE: Because the general waited until late in the battle to order an attack, many soldiers died.

> WHY IT'S BETTER: *Big mistake* and *lots of* are too informal. Also, the fact that soldiers died shows the mistake. The writer does not have to say *big mistake*.

> UNACCEPTABLE SENTENCE: This painting is all about color, a ton of color, and nothing else but color.

> BETTER SENTENCE: The distinctive characteristic of this painting is its color.

> WHY IT'S BETTER: The original version repeats *color* and tries to be cute. Academic writing should be more formal.

Q. Which sentence(s) would be appropriate for an academic or business report?

(A) A great change in family finances has long-term effects.

(B) The effects of a large increase or decrease in family income may last for years.

(C) neither

(D) both

A. (D) Both sentences make a clear point without slang or casual language, so both are acceptable.

Identifying others' ideas

Robbing a bank is a crime. Stealing someone else's ideas is also a crime in the academic world (and sometimes in the business world, too). This crime, *plagiarism,* is a serious offense. Luckily, you can stay on the right side of the law by crediting your sources. You can do so in several different ways.

If you insert someone else's exact words into your own writing, you must be sure that the reader knows you're quoting. Place quotation marks around short quotations and insert them into the text. Take a look at these examples:

> Economist Joan Smith noted, "The economic downturn has led to lowered expectations for a better future and contributed to a rise in crime."

> According to Smith, the trade agreement signed last year "damaged many parts of the economy," bringing hardship to a large number of people.

> "Unemployment for factory workers will not improve for at least five years," she added.

> She claims that the job market is "at crisis level in nearly every area of the country."

The quotation marks tell you what Joan Smith said. If you leave them out, your reader assumes that you linked a bad economy to the crime rate, discovered the consequences of the trade agreement, and analyzed the job market. But you didn't do these things. Joan Smith did. (Joan Smith is just an example, not a real person. Nor is the information about the economy, trade agreement, and job market real.)

As you see in these examples, the quotation may appear at the beginning of the sentence, at the end, or even in the middle. (For more information on punctuating and capitalizing quotations, turn to Chapter 18.)

Quotations that are longer than three lines should be indented from the left margin so that they resemble a block of text. Take a look at this example, which is not from a real source but is something I created just for you:

> Historian Alex Johnson has attempted to determine why the trial attracted so much attention. In *The Trial of Martha Martin,* he writes:
>
>> Some see sexism and the narrow roles assigned to women as the cause. However, economic gain is a more likely reason the media covered the trial

in great detail. All the major television networks sent representatives, and thousands of words appeared in traditional newspapers and magazines. Millions followed the trial on various websites. All these media outlets bring in millions of dollars in advertising money.

Statistics provided by the Advertising Council support Johnson's view. In 2024, rates for social media pop-up ads . . . [The text continues here.]

TIP

Notice that the block quotation isn't surrounded by quotation marks. The blocking takes the place of that punctuation.

If you aren't directly quoting someone else's words in your paper, you may still have to give credit. Information and ideas that are not your own must be identified, even if you change the wording. If you explain Rebecca Dunne's ideas about the Salem witch trials, for example, you must give credit to Rebecca Dunne. (Rebecca Dunne is not a real person. This name is just an example to illustrate the point.) When you mention statistics, identify the person supplying the statistics. You may identify the source in the text ("Rebecca Dunne believes that . . .") or in footnotes or parentheses.

TIP

Sometimes no name is available for a source. Instead, all you know is the name of the organization (the Advertising Council, perhaps). In this situation, give credit to the organization.

Teachers usually ask you to identify the source of a quotation, an idea, or information in a citation. A *citation* is a footnote, a note at the end of a chapter, or a reference in parentheses inserted into the text. Additional information about each source appears in a *bibliography* or source list at the end of the paper or essay. Several systems for formatting citations and bibliographies exist, and every teacher has a favorite. So does every subject area. Before you write, ask which system your teacher prefers. Then check the internet or a reference book for the format, or use a computer program that automatically formats your citation and bibliography according to your teacher's preferred system.

For a longer discussion of research papers and citations, you may want to take a look at *College Research Papers For Dummies,* by Joseph J. Giampalmi (Wiley, 2023).

REMEMBER

Without identifying the source, the reader will think that the idea or information comes directly from you. Give credit where credit is due.

Other formatting issues

Your essay or research paper should have a title. Some teachers don't require this step, but a title helps you focus your ideas. For a long essay or for a research paper, place the title on a separate page. For a short piece of writing, center the title at the top of the page. Don't place quotation marks around the title.

When you write an English, history, or art paper, capitalize all the important words. Place unimportant words — *a, an, the,* and so on — in lowercase. Follow the same system for titles of other works that you mention within your paper. The title of an article should be inside quotation marks. Titles of full-length works (novels, nonfiction books, plays, and so on) should be italicized or underlined.

The title of a science paper, or titles within a science paper, follow different rules, which I explain in a later section "Science reports."

Verb tense also matters when you write an essay or a research paper. In general, use past tense for history papers, except for events that are still going on. Take a look at these examples. The past tense verbs are underlined:

> Rosa Parks <u>was</u> a civil rights activist who <u>played</u> an important role in the Montgomery bus boycott.

> Alexander Fleming <u>discovered</u> penicillin in 1928.

> Julius Caesar <u>was</u> a Roman general and statesman whose victories <u>extended</u> the territory of the Roman Empire to modern Britain and Germany.

If you write about a work of literature or art, present tense is best. Why? The work doesn't change. Every time you open the book or look at the painting, the experience begins anew. Here are some examples, with the present tense verbs underlined:

> Hamlet <u>kills</u> Polonius by accident.

> In Goya's painting, two women <u>stand</u> on a balcony.

> The poet <u>calls</u> darkness "comforting" and "tender."

EXAMPLE

Q. Is the format acceptable or unacceptable? The information in parentheses identifies the element of the essay or paper.

"The Role of the Unreliable Narrator" (title, centered on a line above an essay)

A. **unacceptable** Centered titles should not be placed in quotation marks.

YOUR TURN

Is the format acceptable or unacceptable? The information in parentheses identifies the element of the essay or paper.

1. Henry Peters said, The war illustrated the limitations of troops fighting without proper equipment. (sentence in a research paper)

2. The Dow-Jones Industrial Average is, according to the many economists, the most important indicator of the health of the economy. (sentence from an essay for an economics class)

3. The artist believed that his art was unique, but Arthur Bombech and other experts have identified many influences on his personal style. (sentence from a research paper about a sculptor)

4. "Comic Art in France: A Survey" (title of a research paper, alone on a title page)

5. Jay Gatsby, the title character in Fitzgerald's *The Great Gatsby*, was in love with Daisy. (sentence from an essay for English class)

Science reports

If you're writing a science research paper based on reading articles published by others, the guidelines in the earlier section "Essays and research papers" are mostly the same. One exception is the capitalization of titles. The title of the paper, as well as any titles referred to within the paper, are capitalized in *sentence style*. Only the first word of the title, the first word of the subtitle (if there is one), and proper names are capitalized. Everything else is in lowercase. Here are some examples:

Pneumonia risk in newborns: The influence of nutrition

Population growth of *Orcinus orca* in Puget Sound, 1950–2020

Desert and alpine flora in California: A comparative study

Science has its own system — actually, a couple of systems — for source citations. Ask the teacher or professor about their preferred system and then consult the appropriate website or handbook. Or download an app (computer program) that will do the formatting for you.

From middle school through graduate school, most science courses involve doing lab work — experiments — and writing lab reports. Your teacher or professor may give you a sample lab report and ask you to format your own work in the same way. (If you don't receive a sample, ask for one!) Science lab reports vary somewhat, but a few rules apply to all.

References to others' experiments

Some lab reports begin with a summary of others' work in the same field. If you refer to the titles of scientific papers in your lab report, use sentence style, described earlier in this section. Capitalize the first word of the title of the report, as well as the first word of the subtitle (if the report has one). Capitalize proper names. Everything else appears in lowercase (non-capitals).

Generally, you don't need to quote directly from someone else's scientific paper. Scientists want the information, but the exact words aren't important. Summarize or state the information in your own words. Be sure to credit the source.

Dates are another important element in lab reports. Science constantly moves forward, extending or correcting theories as new information appears. When you refer to someone else's experiment or theory, you should supply the date. The reader then understands how current the information is. Most scientists prefer the date to appear in this order: day-month-year, or, if no day is given, month-year. No commas appear within the date. Here are a few examples of dates in the scientific style:

10 May 1999

26 August 2014

June 2015

If you do not know the day or the month, or if that information isn't relevant, simply write the year.

Q. Which format(s) would be acceptable in a science report?

(A) 15 June 2025

(B) June 15, 2025

(C) both

(D) neither

A. **(A)** Dates in a science report are written without commas. The format is *day month year*.

Reporting your own actions

Most of your laboratory report explains what you did, how you did it, and what results you obtained. When you report your actions, be specific. Also, write about the experiment, not about yourself. Take a look at these sample sentences:

BAD SENTENCE: I added sodium.

GOOD SENTENCE: Sodium was added.

WHY IT'S GOOD: *I* is not appropriate in a lab report.

BAD SENTENCE: We exposed the plant to sunlight.

GOOD SENTENCE: The plant was exposed to sunlight.

WHY IT'S GOOD: The focus of the sentence should be on the action, not on the people performing the action.

BAD SENTENCE: After the plant flowered, Jean measured the stem.

GOOD SENTENCE: After the plant flowered, the stem was measured.

WHY IT'S GOOD: *Jean* is not important. Focus on the action, not on the person.

Notice that the good sentences use past tense. The experiment is over, and the report explains what you did and what happened. Present tense doesn't fit this situation. For the same reason, you should also use past tense when you give information about others' experiments.

Be serious, factual, and formal when you write about an experiment. A science lab report is not the place to make a joke or to let your imagination loose. Present the information clearly.

Q. Are the format and language of this sentence acceptable in a science lab report?

Next, sodium is added to the solution.

A. **unacceptable** The experiment happened in the past, so you need a past tense verb, *was*. Also, how much sodium? That's an important fact and should appear in the report.

Other formatting issues

You have to present information you gathered during your experiment. Often you do so visually, in charts, graphs, tables, or diagrams. Each of these visual elements should be numbered and identified. Here's an example of a table:

TIP

Elsewhere in your lab report, you may refer to "Table 1" as you analyze the information. Capitalize *Table*.

Table 1 Number of flowers with and without fertilizer treatment

Plant type	Number of flowers without fertilizer	Number of flowers with fertilizer treatment	Average width of flowers
Rosa abyssinica	2	8	3 cm
Rosa arkansana	0	3	2.8 cm
Rosa carolina	1	1	6 cm

Numbers often appear in lab reports. As you see in the example, scientists use metric units for size, weight, and volume. In other words, you measure *meters, kilograms,* and *liters,* not *yards, pounds,* or *quarts.* Always abbreviate metric units. Most metric abbreviations are not capitalized. (*L* for liter and *C* for Celsius temperature are exceptions.) Place a space between the number and the metric unit, and omit periods within or after the abbreviation. The same abbreviation works for both singular (one unit) and plural (more than one unit). Take a look at these examples:

8 cm (eight centimeters)

1.5 kg (one-point-five kilograms)

55 ml (fifty-five milliliters)

2 L (two liters)

Take another look at the sample table. The scientific names of the plants (all types of roses) are italicized. All scientific names of plants and animals require italics. Common names, such as *rose,* do not need italics. Generally, the first word of a scientific name, the *genus,* is capitalized and what follows, the *species,* is in lowercase. Sometimes, the first word may be abbreviated. Here are some examples:

Homo sapiens

E. coli

Turdusmigratorius

In case you're wondering, the common names of the items in the preceding list are human beings, a virus, and a robin.

WARNING

If you're writing the report with a pen, don't attempt to reproduce italics by hand. Simply write the name clearly.

EXAMPLE

Q. Is the format of this excerpt from a lab report acceptable? The information in parentheses identifies the element of the report.

Acceleration of falling objects in a vacuum (title, centered alone on a title page)

A. **acceptable** This science title is capitalized properly: only the first word is capitalized, and everything else is in lowercase.

YOUR TURN

Is the format of each excerpt from a lab report acceptable? The information in parentheses identifies the element of the report.

6 Comparison of fertilized and unfertilized *Rosa rubiginosa* plants (title of an experiment, alone on a title page)

7 The fertilized rose totally won, in terms of numbers of flowers. (sentence from the conclusion)

8 The fertilizer, I think, made a difference. (another sentence from the conclusion)

9 Approximately 2 ml of fertilizer were added to the soil every day for a month. (sentence explaining the procedure)

10 Temperature was kept at 4° c. (sentence explaining the procedure)

Get to Work: Writing on the Job

In school, you may pay money (tuition and fees) to write. At work, someone may pay you to write. That's a better arrangement, don't you think? Writing on the job can make or break your career. If you write well, you may advance, but if you write poorly, you may lose your position. In this section, I help you take a close look at the most common types of business writing so that every document you create is perfect.

TIP

Most word processing programs provide templates — basic formats — for many types of business communications. When you bring one up on your screen, everything is in the right place. All you have to do is supply the content. In this section, I show you some standard formats and provide guidelines for how to use them correctly.

TIP

If your job involves writing business reports, follow the guidelines in the section "Essays and research papers," earlier in this chapter. Business reports are similar to the research papers you write (or wrote) in school.

Letters

Email and phone calls may be taking over the business world, but letters on paper are still around. When you write a business letter, you must include some important elements, which can be formatted in several different ways. Your company may have a preferred format, or there may be some room for your own preferences.

Take a look at this sample letter. Each part is labeled in bold. Below the letter are further instructions for each part.

NAME AND ADDRESS OF COMPANY:

Peterman Construction Company

5212 Calla Street

Anytown, New York 10021

DATE:

September 12, 2024

INSIDE ADDRESS:

Mr. George Dodge

1471 Second Avenue

Millerville, VT 05469

GREETING:

Dear Mr. Dodge:

BODY OF THE LETTER:

The repairs to your roof were completed two days ago. We hope that you are satisfied with our work. Please send us the final payment ($1,500) by Friday, October 12, 2024. We look forward to working with you on future projects.

CLOSING:

Sincerely,

NAME OF SENDER:

Herman Denten

TITLE OF SENDER:

Project Manager

PHONE NUMBER AND EMAIL ADDRESS OF SENDER:

212-555-9393 hdenten@dummiesallinone.com

Take a look at each part of the letter:

» **The name and address of the company appear at the top of the letter.** If you're printing the letter on official company paper, or *letterhead,* the top of the paper already provides the company's name and address. If it doesn't, you can add this information yourself. Place the company name, physical address, and web address flush with the left margin.

» **Additional information about the sender may appear after the company name and address or at the end of the letter.** You're the sender, unless someone else asked you to write the letter. Your name and title may appear on one line, followed by your email address and phone number on another line, all flush with the left margin. You can also choose to place the title, email address, and phone number after your name at the end of the letter, as I did in the preceding sample letter.

» **The date should begin at the left margin.** An older but still acceptable style places the date closer to the right margin, more or less in the middle of the page. In the sample you see a month-day-year format *(September 12, 2024),* but you may also use day-month-year *(12 September 2024)* instead. If the day comes first, don't insert commas. Don't write a date entirely with numerals *(9/12/24,* for example). In some countries, the day comes before the month. In others, it follows. Your reader may see *9/12/24* and read it as *September 12, 2024* or *December 9, 2024.*

» **The inside address contains the name and address of the person you're writing to.** Use *Mr., Mrs., Ms., Dr.,* or any other title that fits. Capitalize the abbreviation, and end the abbreviation with a period. Use both the first and last names, if you know them.

» **The greeting in a business letter is formal.** Stay away from *Hi, Hello,* and other such words. *Dear* or *To* are better choices. Generally, omit the first name of the person you're writing to. Attach the title *(Mr., Mrs., Ms.,* or *Dr.)* to the last name. Follow the greeting with a colon (one dot atop another).

» **The body of the letter should be simple and dignified.** Formality and courtesy are important when you write to an employee or a customer. Steer clear of slang, and don't wander off topic. Write the message in simple, clear language.

» **The closing appears alone on a line.** *Sincerely, Yours truly, Kind regards,* and similar formal phrases are fine. *Best,* short for *Best regards,* is a little less formal but still acceptable. Don't write *Your friend* or something similar. In business, you don't have friends! You have co-workers, supervisors, and customers. Follow the closing with a comma.

» **Your name completes the letter.** Include both your first and last names, and a middle initial, if you like. Add a suffix *(Jr., Esq.),* if you use one. If you didn't include your title at the top of the letter, place the title on a separate line after your name. Capitalize your title: *Director of Marketing, Sales Assistant,* and so on. If you didn't place your phone number and email address at the beginning of the letter, place that information on a separate line after your title.

You can adapt this letter format for recommendations, performance reviews, marketing campaigns, and many other situations. The only portion of the letter that changes is the body, where the message appears. Everything else stays the same.

Q. Is this acceptable or unacceptable in a business letter? The information in parentheses identifies the element of the letter.

Dear Maxine, (greeting in a letter to Dr. Maxine Oheria)

A. **unacceptable** The greeting should be more formal: *Dear Dr. Oheria.* Generally, the first name doesn't appear.

Is this acceptable or unacceptable in a business letter? The information in parentheses identifies the element of the letter.

11. Sincerely, (closing)

12. 5/6/24 (date)

13. Dear Ms. Mary North: (greeting)

14. Classic Company 4 Park Road Autton NY 11202 (sender's company and company address)

15. Director Of Marketing (sender's title)

Memos

Memos are communications sent within a company — from boss to employee, employee to boss, or one employee to another. They're more formal than most emails. Your word processing program may supply several memo templates, or you can format your own. Here's one option, with labels capitalized:

PERSON RECEIVING THE MEMO:

To: Samantha Friedman

PERSON SENDING THE MEMO:

From: Arthur Gordon, Vice President of Marketing

SUBJECT LINE:

Re: Performance review

DATE:

Date: June 12, 2024

MESSAGE:

All sales associates will meet with me individually during the month of July for the annual performance review. Please call my secretary (ext. 333) for an appointment.

As you write a memo, keep these ideas in mind:

» **When you fill in the To and From lines, use full (first and last) names.** You may include the job title, if you wish. Capitalize only the important words in the job title. Remember that *To* and *From* should be followed by colons, not commas.

» **If you send a copy to another person, include a CC line.** *CC* is an old abbreviation. It used to mean *carbon copy,* in the days when copies were made with carbon paper. No one uses carbon paper now, but the abbreviation remains. Most often, this abbreviation is capitalized, but lowercase is also fine. (Choose one. Don't capitalize one letter and not the other.) Either way, follow the abbreviation with a colon. Then write the names of the people who should receive copies.

» **Write a clear subject line.** Capitalize the first word in the subject. If you like, you may capitalize all the important words, or leave the rest in lowercase. The subject line should be short, just long enough to let the reader know what the memo is about.

» **Include the date.** Here you see the traditional month-day-year format. You can change that pattern to day-month-year. You may also drop the name of the month and insert a number (*6* instead of *June,* for example). Be careful, though. In some countries, the day precedes the month. In others, it follows. Your reader may see 6/12 and read it as *June 12* or *December 6.*

» **Keep the body of the memo clear, formal, and short.** Get your message across politely, omitting unnecessary words and comments.

» **Initial the memo.** Place your initials next to your name on the From line. If you're working on paper, use a pen. Otherwise, use your word processing program to insert your initials. A memo has no closing or signature line.

EXAMPLE

Q. Is this acceptable or unacceptable in a memo? The information in parentheses identifies the element of the memo.

Re: supply chain (subject line)

A. **unacceptable** You should always capitalize the first word, and you may also capitalize other significant words in the subject line. The correct version of this subject line is *Supply Chain* or *Supply chain.*

Is this acceptable or unacceptable in a memo? The information in parentheses identifies the element of the memo.

YOUR TURN

16 18 March 2024 (date)

17 To Elizabeth Stanton (person receiving the memo)

18 From: Marlon Rabbitti (person sending the memo)

19 Dear Elizabeth, (first line of the message)

20 Update on Order Status (subject line)

Practice Questions Answers and Explanations

1. **unacceptable** The quoted words should be surrounded by quotation marks. Thus, the correct version is *Henry Peters said, "The war illustrated the limitations of troops fighting without proper equipment."*

2. **acceptable** The language is formal, as it should be. No quotation marks are necessary, because no words are quoted and the ideas are attributed to *many economists*.

3. **acceptable** The language is formal, and no quotation marks are needed.

4. **unacceptable** A title that is alone on the page should not be enclosed by quotation marks.

5. **unacceptable** When writing about a literary work, use present tense. Change *was* to *is*.

6. **acceptable** The first word of the title is capitalized, as well as the first part of the scientific name of the plant (a tea rose, in common language). *Rosa* is the genus, a category that includes many types of roses, and *rubiginosa* is the species, a subgroup of the genus. In science writing, capitalize the genus but not the species, and italicize both.

7. **unacceptable** The language is too informal and too general. Instead of *totally won*, give accurate information: *Fertilized plants produced an average of 8.7 blooms per plant, compared to 3.2 for unfertilized plants.*

8. **unacceptable** Don't insert yourself into a lab report! The sentence is also too general. Give information about the observed difference, such as the number of blooms, plant height, and so forth.

9. **acceptable** Everything here is factual and in formal language. The abbreviation for *milliliters* is written without a period, as it should be.

10. **unacceptable** The abbreviation for *Celsius* is *C*, not *c*.

11. **acceptable** The formality of this closing is appropriate for a business letter.

12. **unacceptable** In some countries this is May 6, 2024. In other countries it's June 5, 2024. Clarity is your goal, and you can't achieve that with numerals.

13. **unacceptable** In the greeting, use the title and last name only (*Ms. North*), followed by a comma or colon.

14. **unacceptable** Place the company name and street address on separate lines. Below the street-address line, place the city, state, and zip code on their own line. If separate lines present a problem, insert commas to separate each of these elements, with one exception: No comma appears between the state and the zip code.

15. **unacceptable** Don't capitalize *of* in a title.

(16) **acceptable** Everything is as it should be in this date.

(17) **unacceptable** *To* should be followed by a colon. Thus, this should be *To: Elizabeth Stanton*

(18) **acceptable** Everything's fine with the punctuation and capitalization here.

(19) **unacceptable** Don't place a greeting in a memo.

(20) **acceptable** The word *on* isn't important, so it should be in lowercase. Another acceptable format for this subject line is *Update on order status.*

If you're ready to test your skills a bit more, take the following chapter quiz that incorporates all the chapter topics.

Whaddya Know? Chapter 26 Quiz

Quiz time! Complete each problem to test your knowledge on the various topics covered in this chapter. You can then find the solutions and explanations in the next section.

Decide whether these excerpts from academic or business communications are acceptable.

Excerpt	What It Is	Acceptable or Unacceptable?
1. To Mr. Carmen,	Greeting line in a business letter	
2. "International Travel in 19th Century Europe"	Title of a history research paper, centered on a title page	
3. Peterson 222 Main Street Centerton, NY 11001	Business letter, inside address of the recipient	
4. According to Dr. Higging, the most recent census showed a rise in the number of multifamily dwellings in the metropolitan area.	Sentence from a research paper	
5. Very truly yours,	Closing of a business letter	
6. On 15 July 1972, both parties reached an agreement on the merger.	Sentence from an academic essay	
7. 2024 June 14	Date of a memo	
8. Growth of antibiotic-resistant bacteria in soil following natural flooding	Title of a science paper, centered on the top line	
9. C.C. Lorna Francis	Copy line in a memo	
10. The painting showed the dead man and his murderer.	Sentence in an essay describing a work of art	

Answers to Chapter 26 Quiz

1. **unacceptable** A colon, not a comma, should follow the name in the greeting line of a business letter.

2. **unacceptable** A centered title should not be enclosed in quotation marks.

3. **unacceptable** *Peterson* should not appear all by itself. Add *Mr.* or *Ms.* or whatever title the recipient uses. Also insert the first name, if you know it.

4. **acceptable** The information is credited to the source, *Dr. Higging,* and the language is appropriately formal.

5. **acceptable** This closing is fine for a business letter.

6. **acceptable** The format, tone, and tense are all fine in this sentence.

7. **unacceptable** The year should not appear first. Change to *June 14, 2024* or *14 June 2024.*

8. **acceptable** A centered title should not be enclosed in quotation marks. In a science report, only the first word of the title and subtitle and proper names should be capitalized.

9. **unacceptable** Don't insert periods into the abbreviation *CC.* Place a colon after the abbreviation.

10. **unacceptable** In describing a work of art (painting, novel, poem, and so forth) use present tense. Change *showed* to *shows.*

Index

N

names
  capitalization, 374
  nouns, 38–39
nearly, 269
negative statements, 77–78
neither, 112, 227–228, 242
nevertheless, 423
newspaper articles, titles of, 329
newspapers, titles of, 329
no one, 230, 231
nobody, 230, 242
none, 229–230, 242
nor, 228, 350
nothing, 230, 242
noun clauses, 180
nouns
  about, 37
  adjectives describing, 89
  agreement, 223
  answers to chapter quiz, 50
  attaching "this." these," "those", and "that" to, 45–46
  chapter quiz, 49
  defined, 38, 105
  examples, 10
  identifying, 38–42
  -ing nouns, 251–252
  names, 38–39
  naming ideas and emotions with, 41
  naming things with, 39
  parts of speech and, 10–11
  pinpointing meaning with, 397–398
  places, 39
  plural, 42–45
  possession with proper nouns, 302
  possessive, 303
  practice questions, 42, 44, 45, 46, 398–399
  practice questions answers and explanations, 47–48, 403
  prepositional phrases, 106–107
  replacing with pronouns, 52
  singular, 42–45
  subordinate clauses and, 179
numbers
  contractions, 305
  hyphens, 361
  lab reports, 482
  pronouns, 55

O

object pronouns
  direct objects, 244
  indirect objects, 244
objective complements, 135, 141–142
objects, attaching to verbals, 246
one, 230
one-clause sentences, 176
only, 269
or, 228, 350, 456. *See also* conjunctions
-or word ending, 289
orders, 112
other, 341
ourselves, 241

P

padding, 401. *See also* wordiness
pants, 233
parallelism, 144, 440–441
paraphrase, 316–317. *See also* quotations
part participles, 208–209
participial phrase, 430
participles
  and commas, 342–343
  defined, 272, 430
  examples, 430
parts of sentence, 9, 11–15
parts of speech, 9, 10–11
passive verbs, 67, 209–210
past perfect progressive tense, 198–199
past perfect tense, 198–199
past progressive tense, 192–193, 195
past tense, 192–193, 195, 204–205. *See also* tense
patterns, 438–439
perfect tenses. *See also* tense
  cases
    beginning in the past and continuing in the present, 200–201
    events at two different times in the past, 201–202
    more than two past events, all at different times, 202–203
    two events in the future, 203
  future perfect progressive tense, 199
  future perfect tense, 199
  past perfect progressive tense, 198–199
  past perfect tense, 198–199
  present perfect progressive tense, 197–198
  present perfect tense, 197–198

About the Author

Geraldine Woods has taught every level of English from fifth grade through adult writing classes. She's the author of more than 50 books, including *English Grammar For Dummies*, 3rd Edition; *Basic English Grammar For Dummies*; and *1001 Grammar Practice Questions For Dummies*, 2nd Edition (all published by Wiley). She also wrote *25 Great Sentences and How They Got That Way* and *Sentence. A Period-to-Period Guide to Building Better Readers and Writers*, both published by WW Norton. She blogs at www.grammarianinthecity.com about current trends in language and ridiculous signs she encounters on her walks around New York City. Her current favorite sign reads, "Help Wanted: Grilled and Deli Man."

Dedication

For Harry, who will always live in my heart.

Author's Acknowledgments

I owe thanks to my elementary school teachers — nuns who taught me how to diagram every conceivable sentence and, despite that fact, also taught me to love language and literature. I appreciate the efforts of Tim Gallan, a project editor second to none; Lindsay Lefevere, Wiley's acquisitions editor; Becky Whitney, the copyeditor; and Kelly Henthorne, the technical reviewer.

Publisher's Acknowledgments

Executive Editor: Lindsay Lefevere
Development Editor: Tim Gallan
Copy Editor: Becky Whitney
Technical Reviewer: Kelly Henthorne
Proofreader: Debbye Butler

Production Editor: Mohammed Zafar Ali
Cover Image: © pepifoto/Getty Images